For reference

W9-CAE-597

AMERICANS AT WAR

EDITORIAL BOARD

Editor in Chief
John P. Resch
Professor of History
University of New Hampshire—Manchester

Associate Editors
D'Ann Campbell
Dean of Academics
United States Coast Guard Academy

Richard Jensen
Independent Scholar

Sally G. McMillan
Professor of History
Davidson College

G. Kurt Piehler
Director, The Center for the Study of War and Society
University of Tennessee

AMERICANS AT WAR

Society, Culture, and the Homefront

VOLUME 2: 1816–1900

John P. Resch, Editor in Chief

MACMILLAN REFERENCE USA
An imprint of Thomson Gale, a part of The Thomson Corporation

Detroit • New York • San Francisco • San Diego • New Haven, Conn. • Waterville, Maine • London • Munich

THOMSON
★
GALE
™

Americans at War: Culture, Society, and the Homefront
John P. Resch, Editor in Chief

©2005 Thomson Gale, a part of the Thomson Corporation.

Thomson, Star Logo and Macmillan Reference USA are trademarks and Gale is a registered trademark used herein under license.

For more information, contact
Thomson Gale
27500 Drake Rd.
Farmington Hills, MI 48331-3535
Or you can visit our Internet site at
http://www.gale.com

ALL RIGHTS RESERVED
No part of this work covered by the copyright hereon may be reproduced or used in any form or by any means—graphic, electronic, or mechanical, including photocopy-
ing, recording, taping, Web distribution, or information storage retrieval systems—without the written permission of the publisher.

For permission to use material from this product, submit your request via Web at http://www.gale-edit.com/permissions, or you may download our Permissions Request form and submit your request by fax or mail to:

Permissions Department
Thomson Gale
27500 Drake Road
Farmington Hills, MI 48331-3535
Permissions Hotline:
248-699-8006 or 800-877-4253, ext. 8006
Fax: 248-699-8074 or 800-762-4058

Since this page cannot legibly accommodate all copyright notices, the acknowledgments constitute an extension of the copyright notice.

While every effort has been made to ensure the reliability of the information presented in this publication, Thomson Gale does not guarantee the accuracy of the data contained herein. Thomson Gale accepts no payment for listing; and inclusion in the publication of any organization, agency, institution, publication, service, or individual does not imply endorsement of the editors or publisher. Errors brought to the attention of the publisher and verified to the satisfaction of the publisher will be corrected in future editions.

LIBRARY OF CONGRESS CATALOGING-IN-PUBLICATION DATA

Americans at war : society, culture, and the homefront/John P. Resch, Editor in Chief.
   p. cm.
     Includes bibliographical references and index.
     ISBN 0-02-865806-X (set hardcover : alk. paper)—ISBN 0-02-865807-8 (v. 1)—
     ISBN 0-02-865808-6 (v. 2)—ISBN 0-02-865809-4 (v. 3)—ISBN 0-02-865810-8
     (v. 4)—ISBN 0-02-865993-7 (e-book)
     1. United States—History, Military. 2. United States—Social conditions.
     3. United States—Social life and customs. 4. War and society—United
     States—History. I. Resch, John Phillips

E181.A453 2005
973—dc22   2004017314

This title is also available as an e-book.
ISBN 0-02-865993-7
Contact your Thomson Gale sales representative for ordering information.

Printed in the United States of America
10 9 8 7 6 5 4 3 2 1

ACC Library Services
Austin, Texas

Project Editors: Anthony Aiello and Kristin Hart

Editorial Assistants: Regan Blinder, Sofia Bragg, Sara Constantakis, Steve Cusack, Melissa Hill, Scot Peacock, Ken Wachsberger

Imaging: Randy Bassett, Leitha Etheridge-Sims, Lezlie Light

Sidebar Writer, unless otherwise specified: Jeanne Lesinski

Proofreaders: Robert A. Arlt, Taryn Benbow-Pfalzgraf, Nicolet Elert, Sylvia Engdahl, Ellen Hawley, Jessica Hornik Evans, Tom McMahon, Laura M. Miller, Lucia Vilankulu

Indexer: Wendy Allex

Art Director: Pam A.E. Galbreath

Compositor and Tables: GGS Information Services (York, Pennsylvania)

Permissions: Margaret Chamberlain, Shalice Shaw-Caldwell

Manager, Composition: Mary Beth Trimper

Assistant Manager, Composition: Evi Seoud

Manufacturing: Lori Kessler

Director, New Product Development: Hélène Potter

Vice President and Publisher: Frank Menchaca

EDITORIAL & PRODUCTION STAFF

TABLE OF CONTENTS

VOLUME 1: 1500–1815

VOLUME 2: 1816–1900

VOLUME 4: 1946–PRESENT

Daniel W. Aldridge, III
Davidson College
African Americans (Freed People)
Douglass, Frederick

John K. Alexander
University of Cincinnati
Sons of Liberty

Donna Alvah
St. Lawrence University
Military Families
Vietnam Veterans
Women's Rights and Feminism, 1946–Present

Angelo T. Angelis
Hunter College
Revolution and Radical Reform

Janis Appier
University of Tennessee
Catt, Carrie Chapman

Marie L. Aquila
Ball State University's Indiana Academy of Science,
Mathematics, and Humanities
Music, World War II

Robert A. Arlt
Independent Scholar
Jefferson, Thomas

Stephen V. Ash
University of Tennessee at Knoxville
Occupation of the South

Jeanie Attie
Long Island University
United States Sanitary Commission

Allan W. Austin
College Misericordia
Japanese Americans, World War II
Tokyo Rose

Jean Harvey Baker
Goucher College
Lincoln, Mary Todd
Women's Suffrage Movement

James M. Banner, Jr.
Washington, D.C.
    Federalist Party
    Hartford Convention

Lance Banning
[illegible]
    Jeffersonian Republican Party
    Madison, James

J. L. Bell
Independent Scholar
    Boston Massacre: Pamphlets and Propaganda
    Boston Tea Party: Politicizing Ordinary People
    Hewes, George Robert Twelves

Richard J. Bell
Harvard University
    Republican Womanhood

Scott H. Bennett
Georgian Court University
    Dissent in World War I and World War II

Chad Berry
Maryville College
    Regional Migration, World War I and World War
        II

Michael E. Birdwell
Tennessee Technological University
    York, Alvin Cullum

Mary W. Blanchard
Independent Scholar
    Visual Arts, World War I

Larry I. Bland
Marshall Museum VMI
    Marshall, George C.

Rose Blue
Independent Scholar
    Age of Westward Expansion
    Cochran, Jackie
    Compromise of 1850
    Confederate States of America
    Davis, Angela
    Ford, Henry
    Hiroshima Guilt
    Kirkpatrick, Jeanne
    Madison, Dolley
    New York City Draft Riots
    Pirates and the Barbary War
    United Nations

David Bogen
Emerson College
    Iran-Contra Affair

Mark Boulton
University of Tennessee
    Allies, Images of
    Peace Movements, 1898–1945
    Propaganda, 1898–1945
    Wayne, John

Terry Bouton
University of Maryland
    Civil Liberties: Kentucky and Virginia Resolutions

Charlene M. Boyer Lewis
Kalamazoo College
    Recreation and Social Life

Patricia Bradley
Temple University
    Slavery and the Homefront, 1775–1783

Stuart D. Brandes
Independent Scholar
    Financing, World War I
    Financing, World War II

Dewey A. Browder
Austin Peay State University
    Berlin as Symbol

Margaret Lynn Brown
Brevard College
    Civilian Conservation Corps (CCC)

Mary Lynn McCree Bryan
Duke University
    Addams, Jane

Lisa M. Budreau
St. Anthony's College, Oxford University
    Armistice Day
    Gold Star Mothers Pilgrimage
    Monuments, Cemeteries, Spanish American War
    Monuments, Cemeteries, World War I

Stephanie M. H. Camp
University of Washington
    Slavery

D'Ann Campbell
United States Coast Guard Academy
    Equal Rights Amendment (ERA) and Drafting
        Women

Feminism
Women and World War I
Women and World War II
Women Integrated into the Military

Nicholas J. Capasso
DeCordova Museum and Sculpture Park
Vietnam Veterans Memorial

Lewis H. Carlson
Independent Scholar
Red Scare

John Whiteclay Chambers II
Rutgers University
Wilson, Woodrow

Paul A. Cimbala
Fordham University
Civil War Veterans
Freedmen's Bureau

J. Ransom Clark
Muskingum College
CIA and Espionage

John E. Clark, Jr.
Independent Scholar
Railroads

Craig T. Cobane
Culver-Stockton College
Atomic Energy Commission
Star Wars
Terrorism, Fears of
Think Tanks

David G. Coleman
Miller Center of Public Affairs, University of Virginia
Kennedy, John Fitzgerald

Susan G. Contente
Independent Scholar
Clothing, World War I and World War II

Conrad C. Crane
United States Army War College
Mitchell, Billy
Stewart, Jimmy

Robert E. Cray, Jr.
Montclair State University
Politics and Expressions of Patriotism

Lynda Lasswell Crist
Rice University
Davis, Jefferson

Wayne Cutler
University of Tennessee
Polk, James K.

Ginger R. Davis
Independent Scholar
Vietnamese and Hmong Refugees
Who Served in Vietnam?

Michael Davis
Independent Scholar
Adams, John
Common Sense
Olympics and Cold War

Mary A. DeCredico
United States Naval Academy
Chesnut, Mary Boykin

James X. Dempsey
Center for Democracy & Technology
Civil Liberties, 1945–Present

Victor G. Devinatz
Illinois State University
Labor, 1946–Present

Jose O. Diaz
Ohio State University
Davis, Varina Howell

Jonathan M. DiCicco
Rutgers, The State University of New Jersey
Disarmament and Arms Control, 1898–1945

Ricky Dobbs
Texas A & M - Commerce
Texas, Republic of

Michael B. Dougan
Arkansas State University
Black Codes
Civil Liberties, Civil War

Robert C. Doyle
Franciscan University of Steubenville
Prisons and Prisoners of War, 1815–1900

James D. Drake
Metropolitan State College
King Philip's War, Legacy of

Mara Drogan
University of Albany, SUNY
   Arms Control Debate

Christopher M. Duncan
University of Dayton
   Anti-Federalists

Sylvia Engdahl
Independent Scholar
   Space Race

Thomas I. Faith
George Washington University
   Roosevelt, Eleanor

Victoria A. Farrar-Myers
University of Texas at Arlington
   Bush, George H.W.
   Bush, George W.

Elizabeth Faue
Wayne State University
   Veterans Benefits

Ilene Rose Feinman
California State University, Monterey Bay
   Peace Movements, 1946–Present

Daniel Feller
University of Tennessee
   Jackson, Andrew

Michael D. Fellman
Simon Fraser University
   Lee, Robert E.

Phyllis F. Field
Ohio University
   Political Parties

Gayle V. Fischer
Salem State College
   Clothing

Thomas Fleming
Independent Scholar
   Hamilton, Alexander

Justin Florence
Harvard University
   Quasi-War and the Rise of Political Parties

Ernest Freeberg
University of Tennessee
   Civil Liberties, World War I
   Journalism, Spanish American War

Richard M. Fried
University of Illinois at Chicago
   McCarthyism

Tim Alan Garrison
Portland State University
   Indian Removal and Response

Edith B. Gelles
Stanford University
   Adams, Abigail

Nancy Gentile Ford
Bloomsburg University of Pennsylvania
   Americanization
   Labor, World War I
   Mobilization for War

Delia Gillis
Central Missouri State University
   Education
   Powell, Colin
   Refugees

Andrew D. Glassberg
University of Missouri—St. Louis
   Military Bases

David T. Gleeson
University of Charleston
   Immigrants and Immigration
   Lost Cause

Rebecca Goetz
Harvard University
   Galloway, Grace: Diary of a Loyalist

Eliga H. Gould
University of New Hampshire
   Peace of Paris, 1763

Lewis L. Gould
University of Texas, emeritus
   Great Society
   Johnson, Lyndon Baines
   1968 Upheaval

Charles D. Grear
Texas Christian University
   Blockade, Civil War

Emily Greenwald
Historical Research Associates, Inc. (Missoula, MT)
Dawes Severalty Act

Beth Griech-Polelle
Bowling Green State University
Holocaust, American Response to

David Grimsted
University of Maryland
Violence

Ricardo Griswold del Castillo
San Diego State University
Guadalupe Hidalgo, Treaty of

Michael J. Guasco
Davidson College
Bacon's Rebellion

Allen C. Guelzo
Gettysburg College
Lincoln, Abraham

Joan R. Gundersen
University of Pittsburgh
Brown, Charlotte: Diary of a Nurse
Camp Followers: War and Women
Drinker, Elizabeth

Michael W. Hail
Morehead State University
Poor Relief, 1815–1900
States and Nation Building, 1775–1783

Jeremy L. Hall
Independent Scholar
States and Nation Building, 1775–1783

John Earl Haynes
Library of Congress
Rosenberg, Hiss, Oppenheimer Cases

Sam W. Haynes
University of Texas at Arlington
Manifest Destiny

Kenneth J. Heineman
Ohio University
Americanism vs. Godless Communism
Communism and Anticommunism

Jan Kenneth Herman
Bureau of Medicine and Surgery, Wash DC
Medicine, World War II

Donald R. Hickey
Wayne State College
Embargo
War of 1812

Sarah Hilgendorff List
Independent Historian
Ku Klux Klan
Segregation, Racial, 1815–1900
Whitman, Walt

Sylvia D. Hoffert
University of North Carolina at Chapel Hill
Woman's Rights Movement

Leonne M. Hudson
Kent State University
Food Shortages

Darren Hughes
University of Tennessee
Motion Pictures during World Wars I and II

Jean M. Humez
University of Massachusetts, Boston
Tubman, Harriet

R. Douglas Hurt
Iowa State University
Farming

Samuel C. Hyde, Jr.
Southeastern Louisiana University
Sharecropping and Tenant Farming

Christina Jarvis
State University of New York at Fredonia
Visual Arts, World War II
World War II, Images of

Laura S. Jensen
University of Massachusetts
Veterans' Benefits

Richard Jensen
Independent Scholar
9–11

Herbert A. Johnson
University of South Carolina Law School
Supreme Court
Supreme Court and War Powers

Adam Jones
Center for Research and Teaching in Economics (CIDE), Mexico City
Latinos in the Military, 1946–Present

Steven Jones
Brown University
   Nuclear Freeze Movement
   Weapons of Mass Destruction

John P. Kaminski
University of Wisconsin, Madison
   Washington, George

Angela Frye Keaton
University of Tennessee
   Civil Liberties, World War II

Jennifer D. Keene
Chapman University
   American Legion
   Bonus March
   Demobilization
   Profiteering

Richard Kirkendall
University of Washington
   Truman, Harry S.
   Truman Doctrine

Wendy Kozol
Oberlin College
   Photojournalism

Gregory Kupsky
University of Tennessee
   Prisoner of War Camps, United States

Stanford J. Layton
Weber State University
   Homestead Act

Jama Lazerow
Wheelock College
   Black Power/Black Panthers

James S. Leamon
Bates College
   Armed Conflicts in America, 1587-1815
   Loyalists
   Shays's and Whiskey Rebellions

Daniel B. Lee
Pennsylvania State University
   Television, 1946–Present

Edward Lengel
Independent Scholar
   Memoirs, Autobiographies

Neil W. Lerner
Davidson College
   Music, Civil War
   Music, Musicians, and the War on Terrorism
   Music, World War I

J. E. Lighter
University of Tennessee
   Literature, World War I
   Literature, World War II

Blanche M. G. Linden
Independent Scholar
   Anthony, Susan B.
   Friedan, Betty

Judy Barrett Litoff
Bryant College
   Rosie the Riveter
   Women, Employment of

Ellen M. Litwicki
State University of New York at Fredonia
   Fourth of July
   Memorial (Decoration) Day

M. Philip Lucas
Cornell College
   Elections, Presidential: The Civil War

Ralph E. Luker
Independent Historian
   Churches, Mainstream
   Civil Rights Movement
   Jackson, Jesse Louis
   King, Martin Luther, Jr.
   Nonviolence

Michael Lynch
Cornell University
   Iran-Contra Affair

John Majewski
University of California
   Financing the War

John W. Malsberger
Muhlenberg College
   Cuban Missile Crisis
   Kissinger, Henry
   Nixon, Richard M.

Anthony Maravillas
Independent Scholar
   Tet, Impact of

Rosemary Bryant Mariner
Center for the Study of War and Society
    Conscription, World War II
    National Guard

Norman Markowitz
Rutgers University
    Higher Education
    Labor, World War II

John F. Marszalek
Mississippi State University
    Sherman's March to the Sea

James Marten
Marquette University
    Children and the Civil War

Cathy Matson
University of Delaware
    Continental Congresses

Holly A. Mayer
Duquesne University
    Generals' Wives: Martha Washington, Catharine
        Greene, Lucy Knox

Paul T. McCartney
University of Richmond
    Neo-isolationism
    Triumphalism
    War Powers Act

Richard B. McCaslin
High Point University
    Johnson, Andrew

Michael A. McDonnell
University of Sydney
    Republicanism and War

Gordon B. McKinney
Berea College
    Peace Movements

John R. McKivigan
Indiana University- Purdue University at Indianapolis
    Abolitionists

Sally G. McMillen
Davidson College
    Civil War and Industrial and Technological
        Advances
    Civil War and Its Impact on Sexual Attitudes on
        the Homefront

    Dix, Dorothea
    Family Life
    Stanton, Elizabeth Cady

Daniel T. Miller
Historical Solutions LLC, Indiana
    Alien and Sedition Laws
    Hamilton's Reports

Laura M. Miller
Vanderbilt University
    Arnold, Benedict
    Du Bois, W.E.B.
    Grant, Ulysses S.
    Hemingway, Ernest
    Jackson, Thomas J. (Stonewall)

Randall M. Miller
St. Joseph's University
    Religion, Civil War

D. E. "Gene" Mills Jr.
Florida State University
    Churches, Evangelical, 1946–Present

Curtis Miner
State Museum of Pennsylvania
    Levittown

Susan Moeller
Philip Merrill College of Journalism
    Photography, Civil War
    Photography, World War I
    Photography, World War II

Edwin E. Moise
Clemson University
    Pentagon Papers

John Morello
DeVry University
    Antiwar Movement
    Drugs and Vietnam
    Grunts
    Music, Vietnam Era
    My Lai
    Selective Service

Michael A. Morrison
Purdue University
    Kansas Nebraska Act

James C. Mott
Independent Scholar
    Holocaust Guilt
    Politics and Elections

Malcolm Muir, Jr.
Austin Peay State University
    MacArthur, Douglas

Brigitte L. Nacos
Columbia University
    Hostage Crisis, 1979–1981

Corinne J. Naden
Independent Scholar
    Age of Westward Expansion
    Cochran, Jackie
    Compromise of 1850
    Confederate States of America
    Davis, Angela
    Ford, Henry
    Hiroshima Guilt
    Kirkpatrick, Jeanne
    Madison, Dolley
    New York City Draft Riots
    Pirates and the Barbary War
    United Nations

June Namias
Independent Historian
    Rowlandson, Mary

Michael S. Neiberg
United States Air Force Academy
    ROTC
    Volunteer Army and Professionalism

John Nerone
University of Illinois, Urbana–Champaign
    Newspapers and Magazines

Thomas M. Nichols
Naval War College
    Preemptive War
    Preventive War

Travis Nygard
University of Pittsburgh
    Visual Arts, Civil War and the West

Greg O'Brien
University of Southern Mississippi
    Jamestown: Legacy of the Massacre of 1622
    Legacies of Indian Warfare
    Native Americans: Images in Popular Culture

Christopher J. Olsen
Indiana State University
    Secession

Russell Olwell
Eastern Michigan University
    Manhattan Project

William L. O'Neill
Rutgers University
    Roosevelt, Franklin Delano

Stephen R. Ortiz
University of Florida
    Hoover, Herbert
    Veterans of Foreign Wars

Victoria E. Ott
University of Tennessee
    Widows and Orphans
    Women on the Homefront

Matthew M. Oyos
Radford University
    Roosevelt, Theodore

Chester J. Pach, Jr.
Ohio University
    Eisenhower, Dwight D.
    Korea, Impact of
    Nitze, Paul
    Nonalignment
    Patriotism
    Reagan, Ronald

Richard Panchyk
Independent Historian
    Clinton, William Jefferson
    Conscription, World War I
    Flags
    Fort William Henry Massacre, Cultural Legacy
    Homeland Security
    Men on the Home Front, Civil War
    Monuments, Cemeteries, World War II
    Rationing
    War, Impact on Ethnic Groups
    Washington's Farewell Address

Melinda Lee Pash
Independent Historian
    African Americans, World War I
    American Indians, World War I and World War II
    National Anthem
    Sexual Behavior

Sidney L. Pash
Fayetteville State University
    Economy, World War I
    Economy, World War II

Isolationism
McKinley, William
New Deal
Pearl Harbor Investigation
Public Opinion

Edward Piacentino
High Point University
 Humor, Political

Jim Piecuch
Clarion University
 Commonwealth Men
 Federalist Papers
 Stamp Act Congress

S. W. Pope
University of Lincoln, UK
 Sports, World War I
 Sports, World War II

Charles B. Potter
Independent Scholar
 Cooper, James Fenimore
 The Spy: First American War Novel
 Wyoming Valley Conflict

Caren Prommersberger
Independent Scholar
 Conscription, World War I
 Fort William Henry Massacre, Cultural Legacy
 Monuments, Cemeteries, World War II

Luca Prono
ABC-Clio
 Painters and Patriotism, Late 18th and Early 19th
  Centuries
 Popular Culture and Cold War
 "Who Lost China" Debate

Sarah J. Purcell
Grinnell College
 Battle of New Orleans
 Bunker Hill Monument
 Lafayette's Tour
 Memory and Early Histories of the Revolution
 Montgomery, Richard

Richard J. Regan
Fordham University
 Just-War Debate

John P. Resch
University of New Hampshire—Manchester

Constitution: Creating a Republic
Paine, Thomas
Religion and Revolution
Revolutionary War Veterans

Jason S. Ridler
Royal Military College of Canada
 H-Bomb, Decision to Build

Edward Rielly
Saint Joseph's College of Maine
 Fiction and Memoirs, Vietnam

Stuart I. Rochester
Office of the Secretary of Defense
 POW, MIA

John B. Romeiser
University of Tennessee
 Journalism, World War II

Frank A. Salamone
Iona College
 Civil War and Industrial and Technological
  Advances
 Civil War and Its Impact on Sexual Attitudes on
  the Homefront
 Gays, Civil Rights for, 1946–Present
 Journalism, World War I
 Multiculturalism and Cold War
 Race and Military
 Teenagers, 1946–Present

Walter L. Sargent
University of Minnesota
 Association Test
 Mobilization, War for Independence

Alfred Saucedo
University of Chicago
 Enemy, Images of

Gregory L. Schneider
Emporia State University
 Goldwater, Barry
 John Birch Society

Nancy Schurr
University of Tennessee, Knoxville
 Medicine and Health

Larry Schweikart
University of Dayton
 Aerospace Industry

Ben H. Severance
University of Tennessee, Knoxville
Reconstruction

John Y. Simon
Southern Illinois University Carbondale
Gettysburg Address

Philip L. Simpson
Brevard Community College
Cold War Novels and Movies
Literature

Gerald L. Sittser
Whitworth College
Religion, World War II

Sheila L. Skemp
University of Mississippi
Franklin, Benjamin

David Sloan
Morehead State College
Poor Relief, 1816–1900

Fred H. Smith
Davidson College
Economic Change and Industrialization

John David Smith
North Carolina State
Emancipation Proclamation

Mark M. Smith
University of South Carolina
Stono Rebellion

André B. Sobocinski
Bureau of Medicine and Surgery, Washington, D.C.
Medicine, World War I

Richard C. Spicer
Boston University
Music and the Revolution

Kathryn St. Clair Ellis
University of Tennessee, Knoxville
GI Bill of Rights

Ian K. Steele
University of Western Ontario
European Invasion of Indian North America,
1513–1765

Stephen K. Stein
University of Memphis
Israel and the United States

Christopher H. Sterling
George Washington University
Radio and Power of Broadcasting

Margaret D. Stock
United States Military Academy
Al-Qaida and Taliban
Supreme Court, 1815–1900

Brian D. Stokes
Camden County College
States' Rights, Theory of

Amy H. Sturgis
Belmont University
Monroe, James
Monroe's Tour of New England

Kirsten D. Sword
Georgetown University
Families at War

James Lance Taylor
University of San Francisco
Slavery in America

Athan Theoharis
Marquette University
Federal Bureau of Investigations (FBI)

Rod Timanus
Independent Scholar
Alamo

Lorett Treese
Bryn Mawr College Library
Valley Forge

A. Bowdoin Van Riper
Southern Polytechnic State University
Civil Defense, 1946–Present

John R. Vile
Middle Tennessee State University
Articles of Confederation
Constitution: Bill of Rights
Constitutional Amendments and Changes

Jonathan E. Vincent
University of Kentucky
Red Badge of Courage

Michael Wala
Ruhr-Universität Bochum, Historisches Institut
Containment and Détente

Matthew C. Ward
University of Dundee, Scotland
French and Indian War, Legacy of
Mobilization, French and Indian War

Matt Wasniewski
University of Maryland
Cold War Mobilization
Military-Industrial Complex
NSC #68

Cindy Weinstein
California Institute of Technology
Uncle Tom's Cabin

Patricia Weiss Fagen
Georgetown University
Human Rights

Douglas L. Wheeler
University of New Hampshire
Espionage and Spies

George White, Jr.
University of Tennessee, Knoxville
African Americans, World War II
Imperialism

Stephen J. Whitfield
Brandeis University
Arts as Weapon

Robert C. Williams
Davidson College
Greeley, Horace

Tony Williams
Southern Illinois University, Carbondale
Vietnam Films

Clyde N. Wilson
University of South Carolina
Calhoun, John Caldwell

Mark R. Wilson
University of North Carolina at Charlotte
Business and Finance
Labor and Labor Movements
Preparedness

Meghan Kate Winchell
Independent Scholar
USO

Mitchell Yockelson
*United States National Archives and Records
Administration*
Red Cross, American
Veterans of Foreign Wars

Ronald Young
Georgia Southern University
Declaration of Independence
Foreign Aid, 1946–Present
Latinos, World War I and World War II
Urbanization

Rosemarie Zagarri
George Mason University
Sampson, Deborah
Warren, Mercy Otis

Stephen Zunes
University of San Francisco
Muslims, Stereotypes and Fears of

Preparation for war, war itself, and the legacy of war are among the most important forces shaping American society and culture. Nevertheless, the study of war is often treated as if the only topics of importance were battles and campaigns, results measured in territory, and reputations gained or lost. This four-volume reference set, *Americans at War*, provides students with a different perspective by examining the profound effect of war upon American society, culture, and national identity. The 395 articles in this set, written by leading academic and independent scholars, cover a wide range of topics. We hope that these articles, focused on the effect of war upon society, will provide new insights into the nation's history and character, and will serve as a resource for further study of America's past and for charting the nation's future.

Volume 1 covers the longest period, 1500 to 1815, especially the era beginning in 1607 with the first permanent English settlement at Jamestown. Between 1607 and 1700, apart from frontier skirmishes, raids, and ambushes, colonists from South Carolina through New England were engaged in over a score of declared wars, rebellions, and insurrections. In the eighteenth century Americans were at war more than at peace. Between 1700 and 1800 Americans engaged in seventeen separate conflicts and rebellions, including the 1739 uprising of slaves at Stono, South Carolina, and the Revolutionary War, 1775–1783. Between 1798 and 1825 the United States was at war with Barbary pirates, Seminole Indians, and in the "Second War of Independence," 1812–1815, with Great Britain and Canada.

The articles in this volume examine how those wars, especially the Revolutionary War, influenced American literature, art, and music; affected the role of women; shaped the economy; and challenged the institution of slavery. Articles also examine how dissent and rebellion contributed to America's creed of liberty and the formation of its Constitution. Some articles focus on the effects of war in forming and reinforcing American racial attitudes towards Indians and blacks. Others discuss the effect of war upon civil liberties, such as freedom of speech and politics. The memory of America's wars helped to define the nation's culture and identity through patriotic celebrations, monuments, and memorials, and by honoring Revolutionary war veterans. Wars also reinforced the religious view that the nation was a beacon to the world's suffering and repressed.

The articles in Volume 2, 1816 to 1900, examine how wars in the nineteenth century shaped American society, culture, and identity while the United States changed from a small, nearly homogeneous, agricultural country into a continental, multicultural, industrial nation. American literature and art, the role of women, industry and technology, race relations, popular culture, political parties, and the Constitution were influenced by those wars, especially the Civil War (1861 1865). Protests against the institution of slavery and the spread of slavery affected the nation's expansion westward. The coming of the Civil War changed American politics through the formation of new parties.

In many ways, the Civil War was America's second revolution, fought to preserve and advance the founding principles of the nation. When Lincoln spoke of a "new birth of freedom" at Gettysburg, he addressed the meaning and vitality of America's most cherished ideals and values—values that were tested and refined by that war. Prior to the Civil War women sought equal rights and Abolitionists fought to end the institution of slavery. Whereas women did not secure their rights after the war, Constitutional amendments ended slavery and redefined the rights of citizenship that later generations struggled to achieve.

The Civil War also resolved the Constitutional issue of whether the states had the right to secede from the Union. The South clung to its image of the war as a "Lost Cause" that had impoverished the region and undermined its way of life. One legacy of defeat was the restoration of racial subjugation through "Black Codes," sharecropping, and the Ku Klux Klan. For both North and South, the Civil War became a source for literature, art, music, and public celebrations to memorialize their concepts of conflict and to honor their own veterans. Although the Civil War preserved the Union, society and culture remained divided.

The articles in Volume 3, 1901 to 1945, examine how America's rise as an imperial and then a world power shaped American society, culture, and identity. During this period the United States engaged in four significant overseas wars, the Spanish American War (1898), the Philippine Insurrection (1899–1902), the First World War (1917–1918), and the Second World War (1941–1945). American literature and art, the role of women, industry and technology, race and ethnic relations, popular culture, political parties, and the power of government were profoundly affected by those wars. The First World War produced a mass migration of blacks from the South to northern cities to work in defense industries. Hostility toward the enemy produced public discrimination against citizens with German ancestors. A "Red Scare," meaning the fear of Communist subversion and restriction of civil liberties by our government, followed the Russian Revolution in 1917. Americans became increasingly suspicious of aliens and dissenters. While seeking world peace through treaties promoting disarmament and renouncing war in the 1930s, America turned its back on the League of Nations and aggression in Asia and Europe.

When World War II began in Europe in 1939, the United States remained neutral. Nevertheless, the nation began to prepare for war, which was declared after Pearl Harbor was attacked by Japan. World War II reshaped American society. Massive defense spending and the mobilization of young men and women for military service ended the Great Depression, which had begun in 1929. As a result of defense orders, big business prospered and labor union membership soared during the war years. America achieved a full employment economy during this conflict and this required a large number of women to enter the work force to increase defense production. It also spurred the massive migration of many Americans, especially African Americans, to cities in the North and West. The war effort reinvigorated movements to end racial discrimination and gender inequity. Many of the articles examine the legacy of that war in a wide range of areas that include the expansion of the federal government over the economy and the life of the average citizen as well as fashion, sports, veterans' organizations, medicine, gender roles, race relations, movies, music, patriotic celebrations, veterans, civil liberties, and war widows and orphans.

Volume 4's articles cover 1946 to 2004 and examine how the Cold War (1946–1991) and the War on Terror have formed American society, culture, and identity. For nearly fifty years, United States and its allies contested the Communist Bloc led by the Soviet Union. The "cold" part of the Cold War involved an elaborate worldwide network of alliances and military bases, an arms race to produce nuclear weapons, and the means to deliver those weapons to destroy whole civilizations. The fall of the Berlin Wall in 1989 and collapse of the Soviet Union in 1991 left the United States as the only superpower on the globe. The years after 1991 appeared to begin a new era of peace as fear of a cataclysmic war began to fade. However, since September 11, 2001 a new threat, terrorism, has again led America to an unprecedented form of war that is both foreign and domestic. Homeland security has become a feature of war in the twenty-first century.

The articles in this volume reflect the new role of America after World War II. Unlike the generation following World War I, Americans could not return to isolationism. National Defense became the nation's priority. Safeguarding the nation against subversion and aggression affected all parts of American society, culture and identity. Anticommunism following World War II produced a second Red Scare that again tested the limits of civil liberties and introduced a new term, "McCarthyism." In 1954 Congress amended the Pledge of Allegiance, adding "under God" to the description of "one nation" to underscore the difference between "godless communism" and the religious foundation of American democracy.

An arms race with the Soviet Union contributed to the growth of the federal government, fueled spending on education, and created a significant defense industry. In his farewell address in 1961 President Eisenhower warned of a "military-industrial complex." Films and novels about experiences in World War II, the Korean War, and especially the Vietnam War revealed the traumatic effects of combat on soldiers and their families. During the Vietnam War television brought the images of combat into American homes.

Defeating Fascism and Nazi racialism in World War II energized efforts to close the gap between American ideals of equality and opportunity and social practices that involved racial, gender, and sexual discrimination. During the late 1950s, 1960s, and early 1970s, anti-war and anti-establishment protests as well as the civil rights, feminist, and black power movements, challenged cultural conventions and roiled American society. These conflicts changed American literature and art, gender and race relations, popular culture, the entertainment industry, political parties, and the Constitution. The articles in this volume examine those changes as legacies of the Cold War and America's conflicts since World War II. They also explore the impact of the War on Terror on American citizens through the Homeland Security Act, the implications of the concepts of "just wars" and "preemptive war" on American society, culture, and identity as a nation.

All of the articles in these four volumes are written for the general reader and are supplemented with aids to make the material accessible. A Topic Outline assists readers who wish to focus on a particular issue, such as civil liberties, that appears in all volumes. Additional text appears as sidebars to further illustrate or elaborate portions of articles. A select bibliography follows each article for readers who wish to study the subject further. A general chronology of events from 1500 to 2004 will assist readers in placing the articles they are reading in a larger historical context. An Index will lead readers to

specific subjects. A Glossary defines key terms that might not be clear to younger readers. The editors hope that *Americans at War* will not only assist students and researchers in obtaining information, but will also encourage additional reading about the effect of war upon American society, culture, and identity.

Americans at War is the product of 234 authors and the editorial board. I thank all of the contributors for their fine work and outstanding scholarship. In particular, I wish to express gratitude and admiration to my associate editors for their thoughtful, timely, and untiring work on this project. Sally G. McMillen, Babcock Professor of History at Davidson College, edited Volume 2. Professor G. Kurt Piehler, Director, Center for the Study of War and Society, University of Tennessee, edited Volume 3. Professor D'Ann Campbell, Dean of Academics, U.S. Coast Guard Academy, and Professor Richard Jensen, Independent Scholar, edited Volume 4. I wish to thank Hélène Potter, senior editor at Macmillan Library Reference. She brought this editorial team together early in the process and has provided support, guidance, and encouragement to transform a concept into reality.

I also thank Oona Schmid at Macmillan, who recognized the need for a reference set on the effects of war upon American society and initiated the project. I hope that she, although no longer at Macmillan, feels the satisfaction of seeing her vision come true. The editors thank Anthony Aiello, who was our first project editor and who is also a contributor to the set. Finally, we wish to extend our deep appreciation and thanks to Kristin Hart, our project editor, who assisted us through the final stages of producing the set. Her attention to detail, responsiveness, clarity, and helpfulness were invaluable in the completion of the project. Finally, I thank the Humanities Center at the University of New Hampshire–Durham for its grant of a Senior Faculty Research Fellowship which helped to provide the time for me to devote to this project, and for support from the University of New Hampshire–Manchester.

John P. Resch
Editor-In-Chief
Editor, Volume 1
Professor of History
University of New Hampshire–Manchester

COMING OF AGE: AMERICA, 1820–1890

Warfare is more than combat between armies. It is a force that deeply affects the fabric of nations. The articles in this volume examine how wars in the nineteenth century, especially the Civil War, have shaped American society, culture, and identity. American literature and art, the role of women, industry and technology, race relations, popular culture, political parties, and the Constitution were profoundly affected by those wars. When Lincoln spoke of a "new birth of freedom" at Gettysburg, he addressed the meaning and vitality of America's most cherished ideals and values. In many ways, the Civil War was America's second revolution, for it served to preserve and advance the founding principles of the nation. That war occurred in the midst of the nineteenth century as the United States was transformed from a small, nearly homogeneous, agricultural country into a continental, multicultural, industrial nation on the verge of creating its own empire.

The United States underwent tremendous growth and change in the years between 1820 and 1890, evidenced by the rapid increase of its population, vast geographical expansion, and the emergence of new social, political, and economic institutions. In a sense, the nineteenth century represented the nation's "coming of age" as the United States expanded its borders coast to coast, became home to a larger, more diverse population, confronted myriad social, economic, and political problems, and, as a result of the Civil War, resolved the balance of power between the state and federal government.

THE EXPANSION OF THE NATION

During the nineteenth century, the nation experienced an enormous increase in its population, growing from 9.6 million people in 1820 to almost 63 million people by 1890. This increase was partly due to high fertility, but was also brought about by the millions of immigrants who flocked to the United States before and after the Civil War. These people sought to escape war, famine, political and religious persecution, and limited economic opportunities and to achieve a better life than the one they had left behind. Most immigrants before the Civil War came from Western Europe, but this changed in the late nineteenth century as immigration from Eastern and Southern Europe increased. These waves of people from abroad enhanced the cultural and religious diversity of the nation and created a huge labor force for an industrializing nation. By the late nineteenth century, some observers saw the nation as a "melting pot" due to its diverse racial and ethnic mix. But the influx of newcomers also fostered negative responses from Americans already living here who resented outsiders and the growing competition for jobs.

Another notable event in the nineteenth century was the physical expansion of the United States, undertaken and encouraged by the federal government through wars and military campaigns and through treaties negotiated with foreign nations and Native Americans. For instance, the federal government signed treaties with Great Britain to gain additional land in Florida and, in 1846, to settle the border between Canada and the Oregon Territory. Of more significance was the War with Mexico (1846–1848), for the outcome of that conflict increased the nation's land by a third and gave the United States coast-to-coast territory by adding land in the Southwest and West. The purchase of Alaska from Russia in 1867 and the granting of territorial status to Hawaii in 1898 gave the United States its current landholdings.

The acquisition of new land fostered both opportunities and problems. The discovery of gold in California in 1848, of silver in the Rocky Mountains in the 1860s, and the passage of the Homestead Act in 1862 encouraged Americans and new immigrants to settle the West, drawn by possible riches, a pleasant climate, free land, and the chance to start life over. From the 1840s until the end of the century, millions of people traveled westward by wagon train, ship, and railroad to take advantage of new opportunities. This movement raised a new question as early as 1820, when with the Missouri Compromise, Congress debated whether western lands should be open to slavery or not.

The nation's territorial expansion after the Mexican War only fueled the problem. Most people in the North reluctantly accepted slavery as long as it remained confined to the South, but they did not wish to see slavery expand into new western territories and states. On the other hand, southerners felt that they had the right to take their property (i.e., slaves) wherever they moved. Debates in Congress became increasingly combative over this issue as northerners and southerners argued over the future of these lands, reaching compromises that bought time, such as the Compromise of 1850 and the Kansas-Nebraska Act of 1854, but no successful resolution. The 1850s was an especially uneasy decade in American politics as the new Republican Party emerged and was determined to prevent the expansion of slavery. Few people predicted that it would take a war to resolve this issue and southerners' insistence on states' rights over federal authority.

Transportation rapidly expanded and improved throughout these decades, increasing markets and speeding the travel of goods and passengers. In the early part of the nineteenth century, the nation engaged in building canals, better roads and turnpikes, and steamboats. But it was the railroad that transformed the United States, especially the completion of the transcontinental railroad in 1869, which tied the East and West coasts together and provided faster, more economical travel. The growth of railroads aided farmers and ranchers who now could ship their produce and crops to distant markets.

THE IMPACT OF EDUCATION AND INNOVATION

With the spread of public education and the founding of new private academies, colleges, and universities during the nineteenth century, more of the population could read and write. People gained greater access to the printed word with improved printing presses and inexpensive books and serials. More newspapers and magazines were published; every town seemed to boast at least one paper. The invention and development of the telegraph by the 1850s brought news to more homes and communities, making Americans aware of the events of the day. The literary outpouring of popular authors such as Emerson, Thoreau, Whitman, Beecher, Melville, and Hawthorne created the nation's first literary renaissance.

The economy experienced a major transformation during this period as the nation became more industrialized. Though the United States remained essentially rural even by the end of the nineteenth century, major changes were well underway. New inventions and better technology had a positive impact on the lives of many Americans. New farm inventions—reapers, steel plows, and the cotton gin—vastly increased productivity in the Midwest and South. The invention of barbed wire aided farmers in the West, and the refrigerated railroad car made the raising of cattle a profitable enterprise after the Civil War. The spread of factories in the Northeast, which had begun early in the century, and the invention of steam-driven looms and the sewing machine enhanced the output of manufactured items such as woven textiles and factory-made clothing. The enormous demand for goods during the Civil War increased the output of armaments, uniforms, and consumer products and gave the North an enormous advantage over the agrarian South.

In the late nineteenth century, the invention of the electric light and DC generators transformed homes, factories, and entire cities. Industrial output increased and spread nationwide, evident in the success of textile and tobacco factories in the South and steel production in the North. Manufacturing put more people to work in industries, created more uniform goods, and made manufactured items available to more people at lower prices. The nation's enormous supply of natural resources, its rich farmland that produced food for wage workers, new technological innovations, and a huge labor supply made this industrialized economy possible. Yet the change to an industrialized economy extracted a price in fostering low wages, child labor, and unsanitary, unsafe working conditions.

These decades also witnessed a more self-conscious nation increasingly concerned about its identity and the values it embraced. A number of people, especially both men and women of the urban middle-class, began to ponder how to improve the nation as well as enhance their personal lives. By the second quarter of the nineteenth century, a number of activists, reformers, and religiously-minded individuals engaged in reform efforts to rid the nation of its myriad social problems. Groups of these activists as well as volunteer and religious organizations sought to eradicate the perceived evils of alcohol and prostitution, to expand and improve public education, to create cleaner, more livable cities, and to form institutions to take care of the blind, deaf, orphaned, handicapped, and mentally retarded. A few committed people organized utopian societies, such as the Owenites, Transcendentalists, and Shakers, to achieve a more perfect means to live by adhering to values and morals their founders considered important. A few female activists in the Northeast initiated the women's rights movement at Seneca Falls, New York in 1848, challenging laws and traditions that kept women in a secondary position with few rights and opportunities. There and at subsequent conventions, women activists demanded access to their own property, easier divorce laws, better jobs and schooling, and the right to vote.

Of all reform efforts in the decades before the Civil War, abolition of slavery was the most important and also became the most political issue. Its impact and number of followers increased over time. Abolitionists challenged the nation's conscience. Slavery, which had existed nationwide through the American Revolution, gradually began to disappear in northern states, where it was unprofitable as a labor system. In the South, slavery brought enormous wealth to a minority of privileged whites; most white southerners accepted this institution as a God-given, natural part of life and saw slaves as inferior, almost subhuman beings. Over time, a number of northerners became increasingly troubled by the existence of slavery, not only protesting its spread but, following the lead of other nations such as Great Britain (which had abolished slavery in the 1820s) wanting to put an end to it. A number of abolitionist organizations emerged, with committed activists—male, female, black and white—seeking to convince Congress to end the slave system. The issue was extremely controversial and raised questions about the nation's moral values. For the United States, it took a Civil War and the Thirteenth Amendment to settle the issue.

THE CIVIL WAR AND ITS AFTERMATH

The Civil War, more than any other event or movement, was the defining moment of the nineteenth century—a pivotal, extraordinarily bloody, event for the nation. With the election of Republican Abraham Lincoln in November 1860, eleven southern states in the next few months seceded from the United States and organized their own nation, establishing their own government and writing their own constitution. By going to war, the Confederacy was determined to defend the white southern way of life and protect its institutions (especially slavery) against federal encroachment. The Union, on the other hand, fought to restore national unity under one government and, as of 1863, to abolish slavery. Millions of men fought in this war, and more than 600,000 men died from battle wounds and disease. The Union victory in 1865 assured the unity of the nation and gave nearly four million slaves their freedom.

After the War ended, the North and South continued to move in different directions. The federal government undertook a halting, ultimately rather ineffective effort to reconstruct the South. The nation passed three important constitutional amendments, which ended slavery forever and ensured citizenship and voting rights for African American males. However, the idealism behind Reconstruction soon faltered, and by the 1870s, southern states were left to their own devices. Whites in the South found ways to resist what they regarded as federal meddling, and some resorted to violence to ensure white superiority.

By the end of the century, most southern states had enacted laws that prevented black men from voting and passed Jim Crow laws to ensure the segregation of blacks and whites in public buildings, public transportation, and public schools. Economically, the South faced enormous devastation and widespread poverty. Though now without its slave labor force, the South continued to grow cotton, which had brought great wealth before the war. Sharecropping and tenant farming became the major form of labor for southern blacks and poor whites. The federal government gradually turned its back on the South, giving its attention to more important issues and showing little concern for the plight of African Americans.

The West also brought new challenges to the nation after the Civil War. With more Americans moving west and claiming land, problems with Native Americans intensified. Indians had tried to resist whites' encroachment on their land by signing treaties with the government, moving to reservations, and fighting both settlers and soldiers. Whites, imbued with ideas of manifest destiny and their own sense of racial superiority, claimed any land they saw as rightfully theirs. Violence was the outcome, and misunderstanding and conflict between whites and Native Americans throughout much of the late nineteenth century defined the region. As became all too evident, Native Americans had little chance against superior white forces. The final conflict between white soldiers and Native Americans took place at Wounded Knee in 1890 and virtually ended all physical resistance by Indians.

Racism was also evident in the treatment of Mexicans still living in the American West, who lost most of the land they had owned before the War with Mexico. Chinese immigrants faced persecution over employment and schooling, as state and local governments passed laws that sought to limit their economic opportunities and segregate them from the white population. By the end of the century, the federal government passed a law prohibiting the Chinese from immigrating to this country, the first such law aimed at a specific group of people.

By the end of the nineteenth century, the nation was far different than it had been decades earlier. The United States was becoming truly urbanized and industrialized. Its population was now spread from coast to coast. Life for many Americans appeared far more hurried and chaotic than in the past. People were now better educated, as more of the nation's poor, its minorities, and its women took advantage of public education and as the burgeoning number of high schools, trade schools, and universities expanded nationwide. A true American culture of music, art, and literature had developed. The country began to look beyond its borders for new opportunities, for some observers expressed concern that the nation's frontier was now gone.

The United States was emerging as a major world force, with a strong, industrialized economy to trade and compete with others. And yet, despite the accomplishments, many issues remained unresolved, especially those concerning its diverse population, widespread poverty, and the lack of opportunities for many. The achievements of the nineteenth century, as well as its problems, loomed at the dawn of the twentieth century.

Sally G. McMillen

SYNOPTIC OUTLINE
OF ENTRIES

This systematic outline provides a general overview of the conceptual scheme of *Americans at War,* listing the titles of each entry in each volume. Because the section headings are not mutually exclusive, certain entries in *Americans at War* are listed in more than one section.

VOLUME 1: 1500–1815

AMERICAN REVOLUTION
Association Test
Boston Massacre: Pamphlets and Propaganda
Boston Tea Party: Politicizing Ordinary People
Common Sense
Commonwealth Men
Continental Congresses
Declaration of Independence
Loyalists
Peace of Paris, 1763
Republicanism and War
Revolution and Radical Reform
Sons of Liberty
Stamp Act Congress
States and Nation Building, 1775–1783

BIOGRAPHY
Adams, Abigail
Adams, John
Arnold, Benedict
Cooper, James Fenimore
Drinker, Elizabeth
Franklin, Benjamin
Hamilton, Alexander
Hewes, George Robert Twelves
Jackson, Andrew
Jefferson, Thomas
Madison, Dolley
Madison, James
Monroe, James
Montgomery, Richard
Paine, Thomas
Rowlandson, Mary
Sampson, Deborah
Warren, Mercy Otis
Washington, George

CONSTITUTION
Alien and Sedition Laws
Anti-Federalists
Articles of Confederation
Civil Liberties: Kentucky and Virginia Resolutions
Constitution: Bill of Rights
Constitution: Creating a Republic
Federalist Papers
Hartford Convention
Shays and Whiskey Rebellions

VETERANS
Civil War Veterans
Memorial (Decoration) Day
Prisons and Prisoners of War, 1815–1900

VISUAL ARTS
Photography, Civil War
Visual Arts, Civil War and the West

VOLUME 3: 1901–1945

BIOGRAPHY
Addams, Jane
Catt, Carrie Chapman
Cochran, Jackie
Ford, Henry
DuBois, W.E.B.
Hemingway, Ernest
Hoover, Herbert
McKinley, William
Mitchell, Billy
Roosevelt, Eleanor
Roosevelt, Franklin Delano
Roosevelt, Theodore
Stewart, Jimmy
Tokyo Rose
Wayne, John
Wilson, Woodrow
York, Alvin

CONSTITUTION
Civil Liberties, World War I
Civil Liberties, World War II
Conscription, World War I
Conscription, World War II
Dissent in World War I and World War II
Japanese Americans, World War II
Red Scare

CIVIL LIBERTIES
Civil Liberties, World War I
Civil Liberties, World War II
Dissent in World War I and World War II
Japanese Americans, World War II
Red Scare

DISSENT
Dissent in World War I and World War II
Peace Movements, 1898–1945

ECONOMY
Economy, World War I
Economy, World War II

Financing, World War I
Financing, World War II
GI Bill of Rights
Labor, World War I
Labor, World War II
Profiteering
Rationing
Rosie the Riveter
Women, Employment of

FAMILY AND COMMUNITY
Clothing, World War I and World War II
Gold Star Mothers Pilgrimage
Japanese Americans, World War II
Prisoner of War Camps, United States
Red Cross, American
Refugees
Regional Migration, World War I and World War II
Sexual Behavior
Sports, World War I
Sports, World War II
USO
Widows and Orphans

GENDER
Feminism
Gold Star Mothers Pilgrimage
Rosie the Riveter
Widows and Orphans
Women, Employment of
Women and World War I
Women and World War II
Women's Suffrage Movement

LITERATURE
Literature, World War I
Literature, World War II
Memoirs, Autobiographies

MEDIA
Allies, Images of
Enemy, Images of
Journalism, Spanish American War
Journalism, World War I
Journalism, World War II
Motion Pictures, World War I and World War II
Photography, World War I
Photography, World War II
Propaganda, 1898–1945
Public Opinion
Radio and Power of Broadcasting

MOBILIZATION
Conscription, World War I
Conscription, World War II

Demobilization
Financing, World War I
Financing, World War II
Labor, World War I
Labor, World War II
National Guard
Preparedness
Prisoner of War Camps, United States
Rationing
Red Cross, American
Rosie the Riveter
USO
Women, Employment of

MUSIC
Music, World War I
Music, World War II
National Anthem

PATRIOTISM AND NATIONAL IDENTITY
Americanization
American Legion
Armistice Day
GI Bill of Rights
Holocaust, American Response to
Monuments, Cemeteries, Spanish American War
Monuments, Cemeteries, World War I
Monuments, Cemeteries, World War II
National Anthem
Patriotism
Rosie the Riveter
Veterans of Foreign Wars

POLITICS
Bonus March
Civilian Conservation Corps (CCC)
Conscription, World War I
Conscription, World War II
Disarmament and Arms Control, 1898–1945
Gold Star Mothers Pilgrimage
GI Bill of Rights
Imperialism
Isolationism
New Deal
Pearl Harbor Investigation
Preparedness
United Nations

PRIMARY SOURCE DOCUMENTS
Advice to the Unemployed in the Great Depression
Against the Declaration of War
America's War Aims: The Fourteen Points
Bracero Agreement
Dedicating the Tomb of the Unknown Soldier

Excerpt from "The War in Its Effect upon Women"
Executive Order 8802
Executive Order 9066
Executive Order 9835
Green Light Letter
Lend-Lease Act
Lusitania Note
Neutrality Act
Franklin D. Roosevelt's Fireside Chat on the Bank
    Crisis
Franklin D. Roosevelt's First Inaugural Address
Sedition Act of 1918
Selective Service Act
Servicemen's Readjustment Act of 1944
"Over There"
Wilson Asks Congress for War
Women and the Changing Times
Women Working in World War II
Zimmermann Telegraph

RACE AND ETHNICITY
Americanization
African Americans, World War I
African Americans, World War II
American Indians, World War I and World War II
Japanese Americans, World War II
Latinos, World War I and World War II
Refugees
War, Impact on Ethnic Groups

RELIGION
Holocaust, American Response to
Religion, World War II

SCIENCE AND MEDICINE
Manhattan Project
Medicine, World War I
Medicine, World War II

VETERANS
American Legion
Armistice Day
Bonus March
GI Bill of Rights
Veterans Benefits
Veterans of Foreign Wars

VISUAL ARTS
Motion Pictures, World War I and World War II
Photography, World War I
Photography, World War II
Visual Arts, World War I
Visual Arts, World War II

CHRONOLOGY

Subjects marked in **bold** can be found within *Americans at War*, either in the main body or in the Primary Source Documents in the appendix.

Date	President	Event
1434		Beginning of African Slave Trade by Portuguese.
1494		Line of Demarcation dividing North and South America between Spain and Portugal.
1500–1542		Spanish and Portuguese exploration and conquests in North and South America. Few Spanish and Portuguese migrate to America. Their officials, soldiers, and priests rule native tribes. Plantations established. **Beginning of the decline of the native population** from 20 million to about 2 million due largely to disease.
1517		Beginning of the Protestant Reformation. Martin Luther posts his ninety-five theses challenging the authority of the Roman Catholic Church.
1519–1522		Hernando Cortez conquers the Aztecs in Mexico.
1529		Henry VIII of England separates from the Roman Catholic Church to create the Church of England.
1520s		**Slaves imported from Africa** in large numbers to work on sugar plantations in the West Indies.
1530–1533		Francisco Pizarro and *Conquistadores* defeat Inca civilization on the Western coast of South America, now the countries of Peru and Chile.
1539–1542		Hernando de Soto expedition from Florida to the Mississippi.
1540		Silver deposits discovered in Peru and Mexico. Mined by Indians.
		The Society of Jesus, Jesuits, formed by Ignatius of Loyola. Missioners sent throughout the world to convert people to Christianity, including many sent among the Indian tribes of North America.

Date	President	Event
1540–1542		Francisco Vásquez de Coronado explores the Southwest of what would become the United States.
1541		John Calvin and his Protestant followers take control of Geneva, Switzerland.
1542		Juan Rodriquez Cabrillo explores what would become the California coast.
1555		Peace of Augsburg ends religious wars in the Habsburg Empire and divides the land between Protestants and Catholics.
1564		French Calvinists known as Huguenots establish settlement at Fort Caroline in Florida. The fort is destroyed by Spanish in 1564 and most settlers killed.
1565		Queen Elizabeth I of England encourages colonization of Ireland by English Protestants.
August 24, 1572		St. Bartholomew's Day Massacre in Paris, which began a killing spree of Huguenots by Catholic mobs. Massacres and religious warfare in France follows, leaving 70,000 to 100,000 Huguenots dead.
1584		Richard Haklute publishes *A Discourse Concerning Western Planting,* a report on his voyage to America with Sir Walter Raleigh. Report encouraged English settlement to claim land for Protestantism, expand English trade, and to a find productive work for the unemployed.
1588		Founding of the English colony at Roanoke, Virginia by Sir Walter Raleigh. When the supply ship returns three years later the colony is found mysteriously abandoned and the whereabouts of the settlers unknown. All that is left is the message "Croatoan" on a post, the meaning of which is unclear.
		Defeat of the Spanish Armada by the English. End of Spanish effort to conquer England and restore the Catholic Church.
1598		Edict of Nantes ends religious persecution in France; Huguenots are granted religious rights, which are revoked in 1685.
1603		James I becomes King of England. Favors colonization in America.
1605		French colony established at Port Royal in what is now Nova Scotia, Canada.
1606		Virginia Company of Jamestown and Virginia Company of Plymouth created as joint-stock companies to finance and promote English colonization of America.
1607		**Jamestown** founded—first permanent English colony in North America.

Date	President	Event
1608		Quebec founded by Samuel de Champlain for fur trading. Becomes the capital of New France or Canada.
1608–1609		John Smith becomes head of **Jamestown** colony. Colony suffers from disease, starvation and attacks by Indians.
1609		Henry Hudson explores what is now the New York region and Hudson valley on behalf of the Dutch.
1610		Decision made to abandon **Jamestown**; colonists return when relief ships arrive bringing supplies and settlers.
1614		Lutheran refugees from Amsterdam, Holland, establish a trading post in what is now Albany, New York.
1616		John Rolf and Pocahontas visit England to promote tobacco sales and settlement.
1619		First African **slaves** arrive at **Jamestown.**
1620		Pilgrims land at Plymouth. The day before landing they sign the Mayflower Compact, often described as America' first constitution.
1622		**Massacre of 350 settlers at Jamestown** led by Opechancanough.
1624		Jamestown company disbanded. Virginia becomes a Royal Colony.
1626		Dutch purchase Manhattan Island from Indians; establish New Amsterdam.
1630		Puritans led by John Winthrop settle in what becomes Boston, Massachusetts.
1632		Maryland chartered by Charles I to be refuge for English Catholics.
1635		Roger Williams banished from the Massachusetts Bay Colony, establishes Rhode Island.
1636–1637		Pequot War, the first serious armed conflict between Native Americans and settlers, takes place in New England.
1637		Anne Hutchinson excommunicated.
1642		Beginning of English Civil War between supporters of Charles I and Parliament led by Oliver Cromwell.
1649		Charles I beheaded; England becomes a republic under Oliver Cromwell.
1660		Monarchy restored under Charles II. Navigation Act demands colonial tobacco shipped to England for tax.
1660–1688		England establishes six colonies, including Pennsylvania by Quakers and Carolina by Barbadian planters who receive charter in 1663.

Date	President	Event
1664		Dutch colony surrenders to English. New Amsterdam becomes New York.
1675–1676		**King Philip's War** in New England; 10,000 Indians die.
1676		**Bacon's rebellion.** Uprising in Virginia by settlers to overthrow government that prevents them from seizing Indian land.
1688		Glorious Revolution in England. James II deposed and Parliament's power increased.
1688–1689		John Locke produces his *Second Treatise on Government* professing that individuals have inalienable rights of life, liberty and property.
1692		Salem Witch Trials. By the end, nineteen accused witches had been hung, one was crushed to death, and seventeen more died in prison.
1702–1713		Queen Anne's War—A series of raids by the French and their Indian allies upon New Englanders, including the raid on Deerfield, Massachusetts.
1711–1713		The Tuscarora War—War between Carolina settlers and Tuscarora Indians.
1715–1716		Yamasee War—War between Carolina settlers and Yamasee Indians and their allies in Florida.
1730s–1740s		The religious revival led by Jonathan Edwards and George Whitefield, called the Great Awakening, sweeps through the colonies.
1739		**Stono Rebellion,** slave uprising in Stono, South Carolina.
1739–1743		The War of Jenkins Ear—War between England and Spain on the Georgia-Florida border. Named after Robert Jenkins who lost his ear.
1744–1748		King George's War—War between England and France on American soil. Louisburg on Cape Breton is captured by New England troops, stiking a blow to the French.
1754–1763		**French and Indian War**—Conflict for empire. France is defeated and its lands, especially Canada, become part of the British empire.
1763		Pontiac's War—Indian attacks on English posts and settlers in the Great Lakes region.
1765		**Stamp Act** Passed by Parliament; American protest and resistance to the Stamp Act; "**Sons of Liberty**" formed in Boston.
October 1765		**Stamp Act Congress** approves Resolutions upholding rights as Englishmen.

Date	President	Event
1766		Protest against the **Stamp Act** is successful and the act is repealed.
		Parliament passes the Declaratory Act proclaiming full authority over the American colonies.
1767		Townshend duties passed by Parliament; protests result.
1768		Riots in Boston against the Townshend Duties; British Troops sent to Boston.
1770		**Boston Massacre.**
December 16, 1773		**Boston Tea Party.** English tea is destroyed in Boston harbor by the "Sons of Liberty" in reaction to Britain's Tea Act of 1773.
1774		Britain places Massachusetts under military rule—Parliament approves four laws to quell the Massachusetts rebellion. Laws branded by colonists as the Intolerable Acts.
September 5, 1774		First **Continental Congress** meets in Philadelphia to organize colonial protest and resistance.
October 25, 1774		Edenton, North Carolina tea party by local women protesting British imports. Fifty-one local women met and openly declared "We, the aforesaid Ladys will not promote ye wear of any manufacturer from England until such time that all acts which tend to enslave our Native country shall be repealed."
April 19, 1775		Battles of Lexington and Concord. Beginning of the War for Independence.
January 1776		**Thomas Paine** publishes *Common Sense*. Argues for American independence and formation of a republican form of government; rejected European style monarchy and aristocracy.
July 4, 1776		**Declaration of Independence.**
1776		Virginia creates the first state constitution. It includes a Bill of Rights. Other states follow by making their own constitutions.
1777		Vermont outlaws **slavery.**
November 15, 1777		**Articles of Confederation** agreed to by the **Continental Congress.** Creates the United States as an alliance of independent states.
1778		France allies with the United States after the Americans defeat the British at Saratoga in 1777.
1779		Spain declares war on Great Britain.
October 19, 1781		Cornwallis defeated at Yorktown; last major battle of the Revolutionary War and peace negotiations begin.
1783		**Peace of Paris.** American Independence recognized.

Date	President	Event
1787		Shays's rebellion in Massachusetts. National government under the Articles of Confederation shaken.
May 14, 1787		Constitutional convention gathers in Philadelphia. Proposes to replace the Articles of Confederation with a new constitution.
1788		Constitution adopted.
1789	George Washington, 1789–1797	French Revolution begins.
		French Assembly adopts the *Rights of Man* declaration written by Thomas Paine.
April 30, 1789		George Washington inaugurated as first president of the United States.
1790		First federal census undertaken.
1791		Bill of Rights—First Ten Amendments added to the Constitution.
1792		French Republic proclaimed.
1793		Eli Whitney invents cotton gin.
January 21, 1793		French King, Louis XVI tried and executed; French Revolution takes radical turn.
1794		United States and Great Britain agree to blockade France. Beginning of American quasi–war with France.
		Whiskey rebellion in western Pennsylvania. George Washington and Alexander Hamilton send the militia to put down the protesters against the tax on whiskey.
		"Mad" Anthony Wayne defeats Indians at "Fallen Timbers" near Detroit.
September 26, 1796		Washington's Farewell Address.
1797	John Adams, 1797–1801	
1798–1800		Quasi-War with England and France. Military mobilization proposed. Alien and Sedition laws passed to curtail freedom of speech because of threat of war and subversion. James Madison and Thomas Jefferson respond with the Kentucky and Virginia Resolutions proclaiming the right of states to void federal laws that violate individual or states' rights.
1801	Thomas Jefferson, 1801–1809	John Marshall appointed Chief Justice of the Supreme Court (1801–1835). Generally considered one of the principal architects of American government and cultural values.
1801		Thomas Jefferson inaugurated. Peaceful transfer of power between two opposing political parties, Federalists and Democratic Republicans. Beginning of wars with Barbary pirates (1801–1805; 1815).

Date	President	Event
		Great Revival begins, Cane Ridge, Kentucky.
1803–1815		Napoleonic Wars. War between France and England in Europe and the Western Hemisphere. American ships and men seized by both countries.
April 30, 1803		American purchase of Louisiana territory from France.
1804–1806		Lewis and Clark Expedition to Pacific.
1808		African Slave traded to the United States prohibited.
1809	James Madison, 1809–1817	
1812–1815		War with England. Washington, D.C. occupied by the British and burned.
September 14, 1814		Francis Scott Key composes poem, "Star-Spangled Banner."
1815		Andrew Jackson's victory at New Orleans.
		Hartford Convention. New England protest against the war with England. Demands changes in the Constitution to weaken Congress's power to declare war. Some New England states threaten to secede from the Union if federal power is not reduced.
1816–1826		Outburst of American nationalism and patriotism.
1817	James Monroe, 1817–1825	Monroe's tour of New England and beginning of Bunker Hill monument.
1818		Passage of the Revolutionary War Pension Act to honor and reward veterans.
1020s		Expansion of factory towns and creation of new mill cities in New England.
1820		Missouri Compromise.
1820–1861		Expansion of the market economy in the North and South. Northern manufacturing, commerce, and farming; Southern farming, plantations, and export of cotton. Wage labor in the North; Wage and slave labor in the South.
1822		Discovery of Denmark Vesey's slave conspiracy for a rebellion in Charleston, South Carolina.
1823		Monroe Doctrine proclaimed in 1823.
1824–1825		Lafayette's tour of the United States.
1825	John Adams, 1825–1829	Completion of the Erie Canal connecting Buffalo with New York City. Part of the "Transportation Revolution" that binds the nation by roads, canals, and later railroads.
1826		Second Bank chartered. National Road completed.

Date	President	Event
		James Fenimore Cooper publishes *The Last of the Mohicans*, a tale about the **French and Indian War**, 1754–1763. Beginning of an American **literature**.
July 4, 1826		Death of **John Adams** and **Thomas Jefferson**. Viewed as a time of reflection on the Revolution.
1828		First **railroad** completed, the Baltimore and Ohio.
1829	**Andrew Jackson, 1829–1837**	
1830		Religious revival, "Second Great Awakening," begins in western New York.
		Indian Removal Act; relocate Indians in Georgia.
1831		*Cherokee Nation v. Georgia Supreme Court* decision.
		Nat Turner slave uprising in Virginia.
1832		William Lloyd Garrison founds the abolitionist newspaper, *The Liberator.*
1833		Garrison and **Abolitionists** create the American Anti-Slavery society to end the institution of slavery.
		Nullification Crisis in South Carolina; South Carolina votes to nullify federal law on tariffs.
1834		Mobs attack **abolitionists** in New York City. Race riot in Philadelphia. Female mill workers at Lowell, Massachusetts strike and again in 1836.
1836		Ralph Waldo Emerson publishes *Nature*, first major work on transcendentalism. Part of the effort to create an American **literature**.
March 6, 1836		Defeat of Americans at **Alamo** by General Santa Anna.
1837	**Martin Van Buren, 1837–1841**	
1838		Cherokee Indians forcibly removed from Georgia to Oklahoma; thousands die along the "trail of tears" before arriving.
1840s		Famine in Ireland and failed revolution in Germany in 1848 result in surge of Irish and German immigrants to the United States.
1840		Liberty Party formed. Opposes the spread of **slavery** to the territories. Receives less than one percent of the popular vote.
1841	**William Henry Harrison, 1841; John Tyler, 1841–1845**	
1844		Margaret Fuller publishes *Woman in the Nineteenth Century*, which examines the role of women and argues for **equal rights for women**.

Date	President	Event
1845	James Polk, 1845–1849	Proclamation of **Manifest Destiny** by the United States. Americans feel it is their mission and part of God's plan to spread democracy throughout the continent.
		United States **annexes** Texas, which permits **slavery**.
		Frederick Douglass publishes *Narrative of the Life of Frederick Douglass*, a powerful autobiography that further inspires the **Abolitionist** movement.
1846		United States declares war with Mexico. Anti-war protests divide the nation.
		Wilmot Proviso. Proposal for popular sovereignty to prohibit **slavery** in territories won from Mexico approved by the House of Representatives but defeated in the Senate.
June 10, 1846		Bear Flag Revolt in California. "Bear Flaggers" raise the grizzly bear flag and officially declare the territory free from Mexican rule. The bear flag becomes the official flag of California.
June 15, 1846		U.S. and Great Britain settle Oregon border. The 49th parallel is determined to be the border between Great Britain and the United States, with the exception of Vancouver Island.
1847		Brigham Young leads Mormons to Great Salt Lake, Utah.
1848		**Treaty of Guadalupe Hidalgo** ends war with Mexico and results in the United States acquiring California and what is now the U.S. southwest.
		Free Soil Party formed; opposes the spread of the slave institution. Absorbs the Liberty Party.
		Gold discovered in California, leading to California gold rush of 1849.
July 19, 1848		**Women's Rights Movement** convenes in Seneca Falls, New York. Demands equal rights under the law, including the right to vote.
1849	Zachary Taylor, 1849–1850	Henry David Thoreau publishes *Walden*, an account of man and nature and part of the new American literary genre.
1850	Millard Fillmore, 1850–1853	Compromise of 1850. Intended to resolve the conflict over the spread of **slavery**; California admitted as a free state (prohibited slavery). Fugitive slave law strengthens recovery of runaway slaves in the North.
1851		Herman Melville publishes *Moby-Dick,* a novel that has become an American classic.

Date	President	Event
1852		Harriet Beecher Stowe publishes *Uncle Tom's Cabin*. The novel attacks the institution of **slavery** and increases tension between the North and South.
1853	Franklin Pierce, 1853–1857	American or "Know Nothing" party formed. The party is composed of nativists, people who oppose immigration, Catholics, and citizenship for blacks. Members, when asked about their organizations were suppose to reply they knew nothing, hence the name of the party.
		Gadsden Purchase adds territory in Southwest.
1854		**Kansas-Nebraska Act** opens the west to the possibility of slavery.
		Republican Party formed to oppose the **Kansas-Nebraska Act**. Absorbs the Free Soil Party.
1856		"Bleeding Kansas" erupts as northerners and southerners fight over future of **slavery** in territory.
1857	James Buchanan, 1857–1861	Dred Scott case. **Supreme court** declares that the **Constitution** does not apply to free blacks and that it allows slave owners to take their property (slaves) to any state or territory.
1858		**Lincoln**-Douglas debates in Illinois for Senate seat.
October 16, 1859		John Brown's raid on Harpers Ferry, Virginia. His intent is to arm slaves and to lead a slave uprising. He is captured and later hanged.
1860		**Abraham Lincoln** elected president with 40 percent of the popular vote. South Carolina votes to **secede** from the Union.
1861	Abraham Lincoln, 1861–1865	**Confederacy** formed by **seceded** states. Fort Sumter attacked and **Abraham Lincoln** calls out militia to end rebellion. Civil War begins.
		Harriet Jacob publishes *Incidents in the Life of a Slave Girl*, describing the life of a female under **slavery**.
1862		Bloody battles at Shiloh and Antietam.
		Homestead Act passed by Congress.
January 1, 1863		**Emancipation Proclamation** by Abraham Lincoln, ending **slavery** in territory conquered by northern troops.
July 1863		Battles at Gettysburg and Vicksburg turn the tide toward the Union.
September 2, 1864		Atlanta falls. After several weeks of preparation General **Sherman begins his march to the sea.**
1865	Andrew Johnson, 1865–1869	Congress establishes **Freedmen's Bureau** to assist former slaves. South enacts **Black Codes** to suppress blacks.
		Thirteenth Amendment to **Constitution** ratified, abolishing **slavery**.

Date	President	Event
April 9, 1865		End of Civil War at Appomattox Courthouse. Six days later **Abraham Lincoln** is assassinated.
1866		Founding of Equal Rights Association to seek woman's suffrage.
		Formation of the Grand Army of the Republic composed of veterans of the Union Army. To become an organization for **veterans' benefits.**
		Ku Klux Klan organized as the "Invisible Empire of the South."
1868		**Fourteenth Amendment** added to Constitution, ensuring all male citizens equal protection of the laws and due process of law.
1869	**Ulysses S. Grant, 1869–1877**	Woman's suffrage groups split in two over tactics and issue of black male suffrage; will reunite in 1890.
		Territory of Wyoming allows women to vote.
May 10, 1869		Completion of transcontinental **railroad** in Promontory, Utah.
1870		**Fifteenth Amendment** added to **Constitution**, guaranteeing the right to vote to males regardless of race or color.
1870–1871		Franco-Prussian War.
1876		Westward migration increases conflicts with Indians. Custer defeated at Little Bighorn.
1877	**Rutherford B. Hayes, 1877–1881**	Troops withdrawn from the South. Disputed election of 1876 resolved and Rutherford B. Hayes was determined to have won 185 electoral votes to Samuel Tilden's 184. **Reconstruction** ended.
1881	**James Garfield, 1881; Chester Arthur, 1881–1885**	Helen Hunt Jackson publishes *A Century of Dishonor*—documents the mistreatment of American Indians.
1882		Chinese Exclusion Act passed by Congress.
1885	**Grover Cleveland, 1885–1889**	
1887		**Dawes Severalty Act,** which dissolves Indian tribes and turns tribal lands into private property for Indians—an effort to Americanize Indians.
1888		Edward Bellamy publishes *Looking Backward*—a critical assessment of American capitalism and endorsement of more cooperative society.
1889	**Benjamin Harris, 1889–1893**	
1890		Formation of the National American Woman's Suffrage Association, uniting the two groups working for woman's suffrage.

Date	President	Event
		Jacob Riis publishes *How the Other Half Lives,* an exposé aided by photographs of squalor and exploitation of New York's **immigrants** and poor.
1890–1904		Ex-confederate states pass laws prohibiting Blacks from voting. "Jim Crow" laws enforce **racial segregation.**
December 29, 1890		Battle of Wounded Knee marking last major conflict between Native Americans and federal troops in West.
1893	**Grover Cleveland, 1893–1897**	
1895		Booker T. Washington's "Atlanta Compromise."
		Stephen Crane published *Red Badge of Courage,* a novel giving psychological insights into combat during the Civil War.
1896		*Plessy v. Ferguson* ruling by the **Supreme Court** that **segregation**—"separate but equal"—is constitutional.
1897	**William McKinley, 1897–1901**	
1898		Spanish-American War.
1899–1902		American-Filipino War. Insurrection against American rule.
1900		United States becoming one of the world's leading industrial powers.
1900–1914		**Immigration** averages one million people a year. Many from Eastern and Southern Europe, including Jews and Catholics.
1901	**Theodore Roosevelt, 1901–1909**	
1903		United States acquires the Panama Canal Zone. Construction on canal begins.
December 17, 1903		First powered flight. The age of air transportation and warfare begins.
1904		President **Theodore Roosevelt** issues his "corollary" to the **Monroe Doctrine.**
1904–1917		Progressives expand the regulatory powers of the national government.
1905		The Industrial Workers of the World (IWW) founded.
1908		**Henry Ford** produces the Model T.
		Race riot in Springfield, Illinois.
1909	**William H. Taft, 1909–1913**	National Association for the Advancement of Colored People (NAACP) founded to fight racial discrimination and to secure **civil rights.**

Date	President	Event
1913	**Woodrow Wilson, 1913–1921**	
1014 1010		World War I in Europe.
1914–1917		Unites States remains neutral about the war in Europe.
1917		Russian Revolution begins. Communists under Lenin seize power.
April 6, 1917		United States declares war on Germany in April. **Draft begins.** Security Espionage Act. President Wilson creates the Committee on Public Information (CPI). Over 400,000 blacks serve in armed forces.
1918		**Sedition Act.** Eugene V. Debs, head of the IWW, jailed.
November 11, 1918		World War I concludes. A total of 112,000 American soldiers killed.
1919		**Peace of Paris.** Congress rejects American membership in the League of Nations.
		Widespread labor strikes.
		Race riot in Chicago.
1919–1920		**Red Scare.** Campaign to suppress communists, radicals and socialists. Federal raids to round up aliens.
1920s		Rise of a consumer society; mass marketing and advertising; expansion of highways and automobile travel, and entertainment industry, particularly **movies.**
1920		Marcus Garvey, a Black Nationalist, calls for blacks to create a separate nation within the United States.
		Nineteenth Amendment to the **Constitution** ratified giving women the right to vote.
		Election of Warren G. Harding on the pledge to return America to "normalcy," meaning returning to the pre-World War I society.
		Census reports a majority of Americans live in cities.
1921	**Warren Harding, 1921–1923**	
1922		Benito Mussolini becomes Fascist dictator of Italy.
		United States along with four other great powers agree to limit the size of their navies.
1923	**Calvin Coolidge, 1923–1929**	Adolf Hitler and his Nazi party attempt to overthrow the government in Bavaria. Hitler imprisoned and writes *Mein Kampf*
April 18, 1923		Yankee Stadium opens. Part of era of mass public **sports** in baseball and college football.
1924		Ku Klux Klan achieves a membership of nearly 4 million people.

Date	President	Event
		America **aids European recovery** with the Dawes Plan.
1924–1926		Joseph Stalin rises to power in the Soviet Union.
1925		Hitler rebuilds Nazi party.
		Scopes trial in Tennessee.
1926		**Ernest Hemingway** publishes *The Sun Also Rises* about the "Lost Generation."
1928		Kellogg-Briand Pact. International agreement not to use war as means to fulfill national policies.
1929	**Herbert Hoover, 1929–1933**	Eric Maria Remarque publishes *All Quiet on the West ern Front*, a powerful anti-war **novel**. Made into a popular **film** in 1930.
		Ernest Hemingway publishes *A Farewell to Arms*, another anti-war **novel**.
October 29, 1929		Stock Market crash.
1929–1932		Economic depression spreads through United States and Europe. Unemployment in the United States rises to 25 percent of the work force.
1931		Japan invades Manchuria.
1932		World War I veterans march on Washington. "Bonus Army" dispersed by troops.
		Franklin Roosevelt elected president.
1933	**Franklin D. Roosevelt, 1933–1945**	**Roosevelt's inaugural address** declares that Americans have "nothing to fear but fear itself."
		Adolf Hitler becomes Chancellor of Germany.
1933–1935		First **New Deal**. Prohibition repealed. "Alphabet" measures implemented such as the Agricultural Adjustment Act (AAA), **Civilian Conservation Corps (CCC)**, and Tennessee Valley Authority (TVA). Banking and stock market regulated.
1935		Italy invades Ethiopia.
		Congress passes first of **Neutrality Acts** aimed at keeping the United States out of war.
1935–1937		Second **New Deal**. Social Security Act passed. National Labor Relations Acts (Wagner Act) strengthens unions. Rural Electrification Act brings power to rural America. Works Progress Administration (WPA) provides employment for workers, artists, and performers.
1936		Civil war in Spain. Germany and the Soviet Union aid combatants.
		Germany and Italy agree to form an alliance as "Axis Powers."
1937		Japan invades China.

Date	President	Event
		Neutrality Acts strengthened.
1937–1938		Recovery of the American economy halted. Unemployment approaches 1932 levels.
October 5, 1937		Roosevelt gives his "Quarantine Speech" urging peace-loving countries to unite against aggressors.
1938		Germany occupies part of Czechoslovakia following Munich agreement.
1939		Congress rejects Wagner-Rogers bill to increase **immigration** quotas to allow 20,000 Jewish children in Germany to enter the United States.
September 1, 1939		Germany invades Poland. World War II begins in Europe.
1940		Congress passes the **first peace-time draft**. American rearmament begins.
June 1940		Germany defeats France. Battle of Britain begins.
1941		**Franklin D. Roosevelt** announces the "Four Freedoms."
		Roosevelt proposes that America become the "arsenal for democracy." Congress passes "**Lend-Lease**" legislation to provide arms to Britain.
		Roosevelt creates the Fair Employment Practices Commission (FEPC) to ensure nondiscrimination in industries receiving federal contracts.
		Roosevelt and Winston Churchill agree on the "Atlantic Charter" to create a new world organization to ensure collective security.
December 7, 1941		Japans attacks **Pearl Harbor.** United States declares war. Germany and Italy, allies of Japan, declare war on the United States.
1942–1945		Economic depression begun in 1929 ends. About 15,000,000 people in the armed services. Military remains racially segregated.
1942		**Roosevelt** signs **Executive Order 9066** authorizing **internment of Japanese** on the west coast for reasons of national security.
		Roosevelt creates the Office of War Information (OWI) to oversee **propaganda** and censorship affecting the war.
		Congress of Racial Equality (CORE) formed to secure **civil rights** for blacks.
1943		Many blacks move north. Black employment in defense industries increases. Race riot in Detroit.
1944		Gunnar Myrdal publishes *The American Dilemma* analyzing the depth of racism in America.

Date	President	Event
		Bretton Woods agreement creates a new economic organization for the world.
		GI Bill passed.
June 6, 1944		D-Day. Allied forces land in Normandy.
December 18, 1944		**Supreme Court** declares **internment of Japanese** constitutional in *Korematsu v. United States.*
1945	**Harry Truman, 1945–1953**	Yalta and Potsdam agreements by allies to divide Germany and reestablish governments in Easter Europe. A source of conflict during the **Cold War.**
May 7, 1945		Germany surrenders unconditionally. One day later is V-E Day, Victory in Europe.
August 6 and 9, 1945		United States drops **atomic bombs** on Hiroshima and Nagasaki. Japan surrenders within days.
September 2, 1945		V-J Day, Victory over Japan.
November 1945		Nuremberg trial of Nazi leaders.
December 1945		**United Nations** established.
1946		Baruch plan for international control of atomic power approved by the **United Nations.**
		Atomic Energy Commission created. RAND (Research and Development) "think tank" established.
		Winston Churchill delivers his "iron curtain" speech in Fulton, Missouri.
1947		Beginning of "**Cold War.**" **Truman Doctrine** National Security Act passes creating the Defense Department, National Security Council, and **CIA.** George Kennan outlines the policy of "containment." President Truman issues **Executive Order 9835** to remove "security risks" from government.
		Marshall Plan approved.
		British colonialism ends in India. Pakistan created. New countries emerge as decolonization occurs elsewhere in the world.
		House Un-American Activities Committee conducts hearings to reveal communist influence in the movie and entertainment industry.
		Postwar baby boom peaks at nearly 27 million births. Suburbs expand. **Levittown,** the beginning of mass housing developments.
1948		Soviet Union blockades West Berlin. Berlin airlift begins.
		State of **Israel** created. **Israel** repels attacks.
		Truman issues Executive Order 9981 desegregating the armed forces.

Date	President	Event
1949		Communists under Mao Zedong take control of China.
		Soviet Union detonates its first atomic bomb.
		North Atlantic Treaty Organization (NATO) formed for mutual security against a Soviet invasion of Western Europe.
		George Orwell publishes *1984*—prophesizes the triumph of totalitarianism.
		Major League Baseball integrated.
1950s		Beginning in the late 1940s the "new look" return to women's fashion. Television replaces radio as the principal source of home entertainment.
		Employment of married mothers outside of the home increases.
1950		NSC #68, a top secret policy approved by the National Security Council, which approves use of covert force and encouraging "captive nations" to revolt against Soviet rule. Places the United States on a quasi-war footing.
		Julius and Ethel Rosenberg arrested for treason. Both executed in 1953.
		Passage of the McCarran Internal Security Act.
1950–1953		Korean War.
1950–1954		"McCarthyism." Civil liberties challenged. 1954 Senate censors Senator Joseph McCarthy.
1951		European Coal and Steel Community formed. Beginning of what would become the European Economic Community (known as the Common Market, and later the European Union.
April 1951		Truman removes General McArthur from command in Korea.
1952		Election of Dwight D. Eisenhower as president. First Republican in 20 years.
1953	Dwight D. Eisenhower, 1953–1961	East Germans rise up against Soviet rule. Suppressed by force.
March 5, 1953		Soviet dictator, Joseph Stalin, dies.
1954		French defeated at Dien Bien Phu. French Indochina divided into Laos, Cambodia and Vietnam.
		Historian David Potter publishes *People of Plenty*, describing the rise of American consumer economy and expansion of the middle class.
		Congress adds "under God" to the Pledge of Allegiance.
		Elvis Presley tops the music charts.

Date	President	Event
May 17, 1954		*Brown v. Board of Education.* **Supreme Court** rules that **segregation** in schools is unconstitutional.
1955		Movie *The Blackboard Jungle* warns of social decay caused by youth gangs and rock 'n roll **music.**
December 1, 1955		Rosa Parks refuses to give up her seat on a Montgomery bus. Boycott begins to end **segregation** on the city buses. **Civil rights movement** intensifies. **Martin Luther King, Jr.** and the Southern Christian Leadership Conference emerge as leaders.
1956		Passage of the Highway Act authorizing construction of the interstate highway system to improve American defense and promote commerce.
		Congress approves adding "In God We Trust" to the nation's motto.
		Supreme Court declares **segregation** on public buses unconstitutional.
		Hungarian uprising against **Communist** regime suppressed.
September 1957		Federal troops enforce integration of Little Rock, Arkansas, high school.
October 4, 1957		Soviet Union launches Sputnik, the **first space satellite.** Soviet leadership in missile technology and delivery of atomic weapons feared. Sales of bomb shelters increase in United States.
1958		National Defense Education Act passed to improve the teaching of mathematics and science.
1959		Fidel Castro leads revolution in Cuba. Establishes a **communist** regime.
1960		Young Americans for Freedom (YAF) formed—College activists favoring aggressive American actions to defeat **communism** and to reduce "big government" at home.
1960–1963		Increased **civil rights** activism—sit ins and "freedom rides."
1961	John F. Kennedy, 1961–1963	President **John F. Kennedy** increases American aid to South Vietnam against communist insurgents.
		Construction of the **Berlin Wall.**
January 7, 1961		**President Eisenhower's** farewell speech. Warns of the dangers of a "**military-industrial complex**" dominating American economy and society.
April 17, 1961		**CIA** supports attack on Cuba by exiles defeated at the "Bay of Pigs."

Date	President	Event
1962		Students for a Democratic Society (SDS) formed in response to YAF. Young activists against racial discrimination and social injustices. Becomes part of the "New Left." Beliefs expressed in its "Port Huron Statement."
October 1962		Cuban missile crisis.
1963	Lyndon B. Johnson, 1963–1969	Betty Friedan publishes *The Feminine Mystique* expressing women's dissatisfaction with limitations of domestic life and wish for careers and more active public life.
August 28, 1963		March on Washington where Martin Luther King, Jr. gives his "I have a dream" speech.
September 15, 1963		Bombing of Birmingham, Alabama, church killing four children.
November 22, 1963		Assassination of President Kennedy.
1964		Congress approves Tonkin Gulf Resolution authorizing increased military force in South Vietnam.
		Movie, *Dr. Strangelove: Or How I Stopped Worrying and Learned to Love the Bomb* presents a critical parody of cold war fears and American policy of Mutual Assured Destruction (MAD).
		Passage of the Civil Rights Act. Prohibits racial discrimination in public facilities and discrimination against women.
1965		President Lyndon Johnson announces his "Great Society" program—Medicare, Medicaid, and a "war on poverty."
		Voting Rights Act removes barriers used to restrict Blacks from voting.
		President Johnson orders operation "Rolling Thunder," the limited bombing of North Vietnam. 50,000 more troops sent to South Vietnam.
1965–1970s		Counterculture. Associated with "hippies," "yippies," the anti-war movement. Woodstock Festival in New York.
February 21, 1965		Malcolm X murdered by enemies within his own movement.
1967		Anti-war march on the Pentagon.
1968		Civil Rights Act ending racial discrimination in housing.
		Tet Offensive in Vietnam. A majority of Americans turn against the Vietnam war.
April 4, 1968		Assassination of Martin Luther King, Jr.
June 6, 1968		Assassination of Robert F. Kennedy.
August 1968		Riots at the Chicago convention of the Democratic Party.

Date	President	Event
1969	Richard Nixon, 1969–1974	President **Richard Nixon** begins negotiations with the Soviet Union to reduce nuclear missiles. Strategic Arms Limitations Treaty (SALT) formalized two years later.
		American withdrawal from Vietnam begins.
July 20, 1969		**Americans land on the moon.**
1970		American incursion in Cambodia sets off campus riots and protests. Students killed at Kent State University in Ohio.
June 1971		Daniel Ellsberg leaks the so-called "**Pentagon Papers.**"
1972		**President Nixon** opens relations with Communist China.
1973		Paris Peace Agreement. American troops withdrawn from Vietnam. **POWs** returned.
1973		*Roe v. Wade.*
August 8, 1974	Gerald Ford, 1974–1977	**President Nixon** resigns from office as a result of the Watergate scandal.
1975		South Vietnam falls to the **communists.**
1977	Jimmy Carter, 1977–1981	**Feminist movement** becomes international. First meeting in Houston, Texas.
1980		Microsoft licenses its computer software, MS-DOS (Microsoft Disk Operating System).
1980s		Legal **immigration** of Asians and Hispanics increases social diversity.
		America becoming a "knowledge and service" economy.
		AIDs epidemic begins.
1980–1988		The so-called "Reagan Revolution." A massive build-up of the American military, a more aggressive policy to combat Soviet influence, efforts to restore more political power to the states, and federal tax cuts.
1981	Ronald Reagan, 1981–1989	
1985		Mikhail Gorbachev becomes head of the Soviet Union. Begins programs of reform *glasnost* (openness), and *perestroika* (restructuring) to revitalize the Soviet economy.
April 25–26, 1986		Nuclear power plant at Chernobyl explodes. World's worst nuclear accident.
June 3–4, 1989	George H. W. Bush, 1989–1993	Chinese students demonstrate in Tiananmen Square for more freedoms. Suppressed by military force.
November 19, 1989		Destruction of the **Berlin Wall.**
1990s		Internet moves from college and military use to public use. Contributes to the worldwide computer and digital information revolution.

Date	President	Event
1991		**First Gulf War.** Iraqi forces defeated. Sovereignty restored in Kuwait.
		Ethnic wars and ethnic cleansing begins in the former Yugoslavia.
December 21, 1991		The Soviet Union officially ceases to exist. **Cold War** ends.
February 26, 1993	**William J. Clinton, 1993–2001**	Al-Qaida detonates a truck bomb under the World Trade Center.
1995		The Dayton Accords. NATO forces enforce the peace in the Balkans.
2001	**George W. Bush, 2001—**	American-led forces defeat the **Taliban** in Afghanistan and destroy **al-Qaida** training bases.
September 11, 2001		**Al-Qaida Terrorists** destroy the two World Trade Center towers and damage the Pentagon. Nearly 3,000 people killed. President George W. Bush declares War on **Terror.**
October 26, 2001		USA PATRIOT Act passed.
2002		The Euro becomes the currency for many countries in the European Union.
March 19, 2003		United States-led forces invade Iraq.
2004		The European Union expands from fifteen to twenty-five members.
		An interim regime established in Iraq.
		American policy in Iraq and conduct of the War on **Terror** become key issues in the election campaign for president of the United States.

ABOLITIONISTS

In colonial North America, the nonviolent Society of Friends stood almost alone in condemning slavery, which has led to the common misperception that the American antislavery movement was ideologically committed to nonviolence. In fact, decades of frustrating campaigning eventually led most American abolitionists to accept the proposition that slavery could not be ended peacefully.

VIOLENCE AND NONVIOLENCE

The post-Revolutionary antislavery movement got its start in the early 1830s and condemned slavery largely on evangelically inspired moral grounds. Although it represented a minority of the population, its cause and tactics played a significant role in the outbreak of war in 1861. By means of lecturing agents, petition drives, and a wide variety of printed materials, the American Anti-Slavery Society promoted the cause of immediate emancipation and racial equality. The targets of abolitionist efforts, the individual slaveholders and the national religious institutions, rejected antislavery appeals and attempted to suppress the abolitionist agitation by mob violence and by legal and ecclesiastical enactments.

The widespread rejection of the antislavery program forced abolitionists to reconsider their strategy. Many followed the lead of the Boston abolitionist William Lloyd Garrison and abandoned the churches as hopelessly corrupted by slavery. These Garrisonians adopted pacifist political practices and counseled Northerners to withhold their sanction from the U.S. Constitution by refusing to vote, since the Constitution contained clauses supporting slavery. The Garrisonians also actively championed women's rights and a program of "universal reform," which led them into quarrels with abolitionists who wanted to focus strictly on freeing the slaves. The Garrisonians won control of the American Anti-Slavery Society in 1840 when opponents quit in protest over the election of a female officer.

Some non-Garrisonian abolitionists continued their attempts to reform the churches, but others shifted their energies to the political arena, launching the Liberty Party in 1840. Like the original antislavery societies, the Liberty Party called for an immediate abolition of slavery wherever constitutionally possible and for the repeal of all racially discriminatory legislation. The Liberty Party's presidential candidate, James G. Birney, received just 7,000 votes (0.29 percent) in 1840 and only 62,000 (2.31 percent) in 1844—an indication that the single issue of slavery was not yet strong enough to sway many voters.

The dismissal of antislavery arguments by every major American institution forced abolitionists to reconsider their original nonviolent strategy. Black abolitionists already had been employing violent means to assist runaway slaves and to thwart the capture of fugitive slaves. A small but active minority of white abolitionists also began condoning more militant ways of combating slavery. In the 1840s, public controversy over such issues as the congressional gag rule that tabled all antislavery petitions, the annexation of Texas as a new slaveholding state, and the disposition of territory won in the Mexican War made opposition to slavery more respectable in Northern circles. The Liberty Party merged with Northern Whigs and Democrats who opposed the further spread of slavery into the western territories, creating first the Free Soil Party in 1848 and then the Republican Party in 1854.

VIOLENT ABOLITIONISM

In the 1850s, the apparent inability of antislavery politicians in the newly formed Republican Party to block Democratic Party efforts to bring Kansas into the Union as a slave state spurred the growth of violent abolitionism. A well-organized effort recruited and armed hundreds of antislavery activists to settle in Kansas and thwart proslavery statehood settlers, who were also armed. Out of the guerrilla skirmishes in "bleeding Kansas" emerged John Brown, who killed several proslavery Kansas settlers. In October 1859, leading a small, integrated company, which was financed by a clandestine group of wealthy Northern abolitionists, Brown attacked the federal arsenal at Harpers Ferry in the forlorn hope of sparking a slave insurrection. Such militant abolitionist agitation helped fan the flames of sectionalism and provoke Southern secession in 1861.

The Civil War caused considerable alterations in abolitionist strategies. All abolitionist factions realized that Southern secession made slavery preeminently a political question. In particular, they recognized that the war gave them an unprecedented opportunity to press the federal government to adopt an emancipation policy. Longtime pacifists joined veteran political abolitionists in endorsing the war and in calling on the government for decisive antislavery action. When the Republican Congress and the Lincoln administration hesitated to take such a revolutionary step, abolitionists worked to embolden them by producing evidence of Northern public support for emancipation.

EMANCIPATION

The culmination of this agitation came when Lincoln issued the preliminary Emancipation Proclamation in the fall of 1862. Although it exempted at least one million slaves from its provisions and was surrounded with an aura of expediency, most abolitionists responded favorably to Lincoln's actions. A few, however, complained that Lincoln still shrank from immediate and complete emancipation, and they unsuccessfully attempted to replace Lincoln as the Republican nominee with a more committed antislavery candidate. After Lincoln's reelection in 1864, abolitionists worked for permanent emancipation by lobbying Congress to pass the Thirteenth Amendment, abolishing slavery everywhere.

Abolitionists also actively advocated the use of African-American troops in the Union army. When Lincoln belatedly began recruiting African Americans in 1863, many younger abolitionists volunteered as officers for black units. After the war, abolitionists argued that since African Americans had served in the military they deserved equal rights. Some abolitionists went south to work for Freedmen's Aid societies, and later the Freedman's Bureau, to assist the former slaves in their transition to freedom.

Although Garrison believed the Thirteenth Amendment had fulfilled the American Anti-Slavery Society's original goals, the organization remained active until two additional amendments ensured African Americans' citizenship and (male) suffrage. When Southern white resistance during postwar Reconstruction nullified many of the hard won gains African Americans had made, abolitionists vainly attempted to pressure Northern politicians not to sacrifice racial equality for the sake of sectional reconciliation. The sectional passions unleashed by the Civil War had enabled abolitionists to achieve the partial victory of emancipation, but true racial equality would require additional generations of struggle.

Abolitionism began as a small, idealistic protest movement against slavery, and its proponents used moral suasion, political power, civil disobedience, and in some cases violence to promote their cause. But it was the Civil War that brought their movement to power by adding to the original purpose of the war, which was to restore and preserve the Union, the abolition of slavery and the granting of citizenship to African Americans. With the passage of the Thirteenth, Fourteenth, and Fifteenth amendments, the abolitionists successfully codified the ideals of the Declaration of Independence into the Constitution and helped lay the groundwork for a multiracial society. The success of the abolitionists' struggle marked the end of that movement but also the beginning of a nearly 100 years of struggle by African Americans to achieve the equal rights promised under the law.

BIBLIOGRAPHY

Dillon, Merton L. *Slavery Attacked: Southern Slaves and Their Allies, 1619–1865.* New York: Oxford University Press, 1984.

Harrold, Stanley. *American Abolitionists.* Harlow, UK: Longman, 2001.

McPherson, James M. *The Struggle for Equality: Abolitionists and the Negro in the Civil War and Reconstruction.* Princeton, NJ: Princeton University Press, 1964.

John R. McKivigan

See also: **Douglass, Frederick; Slavery; Stanton, Elizabeth Cady; Tubman, Harriet.**

AFRICAN AMERICANS (FREED PEOPLE)

Although the vast majority of African Americans were slaves until 1865, the relatively small free black community that began to form during the late eighteenth and early nineteenth centuries played a very important role in African American history. The free black community established institutions such as independent black churches, schools, fraternal organizations, and mutual aid societies. Free blacks were also extremely important in the abolitionist movement. African Americans' post-emancipation hopes for full and equal citizenship were ultimately dashed; nonetheless, the freed people developed their own distinct culture and institutions that would shape black American life in the decades that followed.

BACKGROUND: SEVENTEENTH AND EIGHTEENTH CENTURIES

The first African Americans were transported to the Chesapeake colonies of Virginia and Maryland in the early 1600s in order to work as indentured servants on tobacco farms, similar to many European emigrants. However, throughout the 1600s, the practice gradually developed where blacks were presumed to be slaves for life rather than bound for a term of years. By the early 1700s, African slavery was established in all of the British North American colonies, north and south.

While some free blacks, such as the poet Phillis Wheatley and Boston Massacre victim Crispus Attucks, achieved some renown in colonial America, a distinct black community did not emerge until the American Revolution (1775–1783). A number of blacks received their freedom as a result of their fighting in the American Army. Other blacks, particularly in the South, received their freedom by fighting for the British against their patriot masters. Thousands of blacks took advantage of the dislocations caused by the war to run away from their owners. Further, the democratic and egalitarian sentiments spawned by the Revolution led northern states to begin the gradual emancipation of slaves within their borders. While southern states did not abolish slav-

ery as a result of the revolution, some individual slaveowners, such as George Washington, voluntarily emancipated their slaves. By the late 1700s, sufficient numbers of free blacks were present in cities such as New York, Philadelphia, Baltimore, and Charleston, and in rural areas in upper South states such as Maryland, as to permit the emergence of a black community with its own distinct culture and institutions.

After the Revolutionary War, free northern blacks formed institutions that have continued to influence African American life to the present day. The first independent black churches date from this period; the most well known example is the Bethel African Methodist Episcopal Church founded by Richard Allen in Philadelphia in the mid-1790s. Free blacks also founded independent black schools, fraternal organizations such as the Prince Hall Masons, and mutual aid societies such as the Free African Society founded by Absalom Jones and Richard Allen in Philadelphia in the late 1780s. These institutions provided a foundation from which many black community leaders emerged in the first half of the 1800s. Black northerners, however, faced pervasive social discrimination: most states did not permit blacks to vote and they were informally barred from many jobs and public accommodations.

AFRICAN AMERICANS IN ANTEBELLUM AMERICA

There were also free blacks in the slaveholding South during the nineteenth century. Most free blacks in the upper South states of Virginia, Maryland, and Delaware lived in rural areas, although significant numbers of free blacks lived in cities such as Baltimore, Richmond, and Norfolk. A smaller number of free blacks lived in Deep South states such as Georgia, South Carolina, and Louisiana, particularly in cities such as Charleston, Savannah, and New Orleans. Free blacks in the Deep South, unlike those in the North and in the Upper South, often had close ties to the white elite: free blacks in major Deep South cities were often skilled tradesmen, and a small number of Deep South free blacks were slave owners themselves. Free blacks in the South lived under even more restrictive conditions than black northerners because white southerners feared that free blacks would conspire with slaves to harm whites. For instance, some states passed laws to restrict their freedom of movement and ownership of guns.

Free blacks played an important role in the abolitionist movement, which became increasingly prominent after 1830, and helped to cause the Civil War. Frederick Douglass, an escaped slave, was the most well-known free black abolitionist of the period, but free blacks such as Henry Highland Garnet and Martin Delany were also prominent leaders. Free blacks helped slaves escape on

A sharecropper's family on Pettway Plantation, Gee's Bend, Alabama.

the Underground Railroad. Northern free blacks also agitated, with only occasional success, to obtain the right to vote and gain equal employment and housing opportunities.

THE CIVIL WAR AND ITS AFTERMATH

The Civil War was a turning point for the African-American community. Although initially reluctant to use black soldiers, the Union Army enlisted over 180,000 free blacks and escaped slaves who served in all-black units under white officers. Black soldiers faced unequal pay in the Union Army and were frequently executed by Confederate forces that were unwilling to treat black soldiers as prisoners of war. However, blacks served valiantly in the Union cause that began with preserving the nation and ended with the goal of abolishing slavery. Those who survived lived to see both slavery and the Confederacy finally destroyed at the war's end.

The passage of the Thirteenth Amendment in 1865 ended slavery in this country forever. Freedom, however, did not mean equality or economic opportunity. Freed slaves lacked land, education, and employment. As a result, many former slaves continued to work the same land they had worked as slaves, only now as sharecroppers or tenant farmers rather than chattel slaves. Other freed blacks took to the road in order to leave the area in which they had been slaves, to seek opportunities in cities and towns, or to attempt to find relatives who had been sold away during slavery. Now that slavery was ended, it remained to be seen what status free blacks would hold in postbellum America.

After Abraham Lincoln's assassination in April 1865, Reconstruction policy was initially dominated by President Andrew Johnson, a Tennessee Unionist who had little sympathy for blacks. Johnson acquiesced in southern states' passage of "Black Codes" intended to reduce the freed people to a condition much like slavery by preventing them from owning land or traveling freely. Freed blacks were also the target of much violence from angry white southerners in the first several months after the war ended. A particularly heinous incident occurred in Memphis in May 1866 when forty-six black people were killed by a mob led by local policemen. Northern outrage at widespread southern violation of blacks' rights and the return of former Confederate leaders to political power in the South led to a rejection of Johnson's lenient Reconstruction policies in the 1866 elections and to congressional-led Radical Reconstruction (1867–1877).

The Republican-dominated Congress sent federal troops to the South to protect blacks' rights and to establish more democratic governments. The Fourteenth and Fifteenth Amendments to the Constitution were ratified in 1868 and 1870, respectively, with the intent of requiring southern states to give blacks equal citizenship rights and the right to vote. In response, white southerners formed terrorist groups such as the Ku Klux Klan, which instituted a violent campaign against blacks and their white sympathizers. Nonetheless, during Radical Reconstruction, over 1,000 blacks were elected to various offices in southern states, including two U.S. Senators and fourteen members of Congress.

However, this period of black political influence was brief. Unrelenting white terrorist violence in the 1870s led to the recapture of political control in many southern states by white supremacist Democratic regimes. Further, white northerners gradually lost interest in protecting black southern rights throughout the 1870s. By 1876, only Louisiana, Florida, and South Carolina remained under Republican rule.

THE POST-RECONSTRUCTION PERIOD

Radical Reconstruction came to an end after the 1876 presidential election between Democrat Samuel J. Tilden and Republican Rutherford B. Hayes. Although Tilden won the popular vote, Hayes claimed that he had carried Lousiana, Florida, and South Carolina, and therefore had won the election by one vote in the Electoral College. After much dispute, an agreement was reached by which Democrats would accept Hayes's victory in exchange for his promise to remove federal troops from Louisiana, Florida, and South Carolina. Once the troops were removed, white supremacist Democrats immediately seized power in those southern states and Reconstruction was finished.

In the years following 1877, southern states adopted a number of devices, including poll taxes and literacy tests, which effectively prevented nearly all southern blacks from voting. Further, all southern states adopted "Jim Crow" laws which required the segregation of blacks from whites in nearly all aspects of southern life, including housing, schools, and transportation, in order to establish a racial hierarchy in which blacks were clearly subordinated.

Despite the disappointment of Reconstruction, black southerners, in the last third of the nineteenth century, managed to build communities with institutions that would play an important role in black culture and in the civil rights movement of the twentieth century. Black southerners established their own independent churches and Sunday schools in the mid- to late-nineteenth century. Black southerners, often aided by white northern philanthropists, established schools and colleges that trained the next generation of black leaders, such as Fisk University in Tennessee and Hampton Institute in Virginia.

Although frustrated in their search for equality, free blacks in the North and freed slaves in the South established their own distinct culture and institutions that helped them survive difficult times and that would eventually provide the foundation for future gains. The greatest outcome of the Civil War was the freedom of nearly four million slaves. What freedom meant and what this nation would do to ensure freedom and equality to African Americans and all minorities were issues that remained unresolved for decades.

BIBLIOGRAPHY

Foner, Eric. *Reconstruction: America's Unfinished Revolution, 1863–1877.* New York: Harper & Row, 1988.

Horton, James Oliver, and Horton, Lois E. *In Hope of Liberty: Culture, Community, and Protest among Northern Free Blacks, 1700–1860.* New York: Oxford University Press, 1977.

Johnson, Micheal P., and Roark, James L. *Black Masters: A Free Family of Color in the Old South.* New York: Norton, 1984.

Daniel W. Aldridge, III

See also: **Frederick Douglass; Reconstruction; Segregation, Racial, 1816–1900; Sharecropping and Tenant Farming.**

AGE OF WESTERN EXPANSION

At some time in American history, every part of the United States except the easternmost region qualfed as "the West," the last frontier of settlement. As the idea of the West expanded in the public imagination, it became a land of cowboys, buffalo herds, a vast wilderness, and a society that operated on the other side of the law. The West was also the site of frontier warfare between settlers and American Indians. To a large extent, that picture was real, but the American West is far more than just a treasure trove of folklore. It is a vital part of the nation's growth and development, a rich depository of its history.

The age of western expansion refers mainly to the period following the Louisiana Purchase of 1803. Western expansion includes the lands acquired by treaty or warfare west of the Mississippi River. As a result of the war with Mexico (1846–1848), the United States added land in the Southwest stretching from Texas to the Pacific, including California. Although Nebraska, Kansas, and the Dakotas are not generally considered western states today, much of the fighting for land between white settlers and American Indians and much of the trail blazing and cattle drives took place in those states. War and western expansion went hand in hand. That expansion, a form of continental imperialism, not only created modern cultural icons such as the frontiersman, the cowboy, and the homestead family, but also reinforced American identity. Western expansion reinforced the view that American society was superior to all others and that it was the nation's "Manifest Destiny" to spread its institutions across the continent.

THE FIRST GREAT JOURNEY

Thomas Jefferson managed the greatest land bargain in U.S. history when, acting as president, he purchased 828,000 square miles of territory from France in 1803. The boundaries of the purchase were vague; it covered land west of the Mississippi River, comprising what became all or parts of the states of Louisiana, Arkansas, Missouri, Iowa, Minnesota, North and South Dakota, Nebraska, Kansas, Oklahoma, Texas, New Mexico, Colorado, Wyoming, Montana, and Utah. It doubled the size of the United States.

The purchase was real, but no one knew precisely what the United States had bought. So, in 1804, Jefferson sent explorers Meriwether Lewis and William Clark on the first overland expedition to the Northwest. On the twenty-eight month journey from St. Louis, Missouri, to the Pacific Ocean and back, Lewis and Clark kept detailed records of the people, plants, and terrain they encountered. The successful expedition not only provided boundaries for the Louisiana Purchase, but it began the great wave of western expansion that pushed the boundaries of the United States all the way to the Pacific Ocean.

"WESTWARD HO"

Long before Lewis and Clark's expedition, fur trappers had been exploring parts of what became the West. The fur trappers were after the wealth of beaver pelts to be found in the streams of the western wilderness. Some of the trappers became scouts for the army. The military hired experienced mountain men such as Kit Carson and Jim Bridger to lead expeditions during the early and the mid-nineteenth century. The U.S. government had a keen interest in exploring the West and in promoting settlement there. All these explorers and trappers were directly responsible for opening the West to later migration because they established trails through the wilderness. With-

out these trails, the covered wagons that took settlers to the Pacific could not have crossed the dangerous terrain.

On their first expedition, Lewis and Clark carved out much of what became the Oregon Trail, one of the great emigration routes first used by fur traders and missionaries. It wound from Independence, Missouri, to the Columbia River region of Oregon, a distance of some 2,000 miles. By the 1840s, the trail was traveled by some 12,000 emigrants on wagon trains heading west. The journey took from four to six months, with an occasional stop for supplies at various forts set up along the way. Although films of the Wild West generally describe the main hazard on the trail as attacks from American Indians, the emigrants were far more apt to suffer from accidents, wagon breakdowns, and cholera. The Oregon Trail was in use longer than any of the trails west. Even after the railroad began to link both coasts and reduced the need for wagon trains, the trail was still used for cattle and sheep drives heading east.

A route that helped to open the Southwest was the Santa Fe Trail, running from Independence, Missouri, to Santa Fe, New Mexico, although it was used more as a commercial road than an emigration highway. Merchants sent wagon caravans from the Missouri River, following the divide between the Arkansas and Kansas river tributaries, to present-day Great Bend, Kansas, and then along the Arkansas. Three routes turned south at the western end heading for Santa Fe. Use of the trail stopped when the Santa Fe railroad was completed in 1880.

THE MORMON EMIGRATION

During 1846 to 1847, a great wave of migration headed west, following the Oregon Trail for part of the journey. The travelers were followers of the Church of Jesus Christ of Latter-Day Saints, known as the Mormons. Long persecuted for their beliefs, the Mormons, headed by Joseph Smith, Jr., had fled from New York to Ohio, Missouri, and to Illinois. Following Smith's death, the new leader, Brigham Young, led the first wave of migration. Over the next two decades, some 70,000 Mormons made the trek from Nauvoo, Illinois, across Iowa, to the Great Platte River Road at the Missouri River. At Fort Laramie, the Mormons crossed to the south side of the Missouri to pick up the Oregon Trail. After crossing the Continental Divide at South Pass, they left the trail and used a route blazed by earlier groups heading for California. The Mormons followed the faint trail of the ill-fated Donner party into the valley of the Great Salt Lake. The first leg of the trip to the Missouri covered 265 miles; the second to the valley of the Great Salt Lake covered some 1,032 miles. The Mormon trail (much of it no longer visible) is now an historic site, part of the National Trails System. The Mormons settled what is now Salt Lake City, which later became the capital of Utah, and

Joining the tracks for the first transcontinental railroad, Promontory, Utah Territory, 1869. The greatest boost to expansion of the West happened when the Union Pacific Railroad, heading west from Omaha, Nebraska, was joined with the Central Pacific Railroad, heading east from Sacramento, California. NATIONAL ARCHIVES AND RECORDS AD-MINISTRATION

in the surrounding areas. But they also helped to spur migration to California. Prospectors who flocked west after hearing word of gold deposits often stopped for a few days of rest in Salt Lake City.

GOLD RUSH

California's statehood was hastened by the discovery of gold early in 1848. John Marshall, a carpenter from New Jersey, was building a sawmill on land owned by John Sutter on the American River near Coloma. On January 24, he came upon flakes of gold and that started the famed Gold Rush to California, which in turn started the flood of settlement in the West. Although the two men at first tried to keep the gold a secret, by the summer the surrounding hillsides were crowded with some 4,000 tents of would-be prospectors anxious to strike it rich. Some 6,000 wagons made the trek, carrying some 40,000 people. Few of them became rich, but many of them stayed in the area and became westerners. The fact that California joined the Union in 1850, just two years after it had been ceded from Mexico, further spurred the flood of migration to the Pacific.

HOMESTEAD ACT

Even after the Gold Rush and migrations by such groups as the Mormons, the American West was still sparsely populated by the middle of the nineteenth century. Most Americans thought of it as a savage land with impossible terrain, little water, and vast deserts, and populated by American Indians who were, for the most part, unfriendly. Then came the Civil War and the Homestead Act, signed into law by Abraham Lincoln on May 20, 1862. It provided 160 acres of public land free of charge after a small filing fee to anyone 21 years old or head of a family, who was a citizen or had filed for citizenship, and who had lived on and worked the land for at least five years. Before the war, there had been a good deal of opposition to homesteading. Southerners viewed homesteaders as anti-slavery; eastern employers did not want their workers to leave low-paying jobs to travel west; and eastern landowners were afraid that land values would fall if the government gave away land. But as the twentieth century began, more than 80 million acres had gone to the homesteaders and helped to settle the West.

PROMOTING SETTLEMENT

Although the covered wagon played a huge role in transporting emigrants westward, no invention increased western settlement so much as the railroad. In the United States, John Stevens built a steam locomotive in 1825 and demonstrated it on his front lawn in Hoboken, New Jersey. Two years later, the first railroad company in the United States, the Baltimore and Ohio, was chartered. Almost from the beginning, promoters of the railroad saw it as a source of commerce not only for eastern cities, but for western expansion as well.

As other railroads were built, the thrust was westward. The first railroad reached the Mississippi from Chicago in 1854. In 1865, Congress passed the Pacific Railroad Act to provide enormous federal assistance for a transcontinental railroad. Thus, the greatest boost to expansion of the West took place at Promontory, Utah, on May 10, 1869, when the Union Pacific Railroad, heading west from Omaha, Nebraska, met the Central Pacific Railroad, heading east from Sacramento, California. During the following years, nine major routes connected the West Coast to the Midwest and South.

Other inventions promoted development of western lands. A machine to manufacture barbed wire fencing was introduced in 1874 by Joseph Glidden of DeKalb, Illinois. Now ranchers could more easily keep track of their herds in the vast expanse of pasture lands. By 1890, barbed wire fencing had just about replaced the open range in the West, but not without fostering conflicts over land between farmers and ranchers. Improvements in irrigation also helped to promote settlement, especially in dry desert areas, although disputes also arose over who had rights to water.

Another inducement to white settlement was the U.S. government's treatment of American Indians. From the beginning of European migration to North America, different policies were adopted concerning American Indians. Early English law forbid unauthorized confiscation of their land. The Proclamation of 1763 gave all the land west of the Appalachians to the native people. But the Indian Removal Act of 1830 made the first departure from these policies. The act allowed the president to give unsettled western prairie land to certain tribes in exchange for their already settled, and more desirable, territories within the states, especially in the southeast. Trouble arose when the government, especially under the administration of Andrew Jackson, used force to make the exchange of lands, ultimately leading in this case to the forced migration of Cherokees, an event that came to be known as the Trail of Tears.

With the discovery of gold in California, there was no stopping massive white migration westward. Treaties with American Indians were nullified in the rush to claim desirable land. Many horrific battles followed, including the massacre of American Indians at Sand Creek, Colorado, in 1864 and the victory of the Sioux and Cheyenne at the Battle of Little Big Horn in 1876. By 1887, most American Indians had been moved onto reservations and no longer stood in the way of westward expansion.

THE WESTERN IMAGE

Even for those who had no thought of migrating, the American West was a subject of great fascination in the early days of expansion. "Go West, young man," wrote Indiana newspaperman John Soule in 1851. (The quote is usually and wrongly attributed to Horace Greely.) The western image was enchanced by showmen such as Buffalo Bill and by artists such as Frederic Remington. William "Buffalo Bill" Cody was a buffalo hunter and an army scout, who created his image of the West with melodrama. He was a superb showman and organized his first Wild West exhibition in 1883. His enthusiastic audiences were shown what the "real West" was like with an exhibition of fancy shooting, a Pony Express ride, a buffalo hunt, and screaming battles between cowboys and American Indians. Famous rifle shooter Annie Oakley and Chief Sitting Bull later joined his traveling troupe.

Artist and sculptor Frederic Remington won fame for his realistic portrayals of life in the American West. After studying at Yale University art school, he traveled widely west of the Mississippi and devoted his work to life on the plains, including American Indians, cowboys, and soldiers. One of his most famous works is the bronze statue *Bronco Buster*.

SUMMARY

American expansion westward fostered enormous opportunities but also enormous problems for this nation that moved far beyond the acts of migration and settlement. One major problem was the ownership of land, for most white migrants felt they had a right to the most desirable lands, even if American Indians and Mexicans, who had long lived in the West, claimed that land as their own. Expansionist ideas and the demand for more western lands ultimately led to the outbreak of the War with Mexico in 1846. Less directly, by raising the question of slavery in the western territories acquired in the 1848 peace settlement, westward expansion helped to define issues that led to the outbreak of the Civil War in 1861. After the Civil War ended, this relentless quest for western land by white Americans led to many bloody battles between new settlers and soldiers and American Indians, who fought to hold on to tribal lands they felt were rightfully theirs. Thus, western expansion played a significant role not only by contributing to events that led to the Civil War but more importantly, as a source that has helped to define American character. The many and varied conflicts produced by the expansion have been the source of novels, stories, poems, and movies that have created mythical heroes, a national self-image that celebrates the rugged and resourceful individual, and a sense of destiny for the nation as a whole.

BIBLIOGRAPHY

Arrington, Leonard J. *Brigham Young: American Moses.* Urbana: University of Illinois, 1986.

Carrell, Jennifer. "How the Bard Won the West." *Smithsonian* 29 (August 1, 1998): 99-102, 104.

Durham, Michael S. *Desert between the Mountains: Mormons, Miners, Padres, Mountain Men, and the Opening of the Great Basin, 1772-1869.* New York: Henry Holt, 1997.

Lockley, Fred, and Helm, Mike. *Visionaries, Mountain Men & Empire Builders: They Made a Difference.* Eugene, OR: Rainy Day Press, 1982.

Ronda, James. "The OregonTrail." *Columbia* 9, no. 3 (Fall 1995): 39.

Corinne J. Naden and Rose Blue

See also: **Compromise of 1850; Farming; Homestead Act; Indian Removal and Response; Kansas Nebraska Act; Manifest Destiny; Railroads.**

ALAMO

In the late 1820s and early 1830s, hundreds of Americans and Europeans flooded into the northern province of Mexico, known as Tejas (Texas). The American-born colonists, clinging to the political beliefs they had grown up with in the United States, along with many Tejas-born Mexicans, or *Tejanos*, openly opposed any form of government that was not democratic in principle and application. Armed hostilities broke out in late 1835 between the people of Texas and the soldiers of the Mexican dictator, General Antonio López de Santa Anna, who were stationed throughout the province. Santa Anna began to raise a massive army in Mexico City to put down the rebellion.

A ragtag army made up of Texas colonists, volunteers from the United States, and *Tejanos* attacked and defeated the Mexican military garrison at San Antonio de Bexar in December 1835, expelling the soldiers from both the town and the nearby San Antonio de Valero mission, popularly known as the Alamo. At the same time, Santa Anna was driving his army north from Mexico City through an unusually cold winter, intent on crushing this opposition.

The Alamo was a sprawling three-acre compound of stone and adobe whose size and shape made it unsuitable as a fort. Colonel William Barret Travis, a former lawyer, and Colonel James Bowie, known for his adventures and the knife that bore his name, shared command of the small Alamo garrison. Both were determined to defend it against all odds. Among the American volunteers who joined the garrison was David Crockett, former congressman from Tennessee. Santa Anna and advance elements of his army marched into San Antonio on February 23, 1836, and immediately began a siege and continuous

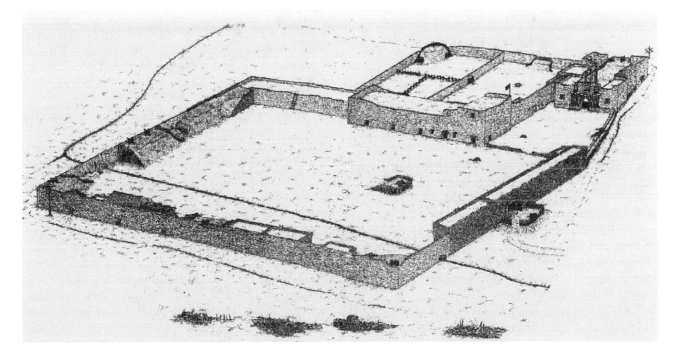

San Antonio de Valero mission, also known as the Alamo. ILLUSTRATION BY ROD TIMANUS

The façade of the church at the Alamo.

artillery bombardment of the Alamo. Bowie fell gravely ill on the first day of the siege, and sole command of the garrison rested with Travis from that day on.

The siege and bombardment of the Alamo continued for twelve days, with additional units of the Mexican army arriving to reinforce the advance troops. Some Texan reinforcements managed to sneak into the Alamo to aid the beleaguered garrison, but Travis's messages for help went largely unanswered. Santa Anna attacked the Alamo on March 6, 1836, in a predawn assault that he hoped would catch the exhausted defenders unprepared. Just before dawn, sixteen hundred Mexican soldiers attacked from all four sides. The defenders, numbering just over two hundred, beat back two attacks, but a third assault breached the north wall and Mexican soldiers poured into the Alamo. The soldiers moved through the compound killing the garrison's defenders in hand-to-hand fighting. Within ninety minutes, all the defenders were dead and the battle was over. Their bodies were burned without ceremony.

Texas won its independence from Mexico on April 21, 1836, when the army of Texas, under the command of General Sam Houston, attacked Santa Anna's camp at San Jacinto while the Mexican soldiers were resting.

The Mexican army had pursued the retreating Texas army for weeks following the battle of the Alamo, and Santa Anna had moved ahead of his main body of troops with a small force of twelve hundred men in an effort to cut off Houston's escape. Houston attacked with less than eight hundred men, routing the Mexican forces and capturing Santa Anna. The Texas battle cry that day was "Remember the Alamo!" As a condition of his immediate safety and eventual release, Santa Anna ordered the entire Mexican army out of Texas and officially recognized it as a free, independent republic.

From 1836 to 1845, the Republic of Texas was the fourth country on the North American continent, along with the United States, Canada, and Mexico. But an ongoing border dispute with Mexico over ownership of lands north of the Rio Grande continued even after Texas was granted statehood in the United States in 1845. In 1846, units of the U.S. army built a fort just north of the Rio Grande, prompting a Mexican army south of the river to cross over and attack a force they considered armed invaders of their territory. A war between the United States and Mexico ensued.

The battle at the Alamo invigorated Americans' determination to achieve independence for Texas, and this ultimately led to the creation of the Republic of Texas, which in turn intensified the settlers' desire to become part of the United States and fostered a major debate over the future of Texas and those Mexican lands situated above the Rio Grande. The resulting concerns led to the Mexican War of 1846, the Compromise of 1850, and the debate over slavery in the territories—all of which contributed to the events leading to the Civil War (1861–1865).

Through the years, however, the battle of the Alamo has been remembered less for its remote link to the coming Civil War than for its battle cry. "Remember the Alamo" has come to symbolize Americans taking a stand for what they believe in and struggling against overwhelming odds for a cause or ideal. The battle cry has become a feature of American identity and the battle itself an icon of American popular culture, illustrating the mythic heroism of ordinary people.

BIBLIOGRAPHY

Chemerka, William R. *Alamo Almanac and Book of Lists*. Austin, TX: Eakin, 1997.

Edmondson, J. R. *The Alamo Story: From Early History to Current Conflicts*. Plano: Republic of Texas Press, 2000.

Timanus, Rod. *An Illustrated History of Texas Forts*. Plano: Republic of Texas Press, 2001.

Rod Timanus

See also: Texas, Republic of.

ANTHONY, SUSAN B.

(b. February 15, 1820; d. March 13, 1906) Women's rights activist and abolitionist.

Susan Brownell Anthony, born on a farm near Adams, Massachusetts, the second of eight children, became a leader in the cause of women's rights and the abolition of slavery. Educated at home and in a district school, she then attended the Friends' Seminary near Philadelphia for four months, learning Quaker tenets of pacifism and the equality of women before God. To help her family, she began teaching at the New Rochelle Friends' Seminary and then, in 1846, at an academy close to her father's new farm near Rochester, New York. As her father often hosted abolitionists like Frederick Douglass and William Lloyd Garrison, Anthony was exposed to reform causes like antislavery, temperance, and women's rights.

In 1848 Anthony attended the Seneca Falls Convention, the first meeting to promote women's rights. She met Elizabeth Cady Stanton two years later. They crusaded for temperance but felt silenced as women in male-dominated organizations. The two then focused on women's rights, attending many state and national conventions. Their lifelong friendship and the collaboration that developed shaped the women's rights movement for the next half century. Anthony applied her organizational skills and Stanton, her powerful writing and oratory. Anthony became the target of ridicule in the press, which presented her as a gaunt, bitter spinster, even as it spared the portly, maternal Stanton, who was married and the mother of seven children.

Devotion to women's rights did not keep Anthony from her antislavery activism. She abandoned Quakerism for Unitarianism when a Friends' meeting weakened its antislavery stance. Closely allied with abolitionists, she served as principal New York agent for Garrison's American Anti-Slavery Society from 1856 until the Civil War. During the Civil War, Anthony and Stanton put their concern for women's rights aside so as to concentrate on abolition. They organized the Women's Loyal National League and gathered hundreds of thousands of signatures demanding the emancipation of slaves.

After the Civil War ended, Anthony became upset when she learned that the Republican Party's reconstruction policy included suffrage for black men but not for women. She denounced the Fourteenth Amendment for ignoring women by inserting the word "male" for the first time into the Constitution. She felt this should have been "woman's hour" because of all that women did to support the Union cause and abolition. Petitions that she presented to Congress in 1866 on behalf of women's suffrage were ignored, as were her efforts to win women the right to vote in Kansas and New York.

Disillusioned, she turned to a wealthy supporter to underwrite an Anthony-Stanton speaking tour and to launch a weekly suffrage magazine, *Revolution*, in January 1868. It advocated support for the Fourteenth and Fifteenth Amendments, provided that they included "educated suffrage irrespective of sex and color," as well as equal pay for equal work regardless of gender, the practical education of girls, opening more occupations to women, and liberal divorce laws. Anthony also used *Revolution* to address women's labor problems. She organized a Working Women's Association in New York City to further unionization for higher wages and shorter hours.

Anthony and Stanton founded the National Woman Suffrage Association in 1869, which held annual conventions. Anthony alienated more moderate women who were less willing to demand a federal law rather than a state-by-state granting of the vote. Moderates led by Lucy Stone countered by forming the American Woman Suffrage Association, creating a schism that lasted for two decades. Anthony further alienated herself from the moderates by casting a ballot

Susan B. Anthony. © BETTMANN/CORBIS

in the 1872 presidential election, which led to her conviction for breaking the law.

Anthony relinquished *Revolution* in 1870 because of its heavy debt and traveled the lecture circuit in the Midwest and Far West to great demand. She rejoiced when the Wyoming Territory granted woman suffrage in 1870, quickly followed by the Utah Territory. She continued to work tirelessly for women's suffrage. The divided women's movement reunited in 1890 as the National American Woman Suffrage Association (NAWSA), pledging to work on both state and federal levels. In 1892 Anthony became its president.

Anthony settled down with her sister in Rochester in 1890 but still traveled to promote issues including unionization and race relations. By then, Anthony attracted acclaim as the matriarch of the women's movement as she triumphantly appeared at the Women's Congress of the 1893 World's Columbian Exposition in Chicago. During the Spanish-American War, she protested women's inability to vote on matters of war and peace. She founded the International Council of Women (1888) and headed the U.S. delegation at meetings in London in 1899 and in Berlin in 1904, where she was lauded as "Susan B. Anthony of the World." While in Berlin, she and Carrie Chapman Catt formed the International Woman Suffrage Alliance, and she was named its honorary president. Anthony turned the NAWSA presidency over to Catt in 1900 and attended her last convention in 1906. When she died at age eighty-six a month after attending the convention, she was eulogized here and abroad.

Anthony's life illustrates the effects of war, and the events leading up to it, on social reform. As an abolitionist, she contributed to the divisions between North and South that led to war in 1861. As an advocate of rights for women and former slaves, she welcomed the expansion of liberties made possible by Northern victory, and spent the remainder of her life fighting to fulfill the cause of women's suffrage.

BIBLIOGRAPHY

Anthony, Susan B., and Harper, Ida Husted, eds. *History of Woman Suffrage.* Rochester, NY: Susan B. Anthony, 1902.

Flexner, Eleanor. *Century of Struggle.* Cambridge, MA: Harvard University Press, 1959.

Gurko, Miriam. *The Ladies of Seneca Falls: The Birth of the Woman's Rights Movement.* New York: Schocken, 1976.

Harper, Ida Husted. *The Life and Work of Susan B. Anthony,* (1898–1908) 3 vols. Manchester, NH: Ayer, 1969.

Lutz, Alma. "Susan Brownell Anthony." In *Notable American Women, 1607–1950: A Biographical Dictionary.* Vol. 1. Edited by Edward T. James, et al. Cambridge, MA: Harvard University Press, 1971.

Blanche M. G. Linden

See also: **Stanton, Elizabeth Cady; Woman's Rights Movement; Women's Suffrage Movement.**

BLACK CODES

Shortly after the Civil War's end, Southern legislatures, which were dominated by ex-Confederates during the presidential phase of Reconstruction (1864–1867), passed laws that for former slaves replaced the authority of slave owners with that of the state. Republicans labeled these laws Black Codes, although Mississippi's 1865 statute was titled *An Act to Confer Civil Rights on Freedmen, and for other purposes.* All acts bestowed at least some minimal civil rights, including the rights to sue and be sued, to testify in court (but not against whites), and to marry (at least each other). In no state were freedmen permitted to vote, hold office, or serve on juries. Northerners objected that the codes also placed severe restrictions on African-American hopes of economic and political advancement.

At the end of the Civil War, a large proportion of the Southern population had been dislocated. Ex-Confederate refugees and soldiers usually had a home site to return to, but the freed people were not always welcomed or anxious to stay on the plantations where they had once worked. In addition, thousands took to the roads in search of lost family members. Finally, the freed people clung to the vain hope that the forty acres and a mule promised by General W. T. Sherman during his march to sea awaited them in the near future. Southern white legislators, faced with what they saw as social unrest and economic ruin, embedded in their codes significant restrictions on African-American economic freedom.

Laws requiring work were nothing new (vagrancy had been punished in England for centuries), and at least three Northern states—Illinois, Indiana, and Ohio—had antebellum statutes directed at African Americans. However, not only did the Black Codes seek to reestablish white control over black labor, but many state and city ordinances effectively froze blacks out of skilled work, professions, and even land ownership. Florida forbade anyone of African origin from owning knives or guns without a license.

Freedman's Bureau officials, Southern Unionists, and radical Republicans immediately objected. The result was the passage of the Fourteenth Amendment to the U.S. Constitution. After its central feature, that freed people were both American and state citizens, came the three key guarantees: the privileges and immunities of citizenship, equal protection of the law, and due process of law. The Black Codes became a dead letter in law.

However, large portions of these codes became part of the structure of Southern society after Reconstruction ended. Restrictions on the freedom to buy land or travel became sunset laws, large posted signs warning those of African-Amercan ancestry that they were expected to be out of town before dark or face the threat of bodily harm. Numerous federal peonage prosecutions in the twentieth century revealed that the labor laws too had been revived. Finally, the segregation found its way back into law in the 1890s and endured until the 1970s. The Civil Rights movement of the 1950s and 1960s was aimed at overturning segregation and the denial of equal rights, which were the legacy of slavery, Black Codes, and the failure after 1877 to apply the Fourteenth and Fifteenth amendments to protect African-American civil liberties.

BIBLIOGRAPHY

Cox, Lawanda, and Cox, John H. *Politics, Principle, and Prejudice, 1865–1866: Dilemma of Reconstruction America.* New York: Free Press of Glencoe, 1963.

Foner, Eric. *Reconstruction: America's Unfinished Revolution, 1863–1877.* New York: Harper & Row, 1988.

Perman, Michael. *Reunion without Compromise: The South and Reconstruction, 1865–1868.* Cambridge, UK: Cambridge University Press, 1973.

Michael B. Dougan

See also: Ku Klux Klan; Reconstruction; Segregation, Racial, 1816–1900.

BLOCKADE, CIVIL WAR

The first action of naval warfare in the American Civil War was the blockade of Southern ports by the Union Navy. Starting on April 19, 1861, the blockade was part of General Winfield Scott's strategy called the Anaconda Plan, which was an effort to reduce the South's ability to make war. Scott knew that the South relied heavily on manufactured goods from the Northern states and foreign countries. In addition, the South relied on them to purchase Southern cotton and other cash crops. With these ideas in mind, the main objectives of the blockade were to prevent desperately needed goods—including war material, manufactured goods, and luxury items—from reaching the South and to stop the exportation of raw cotton to foreign manufacturers.

Accomplishing these objectives in 1861 proved to be a challenge because the Union Navy at the beginning of the war had only thirty-five modern vessels (only three of which were steam powered) to patrol 189 harbors and 3,000 miles of coast. Although at first the blockade proved to be porous, it soon began to affect the South.

The Confederate government was desperate to acquire war material such as guns, powder, cannons, clothes, and other supplies from blockade-runners, but it was difficult for the government to persuade them to ship what it needed. Instead, the blockade-runners preferred to ship luxury items such as silks and liquor, as these goods brought the highest profits. To counter this problem, early in the war the government tried to require blockade-runners to reserve one-third of their load for military supplies. Initially, with the Navy spread so thin, the blockade was not effective and allowed Confederate and foreign blockade-runners to elude capture easily.

As the war progressed, so did the North's ability to make the blockade more effective with the commissioning of almost 700 vessels. Although it never came close to completely cutting the Confederacy off from the rest of the world, it did reduce the usual flow of goods and supplies to the South. The reduced flow of goods led to shortages and higher prices that contributed to civilian discontent. This did not starve the Confederacy, but it did severely hamper its war-making efforts and forced the government in March 1864 to require blockade-runners to allot half of their cargo for military supplies. The blockade succeeded only because of two important achievements: it disrupted interregional trade and denied the Confederacy revenue from exporting raw cotton and other staple products.

Before the war, the South relied on water routes, especially its coastline, to ship goods and products to other regions. The blockade forced the Confederacy to use less effective avenues for trade and transportation, including roads and the railroad system. This increased demand on the railroads increased in turn the cost of transporting goods, thus damaging the Southern economy. The other achievement of the blockade involved restricting the exportation of cotton and other staple products. Prior to the war, the South supplied 75 to 80 percent of the world's raw cotton, and the reduction in cotton revenue severely disrupted the Southern economy and further weakened its ability to wage war. Overall, the Union blockade did not stop all supplies from reaching the Confederacy, but it disrupted the usual flow of supplies into and out of the South enough to severely restrict its ability to make war. The blockade proved to be an effective noncombative means to help the Union win the war.

The Civil War blockade demonstrated that war was no longer a matter only for soldiers, and that the effects of the war were no longer confined to the battlefield. Civilians were now combatants in the sense that war strategy was intended to undermine their morale and their capacity to support conflict. Thus warfare was aimed not only at destroying armies, but also at causing great

The British steamer and Union blockage runner, *Dee* in the harbor at Hamilton, Bermuda, in 1863. © CORBIS

suffering among ordinary people by disrupting the economy and depriving them of goods, even food.

BIBLIOGRAPHY

Carse, Richard. *Blockade: The Civil War at Sea.* New York: Rinehart, 1958.

Surdam, David. *Northern Naval Superiority and the Economics of the American Civil War.* Columbia: University of South Carolina Press, 2001.

Charles D. Grear

BUSINESS AND FINANCE

By the end of the nineteenth century, when it had become the world's leading industrial nation, the United States was home to many of the biggest and most successful business enterprises in the world. Although the Civil War did not directly cause the rise of big business in America, it did change the fortunes of many firms and industries, including some of those that became especially important during the late nineteenth century. The Civil War had a more direct impact on American banking and finance and transformed the ways in which Americans debated the politics of money.

AMERICAN BUSINESS BEFORE AND DURING THE CIVIL WAR

Before and during the Civil War, there were few industrial corporations in America. Although the nation was home to hundreds of mechanized factories by 1860, only a few of these factories employed more than 1,000 people. Most businesses were owned and managed by families or small groups of partners. Many of the wealthiest businesspeople in the economy were commission merchants, who specialized in the marketing of particular goods such as raw cotton, wheat, or textiles.

The beginning of the Civil War, which cut off commerce between the North and the South and limited international trade, hurt most business firms in the short run. Over time, however, the war provided some firms with new opportunities. Although the South experienced shortages of raw materials and relied upon imports for many of its needs, some Southern manufacturers were given a boost by military orders for weapons and uniforms. In the North, hundreds of merchants and manufacturers participated in the war economy as contractors or subcontractors. By the middle of the war, when the economy had rebounded, many Northern businesses were recording high profits. After the war ended in 1865, commercial ties between North and South were re-established, and more businesses began to operate on a national scale.

THE TRANSFORMATION OF BANKING AND FINANCE DURING THE CIVIL WAR

Before the Civil War, the American banking industry was remarkably decentralized. After 1836, when President Andrew Jackson and Democrats in Congress cancelled the charter of the Second Bank of the United States, there was no national bank. There was also no national currency. Instead, hundreds of state-chartered banks issued their own bank notes (paper money). In addition to issuing paper money, banks also kept deposits, issued loans, and negotiated the commercial paper (written promises to pay) that many merchants and manufacturers relied upon to conduct business. Meanwhile, starting in the 1840s, the U.S. government handled its own modest financial needs with a so-called "Independent Treasury," a national network of government vaults that was separate from the banks and used specie (gold and silver) for all transactions.

The Civil War was so expensive that it created new problems in government finance. In the South, where there were fewer banks and businesses, the Confederate government found itself trying to pay for the war mainly by printing money. This policy created terrible inflation that ended up crippling the South's war effort. The North also printed some new paper money to pay for the war, but unlike the South, it was able to cover most war expenses by collecting taxes and selling government bonds.

To pay for the North's war effort, Congress not only raised taxes on imported goods (the tariff), but also created the first federal income tax in national history. But higher taxes were not enough. By the end of 1861, only eight months into the war, Northern banks and the U.S. government started to run out of gold. In 1862, Congress authorized the Treasury to print paper money (called "greenbacks" because of the ink color) that would help pay for the war. Over the course of the war, the Treasury issued about $450 million worth of greenbacks. The Treasury generated even more cash by selling war bonds. It hired Philadelphia banker Jay Cooke, who used a network of hundreds of subagents to sell the government bonds to small investors as well as big banks. By the end of the war, many Americans had become familiar with a variety of new Treasury bonds.

Some Northern war bonds ended up being used as the basis for a new National Banking System. In a series of laws passed between 1863 and 1865, Congress defined the rules under which people would be allowed to create new national banks. After they deposited at least $50,000 worth of bonds with the Treasury, partners in a national bank were allowed to issue national bank notes. Because the old state bank notes were subject to a high tax, these national bank notes soon provided the United States with its first uniform national currency. Although the United

States would not get a true central national bank until the Federal Reserve system was created in 1913, the days of hundreds of different kinds of paper money were over.

THE POLITICS OF MONEY AFTER THE CIVIL WAR

When the Civil War ended in 1865, the U.S. government debt stood at $2.7 billion, up from $60 million at the beginning of the war. Exactly how to settle this huge war debt soon became a major political issue. Creditors, including the actual holders of war bonds and other investors and banks, had an interest in a deflationary monetary policy that would return the country to the gold standard it had abandoned during the war. Debtors, on the other hand, had an interest in keeping money plentiful and cheap. For over thirty years after the end of the Civil War, national politics was shaped by battles between the hard money proponents of the gold standard and the champions of soft money, who called for more use of greenbacks and silver to boost the money supply.

After the country sank into a serious economic depression following the Panic of 1873 (an event caused in part by the failure of the banking business of Jay Cooke, the North's old chief war bond salesman), many people argued that the Republican party's hard money policy was starving the struggling economy of much needed cash. Soon, a new political party known as the "Greenback Party" challenged Republicans over the money issue. Although it had some success in the Congressional elections of 1878, the Greenback party failed to stop the return to the gold standard, and in 1879 one dollar worth of greenbacks became worth exactly one dollar in gold. Nevertheless, soft money supporters continued to fight against the gold standard by calling on the government to create more money in the form of silver coin. The struggle between the forces of gold and the forces of silver culminated in the 1896 Presidential election, in which the "free silver" Democratic candidate William Jennings Bryan lost to William McKinley, a hard money Republican. In that campaign, Bryan declared "You shall not crucify mankind upon a cross of gold."

THE RISE OF BIG BUSINESS IN THE LATE NINETEENTH CENTURY

One of the most important developments in the history of business was the rise of large industrial corporations in the United States at the end of the nineteenth century. Before the Civil War, the biggest businesses in America had been textile mills, cotton plantations, and regional railroads. In the decades that followed the Civil War, Americans saw the growth of enterprises that were much bigger than anything that had been seen before. Although family firms, partnerships, and other smaller-scale enterprises continued

Wall Street in New York City, the center of finance for the United States. AP/WIDE WORLD PHOTOS

to be important parts of the American economy, the new industrial corporations were special because of their unprecedented size and complexity.

The rise of modern big business is often seen as beginning in the 1870s. John D. Rockefeller, who started an oil refining business in Cleveland during the Civil War, founded the Standard Oil Co. in 1870. Just eight years later, Standard Oil controlled 80 percent of the total oil refining capacity in the United States. Gustavus Swift, who started shipping meat out of Chicago by railroad in the late 1870s, built giant slaughtering plants that by 1900 would employ 20,000 people. James Duke, a North Carolina tobacco manufacturer who invested in new cigarette-making machines in the mid-1880s, was selling over 800 million cigarettes a year by 1890. These companies and others like them broke new ground by building national production and distribution networks that allowed them to sell huge quantities of their products. In some cases, these new industrial corporations grew so big that they came to enjoy near-monopoly power over their industries. The Sherman Antitrust Act in 1890, in which Congress authorized the government to break up monopolies, was a response to the rise of giant companies like Standard Oil.

The industrial corporations that emerged in the years after the Civil War not only broke new ground with the size and scope of their operations, but also with their methods of management and finance. Too big and complex to be run by a family or a small partnership, the new corporations were managed by bureaucracies staffed by professional managers. To raise the large amounts of capital they required, many of the new industrial corporations sold stock to the public, something that few companies other than railroads had done before that time. By the 1890s, there were dozens of industrial securities being traded on the New York Stock Exchange; by this time, New York was challenging London for the title of the world's leading financial center.

Over the course of the nineteenth century, as the American economy became more highly industrialized,

there were some remarkable changes in the organization of business and finance. The Civil War, which had the effect of reorganizing the U.S. banking industry and creating new political struggles over national economic policy, did not cause drastic changes in most parts of the economy over the long run. More revolutionary was the rise after the war of industrial corporations, which relied upon mass production and mass distribution, as well as new methods of management and finance. Over the years to come, Americans would continue to grapple with the question of whether these industrial and financial enterprises were compatible with the ideals of political democracy and economic prosperity for the average person.

BIBLIOGRAPHY

Chandler, Alfred D., Jr. *The Visible Hand: The Managerial Revolution in American Business.* Cambridge, MA: Harvard University Press, 1977.

DeCredico, Mary. *Patriotism for Profit: Georgia's Urban Entrepreneurs and the Confederate War Effort.* Chapel Hill: University of North Carolina Press, 1990.

Dew, Charles B. *Ironmaker to the Confederacy: Joseph R. Anderson and the Tredegar Iron Works.* New Haven, CT: Yale University Press, 1966.

Hoffman, Susan. *Politics and Banking: Ideas, Public Policy, and the Creation of Financial Institutions.* Baltimore, MD: Johns Hopkins University Press, 2001.

Koistinen, Paul A.C. *Beating Plowshares into Swords: The Political Economy of American Warfare, 1606–1865.* Lawrence: University Press of Kansas, 1996.

Richardson, Heather Cox. *The Greatest Nation of the Earth: Republican Economic Policies during the Civil War.* Cambridge, MA: Harvard University Press, 1997.

Unger, Irwin. *The Greenback Era: A Social and Political History of American Finance, 1865–1879.* Princeton, NJ: Princeton University Press, 1964.

Mark R. Wilson

See also: **Economic Change and Industrialization; Financing the War.**

CALHOUN, JOHN CALDWELL

⭐ (b. March 18, 1782; d. March 31, 1850) Antebellum statesman; served as vice president and secretary of war; strong spokesman for the southern states.

Although best remembered as the leading spokesman for the South in the controversies leading up to the Civil War, John C. Calhoun played a substantial role in the history of American society in relation to many aspects of war. In a national career of forty years, he was U.S. representative and senator, vice president, secretary of war, and secretary of state. Elected representative from South Carolina in 1811, he immediately became one of the leading "War Hawks," the coalition determined to vindicate the honor of the new United States by armed resistance to British insults and depredations. In 1812 Calhoun wrote Congress's declaration of war against England. His support for the war was not merely verbal. He was so active and energetic in legislative support for the war effort that a leading newspaper referred to him as "the young Hercules who carried the war on his shoulders."

The most important role that Calhoun played in American military history was undoubtedly his service as secretary of war in the cabinet of President Monroe, 1817 to 1825. When Calhoun took over, the War Department, which was the largest and most geographically dispersed part of the federal government, was in administrative, logistical, and financial chaos. With careful planning, Calhoun reorganized the department with an efficient bureau system and laid a foundation that was basic to the U.S. peacetime military establishment for many years to come. His governing principle was the concept of an "expansible army," a small but well-designed peacetime force that could be rapidly expanded under trained officers in case of national emergency. Calhoun's efforts touched every aspect of the army, including supply, health, and education, as well as the combat arms. The prestige of West Point dates from Calhoun's time. He continued to carry out the Jeffersonian policy of toward Native Americans (gradual and peaceful removal to the West). Later, as senator, Calhoun was a strong critic of President Jackson's harsher policy toward American Indians.

In 1825 Calhoun became vice president, but resigned in 1832 to become a senator and take a leading role in his state's conflict with President Jackson's administration, a conflict known as the Nullification controversy. In the South Carolina Exposition in 1828, Calhoun argued that the Southern minority, through the tariff, was being exploited by the majority, and that the remedy for this was

John C Calhoun. © BETTMANN/CORBS

unpopular) opponent of the war with Mexico that broke out in 1846. He abstained from voting on the declaration of war, contending that the war was unnecessary and had been deliberately brought on by the President to preempt the constitutional authority of Congress. This, he warned, was a dangerous precedent for the future.

Calhoun also argued for a negotiated settlement, short of the U.S. army occupying the Mexican capital, and for limited territorial demands. In eloquent speeches he contended that American occupation of foreign countries was more likely to tranform American society from republic to empire than it was to bring freedom to those countries. Further, Mexican territory was "forbidden fruit" because the struggle to control it would bring on unsolvable conflict between the North and the South that would end in war, which was an accurate prophecy.

BIBLIOGRAPHY

Coit, Margaret. *John C. Calhoun: American Portrait.* Columbia: University of South Carolina Press, 1991.

Spiller, Roger J. "John C. Calhoun as Secretary of War, 1817 to 1825." Ph.D. diss., Louisiana State University, 1977.

Wilson, Clyde N. *The Essential Calhoun.* New Brunswick, NJ: Transaction Publishers, 1994.

Clyde N. Wilson

See also: **Indian Removal and Response; Manifest Destiny; Texas, Republic of.**

state action to nullify an unconstitutional federal law. For the rest of his life he developed ideas regarding the restraint of majorities, culminating in his *Disquisition on Government*, which remains of interest to students of politics. For most of the rest of his life, he was a senator from south Carolina. He played an influential role in all controversies of the "Jacksonian era," increasingly focused on rallying the South to resist the Free Soil movement that would ban slavery from all future new states.

The former young "War Hawk" also became, in the last part of his career, a critic of "manifest destiny" and militarism. He argued forcefully against diplomatic and military confrontations with Mexico and with Great Britain over Oregon, two issues many leading politicians were eager to pursue. To Calhoun, there was no need for belligerence. The proper stance, he argued, was "masterful neglect." The natural westward dynamic of the American people would guarantee all the just territorial ambitions of the United States peacefully.

As secretary of state (1844–1845) under President John Tyler, Calhoun initiated the admission of Texas to the Union, which was carried through by the succeeding Polk administration. However, he became a strong (and

CHESNUT, MARY BOYKIN

(b. March 31, 1823; d. November 22, 1886) Author of an important Civil War diary.

Mary Boykin Chesnut penned one of the most significant Civil War diaries ever written. Born to a wealthy planter family in Statesburg, South Carolina, on March 31, 1823, Chesnut enjoyed all the advantages of privilege. Her father, Stephen Decatur Miller, was governor of South Carolina and a leading "nullifier," a states' rights advocate, in the 1820s, so she also received a formidable education in politics. Outgoing, vivacious, and mature beyond her seventeen years, she married James Chesnut, Jr., scion of another prominent South Carolina family, in 1840. Their marriage led them to the center of American and Confederate politics from 1840 until James's death in 1885. Mary Chesnut outlived her husband by one year, succumbing to heart disease on November 22, 1886.

Mary Boykin's marriage to James Chesnut had unanticipated consequences. James Chesnut rose through the ranks of South Carolina politics to become one of the state's most respected leaders. He was also the first U.S.

James and Mary Boykin Miller Chesnut in 1840. THE GRANGER COLLECTION, LTD.

senator to resign his seat after the election of Abraham Lincoln in November 1860. Because of his status and prestige, the Palmetto State elected him to the Provisional Congress of the Confederate States of America. From there, he served in a number of official capacities and ultimately became a military aide to President Jefferson Davis. As a result, Mary Chesnut viewed the rise and fall of the Confederate nation from the vantage point of the highest social and political circles in Montgomery, Richmond, and Columbia.

From the beginning, Chesnut was a staunch defender of the Confederate cause. Despite championing secession and independence, however, the intelligent and ambitious Chesnut became disgusted with the caliber of politicians within the Confederate government. The antebellum elite that governed in Richmond was, to Chesnut, composed of "fossils" instead of "young & active spirits" who were required to lead the South to indepen-

dence. One politician Chesnut did admire was President Jefferson Davis. He and his wife Varina became two of Chesnut's closest friends. Davis sought Chesnut out repeatedly to discuss the Southern cause. Hence she was a frequent visitor to their home and gained an intimate look at the tide of Confederate fortunes. Her diary entries reflect military reverses, include candid discussions of the nature and legitimacy of secession, detail political infighting, and chronicle the downward spiral of morale. Chesnut's accounts also portray the work many Southern women undertook in support of the cause and the very active social life she and members of the elite enjoyed even during the darkest days of the war.

Chesnut's diary also speaks openly about her opposition to slavery. In numerous passages, she railed against Northern abolitionists who invaded the region and sought to conquer the South. Yet Chesnut also assailed her countrymen for embracing an institution that she felt was morally wrong. For all her disgust, however, she, like all members of the Southern elite, was totally dependent on slavery. She might mention her loathing, but she did not rise in the morning, dress, or take a meal without the assistance of a slave.

In 1864 the Chesnuts returned to South Carolina. Here, Mary Chesnut would witness the final downfall of the plantation South. Forced to join the ranks of the refugees, she found herself in an unfamiliar position: she was dependent on strangers and was short of money. She struggled to stay ahead of the advancing Union armies, but with the news of General Robert E. Lee's surrender, Chesnut and her husband returned to their plantation traveling along Sherman's track. It was, as Chesnut recorded it, a journey marked by vistas of desolation.

Like so many Southerners, the Chesnuts lost everything in the aftermath of emancipation. With her former slave, she eked out a small income—$140 a year—with which she supported her husband and various relatives who returned to Camden, South Carolina, and the Mulberry plantation. She continued to revise and rewrite parts of her journals but died before they were finished. Happily, she entrusted them to a friend who saw to their eventual publication.

Mary Chesnut's life highlights the paradoxes of the Confederate experience and many Southerners' way of life. She championed liberty and scorned slavery, but her survival depended in every way on the institution. She contributed to the war effort, but never let those contributions intrude on her very active social life. Finally, she was forced to flee in the face of Sherman's juggernaut and experienced the very difficult life of a refugee. In her life and experiences, we can see a microcosm of the Confederate nation.

BIBLIOGRAPHY

DeCredico, Mary A. *Mary Boykin Chesnut: A Confederate Woman's Life.* Lanham, MD: Rowman and Littlefield, 1996.

Rable, George C. *Civil Wars: Women and the Crisis of Southern Nationalism.* Champaign: University of Illinois Press, 1991.

Woodward, C. Vann, ed. *Mary Chesnut's Civil War.* New Haven, CT: Yale University Press, 1982.

Mary A. DeCredico

See also: **Sherman's March to the Sea.**

CHILDREN AND THE CIVIL WAR

The Civil War lent excitement to the lives of Northern children, imposed hardships and limitations on Southern white children, and changed the lives of African-

American children forever. Although there were, of course, numerous large and small exceptions to such vast generalizations, these broad outlines accurately capture the experiences of children and youth on the Civil War home front.

Although the differences in the experiences of Northern white, Southern white, and Southern black children are most notable, there were, of course, similarities. Children of both races and in both sections eagerly gathered to watch newly formed local companies drill on village and town squares and to watch regiments march off to the front. Many formed their own "boys' companies." Newspapers and parents' letters commented on youngsters' martial enthusiasm, and children's magazines like *The Student and Schoolmate* encouraged it. Few memoirs by Civil War children fail to mention this combination of war and play, and a number of female memoirists recalled their girlhood fascination with military affairs. Many children in both sections also mentioned "picking" or "scraping" lint (which would be used to bandage wounds) and participating in other aspects of the home front war effort. Teenage boys (and, in the South, girls) found work in ammunition factories and government offices; younger children raised money, collected food and supplies, and in many other ways supported local regiments and hospitals. In the North, many children and youth took part as performers, volunteers, and consumers in fairs sponsored by the United States Sanitary Commission. In addition, throughout the country, but especially in the South, youth managed farms and plantations, cared for younger siblings, and provided for their families in the absence of fathers and brothers.

But even the similarities created differences, as the degree to which children suffered, or enjoyed, or participated in the war varied greatly. Northern children who did not suffer the loss of a father or brother could enjoy the excitement of the war culture that gripped the country. Children's magazines were filled with articles, stories, and games about the war, while authors such as Oliver Optic and J. W. Trowbridge produced novels and histories of the war. Panoramas with names such as "The Grand Panopticon Magicale of the War and Automaton Dramatique" presented series of giant paintings accompanied by special effects and dramatic narratives depicting the military highpoints of the war.

Southern children could also attend panoramas and plays, but their lives were more likely to be directly affected by the war. Many became refugees, while others had to quit school because of family finances or a shortage of teachers. Families who lived in the path of invading armies often went hungry. At least a few children were hurt or killed during the sieges of cities such as Vicksburg, Atlanta, and Petersburg. In addition, white children were forced to adjust both to the presence of

Yankee military occupation (these soldiers often formed warm friendships with the youngest Rebels) and to the destruction of pre-war relationships with their slaves.

As it did for their elders, the war affected the lives of slave children in sometimes confusing ways. All Southerners, and especially slaves, went without adequate food and clothing as Confederate resources dwindled, while the absence of white men from Southern plantations sometimes loosened discipline. Children were among the tens of thousands of slaves relocated to isolated parts of the Confederacy, especially Texas. But the most dramatic experiences of slave children came when they were brought under the protection of Union troops, either by escaping with their parents or when Union troops occupied their plantations. Freedom brought wildly varied experiences. Some African-American youngsters could attend schools in occupied areas, often taught by Northern men and women working for the American Missionary Association and other religious organizations, and could live without the threat of being sold away from their families. But many also had to endure the brutal conditions of the "contraband camps" formed near towns or Union army garrisons, where the death rate often rose as high as 30 percent.

Finally, the experiences of one group of Civil War children became living monuments to the sacrifices of the men who fought to save the Union. For decades after the war, the orphans of Northern soldiers killed in the war or of veterans who died later were housed in soldiers' orphans' homes established by most Northern states, where they represented the nation's efforts to repay the debt owed to Union soldiers.

BIBLIOGRAPHY

King, Wilma. *Stolen Childhood: Slave Youth in Nineteenth-Century America.* Bloomington: Indiana University Press, 1995.

Marten, James. *The Children's Civil War.* Chapel Hill: University of North Carolina Press, 1998.

Marten, James, ed. *Lessons of War: The Civil War in Children's Magazines.* Wilmington, DE: Scholarly Resources, 1999.

Werner, Emmy E. *Reluctant Witnesses: Children's Voices from the Civil War.* Boulder, CO: Westview Press, 1998.

James Marten

See also: **Education; Family Life.**

CIVIL LIBERTIES, CIVIL WAR

The outbreak of the Civil War on April 12, 1861, created a major civil liberties crisis. Although President Abraham Lincoln never formally declared war, he used his authority as commander in chief to expand the powers of the presidency. Even before Congress convened on July 4, Lincoln called for volunteers, spent money unauthorized by Congress, ordered a blockade of Southern ports, and violated civil liberties guaranteed in the Constitution.

All the civil liberties guaranteed by the Bill of Rights and other sections in the Constitution rested on the protection found in Article 1, Section 9: "The privilege of the writ of habeas corpus shall not be suspended, unless in cases of rebellion or invasion the public safety may require it." Known from English history and widely revered as the Great Writ, the writ of *habeas corpus ad subjicienolum* is a court order directing that a detained individual be brought before the court so that the reason for the detention can be explained and justified. However, the suspension of the writ was listed under the powers of Congress, not the president. Lincoln nevertheless suspended the writ in parts of the country so that those allegedly planning or engaging in treasonous practices could be detained. Maryland—where Union army officers arrested a number of secessionists, including John Merryman—provided the earliest cases.

After United States Supreme Court Chief Justice Roger B. Taney heard the case of *Ex parte Merryman* (1861), he ordered the military to produce the accused railroad bridge burner. Union officers, acting under Lincoln's orders, refused to comply. Taney then published a decision in which he argued that only Congress could suspend the writ. The president, he maintained, was bound by the constitution to see that the laws were faithfully carried out and could not ignore the civil authorities by substituting military rule. Lincoln's attorney general, Edward Bates, countered that the presidential oath, to "preserve, protect, and defend the Constitution" gave Lincoln the power he needed. On July 4, Lincoln told Congress that it was better to violate a single law "to a very limited extent" rather than have "the Government itself to go to pieces" (Richardson, p. 3236).

Lincoln continued to suspend the writ on his own authority, and his generals imposed martial law. Approximately one out of every one hundred males in Missouri ended up in detention, and in 1862, in anticipation of opposition to the militia draft of that year, Secretary of War Edwin Stanton suspended the writ until the draft quota was met that fall.

The federal draft law of 1863 prompted a new round of opposition to federal authority and prompted the passage of the Habeas Corpus Act of 1863. This legitimated past executive actions and, since some state officials were trying to thwart the draft by issuing the writ, provided federal officials with immunity from state prosecution in carrying out their duties. The administration did provide review commissions to weed out many of those taken into custody. No accurate figures can be deduced on the number of persons detained but at least 16,000 persons were imprisoned on suspicion and held indefinitely without trials. Most of those in custody had been caught trading with the enemy, defrauding the military, or selling liquor to soldiers.

As the Civil War dragged on, opposition by Northern Democrats became more vocal. Demands for a cease-fire and a negotiated peace—or indeed any criticism of the administration—could be looked upon as treasonous. In 1863, prominent Ohio Democrat Clement L. Vallandigham was arrested and tried by a military commission for expressing views considered to be disloyal. His conviction was appealed to the Supreme Court, which, in *Ex parte Vallandigham* (1864), refused to review the judgment on the grounds that the commission was not a court. Despite infringements on civil liberties, the Civil War also produced a landmark decision to protect individual rights in time of war. In 1866, the Supreme Court ruled in *Ex parte Milligan* that a military court could not replace civil courts where those civil courts, far from the war itself, were open and functioning. In this case, a military court in Indiana had sentenced a citizen to death without a grand jury indictment and with no right of appeal. In overturning the conviction, the Supreme Court created a landmark in protection of civil liberties in time of war.

Habeas corpus and martial law also figured prominently in the Confederate States of America. On April 14, 1861, the Confederate general Braxton Bragg arrested a newspaper correspondent whom he accused of treason during the course of the war. More than 4,108 civilian prisoners were taken into custody. Confederate President Jefferson Davis at first roundly castigated his Northern counterpart for engaging in tyrannical acts but soon found it necessary to follow suit. Davis tried to maintain the legal fiction that declaring martial law in specific areas was not the same as suspending the writ of habeas corpus. In the Habeas Corpus Act of 1862, the Confederate Congress granted a power to the president who could use it to cover large areas not necessarily under military control. Provost marshals required that travelers carry passports, arrested spies and deserters, and tried to enforce the Confederacy's prohibition of alcohol.

The war's end led to three important developments. First, the assassination of Lincoln turned him into a martyr, and not until the twentieth century did academics begin to raise questions about his civil liberties record. Second, the sweeping language of *Ex parte Milligan* fostered a libertarian climate about the nature of a citizen's rights in wartime, which has remained strong in theory even though it was breached egregiously for individuals in World War I and for an entire group—Americans of Japanese ancestry—in World War II. Third, a thorough understanding of the Confederate experience diminishes the luster on the halo of the Lost Cause, making the South look as intolerant as most states are in time of war and imminent danger.

BIBLIOGRAPHY

Neely, Mark E., Jr. *The Fate of Liberty: Abraham Lincoln and Civil Liberties.* New York: Oxford University Press, 1991.

Neely, Mark E., Jr. *Southern Rights: Political Prisoners and the Myth of Confederate Constitutionalism.* Charlottesville: University Press of Virginia, 1999.

Randall, James G. *Constitutional Problems under Lincoln*, revised edition. Urbana: University of Illinois Press, 1951.

Richardson, James D., ed. *A Compilation of the Messages and Papers of the Presidents.* New York: Bureau of National Literature, 1897.

Michael B. Dougan

See also: **Blockade, Civil War; Lincoln, Abraham; Supreme Court, 1815–1900.**

CIVIL WAR AND INDUSTRIAL AND TECHNOLOGICAL ADVANCES

The Civil War used the advances of the Industrial Revolution to foster great changes in industrial and technological development. Both the North and the South made use of advances in railroad and riverine transportation. The Union, however, was far more advanced technologically than the Confederate states. Consequently, the Union made greater and more effective use of progress in transportation, military medicine, and field artillery than did the Confederacy. Indeed, the industrial might of the Union states proved a major factor in the northern victory.

Historians generally agree that the Civil War was the first modern war, meaning the first in which technology and industrial strength played a significant role. But the nature of their industry and technology distinguished the two sides, which represented different economic conditions and ways of life.

The North had developed a mixed economy that was becoming increasingly industrialized. By the first quarter of the nineteenth century, large factories and facilities to house workers sprang up there. Lowell, Massachusetts, for example, had enormous textile mills employing hundreds of laborers, many of them women. Moreover, most of the prospering merchant shipping industry was located in the North.

The first half of the nineteenth century was a time of great expansion and improvement of transportation

The cotton gin, developed by Eli Whitney in 1793, made slavery profitable. The success of the cotton gin helped separate the North and the South by fostering slavery.

systems, again, mainly in the North and upper Midwest. States chartered and built overland roads and turnpikes. Canals, such as the 364-mile Erie Canal, tied New York City to the Great Lakes in 1825. Steamboats and railroads improved the movement of goods and people, forging ties that served both sides well during the Civil War. Better transportation fostered increasing trade within the country but brought little government regulation.

To be sure, the industrial revolution fostered social problems. Urban poverty became a growing concern. Fac-

tory wages were scarcely adequate for family survival, and many urban residents experienced hunger and destitution. Among the poor, child labor was common. Southerners often cited these factors as well as urban crime whenever the North challenged its institution of slavery. White southerners claimed that their slaves were far better off than were wage workers in the North.

The Industrial Revolution brought Southern landowners an invention that they adopted and embraced: the cotton gin. The cotton gin made slavery profitable and made cotton the nation's number one export before the Civil War. The South also adopted the steam engine, mainly to aid the cotton gin and to use on steamships to transport cotton. Ironically, the success of the cotton gin, by fostering slavery, helped to separate the two sides of the country and bring about the Civil War.

The federal government began to encourage agriculture and science well before the Civil War, though its efforts were generally modest. For example, in 1839, Congress voted $1,000 for the patent office to collect agricultural statistics and conduct investigations for promoting agriculture and rural economy. In 1829, a French-born Englishman and scientist, James Smithson, left his fortune to the people of the United States (about $500,000 in the currency of the day) to found an institution for the greater "increase and diffusion of knowledge." President Andrew Jackson announced this bequest in September 1835. After some wrangling between northern and southern senators, the money was accepted and used to found the Smithsonian Institution in Washington, D.C., which opened in 1846.

The pace of immigration also stimulated economic growth while increasing differences between North and South. Immigrants, mostly from Europe at this time, supplied low-cost labor and had an enormous impact on the Industrial Revolution in America. Most immigrants settled in the North where jobs were available. The use of standard, interchangeable parts, especially important in the manufacture of guns, clocks, and sewing machines, allowed the nation to advance technologically by using unskilled workers. The pace of immigration slowed during the Civil War but the North's victory in 1865 and the growing demand for cheap and plentiful labor increased the flow of immigration in the post war years.

Also aiding economic expansion in the North and Midwest was the mechanization of farming. By 1861, 125,000 McCormick reapers manufactured between 1856 and 1861 were in use, mostly in Northern states. During the Civil War, another 230,000 reapers were sold. Wartime devastation led to increased demand for agricultural mechanization by the 1870s. The number of farms in the country increased greatly in the post war years, as did industrial expansion in general.

During the Civil War, with Southern members of Congress gone and the Republican Party controlling both houses of Congress and the presidency, the government set about to aid business and technology. In 1862, the Department of Agriculture was founded. It provided a national center to coordinate agricultural development and promote scientific farming. Additionally, scientific farming received a further boost from the idea of land grant colleges through the Morrill Act, which Congress passed that same year. It provided federal land for colleges in order to stimulate agricultural and technical development and represented a new role for the federal government. When the war ended, the practical results of the Morrill law became evident.

Industrialization and technology that helped ensure Northern victory continued after the war. The United States began to make enormous strides in the world of science, technology, and industry. Many pre-Civil War institutions and initiatives continued through the Gilded Age in the late nineteenth century. Robber Barons made use of growing concentrations of business capital and of the nation's extensive natural resources. Cheap immigrant labor again flooded the nation's markets, enabling the building of the transcontinental railroad in 1869, of more factories, and of America's expanding cities. The Civil War furthered the expansion of the Industrial Revolution and eventually made the United States the most powerful industrialized nation in the world.

BIBLIOGRAPHY

Andreano, Ralph, ed. *The Economic Impact of the American Civil War.* Cambridge, MA: Schenkman Pub. Co., 1962.

Basler, R. P. *A Short History of the American Civil War.* New York: Basic Books, 1989.

Goode, George B., ed. *The Smithsonian Institution, 1846–1896.* Washington, DC: Smithsonian Institution, 1897.

Hounshell, David A. *From the American System to Mass Production, 1800–1932: The Development of Manufacturing Technology in the United States.* Baltimore, MD: Johns Hopkins University Press, 1984.

Licht, Walter. *Industrializing America: The Nineteenth Century.* Baltimore, MD: Johns Hopkins University Press, 1995.

Lynch, G. J. and G. Horwich, eds. *Food, Policy, and Politics: A Perspective on Agriculture and Development.* Boulder CO: Westview Press, 1989.

McPherson, James M. *Battle Cry of Freedom: The Civil War Era.* New York: Oxford University Press, 1988.

Stearns, Peter N. *The Industrial Revolution in World History.* Boulder, CO: Westview Press, 1998.

Frank A. Salamone and Sally G. McMillen

See also: **Medicine and Health; Railroads.**

CIVIL WAR AND ITS IMPACT ON SEXUAL ATTITUDES ON THE HOMEFRONT

Gender relationships and sexual behavior were well prescribed throughout much of the nineteenth century. White men controlled the economic, legal, and political structure of the nation. Women could not vote; their educational opportunities were limited; and few women held jobs outside the home. Married women by law, tradition, and faith were considered inferior to their husbands and could not lay claim to their property, wages, or children (in rare cases of divorce). Women were supposed to uphold the moral values of the nation and to behave in a virtuous, pious manner. Their primary role was to care for their families and homes rather than to engage in the rough and tumble of public life. The double sexual standard prevailed, giving men but not women the ability to transgress sexual boundaries without serious repercussions. Before and after the Civil War, medical advisors published numerous tracts that presented dire consequences if any woman became "unsexed" by acquiring too much education or overstepping her social and legal boundaries.

Yet society and sexual behavior did not always function as prescribed. Many poor women had to work for wages in order to survive. Not all women were virtuous; prostitution was a problem in cities, army camps, and western towns and mining camps. White males took sexual advantage of slave women. Female slaves and poor farm women could not conform to ideal female behavior since they often worked in fields and performed what many whites considered to be masculine tasks.

With the woman's rights and abolition movements in the late 1840s, a few northern women became more political and outspoken. A handful of them were soundly criticized for challenging prevailing fashion and donning "bloomers," or pants, that allowed them to discard corsets and tight lacing. Utopian communities that sought to create a more perfect society offered alternate forms of sexual behavior. Shakers insisted that men and women live apart and forgo sexual intimacy, and the Oneida Community promoted "complex marriages," permitting sexual relations between any man and woman in that community. The Mormons allowed polygamy.

During the Civil War, traditional gender roles underwent significant change. Women made major contributions in the war, demonstrating their effectiveness as battlefield nurses (a profession that had been male), and a few even dressed as soldiers and engaged in armed conflict. Female spies' records of daring matched that of their male counterparts. A number of women worked in factories and government offices. Women on the homefront took charge of their farms and families. These examples suggest that rather than being innate, the capabilities of the sexes depended on social and cultural circumstances.

The active roles that women assumed in the Civil War—due to necessity, desire, or a combination of both—worried Americans who were bound by strict ideas of proper gender and sexual behavior. They feared that masculine behavior by women would carry over into the postwar period, making those women unfit wives and mothers.

Whereas some Americans understood that such women were acting out of necessity and appreciated what they did during wartime, they believed that women should assume male roles only in dire emergencies. The general opinion was that men should protect and defend women.

Of course, the Civil War fostered prostitution in both cities and army camps. Often prostitutes in camps also filled conventional female roles. They cleaned for the men, did laundry, cooked, and performed other domestic services. Many soldiers wrote rather sympathetically of these women, whom they viewed as having been forced into prostitution as a result of the exigencies of war.

An improved situation after the Civil War was experienced by African American women. With freedom and the legality of their marriages assured, black women were less likely to become victims of white men's sexual needs. The end of slavery in 1865, however, made whites nervous, and a number of northern and southern states banned marriage and sexual relations between people of different races (miscegenation). Nevertheless, coercive sex between members of the dominant white race and any subordinate race continued into the twentieth century.

As might be expected, a reaction set in after the Civil War against what the public perceived as a loosening of moral standards. In the 1870s, New York City's Anthony Comstock and his Purity Crusade against "smut" sought to suppress pornography, abortion, contraception, and prostitution. Comstock and his followers encouraged the passage of state and local laws against prostitution and abortion as well as federal laws against the selling and importation of contraceptives and the mailing of obscene literature. However, opposition to these laws also arose. Counter movements challenged the nation's ideas of appropriate sex roles and sexual behavior. Americans of this era also worried about what they perceived to be the feminization of men and viewed aberrant male sexual behavior, such as masturbation and homosexuality, as an illness. Churches, Sunday schools, and male organizations such as the YMCA offered activities to foster masculine behavior.

Every major war has affected America's views on gender and sexual relationships. War provides an opportunity to both reassert and question basic assumptions about the roles of men and women. The Civil War was no different in that regard. However, just as it differed from other wars in fundamental ways, so, too, was its effect on male-female relationships appreciably greater.

BIBLIOGRAPHY

Clinton, Catherine and Silber, Nina, eds. *Divided Houses: Gender and the Civil War.* New York: Oxford University Press, 1992.

D'Emilio, John and Freedman, Estelle. *Intimate Matters: A History of Sexuality in America*. New York, Harper & Row, 1988.

Griggs, Claudine. *S/he: Changing Sex and Changing Clothes*. New York: Berg, 1998.

Posner, Richard A. *Sex and Reason*. Cambridge, MA: Harvard University Press, 1992.

Pyron, Darden Asbury, ed. *Recasting: Gone with the Wind in American Culture*. Miami: University Press of Florida, 1983.

Wells, C. A. "Battle Time: Gender, Modernity, and Confederate Hospitals." *Journal of Social History*, 35, no. 2 (2002), 409 ff.

Frank A. Salamone and Sally G. McMillen

CIVIL WAR VETERANS

Over the course of the Civil War, from 2.1 to over 2.4 million men served in the United States Armed Forces. In addition, from 850,000 to over 1,000,000 men served for some period of time in the Confederate Army and Navy. Significantly, of the men who served in the United States Army, over 180,000 were African Americans; another 24,000 blacks served in the United States Navy. More than 86,000 white men from Confederate states served in the United States Army. About 620,000 servicemen died in combat or from wounds or disease, but hundreds of thousands of soldiers returned to their civilian lives transformed by their memories of battle, the enemy, and military life.

Veteran soldiers began to return to civilian life while the fighting continued because terms of service, wounds, and other disabilities allowed men to leave the armed forces before the end of the war. Both governments, however, made an effort to keep experienced soldiers in the ranks. In 1864, the Confederate Army established an invalid corps that placed wounded soldiers on light duty. In late 1864, the United States government offered a special bounty to veterans who would enlist in General Winfield Scott Hancock's Veteran Corps; for various reasons only 4,422 men joined this corps by the end of the war. A more successful effort was the U.S. War Department's Invalid Corps, established in April 1863 to keep wounded or sick veteran soldiers who might otherwise have received discharges on duty in rear echelon jobs. A total of 57,000 enlisted men served in what became known as the Veteran Reserve Corps. By fall 1865, 1,036 officers had received commissions in the corps. During Reconstruction, this corps' officers actively competed for service in the Bureau of Refugees, Freedmen, and Abandoned Lands. They made up the majority of the officers on duty in that organization and, along with many agents who were also Union veterans, committed themselves to the task of securing the fruits of victory, including civil rights for the ex-slaves.

The transition to civilian life was not easy for either Union or Confederate veterans. Many camp-hardened Union veterans first passed through a bureaucratic morass of paperwork; some engaged in boisterous drunken behavior on their routes home. Confederate soldiers drifted home through a desolate countryside and along the way stole from government warehouses and civilians to feed themselves. Some Northern and Southern civilians worried that the war had made these men unfit for civil society.

Physical and emotional scars compounded the problems of adjustment. Over 200,000 Union soldiers returned home with wounds. Many Confederate soldiers returned home in similar condition. A number of veterans continued to be troubled by unhealed amputations, disease, or psychiatric problems; some of them resorted to drugs and alcohol to ease their pain.

NORTHERN VETERANS

Once home, veterans confronted unemployment and their own concerns about making their way in civilian society. Disabled Northern veterans found assistance in the federal government's pension program, first established in 1862 and expanded over the years by subsequent legislation. The federal government also established veterans' homes for disabled and psychologically scarred soldiers. Some veterans attempted to revive the camaraderie of the service by joining organizations such as the Military Order of the Loyal Legion of the United States, founded in 1865, and the more popular Grand Army of the Republic (GAR), founded in 1866. These organizations did not attract large memberships at first, an indication perhaps that Northern veterans were initially more concerned with putting the past behind them. However, during the latter decades of the century, these fraternal organizations grew. The GAR, which in 1890 claimed more than 400,000 members, became an important political voice for veterans' concerns, an influential supporter of Republican Party candidates, and an advocate for preserving the history of the war and for teaching patriotic values to new generations. In 1871 Union veterans also founded the National Rifle Association to develop the marksmanship of future soldiers. A number of Civil War veterans served in federal units in the West to subdue American Indians and ease white settlement of the frontier.

BLACK VETERANS

African-American Union veterans faced problems similar to those of whites, but they found their prospects restricted by the racism they encountered in Northern and Southern society. Black veterans commonly found themselves in separate GAR posts; on celebratory occasions

CIVIL WAR MEMORIALS

The problem of burying soldiers killed during the Civil War not only brought about the establishment of a national cemetery system, but led to the ongoing effort to memorialize America's war dead that has since been taken for granted. While the war lasted there was no formal procedure for dealing with the dead; they were hastily buried in fields, churchyards, or plots donated by private cemeteries near the places where they died. Many of the bodies were unidentified. After hostilities ceased, the army searched the countryside to find Union dead and reinter them with honor, a process that took five years. Southerners, too, made efforts to retrieve and rebury their dead.

Originally, the aim of the national cemeteries was simply to provide a decent resting place for those who had given their lives in the service of their country. However, because many of these cemeteries were located on the sites of historic battles, their dramatic associations gave them a memorial significance that had not been foreseen in 1862 when their purchase was authorized by Congress. Prominent among these was the cemetery at Gettysburg, Pennsylvania, which was dedicated by President Abraham Lincoln in his famous Gettysburg Address. That site and many others were frequently visited by Americans other than families of those buried there. The custom of decorating soldiers' graves with flowers on Decoration Day, later to become Memorial Day, began in 1864 and spread rapidly throughout both the North and the South.

The best known of the national cemeteries is Arlington, across the Potomac River from Washington, D.C., which was established in 1863 on land formerly belonging to the stepson of George Washington and, later, to Confederate General Robert E. Lee. At the beginning it was not a prestigious burying place; like the others it was used only for unidentified war dead and those whose families could not afford to transport them to their northern home states. However, in 1873 Congress passed legislation granting all honorably discharged Civil War veterans the right to be buried at no cost in national cemeteries, and burial at Arlington, in the nation's capital, gradually came to be viewed as an honor. Later, it was opened to those who served in other wars and their dependents; many well-known people, including President John F. Kennedy, are buried there. It is the site of the famous Tomb of the Unknown Soldier built after World War I, but also contains the tomb of over two thousand unknowns from the Civil War—probably including the remains of Confederate as well as Union soldiers.

The national cemeteries, important though they have been to the nation as a whole, were not the primary means through which Americans memorialized the Civil War. Most memorials—monuments, equestrian statues of heroes, and simpler statues of individual soldiers—were created at the local level and served as focal points around which people of a particular community could gather to remember what the conflict and its sacrifices had meant to them. Built to foster unification and reconciliation, these memorials were dedicated in impressive ceremonies attended by large crowds with parades, music and emotion-inspiring speeches. Because raising funds for a local statue often took years, many, particularly in the South, were not erected until the late nineteenth century or even the early twentieth; by Southerners these were increasingly looked upon as symbols of traditional southern values and of the Lost Cause. Thousands of Civil War memorials still exist throughout the states that were involved in the war. Over time, they have played an important role in reaffirming both national and regional identity.

Sylvia Engdahl

---

they were left no choice but to bring up the rear of parades. They also found themselves in conflict with former officers who challenged the notion of black suffrage. In the South, black veterans shared the fate of all blacks throughout the region, although some rose to positions of community leadership because of their military experience. That experience, however, also made them targets for violence, as in the case of veterans attacked by whites in May 1866 in Memphis, Tennessee. By the end of the nineteenth century, black veterans lost what rights they believed they had won by means of their service, including the right to vote.

SOUTHERN VETERANS

In the postwar South, concerns about poverty and the meaning of defeat, as well as a new kind of race relations,

Veterans of the Union and the Confederate armies, ca. 1913. © CORBIS

shaped the adjustment of Confederate veterans to civilian life. Resentment of emancipation and Reconstruction (1865–1877), which gave freed slaves economic and political power, prompted some Confederate veterans to conduct a low-level guerrilla campaign against their Yankee occupiers and freedpeople who challenged the former racial status quo, providing recruits for organizations such as the Ku Klux Klan.

As in the North, Southerners did not join veterans' organizations in large numbers immediately after the war, as their main concerns were rebuilding their lives and regaining control of their communities rather than remembering their hardships. However, in the later years of the nineteenth century, they joined organizations that glorified, perpetuated, and shaped the memory of their wartime sacrifices. In 1889 Southern veterans formed the United Confederate Veterans (UCV), which attracted a significant following. The UCV lobbied for assistance for its less fortunate brothers and their families and helped to reshape the idea of the war memorial as a commem-

oration not only of the war dead, but also of the common Confederate soldier. Like the GAR, the UCV was also concerned with developing a "correct" memory of the war. To that end, in 1899 it sponsored the publication of the twelve volumes of *Confederate Military History*. Unlike their Union counterparts, who received federal pensions, needy Confederate veterans had to rely on state assistance. Southern state governments provided artificial limbs for amputees and eventually small pensions for veterans. States also established veterans' homes across the South, which came to serve as focal points of memorial celebrations for the Lost Cause.

VETERANS AND NATIONAL MEMORY

Veterans brought away from the war varying degrees of hate and respect for their enemies. But toward the end of the nineteenth century, Blue and Gray reunions brought them together in a celebration of national unity. In 1898, the participation of Southerners and Northerners, including Civil War veterans, in the Spanish American War further solidified that spirit of unity. Once again, veterans identified themselves as soldiers, recognized themselves in their former enemies, and selectively remembered their wartime experiences. In the process, white Union and Confederate veterans significantly contributed to the construction of a Civil War history that ignored the centrality of the slavery issue, obscured the purpose of Reconstruction, and diminished the contributions of black Union veterans.

BIBLIOGRAPHY

Blight, David W. *Race and Reunion: The Civil War in American Memory.* Cambridge, MA: Harvard University Press, 2001.

Cimbala, Paul A., and Miller, Randall M., eds. *Union Soldiers and the Northern Home Front: Wartime Experiences, Postwar Adjustments.* New York: Fordham University Press, 2002.

Cimbala, Paul A. "Lining Up to Serve: Wounded and Sick Union Officers Join Veteran Reserve Corps during Civil War, Reconstruction." *Prologue* (spring 2003): 38–49.

Dean, Eric T., Jr. *Shook Over Hell: Post-Traumatic Stress, Vietnam, and the Civil War.* Cambridge, MA: Harvard University Press, 1997.

Foster, Gaines M. *Ghosts of the Confederacy: Defeat, the Lost Cause, and the Emergence of the New South, 1865–1913.* New York: Oxford University Press, 1987.

Logue, Larry M. *To Appomattox and Beyond, the Civil War Soldier in War and Peace.* Chicago: Ivan R. Dee, 1996.

McConnell, Stuart. *Glorious Contentment: The Grand Army of the Republic, 1865–1900.* Chapel Hill: University of North Carolina Press, 1992.

Rosenburg, R. B. *Living Monuments: Confederate Soldiers' Homes in the New South.* Chapel Hill: University of North Carolina Press, 1993.

Paul A. Cimbala

See also: **Lost Cause; Medicine and Health; Memorial (Decoration) Day; Poor Relief, 1816–1900.**

CLOTHING

Scholars debate how much influence the Civil War had on clothing and how much impact clothing had on the Civil War. One argument contends that women's participation in the war effort stimulated reform in their apparel; another insists, with some exceptions, that those who could afford to do so followed the vagaries of fashion in a normal manner. As the war raged on, fashion magazines increasingly emphasized mourning attire, and the demand grew for mourning veils and black yard goods. Matters related to dress and textiles figured in every sector of the war from the battlefield to the home front and did not only concern fashionably-attired women.

Uniforms, more than any other item of clothing, affected the war effort. When the Civil War broke out in April 1861, state volunteer regiments on both sides marched into battle wearing an array of colorful uniforms; this lack of standardized uniforms often had tragic repercussions. By 1862, the two sides had sorted themselves into blue and gray, and uniforms evolved into a functional form. Some of the more flamboyant units such as the Zouaves, the Butterfly Hussars, or the 79th New York Cameron Highlanders (who wore full Highland dress that included kilts) modified their uniforms to become more like the standard uniforms. However, a number of state militias continued to use extravagant uniforms of such units as a recruiting ploy—attracting volunteers by offering them fancy uniforms with which to impress admirers. As the war dragged on, soldiers on both sides generally wore whatever they could find.

Although they could not officially join the troops, approximately 400 women donned military uniforms, passed themselves off as Union or Confederate soldiers, and fought in the war. Some women, perhaps those who wanted to work for the war effort but did not want to wear male apparel, became spies, and female fashions—from parasols and crinolines to corsets and metal buttons—proved highly conducive for spying. One Federal agent complained, "A girl could hide a fair-sized arsenal under her hoop skirt."

In addition to uniting and recruiting military personnel, Civil War uniforms also led to important advances in men's ready-made clothing production, which had begun to develop earlier in the century. Standardized sizing and the large-scale use of the sewing machine enabled manufacturers to create masses of clothing; in particular, for Union uniforms. Poverty pushed many women into these new factories where they might earn one dollar per dozen shirts sewn. At the conclusion of the war, demand for uniforms ceased, and companies diverted their production to civilian garments and made a wide choice of ready-made clothing available to men. Most women, however, continued to obtain their garments from dressmakers or make their own clothing; factory-made feminine attire did not lose its negative associations until the beginning of the twentieth century.

Underpaid factory operatives were not the only women who stitched for the war effort. "Leisured ladies" also sewed and knitted for the soldiers, but in a significantly different way. Thousands of "war work" societies sprang up to augment existing sewing, knitting, and church circles; Northern black and white women also used their quilting skills to raise funds, first for abolition and later for the war. Southern women gathered in neigh-

Clara Barton, ca. 1860s.

borhood groups to sew uniforms and clothing for Confederate soldiers. Additionally, the Women's Patriotic Association for Diminishing the Use of Imported Luxuries pledged to support Union manufacturers by refusing to purchase imported textiles. Mary Todd Lincoln attempted to bolster Union morale by projecting the image of a fashionable first lady, and Varina Howell Davis, wife of Confederate president Jefferson Davis, continued to dress in fashionable attire. Critics pointed out that while these first ladies purchased jewelry and clothing, American women were sewing, scraping lint, and making bandages. Widespread shortages forced loyal seamstresses, especially in the South, to be innovative in their quest for fabric and yarn. Desperate to clothe their ill-clad troops, women unraveled blankets, dresses, draperies, upholstery, even carpets for their valuable threads. The lack of clothing, blankets, and bandages for the soldiers had an effect on the outcome of the war by weakening morale.

Most fashion magazines made few, if any, references to the national situation during the war years and continued to publish the styles designed abroad; the Civil War had little direct impact on how white women's fashionable apparel evolved. In the aftermath of the Civil War, changes related to clothing were measured in the increase in ready made production, the standardization of clothing sizes, the increased use of the sewing machine, the surplus of female seamstresses, and the popularity of the military cap—a vestige from the military uniform. The most significant postwar clothing transformation came about as whites witnessed newly freed black women and men proudly wearing fashions that had once been denied them.

BIBLIOGRAPHY

Banner, Lois. *American Beauty.* Chicago: University of Chicago Press, 1983.

Bullough, Vern L.; and Bullough, Bonnie. *Cross Dressing, Sex, and Gender.* Philadelphia: University of Pennsylvania Press, 1993.

Daves, Jessica. *Ready-Made Miracle: The Story of Fashion for the Millions.* New York: Putnam, 1967.

Hall, Richard. *Patriots in Disguise: Women Warriors of the Civil War.* New York: Paragon House, 1993.

Leonard, Elizabeth D. *Yankee Women: Gender Battles in the Civil War.* New York: W.W. Norton, 1995.

Martin, Paul. *Military Costume: A Short History.* Stuttgart, Germany: W. Keller & Co., 1963.

Masson, Ann, and Bryde Reveley. "When Life's Brief Sun Was Set: Portraits of Southern Women in Mourning—1830–1860." *Southern Quarterly* 27 (Fall 1988): 33–56.

Wasowicz, Laura. "The Tatnuck Ladies' Sewing Circle, 1847–1867." *Historical Journal of Massachusetts* 24 (Winter 1996): 19–46.

White, Shane; and White, Graham. *Stylin': African American Expressive Culture from Its Beginnings to the Zoot Suit.* Ithaca, NY: Cornell University Press, 1998.

Gayle V. Fischer

See also: **Davis, Varina Howell; Lincoln, Mary Todd.**

COMPROMISE OF 1850

The Compromise of 1850 was passed by the U.S. Congress to settle slavery issues and to avert the dissolution of the Union. It stemmed from the request for statehood by the territory of California in 1849, which included a constitution banning slavery. California's admission to the Union would tip the balance in favor of free states—sixteen free states to fifteen slave states. A balance had been achieved with the Missouri Compromise of 1820, which tried to settle the growing slavery issue at that time by admitting Missouri as a slave state and Maine as a free state. The proposed admission of California in 1850 was further complicated by unresolved slavery questions in the vast southwestern territory that had been ceded to the United States after the war with Mexico ended in 1848 with the Treaty of Guadalupe Hidalgo.

As he had done with the Missouri Compromise thirty years earlier, U.S. Senator Henry Clay of Kentucky attempted to find a solution in 1850. This time the stakes were higher—the real possibility that the Union would break apart. Now seventy-one years old and in ill health, Clay gave his last great speech to the Senate on February 5–6, 1850, outlining the many features of the compromise, which once again tried to give satisfaction to both sides, and staking his reputation upon its passage. It was Senator Stephen Douglas of Illinois, though, who successfully crafted the measures.

The Compromise of 1850 called for the admission of California as a free state as well as the organization of the ceded southwestern land into the territories of New Mexico and Utah, without mention of slavery. It stated that, when the territories became states, voting citizens living in those territories could then decide on their slavery status, a solution known as *popular sovereignty.* The compromise also settled the boundary dispute between Texas and New Mexico and called for prohibition of slavery in the District of Columbia.

But by far the most contentious part of the Compromise of 1850 was the Fugitive Slave Act. It was the second of such acts, the first having been passed in 1793. Southern states demanded it largely in response to the growing number of fugitive slaves who were escaping to freedom in the North or into Canada. The act not only called for the return of runaway slaves, as the previous law had done, but prohibited the fugitives a trial by jury or even to testify in their own behalf. In addition, marshals in the North who did not enforce the law were given heavy penalties, as were those who helped slaves to escape.

The act was so severe and the outrage against it in the North so intense that it led to heavy abuses and therefore defeated its own purpose. Some Northern states passed personal liberty laws to defy the Fugitive Slave Act. The number of escapees increased, as did the number of abolitionists who took up the cause against slavery. Putting the law into effect only led to more animosity between North and South, and when South Carolina justified its secession from the Union in December 1860, it listed the personal liberty laws as one of its grievances. The Fugitive Slave Act was not repealed until June 28, 1864, well into the Civil War. The Compromise of 1850, created in an effort to stave off war, actually may have fostered sectional tensions. Ultimately, it led to a Republican victory in 1860 and to Southern secession.

BIBLIOGRAPHY

McPherson, James. *The Battle Cry of Freedom.* New York: Oxford University Press, 1988.

Potter, David M. *The Impending Crisis, 1848–1861.* New York: Harper and Row, 1976.

Internet Resources

Calhoun, John C. "The Clay Compromise Measures." National Center for Public Policy Research. Available from <http://www.nationalcenter.org>.

"The Compromise of 1850 and the Fugitive Slave Act." In *Africans in America, Part 4: 1831–1865.* PBS Online. Available from <www.pbs.org>.

Rose Blue and Corinne J. Naden

See also: Slavery.

CONFEDERATE STATES OF AMERICA

As the presidential election of 1860 drew near, the Southern states faced what they saw as a growing threat to their way of life. When Republican Abraham Lincoln won the presidency in November, there was no longer room for compromise. The South was convinced that Lincoln would use the power of his office to destroy slavery. Accordingly, in the months following his election, seven states of the Deep South seceded from the United States of America. South Carolina left in December; Missis-

sippi, Florida, Alabama, Georgia, and Louisiana in January 1861. Texas seceded on February 1 before Lincoln's inauguration in March.

The new president waited a month before he sent reinforcements to protect the federal arsenal at Fort Sumter in the harbor of Charleston, South Carolina. When Charleston guns fired on the fort on April 12, the Civil War began. Lincoln immediately called for volunteers in response to this. Forced to choose between staying in the Union or joining the seven states that left it, four additional Southern states—Virginia, North Carolina, Arkansas, and Tennessee—seceded as well. They would wage a long and devastating war that cost over 620,000 lives. The Union victory in 1865 would finally reunite the country, but leave cultural and political scars that still affect Americans today.

BUILDING A CONFEDERATE GOVERNMENT

On February 4, two months before the attack on Fort Sumter, six states of the Deep South met in Montgomery, Alabama, to form a provisional government. The constitution for the Confederacy was similar to the U.S. Constitution of 1787, which Southerners generally revered, although they felt the abolitionist North wrongly interpreted it. There were some differences, however. The president of the new nation was elected for a single term of six years. He was given veto power over the budget. Amendments could be passed with a two-thirds majority instead of three-fourths. Slavery was protected, except that the external African slave trade was prohibited, and Congress could not pass a law infringing on slave owners' rights.

The Confederacy chose Jefferson Davis as its first president. He was born in Kentucky and graduated from the U.S. Military Academy at West Point in 1828. He had served in Congress and was wounded in the war with Mexico. Davis believed that Lincoln's election spelled disaster for the South. The vice president was the frail and sickly Alexander H. Stephens of Georgia who defended slavery, but opposed the dissolution of the Union.

As the business of forming a government progressed, it became increasingly clear that the city of Montgomery was not the best choice for the new capital. The climate was hot, and the hotel facilities were poor. It also was not well located within the eleven confederate states. In May 1861, after Virginia joined the Confederacy, the capital moved to Richmond, which had a population of about forty thousand people. Davis had opposed the move, but Congress overrode his veto. Afterward, presidential and congressional elections were held in November. Davis and Stephens, who ran unopposed, were pointedly re-inaugurated on George Washington's birthday, February 22, 1862.

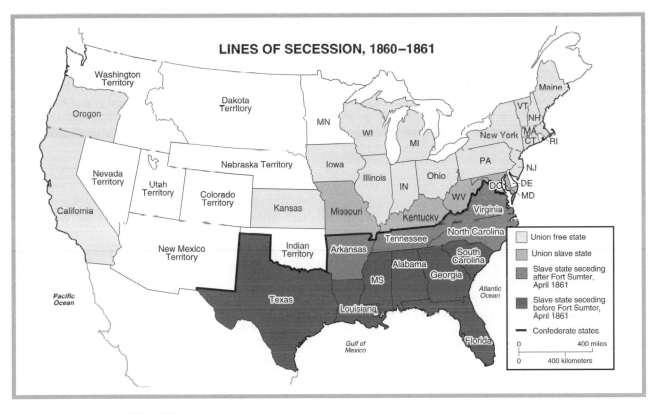

Lines of Secession, 1860–1861. GALE GROUP

The South was seemingly united on the cause of slavery, although most Southerners would have said they were fighting not to save that institution, but to protect states' rights. However, there was friction among groups almost immediately. Lacking any established political parties, the result was disorganization and confusion. Some thought Davis was too dictatorial; some backed the war effort but disliked him personally; others wanted the government to negotiate with the North for peace.

MANPOWER AND ECONOMICS
The most immediate concern of the newly formed Confederate States of America was to raise and equip an army. At first, it was assumed that intense patriotism would fill the military ranks with volunteers. However, after the first few clashes on bloody battlefields, the desire for volunteering waned somewhat and conscription was begun in April 1862. It was the first such law in American history and was mainly aimed at stopping twelve-month volunteers from leaving the military. The draft law called up able-bodied white men, ages eighteen to thirty-five, for a three-year period. Most Southerners bitterly opposed it, for they regarded being drafted as a disgrace, and disliked the government dictating control over their lives. Nevertheless, it overwhelmingly passed through Congress, which regarded it as a necessary evil.

Southern leaders well knew that they were far inferior to the North in terms of manpower and economic resources. The population of the eleven Confederate states was about five and a half million whites and nearly four million black slaves. The Union had a population of twenty-two million. The estimated total number (over the entire duration of the war) of Southerners who served in the Confederate army was 750,000; twice that many troops served in the Union army. The Confederate Army reached its top strength in June 1863 just before the Battle of Gettysburg. After that loss, Southern military power began to decline.

In addition to needing soldiers to fight the war, the Confederacy needed funds. Its first attempt to obtain money was to print it. Hampered by constitutional limits, the Congress issued paper money, which brought on rampant inflation. For instance, in August 1863, the Confederate dollar was equal to eight cents in gold; by March 1865, it was less than two cents. In comparison, although the northern greenback also depreciated, it never lost more than two-thirds of its value. As a result of the collapse, the southern population suffered greatly: flour cost $275 a barrel and bacon was $9 a pound.

What was even worse than inflation was the inability of the Confederacy to provide adequate food for the troops or for the families of poor soldiers. This was due in part to having to convert fields from growing cotton to growing food crops. Soldiers destroyed railroad lines, thus delaying the delivery of food. In addition, hundreds of acres of cotton were burned to prevent them from falling into the hands of Union troops. The South had been confident that foreign countries such as England and France would recognize the Confederacy because of their dependence on American cotton, but that never materialized. The scarcity of food greatly contributed to a loss of morale in the last months of the Civil War.

STATES' RIGHTS

In addition to its manpower and economic shortages, the Confederacy faced the very real problem of winning a war while adhering to the ideal of states' rights. The traditions of the South sought to protect individual property rights and stood against a powerful central government. In fact, the new constitution did not give Congress the power to overrule state court decisions. Yet, a strong government with the power to pass laws infringing on the rights of the states for the good of the Confederacy was exactly what was needed to win a war.

The conflict between advocates of states' rights and the need for a strong central authority to fight the war put the Confederate government in a position of often being at war with its own people; the doctrine of states' rights is usually given as a major factor in the defeat of the South. The conflict first flared up when the conscription law was passed. As the war progressed, plantation owners became reluctant to send out their slaves to work on war projects or in factories. Acts of impressment—seizing private citizens for duty—plus mounting battle losses, so enraged the people of South Carolina that by 1864, only one paper in the entire state (the Charleston *Courier*) backed Jefferson Davis. In fact, Congressman William W. Boyce proposed a revolt against the president and later called publicly for a convention between the North and South to talk about peace terms.

THE LINGERING EFFECTS

The Civil War began at 4:30 on the morning of April 12, 1861, at Fort Sumter, South Carolina. The Confederate government effectively collapsed when Richmond fell on April 2, 1865. The war formally ended on the afternoon of April 9, 1865, when General Robert E. Lee surrendered to General Ulysses S. Grant at Appomattox Court House, Virginia. More than 620,0000 Americans died due to battle casualties, disease, and other causes. About 400,000 on both sides were wounded. It was the worst conflict ever fought on American soil.

A large part of the southland was in ruins. Soldiers returned home to burned out homes, and plantation fields, once tended by slaves, were left unplanted. The lawless roamed the streets. Railroads no longer ran; banks shut down. Thousands were homeless. The war was over, but a long period of reconstruction, which left the white Southern population bitter and resentful toward the North, was just beginning. African Americans were jubilant, for the Confederacy's demise and the passage of the Thirteenth Amendment brought them freedom and immediate hope for the future.

Most of the novels of that period focus on the great suffering of the South, although the North endured great suffering as well. But the war was fought mainly on Southern land; as depicted in the classic novel and motion picture, *Gone With the Wind*, the lives of both whites and blacks were turned upside down as people struggled to find a way to rebuild their lives in a society that was no longer understood by either side.

BIBLIOGRAPHY

Davis, William C. *The Cause Lost: Myths and Realities of the Confederacy.* Lawrence: University Press of Kansas, 1996.

Eaton, Clement. *A History of the Southern Confederacy.* New York: Macmillan, 1954.

Rable, George C. *The Confederate Republic: A Revolution Against Politics.* Chapel Hill: University of North Carolina Press, 1994.

Internet Resources

"Confederate States of America." Available from <http://college.hmco.com/history/readerscomp>.

"Overview of the Confederacy." Available from <http://www.civilwarhome.com>.

Corinne J. Naden and Rose Blue

See also: **Davis, Jefferson; Davis, Varina Howell; Mobilization for War; Secession; States' Rights, Theory of.**

CONSTITUTIONAL AMENDMENTS AND CHANGES

The controversies over interposition, nullification (both involving claims that states could defy Federal laws), secession, and slavery that led to the Civil War were settled on the battlefield but confirmed later by amendments to the Constitution.

THE THREE POSTWAR AMENDMENTS

From 1865 to 1870, the states ratified three critical amendments. The first of these, the Thirteenth Amendment, abolished involuntary servitude in the United States except as a punishment for crimes. The Fourteenth Amendment, ratified in 1868, applied citizenship to all persons born and naturalized within the United States and guaranteed all such individuals certain fundamental rights, including equal protection under the law. The Fifteenth Amendment guaranteed that no citizen would be denied the right to vote on the basis of "race, color, or previous condition of servitude." Each of these amendments vested Congress with enforcement powers.

Conflict over slavery was a major factor in the events leading up to the Civil War (1861–1865). Despite Lincoln's assurance that he did not plan to eliminate slavery from the states where it currently existed, Southern states seceded from the Union after he won the presidential election of 1860. Lincoln considered himself bound by oath to support the continuation of the Union by forcing the seceding states to rejoin it.

As casualties mounted, Lincoln considered ending slavery one of the larger purposes the war might serve. With the Emancipation Proclamation (January 1, 1863), he used his war powers to declare an end to slavery behind enemy lines, but this limited proclamation lacked the security that an amendment firmly planted in the Constitution could provide. By the war's end, even the Confederacy had considered abolishing slavery as a war measure. Slavery had already led to one conflict, and the nation could not allow it to continue and thus lead to another. In January of 1865, Congress proposed the Thirteenth Amendment, which was ratified that December. At the time, its passage was thought sufficient not only to end slavery but to entitle freed slaves to the rights of all American citizens. The legacy of the culture of slavery, however, was not removed by abolishing the institution of slavery.

After the war, many Southern states began to enact Black Codes restricting the rights of former slaves to own property and move freely. In 1866, Congress passed the Civil Rights Bill over President Andrew Johnson's veto to ensure the property and personal rights of African Americans. In addition, in 1866 Congress extended the life of the Freedmen's Bureau, also over Johnson's veto, to aid former slaves who were often uneducated and tied to the land by sharecropping agreements.

Although the intent of the Civil Rights Act of 1866 was to extend full citizenship to free African Americans, the legislation could not guarantee protection in the future because it was vulnerable to repeal. More significantly, the legislation was at odds with the Constitution as it had been defined in the landmark Dred Scott decision of 1857, in which Supreme Court Chief Justice Roger Taney had ruled that African Americans were not and could not be U.S. citizens, thus excluding all African Americans, whether free or slave, from the protections of the Constitution. The Fourteenth Amendment was intended to incorporate the provisions of the Civil Rights

Act of 1866 into the Constitution. Its first sentence overturned the Dred Scott decision by confirming the citizenship of all persons born or naturalized within the United States. Section 1 further conferred the privileges and immunities of citizens, the right of due process of law, and the equal protection of the law upon all such citizens. Section 2 negated the three-fifths clause in the Constitution (Article 1, Section 2), which had counted slaves as three-fifths of a person for the purpose of determining the number of representatives a state could send to Congress.

Free African Americans added hundreds of thousands of new voters to the political process and they became a new political force in the South; they were, however, often exploited by ambitious and corrupt politicians. The rise of African Americans to power was aided by federal enforcement of the Civil Rights Act and the Fourteenth Amendment, which included a provision that prohibited any person who had "engaged in insurrection or rebellion" against the United States from holding public office. A significant number of African Americans voted and were elected to office during Reconstruction. A backlash, however, including intimidation by the Ku Klux Klan, resulted in efforts to deny African Americans the right to vote. In 1870, Congress responded by passing the Fifteenth Amendment, which stated that no state could deny the right of citizens to vote "on account of race, color, or previous condition of servitude." This was the first of a number of subsequent amendments (the nineteenth, twenty-third, twenty-fourth, and twenty-sixth) liberalizing voting rights.

The three post–Civil War amendments transformed the relationship between the national government and the states, diminishing the rights of states. They all, but especially the Fourteenth Amendment, created a new role for the national government by extending the protections of the Bill of Rights to all citizens of the nation. They also left legacies that have fundamentally affected American society and culture to the present day.

One immediate effect was that women who had supported Abolition and rights for African Americans felt betrayed when the vote was extended to African Americans but not to women. Although women had been fighting for the right to vote since the Seneca Falls Convention of 1848, they had to wait until the ratification of the Nineteenth Amendment in 1920 to gain that right. Another effect was seething resentment in the white South against these amendments, which not only overturned the previous planter-slave culture but were forced on the Southern states by Congress's requirement that the Southern states approve them before they could have their military governors replaced with civilian authorities. Despite these fundamental changes in the Constitution, however, the national will to enforce these amendments largely dissipated when the national government withdrew the last federal troops from the South in 1877, thereby ending Reconstruction.

WANING ENFORCEMENT OF THE FOURTEENTH AND FIFTEENTH AMENDMENTS

Even prior to the end of Reconstruction in 1877, the national government began to withdraw its protection of African-American civil rights. In 1873, the Supreme Court had given a very narrow reading to the privileges and immunities clause of the Fourteenth Amendment in the Slaughterhouse Cases in which the court held that the clause did not protect the interests of butchers who were forced to conduct their business in state-approved slaughterhouses. This interpretation was made easier by a system of government that valued federalism and the exercise of state prerogatives over matters considered to be local in nature. The Supreme Court actively utilized the due process clause of the Fourteenth Amendment through early 1937 but applied it primarily to striking down what it considered to be arbitrary interference with economic rights rather than to guaranteeing the rights of racial minorities. In the Civil Rights Cases of 1883, the court further invalidated the Civil Rights Act of 1875, which had outlawed racial discrimination in places of public accommodation, on the basis that the amendment's provision of equal protection only vested government with the right to strike down discriminatory state (as opposed to private) action. Perhaps more significantly, in *Plessy v. Ferguson* (1896), the Supreme Court upheld the proliferating Jim Crow laws that provided for racial segregation and separate facilities as long as such separate facilities were equal. This decision remained law until the court's historic decision in *Brown v. Board of Education* (1954), which struck down laws segregating schools.

For decades, the Fifteenth Amendment was even less effective than the Fourteenth. States adopted literacy tests, understanding clauses (both of which were applied in a discriminatory fashion), grandfather clauses (requiring such tests only of individuals, like the descendants of slaves, whose grandfathers had not voted prior to the abolition of slavery), poll taxes, and all-white primaries, supplemented by physical intimidation by groups like the Ku Klux Klan, to prevent African Americans and other racial minorities from voting. Although federal courts eventually struck down some discriminatory measures, including grandfather clauses and all-white primaries, African-American voting remained severely depressed well into the 1960s, when the force of the Voting Rights Act of 1965 and other federal legislation, supplemented by civil rights marches and voter registration drives, finally began to alleviate the situation.

LEGACY OF THE POSTWAR AMENDMENTS

The post-Civil War amendments were revived in the twentieth century. In *Gitlow v. New York* (1925) and subsequent cases, the Supreme Court began applying the guarantees of the Bill of Rights to the states through the due process clause of the Fourteenth Amendment. Court rulings significantly expanded federal oversight of areas once entrusted almost exclusively to state control. African-American troops returning from World War II brought with them a renewed sense that it was hypocritical for the nation to pursue equality abroad and deny it at home. In *Brown v. Board of Education* (1954), the Supreme Court reversed the doctrine of separate but equal and insisted on racial desegregation in public schools. Soon the principle was applied to all public accommodations.

As the Civil Rights movement, sparked by the Brown decision, gained power in the mid-1950s and early 1960s, Congress again turned to ensuring that African Americans had the same personal and property rights as other citizens, including access to public accommodations. In 1964, it passed the most sweeping civil rights bill since the Civil War, making it illegal to deny African Americans access to public facilities such as lunch counters. In 1965, Congress turned to the issue of voting rights, which had been guaranteed under the Fifteenth Amendment. Despite that amendment, most African Americans in the South had been denied the right to vote. The 1965 act removed all the barriers that had been erected to keep African Americans from the polls. Nearly a hundred years after the Civil War, and after years of struggles by African Americans, the nation's promise to guarantee equal rights to slaves was kept to their descendants.

Of all America's wars, the Civil War may have had the most profound effect on America's culture, society, and identity. The three amendments passed as a result of that war ended slavery, fundamentally changed the Constitution, helped create a biracial society on a scale never before seen in history, contributed to the expansion of voting rights that later included women, laid the foundation for the decline of sectionalism and states' rights that had divided the nation, and defined the concepts of liberty and citizenship in ways that shape American political culture and society in the twenty-first century.

BIBLIOGRAPHY

Flack, Horace E. *The Adoption of the Fourteenth Amendment* (1908). Gloucester, MA: Peter Smith, 1965.

James, Joseph B. *The Ratification of the Fourteenth Amendment.* Macon, GA: Mercer University Press, 1984.

Kyvig, David E. *Explicit and Authentic Acts: Amending the Constitution, 1776–1995.* Lawrence: University Press of Kansas, 1996.

Maltz, Earl M. *Civil Rights, the Constitution, and Congress, 1863–1869.* Lawrence: University Press of Kansas, 1990.

Nelson, William E. *The Fourteenth Amendment: From Political Principle to Judicial Doctrine.* Cambridge, MA: Harvard University Press, 1988.

Richards, David A. J. *Conscience and the Constitution: History, Theory, and Law of the Reconstruction Amendments.* Princeton, NJ: Princeton University Press, 1993.

Vorenberg, Michael. *Final Freedom: The Civil War, the Abolition of Slavery, and the Thirteenth Amendment.* Cambridge, UK: Cambridge University Press, 2001.

John R. Vile

See also: **African Americans (Freed People); Black Codes; Reconstruction; Women's Rights Movement.**

DAVIS, JEFFERSON

(b. June 3, 1808; d. December 5, 1889) U.S. representative and senator, Mexican War hero, and president of the Confederacy.

Jefferson Davis, best known as president of the Confederate States of America, is credited with shaping the Confederacy and leading it in the Civil War. In the years before the war, he served as Mississippi representative and senator, and was also a hero in the Mexican War. The defeat of Davis's Confederacy reshaped American society and government as well as the U.S. Constitution.

Born in Kentucky to a farmer of modest means, Jefferson Davis moved to Mississippi as a child and is most identified with that state, which was then on the frontier. He was educated at Transylvania College and the U.S. Military Academy at West Point, graduating in 1828. Afterward, he was an army officer, serving in the infantry and the dragoons in the Northwest (now Wisconsin and Michigan) and Southwest (now Oklahoma), until 1835. He resigned to marry his first wife, who died soon after their marriage. He then became a successful cotton planter at Davis Bend, near Vicksburg, Mississippi. He married Varina Howell in 1845, and they eventually had six children, only one of whom survived to marry and have children of her own.

In the early 1840s Davis became interested in politics and joined the Democratic Party, of which he was to be a lifelong member. He was in his first term in the House of Representatives when he was elected to lead a volunteer regiment in the Mexican War. As colonel of the Mississippi Rifles he fought heroically in the Battle of Monterrey and again in the Battle of Buena Vista, where he was seriously wounded. Soon after Davis returned home in 1847, the governor of Mississippi appointed him to represent Mississippi in the Senate, and he was soon elected to that position. He was an effective chairman of the Military Affairs Committee and a strong defender of Southern interests, including the extension of slavery. In 1851 he ran for governor, losing in a very close race. In 1853 President Franklin Pierce appointed him secretary of war. He was a success in this position, upgrading the course of study at West Point, increasing the size of the army and its pay, surveying various possible routes to the Pacific for railroads, importing camels for army use in the deserts of the West, and supervising many construction projects in Washington, such as the new dome for the Capitol and the Washington Aqueduct. He also took a great interest in

Jefferson Davis.

scientific inventions and was a trustee of the Smithsonian Institution.

In 1861, while Davis was serving as senator, Mississippi voted to secede from the United States. Davis left Washington reluctantly to follow his state. He hoped for a high military appointment in the Confederate army, but because of his experience in politics he was elected president of the new nation. During the four years of the Civil War, he was devoted to the Confederate cause. Despite his dedication, he was criticized for being too concerned with details, too rigid, and too loyal to old friends; but he won admiration for his military skills, his convictions, his honesty and integrity, and his choice of Robert E. Lee to command the Army of Northern Virginia. Davis's overriding belief in the power of the states over that of the central government proved quite a stumbling block when he found himself in charge of a national administration, the strength of which was essential to waging war.

During the conflict, the South was overwhelmed by the North's much larger resources in manpower, money, and industry. The protection and extension of the institution of slavery, which white Southerners believed key to their economy and way of life, were the underlying reasons for war. In the end, these goals proved indefensible, both practically and morally. Also, the existence of slavery made it all but impossible to secure the foreign aid from England or France, along with other foreign nations, that would have helped the South.

In April 1865 Union forces seized Richmond, Virginia, the Confederate capital. Davis fled southward but was captured in May. He was indicted for treason and for a time was believed to be involved in the plot to assassinate Abraham Lincoln. Imprisoned for two years, Davis was never tried and never regained his U.S. citizenship. He traveled, became the president of an insurance company, wrote his memoirs, *The Rise and Fall of the Confederate Government* (1881), and retired to the Mississippi Gulf Coast. He died in New Orleans in 1889 and is buried in Richmond.

BIBLIOGRAPHY

Cooper, William J., Jr. *Jefferson Davis, American*. New York: Knopf, 2000.

Davis, Jefferson. *Jefferson Davis, Constitutionalist: His Letters, Papers and Speeches*, edited by Dunbar Rowland. 10 vols. Jackson, MS: Department of Archives and History, 1923.

Davis, Jefferson. *The Papers of Jefferson Davis*, edited by Haskell M. Monroe, Jr., et al. 11 vols. Baton Rouge: Louisiana State University Press, 1971–2003.

Davis, Varina Howell. *Jefferson Davis, Ex-President of the Confederate States of America: A Memoir*. 2 vols. New York: Belford Co., 1890.

Davis, William C. *Jefferson Davis: The Man and His Hour*. New York: HarperCollins, 1991.

Internet Resource

"The Papers of Jefferson Davis." Rice University. Available from <http://jeffersondavis.rice.edu>.

Lynda Lasswell Crist

See also: **Confederate States of America; Davis, Varina Howell.**

DAVIS, VARINA HOWELL

(b. May 7, 1826; d. October 16, 1905) First Lady of the Confederate States of America.

Varina Ann Howell, later Varina Ann Howell Davis, was born at the Briars, near Natchez, Mississippi, on May 7, 1826. Her parents, William Howell and Margaret Kempe, occupied a respectable place among Mississippi's slave-owning class. Varina Howell was educated at Madame D. Grelaud's Female Seminary in Philadelphia and also had a private tutor. By the age of seventeen she outwardly fit the model of a perfect Southern lady: vivacious and well mannered, she could play the piano and read French and Latin. But throughout her life Varina Howell Davis was somewhat at odds with the ideal of

44 A M E R I C A N S A T W A R : 1 8 1 6 – 1 9 0 0

southern womanhood and resented a social order that expected women to comply with men.

At a Christmas gathering in 1843, she met the equally well-connected Jefferson Davis, a West Point Academy graduate and plantation owner. The future president of the Confederate States was seventeen years older than Howell and, like her, well positioned in Mississippi's antebellum society. By the time they met, Davis had shaken off the melancholy that followed his first wife's death and seemed willing to give marriage a second try. Following a two-year courtship, they married on February 26, 1845.

The Davis family settled in Mississippi near the home of Davis's older brother and father figure, Joseph Davis. As the family elder, Joseph Davis ruled his property and family autocratically—a style that did not sit well with Varina Davis, and this led to tense relationships in the Davis household. In 1846, Jefferson Davis obtained a commission to fight in the Mexican American War and in 1847 returned home a war hero. By the early 1850s, the family had moved to Washington, D.C., where Jefferson Davis served first as secretary of war under Franklin Pierce and then as senator from Mississippi. Varina Davis enjoyed life in the nation's capital and in 1852 bore the first of the couple's six children.

In 1861, when the nation split over the issue of slavery and Mississippi seceded, Jefferson Davis renounced his senate seat and the Davis family returned to Brierfield, their Mississippi plantation. Shortly thereafter, the newly formed Confederate States of America elected Jefferson Davis as their first president. The family moved first to Montgomery, Alabama, the Confederacy's first seat of government, and then to Richmond, Virginia, the permanent capital. Initially, life in Richmond pleased Varina Davis. She became reacquainted with old friends from Washington, D.C., and enjoyed the prominence and adulation that came with her new role. But as the war progressed and living conditions worsened in the Confederacy, public support for Jefferson Davis tumbled, and public disapproval was not confined to the president. Rumors and innuendo directed at Varina Davis flourished. Her detractors accused her of exercising undue influence over her husband and of poorly managing the Confederate White House. Even her loyalty to the cause was questioned. But despite the public's condemnation, political turmoil, and the accidental death of one of their children, Varina Davis continued to support the Confederate armies on the field. She provided succor to soldiers in the hospitals and maintained the dignity of her position.

Following the collapse of the Confederacy in April 1865 and a harrowing escape attempt, Union troops caught up with Jefferson Davis and his family in Ir-

Varina Howell Davis. © CORBIS

winville, Georgia, arresting Jefferson Davis and sending Varina Davis and the children to Savannah, which she was forbidden to leave. Her time in Georgia was unhappy. The family was subjected to the taunts and abuses of Unionists. She eventually sent her children to Canada and worked tirelessly to gain her husband's release from prison.

The end of the war found the Davises nearly bankrupt. Upon his release from prison, the former Confederate president tried to establish himself as a businessman but had little success. With the assistance of friends, the Davises purchased Beauvoir, the Mississippi estate to which they eventually retired. After her husband's death in 1889, Varina Davis stayed at Beauvoir for a few years but ultimately bequeathed the home to confederate veterans. She moved to New York City, where she worked as a writer until her death in 1905. A company of artillery from Governor's Island, New York, escorted her funeral procession through the streets of city, and the New York Camp of the United Confederate Veterans joined the procession. In Richmond, thousands lined the streets that led to Saint Paul's Church. Even though she occupied a privileged position as first lady of the Confederacy, Varina Howell Davis's life reveals how the Civil War caused Southern women to confront personal challenges and tragedies that changed their lives forever.

BIBLIOGRAPHY

Cashin, Joan E. "Varina Howell Davis (1826–1905)." In *Portraits of American Women*, Vol. 1: *From Settlement to the Civil War*, edited by G. J. Barker-Benfield and Catherine Clinton. New York: St. Martin's, 1991.

Ross, Ishbel. *The First Lady of the South.* Westport, CT: Greenwood, 1973.

Jose O. Diaz

See also: **Confederate States of America; Davis, Jefferson; Women on the Homefront.**

DAWES SEVERALTY ACT

Over the first century of its existence, the United States government tried various strategies to solve what it often called the "Indian problem"—the persistence of Native American communities in the face of expanding Euroamerican settlement. Early policies were informed by a belief that Euroamericans and Indians could not coexist. Initially, the federal government sought to remove Indians from lands Euroamericans desired. As Euroamerican expanded to every part of U.S. territory, policy shifted from removal to that of creating reservations, small islands of Indian land surrounded by a sea of Euroamerican settlement. Pressure grew in the late nineteenth century both to open up reservations to settlers and to find a way for Indians and Euroamericans to coexist peacefully. Policy makers and reformers alike began to promote allotment in severalty—the division of Indian lands into individually owned parcels—and the sale of leftover lands as a final solution to the "Indian problem." These ideas were incorporated into the 1887 General Allotment Act.

The General Allotment Act sought to impose private property ownership on Native Americans by dividing their reservations into individual farms. Its more familiar name, the Dawes Act, pays tribute to Massachusetts Senator Henry L. Dawes, who promoted the legislation. The Dawes Act fit into a broader federal policy of assimilating Indians into the American mainstream, and it dovetailed with government-sponsored education programs and Christian mission work in the last quarter of the nineteenth century.

Although the ideas underlying the assimilation policy had long existed, Congress and reformers alike showed renewed interest in assimilation in the aftermath of military conflicts like the Battle of Little Big Horn (1876) and the Nez Perce conflict (1877). They sought a more humane way to coexist with (or dispossess) Indians. Many reformers and politicians believed that private property was essential to what they considered "civilized" life and thought Indians were doomed to perish if they held land collectively. Other supporters of the legislation believed that Indians controlled more land than they could or would use productively, and these supporters wanted Indians' holdings reduced to family farm-sized parcels. The Dawes Act became law because it incorporated both humanitarian and expansionist ideals.

Under the act's terms, the president used his discretion to identify which reservations would undergo allotment in severalty. The original legislation specified varying amounts based on a person's age and family status, but it was amended in 1891 to provide at least eighty acres to each person. The federal government could purchase so-called "surplus" land—anything remaining after the allotments were made-but the allotments themselves were to be held in trust for twenty-five years. At the end of the trust period, Indians would receive fee patents—full ownership rights—to their lands. Subsequent amendments eroded the trust period and permitted allottees to lease or sell their lands. Between the sale of "surplus" land and the sale of allotments, many tribes lost substantial portions of their reservations.

Scholars generally agree that the Dawes Act was poorly implemented and that it failed to achieve its assimilationist goals. In addition, some tribes successfully resisted allotment, while others escaped it because their land was of little interest to non-Indians. Congress officially overturned the allotment policy in 1934 and indefinitely extended the trust period on existing allotments. Since then, tribes have actively confronted the problems of checkerboarding (the intermixing of Indian and non-Indian lands) and fractionation (the division of inherited trust allotments into uselessly small shares).

At the beginning of the twenty-first century, the Dawes Act has featured prominently in a new battleground: the courtroom. The class action lawsuit *Cobell v. Norton* (filed in 1996) involves individual accounts that were established primarily to hold revenue generated from the lease and sale of Indian land allotments. The plaintiffs charge that the United States has mismanaged individual Indian moneys and cannot provide a proper accounting of the funds. Although the Dawes Act was intended to be the ultimate solution to the "Indian Problem," it has instead generated ongoing conflict.

BIBLIOGRAPHY

Greenwald, Emily. *Reconfiguring the Reservation: The Nez Perces, Jicarilla Apaches, and the Dawes Act.* Albuquerque: University of New Mexico Press, 2002.

McDonnell, Janet A. *The Dispossession of the American Indian, 1887–1934.* Bloomington: Indiana University Press, 1991.

Meyer, Melissa L. *The White Earth Tragedy: Ethnicity and Dispossession at a Minnesota Anishinaabe Reservation, 1889–1920.* Lincoln: University of Nebraska Press, 1994.

Otis, D.S. *The Dawes Act and the Allotment of Indian Lands.* Norman: University of Oklahoma Press, 1973 [1937].

Emily Greenwald

See also: **Indian Removal and Response.**

DIX, DOROTHEA

(b. April 4, 1802; d. July 17, 1887) Superintendent of Women Nurses during the Civil War.

Dorothea Dix was a leading social reformer who advocated humane treatment of prisoners and the mentally ill before the Civil War and became the Union's Superintendent of Women Nurses during that war.

She was born in Hampton, Maine, and raised in Massachusetts. Due to her family's poverty, her father's frequent absences, and her mother's semi-invalidism, Dix also spent time with her grandparents in Boston and with an aunt in Worcester. She eagerly sought an education and studied hard. Responding to her intense desire to teach, she opened a school for young children when she was only fourteen years old. In 1819, she went to live with her widowed grandmother and opened a school in Boston. She found in Unitarianism an outlet for her strong sense of faith. During the 1820s, Dix wrote an elementary school science textbook, books of a devotional nature, and a collection of children's short stories.

A serious bout with tuberculosis forced her to seek refuge in Rhode Island and, later, on St. Croix in the Virgin Islands. Dix returned to teaching, but within a few years, her health suffered and illness drove her to collapse. To recover, she went to England. There she encountered individuals who had committed their lives to prison reform and aid for the criminally insane.

When her grandmother died in 1837, Dix returned to the United States. An inheritance gave her freedom from teaching. Beginning in the 1840s she became involved in prison reform, inspired by what she had seen in England and appalled by the conditions in American jails. She launched a remarkable career as a champion of the indigent mentally ill, who had traditionally been kept under a family's care or incarcerated. Dix believed inmates who were mentally ill deserved far more humane treatment. She personally inspected hundreds of prisons and became widely known for her tireless efforts on behalf the mentally ill.

Through this work Dix had her greatest impact, traveling tens of thousands of miles to visit prisons, raise money, and lobby states to build hospitals for the mentally ill. In the late 1840s, she began seeking help at the

Dorothea Dix.

federal level, urging Congress to pass a law that would set aside public lands for the mentally ill, the blind, the deaf, and the mute. Congress initially turned down her request; a subsequent bill did pass in 1854 but was vetoed by President Franklin Pierce.

With the outbreak of the Civil War, Dix volunteered to serve the Union. She was appointed Superintendent of Women Nurses in June, 1861. During the war, she trained some 180 women for the nursing profession. Yet her efforts were riddled with discord and frustration. There were frequent conflicts with Army physicians, many of whom opposed female nurses and sought to limit their authority. Dix clashed with doctors who felt they, rather than she, should have control of medical facilities. Physicians harassed Dix's nurses and turned to Catholic nuns and female volunteers who assisted without official status.

Dix showed little respect or patience with those whom she felt were less committed to the effort than she was. Her criteria for nurses were strict: She preferred the plain-looking and women who were over thirty, desiring to employ no young woman who envisioned the nursing of soldiers as a romantic adventure. Furthermore, she insisted on dismissing all volunteer nurses, whom she had not hired. She eventually lost the support of the United States Sanitary Commission and other groups, which initially had helped her recruit and train nurses.

In October, 1863, the War Department authorized the Surgeon General, as well as Dix, to appoint female nurses and gave physicians control over the assignment of nurses to hospitals, thus undercutting Dix's authority. After that point, her role as Superintendent of Women Nurses was primarily symbolic, though nonetheless potentially significant. With the war's end, she submitted her resignation in August 1865. She was later elected president for life of the Army Nurses Association, but took little interest in the organization and opposed its petitions to get pensions for female nurses and to promote women's suffrage.

Dix spent her later years visiting mental hospitals and prisons and continued to promote good care for the mentally ill. But her energy and stamina declined. She spent her final years in poor health, living in Trenton, New Jersey, where she died July 17, 1887.

Dorothea Dix brought her considerable skills to her service in the Civil War, but her personality, impatience, and take-charge attitude often had a negative effect on those with whom she worked. Nevertheless, she did hire, train, and oversee nearly 200 women who served as nurses during the war, and through that effort helped to open the nursing profession to women.

BIBLIOGRAPHY

Brown, Thomas J. *Dorothea Dix, New England Reformer.* Cambridge, MA: Harvard University Press, 1998.

Sizer, Lyde Cullen. *The Political Work of Northern Women Writers and the Civil War, 1850–1872.* Chapel Hill: University of North Carolina Press, 2000.

Sally G. McMillen

See also: **Medicine and Health; United States Sanitary Commission.**

DOUGLASS, FREDERICK

(b. ca. February, 1818; d. February 20, 1895) Former slave, political leader, and civil rights advocate.

Frederick Douglass, the foremost African-American political leader of the nineteenth century, was a lifelong advocate of freedom and civil rights for African Americans as well as a strong supporter of equal rights for women. Douglass's 1845 autobiography *Narrative of the Life of Frederick Douglass* is the most renowned and widely read slave narrative as well as a classic work of American literature. His autobiography and his work as an abolition-

Frederick Douglass.

ist speaker and publisher contributed to the nation's debate over slavery and thus to the events that led to the Civil War (1861–1865).

Born a slave on Maryland's Eastern Shore, Frederick Bailey was the son of Harriet Bailey, a slave of Captain Aaron Anthony who, according to rumor, may have been Frederick Bailey's father. In 1826, Frederick Bailey was sent to live in Baltimore, where he secretly learned to read and write. He eventually became a shipyard worker. Increasingly dissatisfied with having to turn his wages over to his owner, and with his slave status in general, Frederick Bailey escaped by taking a train from Baltimore to Philadelphia disguised as a free black sailor.

Frederick Bailey took the name Douglass from a character in Sir Walter Scott's poem "The Lady of the Lake," using it to evade slave catchers. He eventually settled in New Bedford, Massachusetts. Douglass began to attend abolitionist meetings, and after meeting abolitionist leader William Lloyd Garrison he became a major speaker on the abolitionist circuit. Some doubted that such a powerful and articulate speaker could ever have been a slave, and Douglass wrote his 1845 *Narrative*, which provided the actual names and locations of his former owners, in part to authenticate his slave experience. The *Narrative* was an immediate success and it established Douglass as a national and international figure. He gradually emerged from under Garrison's wing and in 1847 moved to Rochester, New York, where he published an antislavery newspaper the *North Star* (later renamed *Frederick Douglass's Paper*) from 1847 to 1863.

Douglass was also an early advocate of voting rights for women. He attended the 1848 Seneca Falls Convention, which is often cited as the beginning of the modern feminist movement, and was a lifelong friend of Susan B. Anthony, Lucretia Mott, and other feminist leaders.

Douglass had always strongly supported full citizenship rights for African Americans and sharply disagreed with black leaders of the 1850s, such as Henry Highland Garnet, who supported black emigration to Africa. When the Civil War broke out in 1861, Douglass fought to have the abolition of slavery made a central war aim, and to have African Americans fight in the Union Army. He believed that military service on behalf of the Union and their own freedom would greatly bolster African Americans' claims for full and equal citizenship. Douglass's sons fought in the Union Army although his own desire for a military commission was never granted. Douglass was elated by the South's defeat in April 1865 and by the subsequent abolition of slavery, but he soon found that his work was not yet finished.

During the Reconstruction Era (1865–1877) Douglass was a tireless advocate of full voting rights for African Americans and an opponent of the Ku Klux Klan and other terrorist groups that sought to deny the freedpeople's constitutional rights. Douglass's support of the Fifteenth Amendment (1870), which guaranteed black males' right to vote without granting women the same right, helped cause a permanent split between the abolitionist and feminist movements. After Reconstruction came to an end with Republican President Rutherford B. Hayes's 1877 removal of the remaining federal troops from the South, Douglass remained loyal to the Republican Party while speaking out against the government's abandonment of African Americans to white supremacist southern Democratic governments.

In his later years, Douglass continued to write and speak and served as marshal and recorder of deeds in Washington, D.C., and as U.S. consul to Haiti from 1889 to 1891. He spoke out against the nation's retreat from the promises of the Reconstruction Era, including the U.S. Supreme Court's 1883 decision that invalidated most of the Civil Rights Act of 1875, which had given African Americans the right to equal treatment in public accommodations. Douglass generated some controversy when he married Helen Pitts, a white woman nearly twenty years his junior, in 1884, a year after his first wife, Anna Murray Douglass, died. When he died of a heart attack in his stately Washington D.C. home, Cedar Hill (now a national historical site) in 1895, an important period in American history ended with him. The period up to and including the Civil War had opened new opportunities for a few African Americans to play a significant role in ending slavery and engaging in a dialogue about their future. Frederick Douglass was the leading African-American spokesperson in these efforts, a man whose voice and ideas had a lasting impact on the nation.

BIBLIOGRAPHY

Diedrich, Maria. *Love across Color Lines: Ottilie Assing and Frederick Douglass.* New York: Hill and Wang, 1999.

Douglass, Frederick. *Narrative of the Life of Frederick Douglass.* Mineola, NY: Dover, 1995.

McFeely, William S. *Frederick Douglass.* New York: Oxford University Press, 1987.

Daniel W. Aldridge, III

See also: **Abolitionists; Anthony, Susan B.; Constitutional Amendments and Changes; Ku Klux Klan; Reconstruction.**

ECONOMIC CHANGE AND INDUSTRIALIZATION

The United States entered the nineteenth century as an agrarian nation of five million residents. Within one hundred years, the United States transformed itself into the world's leading industrial power with a population of nearly seventy-six million. While America's transformation from an agrarian nation to an industrial power is noteworthy because of the pace at which it occurred, it is more remarkable because it did not transpire in all regions of the nation. Indeed, by 1900 the United States effectively contained two separate economies—the industrialized North and the agrarian South. To understand America's economic transformation it is necessary to examine three separate snapshots of the American economy: The antebellum economy, the American economy during the Civil War, and the postbellum economy.

THE ANTEBELLUM ECONOMY

In 1800, the United States was a nation of farmers. Manufacturing was completed at home, in small mills (for the production of lumber and textiles), or in craft shops (for leather products and other household items). American manufacturing continued on a small scale until 1807, when President Jefferson's trade embargo halted the importation of European goods because American merchants were caught in the middle of the war between England and France. Because European products, particularly English textiles, were no longer available to American consumers, American firms had an opportunity and an incentive to grow. As a result, textile factories sprouted in New England during the 1810s and especially during America's war with England (1812 to 1815), which again cut off British imports. Although textile factories (and later, factories producing iron and other products) were born and thrived during the antebellum period, the manufacturing sector lagged well behind the agricultural sector in total employment. By 1860 the manufacturing sector employed one and a half million Americans; the agricultural sector employed nearly 5.8 million workers.

Ultimately, the rise of the American manufacturing sector was limited by firms' ability to transport their goods to distant markets. In 1800, products could be moved between American cities via the ocean or inland waterways. Overland transportation was extraordinarily costly and impractical. However, two developments in the antebellum period led to a dramatic change in the way producers shipped their goods to American markets. First, the Erie Canal opened in 1825. The completion of the canal allowed farmers to ship agricultural products from Midwestern farms to Eastern markets, and it also allowed manufacturers to ship goods from Eastern factories to Midwestern cities. The success of the Erie Canal led to a canal building boom in the United States, although none of the canals built after the completion of the Erie had a similar economic impact on the nation. Second, in the early 1830s, the railroad appeared on the American landscape. Canals had opened markets on waterways, but the railroad allowed manufacturers to sell products in markets throughout the country.

Manufacturing was not limited to the North in the antebellum period, but the Northeast and Middle Atlantic States possessed a manufacturing capital stock seven times that of the South. In the South, agriculture was the dominant sector of the economy. Tobacco was the South's leading crop at the turn of the century, but by 1820, cotton was king in the South. Cotton reached its position of primacy in part due to ideal soil conditions and Eli Whitney's cotton gin. Slavery (the "peculiar institution") also played a major role in the success of cotton. In fact, research completed by economic historians Robert Fogel and Stanley Engerman shows that large southern plantations (those that possessed more than fifty slaves) were uncommonly productive because of the use of gang labor. According to their estimates, antebellum southern farms were, on average, forty-one percent more efficient than their northern counterparts.

Differences between the Northern and Southern economies created the foundation for the Civil War, but it was a disagreement over the resource-rich territories of the West that would eventually lead to the outbreak of hostilities. The gold rush of 1849 caused Americans to pour into California; it also called attention to the enormous value of natural resources contained in the western territories. Neither the South nor the North wished to relinquish control over the territories, and Southerners viewed slavery in the territories as critical for the institution's survival. The issue of slavery in the territories led to a bitterly contested Presidential election in 1860, and South Carolina's secession in December 1860. Four months later, in April 1861, the bloodiest conflict in American history had started.

THE WAR ECONOMY
On the eve of the Civil War in 1860, the South had invested an estimated $2.7 billion in slaves. This represented an outlay of three times the total capital investment made by the manufacturing sector in the entire United States. Thus, it is not surprising that southerners were willing to fight to preserve the institution of slavery.

Economists Claudia Goldin and Frank Lewis have estimated that the Civil War cost the American people $6.6 billion. (Measured in 2003 dollars, the cost would be between $115 and $140 billion.) This estimate takes into account the direct expenditures on the war (guns, uniforms, and ammunition), the destruction of property, and the loss of human life. While the war was extremely costly, it did serve as a catalyst for several important changes in the American economy.

With the daunting task of having to pay for the war, the federal government faced a serious fiscal crisis. In response, the federal government levied the first personal income tax in the nation's history. It also engaged in large scale borrowing. The magnitude of the federal government's debt had a profound impact on the nation's financial markets, and, ultimately, it caused the government to suspend the use of gold and silver coins as a form of currency for everyday transactions. The war also led to increased economic activity in several industries. The primary beneficiaries of the Civil War were the textile firms of the Northeast and the farms of the Midwest. However, the war did very little to stimulate growth in most of the industries in the manufacturing sector.

While economists agree on what the Civil War cost the American people and the impact the war had on the American economy during the 1860s, there is disagreement on the impact that the war had on the postbellum economy. For some historians and economists, the Civil War was a watershed event that sent the South and the North on divergent paths of economic development. However, many others believe that the postbellum economy continued trends that had begun in the antebellum period. Empirical evidence suggests that the latter interpretation is correct.

THE POSTBELLUM ECONOMY
In 1860, personal income per worker was approximately ten percent higher in the South than in the Midwest. A mere ten years later, a southerner's income was only seventy percent of a midwesterner's. Finally, at the turn of the century, this figure had fallen to fifty percent. There are several reasons for this radical reversal of fortune in the South.

Conventional wisdom often attributes the South's poor economic performance in the postbellum period to the wartime destruction of its cities, infrastructure, and capital stock. However, this explanation is inadequate. Northern armies destroyed Charleston, Atlanta, and Richmond, and they also did extensive damage to Southern infrastructure and capital stock. Nonetheless, the southern transportation network had been restored to its prewar condition by 1870, and the damage to the capital stock and southern cities was repaired in an equally timely fashion. Indeed, economic historians Jeremy Atack and Peter Passell point out that Japan and Germany recovered very rapidly from much more extensive physical damage caused by fighting during World War II. The decline of the southern economy cannot be attributed only to the wartime destruction of cities, capital, and infrastructure.

Economic historians attribute the decline of the southern economy to many different factors, but three stand out: a reduction in the supply of labor in the southern economy, a decrease in demand for the South's staple crop, cotton, and a dramatic transfer of wealth from slave owners to African Americans. The reduction in the supply of labor in the postbellum southern economy may be attributed to the emancipation of the slaves. In the antebellum economy, slaves on large plantations worked in gangs, and the gang labor system was extraordinarily productive. However, it was not productive simply because of the number of workers (slaves) involved. Rather, the gang labor system was extremely productive because of the intense effort and long hours put in by slaves. With emancipation it became possible, at least to some extent, for an African-American worker to choose how long and how hard he or she worked. While plantation owners in the South tried to encourage African Americans to continue working under the gang labor system, land owners were unwilling to pay the wages that would be needed to entice workers to spend such long, hard days in the field. Ultimately, the supply of labor in the South decreased because emancipated slaves were unwilling to work as many hours as they had once been forced to work.

A reduction in the demand for southern cotton was the second major factor leading to a decline in southern economic output in the postwar era. Before the Civil War, England had been the leading importer of southern cotton. During the Civil War, England was forced to find alternative sources of cotton, so imports from India, Brazil, and Egypt increased dramatically. The South regained its antebellum market share by the late 1870s; however, by that time the price of cotton was declining. As a result, southern incomes did not return to their antebellum level.

Finally, there was a dramatic transfer of wealth from slave owners to former slaves. Before the passage of the Thirteenth Amendment slaves were "capital" assets possessed by their owners. Granting slaves their freedom immediately reduced a slave owner's personal wealth by the value of his or her slave holdings. This was not a net loss to the southern economy, for the slave owners' wealth, namely the ability of the slaves to perform hard work, was transferred back to its rightful owners—the freed slaves themselves. This did, however, have the effect of reducing the "capital stock" in the southern economy.

Former slave owners who might have wished to sell one or more of their slaves in order to invest in other types of capital (machinery, land, or buildings) no longer possessed an asset to sell. Therefore, the South, already lagging behind the North in capital accumulation, continued on its path to being a region rich in labor but poor in capital.

As the southern economy struggled with institutional changes caused by emancipation and economic changes dictated by the market for cotton, the northern economy flourished. The production of the agricultural sector increased rapidly, and so did the output generated by the manufacturing sector. Indeed, by 1880 the value of northern manufacturing output exceeded the value of northern agricultural output.

The increase in agricultural and manufacturing output may be traced to the spatial expansion of several sectors. The Homestead Act of 1862 led to an expansion in the number of improved acres of farm ground, and an increase in the demand for manufactured products led to the development of regional manufacturing centers. Furthermore, between 1860 and 1890, U.S. manufacturing firms took advantage of an ever-improving transportation network that allowed goods to be sold in any corner of the nation. In fact, by 1894, the United States had become the world's largest producer of manufactured goods.

CONCLUSION

The divergent paths taken by the northern and southern economies in the nineteenth century cannot be attributed to the Civil War. While the Civil War increased the pace at which these two economies grew apart, it is critical to recognize that the economic rift between the North and the South had its origins in the antebellum period. Quite simply, southerners tied their economic fortunes to the production of a single crop—cotton. As a result, the South was ill suited to adapt to a world economy that was rapidly changing in the postbellum period. While southerners chose their economic path in the antebellum period, economic development in the postbellum South period could have been much more substantial than it turned out to be. Between 1865 and 1900 (in fact well into the twentieth century), the South struggled with the institutional changes brought about by emancipation. Ultimately, African Americans were treated as second-class citizens. As a result, the South failed to make full use of a precious resource (the talents and energies of freed slaves) and suffered through decades of economic stagnation.

BIBLIOGRAPHY

Atack, Jeremy, and Passell, Peter. *A New Economic View of American History: From Colonial Times to 1940.* New York: Norton, 1994.

Fogel, Robert, and Engerman, Stanley. *Time on the Cross: The Economics of American Negro Slavery*. New York: Norton, 1989.

Goldin, Claudia, and Lewis, Frank. "The Economic Cost of the American Civil War: Estimates and Implications." *The Journal of Economic History* 35 no. 2 (1975): 299–326.

Walton, Gary, and Rockoff, Hugh. *History of the American Economy*, 9th edition. Fort Worth, TX: Harcourt College Publishers, 2001.

Fred H. Smith

See also: **Farming, Financing the War; Labor and Labor Movements.**

EDUCATION

The American Revolution created a republic that in theory placed sovereignty in the people rather than an elite, which in England was composed largely of a hereditary aristocracy and landed gentry. Republics, theorists stated, depended upon the wisdom and virtue of an educated populace. As early as the 1780s the founders of the United States argued that public education was essential for the prosperity and survival of the new nation. Thomas Jefferson in particular believed Americans should consider mounting a "crusade against ignorance." Jefferson was the first American leader to suggest creating a system of free schools that would be publicly tax-supported. However, Jefferson's plans for publicly funded universal education did not take root until the 1830s.

EDUCATION IN THE EARLY NINETEENTH CENTURY

Throughout much of the nineteenth century, many American children—regardless of race, class, or gender— did not attend school because they had to work or because their parents could not afford to pay the required fees. Those children who did become educated were taught at home by a parent or tutor, went to a school run by a church or charity, or attended a privately-run school. "Subscription schools" were supported by middle class families and charged a fee based on the number of children enrolled. The poor, if their children did attend school, had to sign documents stating that they were "paupers" in order for their children to be admitted to poverty schools. Most institutions provided schooling only for privileged white boys. A small number of young men could go on to one of several colleges established in America, such as Harvard or Yale, to receive a more substantial, often specialized, education.

By the 1830s, Americans expressed a desire to improve the existing educational system. Reformers found the lack of universal education unsuitable for a growing democracy. In 1846, attorney and politician Horace Mann, the father of American public education, argued that public education was an obligation, "a worthy public expense" that reaped substantial benefits for an emerging industrialized and urban society. Mann argued that a solid public education ultimately meant more productive workers. Americans also believed that citizens needed an education in order to participate fully in the political and economic growth of the country. Reformers argued that schools should be free, paid for by taxes and state supported.

Common schools, or publicly financed elementary schools, gradually emerged in the northeast and midwestern United States, although even by the mid-nineteenth century, no state had a statewide school system and local districts ineptly managed their own. In the South, few public schools existed before the Civil War. Public elementary schools provided basic instruction in reading, writing, and math, along with training in citizenship. The publication of the Reverend William Holmes McGuffey's *Reader*, which sold nine million copies between 1836 and 1850, augmented efforts to educate the masses. McGuffey's *Reader* emphasized reading, writing, spelling, and good manners.

EDUCATION OF BLACKS AND WOMEN PRIOR TO THE CIVIL WAR

Because of racial and gender discrimination, African Americans and women not only struggled to acquire an education but had to combat stereotypes concerning what type of education was most suitable for them. The 1800s witnessed important changes in their education. Prior to the Civil War, Catharine Beecher emerged as one of the most important advocates of female education, promoting it as preparation for women's role in expanding their power in the home and in teacher training.

Most Americans considered teaching as a natural extension of women's maternal role, moving them from the private to the public sphere. Yet some women saw teaching not as a "calling" but as a way in which to support themselves. Such was the case with African American feminist Maria Stewart, who taught school beginning in the 1830s after the death of her husband. Stewart later warmed to her new career and in 1853, opened a school for blacks in Washington, D.C.

Women's education and career options, especially for the middle and upper classes, were aided by the founding of academies and seminaries for girls. In 1821, Emma Willard established the Troy Female Seminary in New York, the first endowed educational institution for women in the United States. In 1823, Catharine Beecher opened the Hartford Female Seminary and later founded seminaries in Cincinnati and Milwaukee. In 1837, Mary Lyon established the Mount Holyoke Seminary with a curriculum that emphasized domesticity, piety, and teaching. Mount Holyoke enrolled girls from both wealthy and poor families; it was the first institution to challenge class discrimination. Founding schools for African American women often proved a challenge. At one Connecticut school for black girls that opened in 1833, a white mob attacked the school to protest the educating of African Americans, forcing the school's closure.

Regardless of race or class, women who attended these early seminaries and academies learned how to be better wives and mothers, often acquiring skills in cooking and sewing. As the curriculum expanded, they took courses like those offered to young men in languages, history, geography, math, and science. Not only did schools for women expand and improve their curriculums, but teacher education for women improved as well, creating a feminine teaching corps by the late nineteenth century. In 1855, the first normal schools were established to provide teacher training for young women.

Except at Oberlin College in Ohio and Berea College in Kentucky, blacks and women had little or no access to white male institutions. In 1837, Oberlin College admitted its first female students, making it the first coeducational institution in the country. Vassar College was established in 1861 for women, and the first women's graduate school opened in 1880 at Bryn Mawr College. Despite racial discrimination, some blacks did attend Middlebury, Amherst, Bowdoin, and Ohio University. For African-Americans, Lincoln University (Pennsylvania), Cheyney State, and Wilberforce College were among the few institutions specifically established for blacks before the Civil War.

Women and blacks often faced difficulties in using their education effectively. Well-educated white women were often considered unsuitable for marriage and motherhood. Most schools required teachers to resign when they married.

THE CIVIL WAR AND THE EDUCATION OF BLACKS

The Civil War and Reconstruction period had a profound effect on the education of blacks in the South. The Thirteenth Amendment ended slavery and the Fourteenth and Fifteenth Amendments granted equal rights to freed slaves. Many sought to take advantage of their new freedoms, especially the opportunity to acquire an education.

The reconstruction era witnessed major advances in segregated education for African Americans. Before the Civil War, education for blacks was practically nonexistent in the South, and several southern states had laws

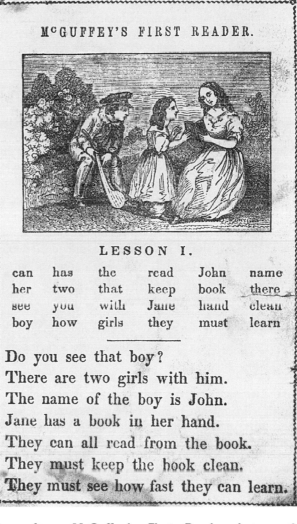

Page from *McGuffey's First Reader*, Lesson 1.
© BETTMANN/CORBIS

against teaching slaves to read and write. Schools in the North were segregated. African American ingenuity and perseverance produced some notable exceptions. For instance, Milla Granson of Natchez, Mississippi, a slave who had learned to read and write from her master's children, operated a school late at night when her master slept and slaves had finished working in the fields.

During the Civil War, both African American and white teachers began the arduous but rewarding task of educating southern blacks. Indeed, freedmen's education began in army camps. Mary S. Peake began teaching freed slaves at a Fort Virginia School in 1861. Susie King Taylor, a former slave who learned to read and write, taught black soldiers in the army. After the war, some white northern women used their education by moving south to teach the freed slaves. Laura Town was the first to do so; in 1862, she established the Penn School on the South Carolina Sea Islands, which she ran for forty years. The African American educator Charlotte Forten Grimke joined her. In her diary, Forten remarked "I never before saw children so eager to learn." Such was the case with most black children throughout the South. The number of black teachers increased as more African American became educated.

Changes came during Reconstruction as Radical Republicans in Congress pushed southern states to create a system of state-funded public schools. Former slaves and black politicians who were elected during Reconstruction were also major promoters of public schools in the South. They were aided in their quest by black schools founded by the American Missionary Association (AMA) and the Freedmen's Bureau, such as Morehouse, Biddle (Johnson C. Smith), and Howard. Despite individual, public, and private support, public education improved, but remained segregated in the United States and in the South in particular. Nevertheless, blacks of all ages who had been denied an education for centuries flocked to these schools to learn to read and write. In contrast to the practice in white schools, co-education was the norm for black students.

THE EXPANSION OF HIGHER EDUCATION

During the mid-nineteenth century Americans increased their interest in developing high schools and expanding institutions of higher learning. In 1839, the University of Missouri was founded as the first public university west of the Mississippi River. A growing number of male colleges were founded in the antebellum period, such as Haverford, Davidson, and Kenyon.

In 1862, in the midst of war, Congress passed the Morrill Act granting each Union state 30,000 acres for each of its senators and representatives. The land was to be sold and the proceeds used to establish colleges in engineering, agriculture and military science. While it did not have special provisions for African Americans, the Morrill Act enabled the development of a few southern institutions. Additional private colleges, such as the Seven Sisters in the Northeast and a number of both public and private universities, such as the University of California, Johns Hopkins, and Stanford, were founded in the latter part of the nineteenth century. In 1890, the second Morrill Act was passed to include the sixteen southern states. Land grant colleges included a liberal arts curriculum, but emphasized agriculture as well as the industrial and mechanical arts.

As the United States entered the twentieth century, it had adopted a framework of publicly supported elementary and secondary schools and had seen a significant increase in the number of colleges and universities nationwide.

BIBLIOGRAPHY

Altenbaugh, Richard J. *The American People and Their Education: A Social History.* Upper Saddle River, NJ: Merrill/Prentice Hall, 2003.

Anderson, James D. *The Education of Blacks in the South, 1860–1935.* Chapel Hill: University of North Carolina Press, 1988.

Butchart, Ronald E. *Northern Schools, Southern Blacks, and Reconstruction: Freedmen's Education, 1862–1875.* Westport: Greenwood Press, 1980.

Christy, Ralph D. and Williamson, Lionel, eds. *A Century of Service: Land-grant Colleges and Universities, 1890–1990.* New Brunswick, NJ: Transaction Publishers, 1992.

DeBoer, Clara Merritt. *His Truth is Marching On: African Americans Who Taught Freedmen for the American Missionary Association, 1861–1877.* New York: Garland, 1995.

Durrill, Wayne K. "New Schooling for a New South: A Community Study of Education and Social Change, 1875–1885." *Journal of Social History* 31 (1997): 156–81.

Hoffman, Nancy. *Woman's True Profession: Voices from the History of Teaching.* 2d edition. Cambridge, MA: Harvard Education Press, 2003.

Jones, Jacqueline. *Soldiers of Light and Love: Northern Teachers and Georgia Blacks, 1865–1873.* Chapel Hill: University of North Carolina Press, 1980.

Reilly, Wayne E., ed. *Sarah Jane Foster, Teacher of the Freedmen: A Diary and Letters.* Charlottesville: University Press of Virginia, 1990.

Solomon, Barbara Miller. *In the Company of Educated Women: A History of Women & Higher Education in America.* New Haven, CT: Yale University Press, 1985.

Urban, Wayne J. and Waggoner, Jennings L., Jr. *American Education: A History.* 3d edition. New York: McGraw Hill, 2004.

Delia C. Gillis

See also: **African Americans (Freed People); Children and the Civil War; Reconstruction.**

ELECTIONS, PRESIDENTIAL: THE CIVIL WAR

The election of 1860 attracted enormous attention across the nation. All four presidential candidates were men of good intentions but with very different solutions for the crisis America faced. The Republican Party nominated Abraham Lincoln. A relatively new political organization, the Republican Party, first organized in 1854, arose from the outrage over the Kansas-Nebraska Act (1854) which, through the concept of popular sovereignty, permitted slavery in those newly created territories. By 1860 the Republicans had devised two effective strategies. What they did not recognize was how far they brought the nation to the verge of civil war.

The first Republican strategy was to energize the North against an enemy the party called the "Aggressive Slavocracy." Many Northerners were apathetic toward enslaved African Americans, but they did not want slavery spreading to the West. Furthermore, many Northerners were appalled at the influx of immigrants, particularly Catholics from Ireland and Germany, who had arrived over the past decade. Republicans argued that there was an "Aggressive Slavocracy" that conspired to pervert the Constitution and favor the will of Southern slave owners over the liberties of the northern people. In the minds of Republicans, these wealthy Southerners with their immigrant allies, who controlled the Democratic Party, truly threatened the nation. Whether one hated Catholics, slavery, or Democrats, one could find a home in the Republican Party. There was no conspiracy, of course, but this anti-South rhetoric was effective, and it deeply offended Southerners.

The second goal was to choose an electable candidate. The nomination of Abraham Lincoln of Illinois was designed to capture midwestern states the party had lost in 1856. The relatively unknown Lincoln was a fresh face for a new and energetic party. Lincoln believed his political relationships with former Whigs (a party that had died out in the mid-1850s) in the South would prevent any trouble once he won the election. Neither he nor the Republican party understood the depth of animosity generated south of the Mason-Dixon Line towards them.

Southern anger, in fact, tore apart the Democratic Party. At the Democratic convention in Charleston, South Carolina, in May 1860, Southern delegates refused to support Stephen A. Douglas's candidacy because he would not pledge the unconditional protection of slavery in the Southern states and all territories. Southerners were scared by Republicans who, they felt, were abolitionists and supporters of John Brown's attack on the Harper's Ferry arsenal in 1859. Brown had planned to arm slaves with the arsenal's weapons and begin an insurrection. Southerners feared the Republican party was composed of others who would bring death and destruction to the entire region.

When the Charleston convention failed, Southern Democrats nominated John C. Breckinridge of Kentucky. Northern delegates reconvened in Baltimore and selected Douglas. When the Democratic Party broke apart, the final means for intersectional communication broke down. Breckinridge's campaign focused on protecting the South. Douglas, on the other hand, recognized the possibilities of disaster and made an heroic attempt to keep Democrats and the nation together.

The final candidate, John Bell of Tennessee, ran under the Constitutional Union Party label. A former Whig like Lincoln, Bell wanted to avoid the slavery issue and focus on economic and social issues. Frightened Americans, however, ignored Bell's traditional appeals. Republicans feared the "slavocracy" would destroy liberty, while Southerners, slaveholders and non-slaveholders alike, viewed the Republicans as destroyers of their property rights, society, and economy.

Over eighty percent of the eligible voters cast ballots. Lincoln captured 180 of 183 Northern electoral college votes, which gave him the election. He received only 39 percent of the total popular vote. The Southern states backed Breckinridge. Douglas received the second highest number of popular votes, but they were spread throughout the entire nation and he finished last in electoral votes. Fearing a Republican president would annihilate their constitutional rights, South Carolina in December 1860 and Deep South states in early 1861 seceded from the Union. Although Lincoln issued no controversial statements, there was nothing he could have said to calm the waters. Lincoln's call for troops after Fort Sumter fell convinced Virginia, North Carolina, Tennessee, and Arkansas that Republicans were indeed the threat that had been so often discussed in the 1860 presidential campaign; they also seceded. The war no one wanted or anticipated had begun. The country's deep divides spurred the transition of America's national political parties into sectional organizations and allowed the election of a president who had the support of only one section of the country and little more than one-third of the popular vote.

1864 ELECTION

Three years of war had a profound effect on society and presidential politics. Presidential contenders in 1864 had to explain how to achieve victory. Since Lincoln did not doubt the outcome, he knew another vital issue was how to bring rebellious Southerners and millions of freed slaves into a reinvigorated and stable Union.

With the secession of the Southern states, the Democratic Party in the North was vastly outnumbered. A noisy minority, the so-called Peace Democrats, wanted an immediate end to the war. Republicans called them Copperheads, suggesting they were traitorous, venomous snakes who would kill the United States. Leaders of this faction, such as Clement Vallandigham of Ohio, portrayed the president as an incompetent radical who was more interested in freeing slaves than saving the nation. Peace Democrats believed that time would heal all wounds and the United States would be united again.

Most Northern Democrats supported the restoration of the Union through war, but they also felt that Lincoln's military policy caused too much bloodshed. Their eventual nominee, General George B. McClellan, argued the war could be won by careful maneuvering and training, not by the butchery seen at battles such as Fredericksburg and the Wilderness. War Democrats also castigated Lincoln for his Emancipation Proclamation and the social disaster that they believed would necessarily follow as millions of former slaves became citizens. Reconciling these two groups of Democrats was nearly impossible. The party platform condemned "the experiment of war" and called "for a cessation of hostilities" with later negotiations to restore the Union. On the first ballot, McClellan was nominated with a Peace Democrat, George H. Pendleton of Ohio, as his running mate. McClellan immediately renounced the peace plank of his party's platform and ran as a War Democrat.

Some historians have argued that Lincoln's reelection was far from certain, but the Republicans had few reasons for pessimism. It is true that some conservative Republicans wanted Lincoln to backtrack on the Emancipation Proclamation. On the other hand, many radicals saw Lincoln as too slow and incompetent, and attempted to promote Secretary of the Treasury Salmon P. Chase or General John C. Fremont as a candidate, but only failed miserably. An indication of Lincoln's future plans was his acceptance of former Tennessee Senator Andrew Johnson for his running mate. Republicans wanted to recast themselves as the "Union Party" in order to attract War Democrats, and Johnson was an appealing symbol.

The ebb and flow of the military campaigns alternately energized and discouraged each political party. General William T. Sherman's slow progress toward Atlanta and the awful bloodletting as General Ulysses S. Grant pushed General Robert E. Lee back towards Richmond caused Lincoln to despair. Republican spirits soared, however, when Atlanta fell in September. Some feel this victory assured Lincoln's reelection.

It is also quite significant for what did not happen in 1864. Despite being in the midst of a horrible war, the American people conducted politics as usual. War added salient issues about military competence, emancipation, and reconstruction, but no one thought to delay or cancel the presidential election. The two-party system remained the best setting to resolve deep political divisions among the northern electorate. The fate of the Union was in dispute, but not the political processes outlined in the Constitution.

1876 ELECTION

Questions about how to reconstruct the Union began to be asked as soon as the war began. The subsequent history of reconstruction is long and complex, but many of the issues were settled by the presidential election of 1876. The eventual election of Rutherford B. Hayes of Ohio was an equally tangled affair.

Ulysses S. Grant's presidency had been a failure, marred by the corruption of his supposed friends serving in his administration. Republicans were frantic to distance themselves from it. The party convention in Cincinnati in June 1876 was deadlocked until Governor Hayes of Ohio, a former Union general and an untainted war hero, received the nomination on the seventh ballot. What the Republican party stood for, however, had been muddled by the pursuit of office.

Democrats chose Governor Samuel J. Tilden of New York as the antidote for all Republican ills. Tilden's reputation for honesty stemmed from his eliminating the Tweed Ring and corrupt officeholders in his state. Tilden also supported "home rule" for the ex-Confederate states. This did not bode well for the remaining Southern state administrations that protected the freedmen. The Democratic platform did accept the Thirteenth, Fourteenth, and Fifteenth Amendments to the Constitution ending slavery and guaranteeing black rights, but it also condemned "the rapacity of carpet-bag tyrannies" in the South. Democrats were further encouraged by their party's capture of the House of Representatives in the 1874 elections. Many Northern voters seemed to be weary of the Civil War's remaining problems and federal corruption.

On election day, Tilden received over 250,000 more votes than Hayes. The Electoral College tally, however, was terribly unclear. The election was plunged into chaos because of the violence and fraud that Southern whites used to seize control of the last three carpet-bag administrations in South Carolina, Louisiana, and Florida. If those three states were counted for Hayes, he would be the victor.

Democrats who controlled the House of Representatives refused to cooperate with the Republican Senate in counting the votes. Both political parties, however, were desperate to settle Civil War issues. The stalemate was broken in March 1877 when Hayes assured Southern Democrats that they would have "home rule" under his administration as well as political appointments and federal money for rebuilding war damages and for railroads. Since Hayes also promised to remove the last federal troops in the South, African Americans would not be seeing many of the benefits of post–Civil War legislation. Upon these conditions, Southern Democrats threw their support to a Republican president a few days before the inauguration.

The Civil War left powerful memories in the North and the South. Presidential candidates for the rest of the century would draw upon those feelings, but the election of Hayes in 1876 left most people satisfied that the Civil War was finally over and the nation could attend to other business. Nevertheless, presidential election campaigns for the remainder of the nineteenth century would often remind voters of the legacy of the Civil War.

BIBLIOGRAPHY

Donald, David Herbert. *Lincoln*. New York: Simon & Schuster, 1995.

Holt, Michael F. *The Political Crisis of the 1850s*. New York: Wiley, 1978.

Hyman, Harold M. "Election of 1864." In *History of American Presidential Elections, 1789–1968*, vol. 2, edited by Arthur M. Schlesinger, Jr. New York: Chelsea House, 1971.

McPherson, James M. *Battle Cry of Freedom: The Civil War Era*. New York: Oxford University Press, 1988.

Morison, Elting. "Election of 1860." In *History of American Presidential Elections, 1789–1968*, vol. 2, edited by Arthur M. Schlesinger, Jr. New York: Chelsea House, 1971.

Neely, Mark E., Jr. *The Union Divided: Party Conflict in the Civil War North*. Cambridge, MA: Harvard University Press, 2002.

Pomerantz, Sidney I. "Election of 1876." In *History of American Presidential Elections, 1789–1968*, vol. 2, edited by Arthur M. Schlesinger, Jr. New York: Chelsea House, 1971.

Silbey, Joel H. *A Respectable Minority: The Democratic Party in the Civil War Era, 1860–1868*. New York: Norton, 1977.

Trefousse, Hans L. *Rutherford B. Hayes*. New York: Times Books, 2002.

Waugh, John C. *Reelecting Lincoln: The Battle for the 1864 Presidency*. New York: Crown Publishers, 1997.

Woodward, C. Vann. *Reunion and Reaction: The Compromise of 1877 and the End of Reconstruction* (1951). New York: Oxford University Press, 1991.

M. Philip Lucas

See also: **Davis, Jefferson; Grant, Ulysses S.; Johnson, Andrew; Lincoln, Abraham; Political Parties.**

EMANCIPATION PROCLAMATION

President Abraham Lincoln's preliminary Emancipation Proclamation of September 22, 1862, became federal military policy on January 1, 1863, prompting Secretary of the Navy Gideon Welles to describe it as "a broad step . . . a landmark in history" (Welles, vol. 1, p. 212). The edict transformed the Civil War into a war of African-American liberation. On New Year's Day, "all persons held as slaves within any State . . . then . . . in rebellion against the United States" became "thenceforward, and forever free" (Basler, vol. 5, p. 434). Although in 1861 Lincoln had repeatedly asserted that his responsibility as president was to suppress the South's rebellion and reunite the nation, not to free its slaves, by late 1862 the realities of war forced him to incorporate emancipation into national policy. Emancipation was both a military tactic and a humanitarian act.

At this point in the war, the armies stood locked in a stalemate and Northern morale was low. England was threatening to recognize Confederate President Jefferson Davis's new government, which could have turned the Civil War into an international conflict. Lincoln needed more men to fill depleted Union regiments, and the Confederacy's military successes depended heavily on slavery: Bondsmen and women provided the agricultural and industrial labor that equipped, fed, and supplied its armies. Slaves constructed fortifications, repaired railroads, and freed up Southern whites to serve in the army.

Union Major General George B. McClellan's tactical draw against Confederate General Robert E. Lee at the Battle of Antietam on September 17, 1862, provided the breakthrough Lincoln sought. Five days afterward, Lincoln issued the preliminary Emancipation Proclamation. In doing so, he gave the rebellious states an ultimatum: If after January 1, 1863, they did not stop fighting and continued to resist federal forces, their slaves would be freed. When the Confederates failed to surrender upon Lincoln's deadline, the emancipation of the South's four million slaves became a Northern war aim.

Confederate President Jefferson Davis damned Lincoln's Emancipation Proclamation as an effort to cause a slave uprising and race war within the Confederacy. In the North, however, abolitionists, African Americans, and others sympathetic to the slaves welcomed Lincoln's proclamation. "We are all liberated" by the Emancipation Proclamation, black abolitionist Frederick Douglass declared. "The white man is liberated, the black man is liberated, the brave men now fighting the battles of their country against rebels and traitors are now liberated, and may strike . . . the Rebels, at their most sensitive point" (Foner, vol. 3, p. 322).

Many Northern Republicans nonetheless expressed disappointment that the president justified his proclamation on the grounds of military necessity, not on the grounds of a commitment to racial equality. They complained that it technically freed slaves only in territory still under Confederate control. In fairness to Lincoln, however, the Emancipation Proclamation did free many slaves along the Mississippi River, in eastern North Carolina and the Sea Islands along the Atlantic coast, and in areas that fell to Union armies throughout the Confederacy.

In addition to freeing Confederate slaves, Lincoln's final Emancipation Proclamation also decreed that suitable emancipated slaves "will be received into the armed service of the United States to garrison forts, positions, stations, and other places, and to man vessels of all sorts in said service" (Basler, vol. 6, p. 30). This signaled a major reversal in policy, because since the start of the war the U.S. Army had turned away free black volunteers.

After 1863, both free African Americans and slaves rushed to join the U.S. Army. They were determined to bury slavery, defeat the Confederacy, prove their manhood, and earn full citizenship. By war's end the army had raised 178,975 African-American troops.

The wartime emancipation of Confederate slaves, coupled with the military service of the African-American troops, paved the way for the passage of the Thirteenth Amendment of the Constitution (December 1865). The Emancipation Proclamation has come to symbolize the destruction of slavery. It commenced the halting and slow, but eventually successful, integration of African Americans into every aspect of American life.

BIBLIOGRAPHY

Basler, Roy P., ed. *The Collected Works of Abraham Lincoln.* 9 vols. New Brunswick, NJ: Rutgers University Press, 1953–1955.

Foner, Philip S., ed. *The Life and Writings of Frederick Douglass.* 5 vols. New York: International Publishers, 1952–1975.

Franklin, John Hope. *The Emancipation Proclamation.* Garden City, NJ: Doubleday, 1963.

U.S. War Department. *The War of the Rebellion: A Compilation of the Official Records of the Union and Confederate Armies.* 128 vols. Washington, D.C.: Government Printing Office, 1880–1901.

Welles, Gideon. *Diary of Gideon Welles: Secretary of the Navy under Lincoln and Johnson.* 3 vols. Boston: Houghton Mifflin, 1911.

John David Smith

See also: **Constitutional Amendments and Changes; Lincoln, Abraham; Slavery.**

ESPIONAGE AND SPIES

Espionage occurs in societies at peace and at war. Nations at peace use spies to gather information on a country's military preparations and plans for war. During war espionage is used to gather information about opposing armies and to mislead opponents through counterintelligence. Those engaged in spying risk imprisonment and death if convicted of treason. Although vital to ensure American security in war and peace, spying—part of intelligence gathering—raises important issues such as the extent civil liberties may be reduced to allow the government to catch spies. The American Civil War marked the beginning of extensive civil and military espionage. The intelligence operations during the Civil War were pre-modern, amateurish, and even eccentric by twenty-first century standards, but elements of this odd secret war foreshadowed the later modernization of America's novice intelligence services.

Although spies could be useful to resourceful commanders, in general commanders employed more traditional battlefield means of acquiring intelligence. Two key methods were cavalry reconnaissance, a skill at which the Confederates tended to be superior, and the systematic interrogation of prisoners and deserters. Such methods were supplemented by dispatching spies to cross enemy lines to discover "what is on the other side of the hill." In attempting this, Civil War spies had certain advantages. The two sides had a common language and culture. And in border states, such as Missouri and Maryland, loyalty to either cause was ambiguous and the recruitment of spies relatively easy. In addition, Union spies assumed convenient cover occupations in Confederate territory, which was experiencing shortages in manpower and military goods. The infiltrators found cover as smugglers or deserters.

The fledgling intelligence services were novelties and did not survive the four-year conflict. The federal organizations, despite their limited jurisdiction and scope, were more effective than the Confederates' service, the so-called Secret Service Bureau. The principal federal services were Allan Pinkerton's Detective Bureau of General McClellan's Army of the Potomac (1861–1862) and General Hooker's Bureau of Military Information (1863–1865), managed by Colonel George Sharpe, 120th New York Regiment. Although both organizations functioned only as part of one army, Hooker's Bureau of Military Information was an improvement on Pinkerton's organization, which was limited to only two functions: spying and interrogation of prisoners of war. Sharpe improved these activities and added more, including the key interception of flag signaling. A Scottish-born master detective, Pinkerton was effective in counterespionage and security. In early 1861 Pinkerton's service helped save the life of President-elect Abraham Lincoln as he traveled through Baltimore to the nation's capital. Pinkerton was talented in penetrating conspiracies but his military intelligence work for the Army of the Potomac and his field estimates of Confederate military strength were inaccurate.

Several Confederate spies long ago entered the realm of myth, in part because of the exaggerations and fabrications of their published memoirs. Secret agent Rose Greenhow, a prominent socialite and Confederate sympathizer in Washington, D.C., produced useful intelligence for General Pierre Beauregard early in the war, but Pinkerton's counterspies were easily her match, and she was arrested and jailed. As was the case with a number of female spies, however, she was released and then escaped to England to pursue a propaganda war against the Union. Another celebrated Confederate female spy was Belle Boyd, who created her own legend as an agent. She was lauded in literature as La Belle Boyd and the Cleopatra of the Confederacy, despite her modest contributions to Confederate intelligence. Her postwar published memoirs promoted her legend, enhanced by her later performances on the stage. On Belle Boyd's tombstone was inscribed "Confederate Spy." But by far the most effective Confederate spy, who never became a celebrity, was thirty-one-year-old Mississippian, Henry T. Harrison, who spied for General James Longstreet and provided accurate reports on federal army movements before the Battle of Gettysburg.

The most successful secret agent of all, however, was Miss Elizabeth Van Lew, a federal spy in Richmond, Virginia, who co-headed a Union spy ring from 1864 to 1865. Using an effective cover personality as an eccentric, even deranged, lonely spinster, she deceived observers and provided vital intelligence to a number of Federal generals. Enhancing her cover personality was her open expression of pro-Union sympathies and her providing federal prisoners in Richmond with food and clothing. After the war Van Lew, known as Crazy Bet as part of her myth, was rewarded with a position in the Federal Postal Service.

By the time of the battle of Chancellorsville in early May 1863, General Hooker's Bureau of Military Information's performance in field intelligence had greatly improved. This service was now more effective in discovering three key intelligence elements about the enemy: the location of its forces, the strength and composition of those forces, and commanders' intentions. Sharpe's spies assisted in Hooker's superb coup of placing a large federal army in the rear of the Confederates, undetected by Lee. Good intelligence helped Hooker's plan, though he lost the battle of Chancellorsville to Lee. It was at the Battle of Gettysburg in July 1863, only weeks later, that federal intelligence truly came into its own. By this time federal intelligence officers had compiled the most complete order-of-battle chart of Lee's army. During this campaign three elements provided vital information to General George Meade: federal soldier-spies behind Confederate lines; organized groups of citizen-scouts in south-central Pennsylvania who observed Confederate movements; and effective cavalry scouting, which detected the enemy's approach to Gettysburg. Meade's use of this intelligence, backed by military strength, was an important factor in the Confederates' defeat at Gettysburg.

The Civil War proved to be a turning point for the government's role in intelligence gathering. First, the North's victory over the South was partly the result of the North's superiority in both tactical and strategic means for observing enemy troops. The North used the interception and deciphering of Southern telegrams and flag signals to its advantage, just as the Allies' breaking of Japanese and German codes in World War II contributed to victory. After the Civil War, in 1885, military intelligence was reorganized to incorporate new technology. Second, despite some objections, Americans accepted the necessity of reducing temporarily some civil liberties during time of war to aid in the detection and capture of spies. In the twenty-first century's War on Terror, Americans face an even greater challenge in balancing individual privacy and civil liberties with security.

BIBLIOGRAPHY

Bakeless, John. *Turncoats, Traitors and Heroes*. Philadelphia: Lippincott, 1959.

Fishel, Edwin C. "Myths that Never Die." *International Journal of Intelligence and Counterintelligence* 2, no. 1 (spring 1988): 27 58.

Fishel, Edwin C. *The Secret War for the Union. The Untold Story of Military Intelligence in the Civil War*. Boston and New York: Houghton Mifflin, 1996.

O'Toole, G. J. A. *The Encyclopedia of American Intelligence and Espionage*. New York: Facts on File, 1988.

O'Toole, G. J. A. *Honorable Treachery: A History of U.S. Intelligence, Espionage and Covert Action from the American Revolution to the CIA*. New York: Atlantic Monthly Press, 1991.

Varon, Elizabeth R. *Southern Lady, Yankee Spy: The True Story of Elizabeth Van Lew, a Union Agent in the Heart of the Confederacy*. New York: Oxford University Press, 2004.

Douglas L. Wheeler

FAMILY LIFE

The coming of war, war itself, and the aftermath of war have profound effects upon individual families and family life generally. Such was the case in the nineteenth century, especially with respect to the Civil War (1861–1865).

The nineteenth-century family was as important and complicated as families are today. Most people regarded marriage as both desirable and necessary. A legal or religious ceremony usually formalized marriage, though some couples in far-flung areas merely moved in and lived together as husband and wife. Among rich and poor alike, the household often included aging parents, single brothers and sisters, and parentless nieces and nephews. Newly married couples often lived with parents until they could establish their own households. According to coverture laws, wives were secondary to their husbands and could not claim their own property.

Divorce rarely disrupted family life, but not because married couples were happier than they are today; people of that era did not expect that marriage would necessarily mean lifelong happiness. Obtaining a divorce was extremely difficult, and women found it hard to survive independently because job opportunities were limited. The major cause of family instability in the nineteenth century was death, for mortality rates were high, especially among infants and young children and women of childbearing age. Over the course of the century, as health and medical care improved, mortality declined, more babies survived infancy, and adults lived longer.

Nineteenth-century families tended to be large, especially in rural areas where children were expected to be productive workers. Though birth control methods were unknown to most people and were generally ineffective, the number of children born to women of childbearing age declined significantly during the nineteenth century, which suggests that couples made some effort to limit family size.

Among the poor, roles tended to overlap, and everyone pitched in to ensure family survival. Women and children often worked in the fields, and older children cared for younger siblings. For the middle and upper classes, society defined proper family roles. Fathers were to support the family. As the nation urbanized and industrialized, more men began to work outside the home, and their day-to-day contact with the family declined. Mothers had charge of nurturing their children, inculcating moral and religious views, and overseeing domestic chores. Men left most household and child-related responsibilities to their wives. Often mothers home-schooled their offspring until children were old enough to go to a more advanced school. Attending boarding school was common among privileged children.

IMPACT OF THE CIVIL WAR

The Civil War had an enormous impact on family life. With millions of men participating in the four-year war, eligible young women found it difficult to find partners. Women whose husbands served in the military were left alone to oversee the family and, in rural areas, to run the farm. With the death of some 618,000 men, the war created many widows who now had permanent charge of their families. Those who did welcome home a returning soldier often found him physically or psychologically wounded. Thus, at least temporarily, women often became the major bread-earners in their families or turned to their surviving children for help. In the South in particular, both rich and poor families encountered severe poverty and the loss of their homes, crops, and farm animals due to four years of war fought on their soil.

The importance of the family was especially evident after slaves gained their freedom in 1865, for many African-American spouses who had been separated before the Civil War traveled widely in search of their partners and children. Slave owners had controlled slave marriages and family life and encouraged family formation in order to enhance the stability of the slave community and foster reproduction. Special laws dictated family structure. For instance, slave children fathered by free men had the status of their slave mother. Laws stated that slave marriages were not legally binding, for this would have prevented an owner from selling a married slave. Nevertheless, slaves did marry, either in an actual ceremony or by moving in together. Because slave marriages were not legal, they could dissolve easily merely by one party leaving the relationship. A number of slave families had both a father and mother present. But slave sales and "abroad marriages" (when a husband and wife lived on different plantations) created many single-parent slave families. Many children were raised by their mothers, perhaps with the help of extended family members living on the same plantation. Slave children were always accountable to two "fathers"—their biological father and their master. After the Emancipation, the family continued to be an important tool for survival as African Americans eked out a living as sharecroppers and tenant farmers.

By the late nineteenth century, families experienced some change. New state laws passed after the Civil War gave women greater access to their own property and wages. Divorce procedures became easier. The family became more child-centered, suggesting that perhaps those who had lived through the Civil War were well aware of the fragility of life and began to express more concern for their offspring. Society placed increasing emphasis on the importance of early nurturing and the need for institutions to play a greater role in a child's upbringing. Public schools, kindergartens, Sunday schools, and literature published especially for children reflected this trend. Families, then as now, were an important institution for survival, love, education, and support, and were both resilient from and vulnerable to the destructive effects of war.

BIBLIOGRAPHY

Censer, Jane Turner. *North Carolina Planters and Their Children, 1800–1860*. Baton Rouge: Louisiana State University Press, 1984.

Degler, Carl N. *At Odds: Women and the Family from the Revolution to the Present*. New York: Oxford University Press, 1980.

Gutman, Herbert G. *The Black Family in Slavery and Freedom, 1750–1925*. New York: Pantheon Books, 1976.

Malone, Ann Patton. *Sweet Chariot: Slave Family and Household Structure in Nineteenth-Century Louisiana*. Chapel Hill: University of North Carolina Press, 1992.

Marten, James Alan. *The Children's Civil War*. Chapel Hill: University of North Carolina Press, 1998.

McMillen, Sally G. *Motherhood in the Old South: Pregnancy, Childbirth and Infant Rearing*. Baton Rouge: Louisiana State University Press, 1990.

Mintz, Steven and Kellogg, Susan. *Domestic Revolutions: A Social History of American Family Life*. New York: Free Press, 1988.

Sally G. McMillen

See also: **Children and the Civil War; Education; Slavery.**

FARMING

Farmers in antebellum America were committed to a mix of subsistence and commercial production. Slavery and the cotton gin drove the rapid expansion of cotton farming in the South. Slavery and the plantation system also created profitable markets for northern farmers, particularly for the sale of corn and pork. Midwestern farmers increasingly specialized their production for local and regional markets, and the emerging railroad network carried farm products to eastern markets cheaply and efficiently. Northeastern farmers could not compete with Midwestern farmers who raised cattle, hogs, and grain, and they began to specialize in dairy, hay, and fruit production. Rapid technological change and settlement be-

Frontier prairie farmers near Lexington, Nebraska, ca. 1890. © BETTMANN/CORBIS

tween the Appalachian Mountains and the Mississippi River also characterized agriculture during the antebellum years. Periodic economic depressions caused financial problems but most farmers experienced general economic improvement during the antebellum period. Prior to the Civil War, wars against the American Indians, forcible removal of American Indians from native lands, the war with Mexico (1846–1848), and the expansion to the Northwest were partly motivated by American desire for more agricultural territory.

When the Civil War began in April 1861, approximately half of the U.S. population of 31.4 million lived on farms. Agriculture provided seventy-five percent of the nation's exports by value. Three farmers out of four owned their own land. In the North and border states, self-sufficient farms prevailed, but farmers also produced for the market economy to make a profit by raising wheat, corn, oats, hay, hogs, and beef and dairy cattle. In the South, large-scale plantations emphasized specialized production of cotton, rice, tobacco, and sugar cane with the use of slave labor. Small-scale farmers often raised cotton or tobacco for the market and corn for home consumption and livestock feed.

In 1861 few people believed that agriculture would affect the outcome of the war for the Union or Confederacy. Northerners expected the war to end quickly in their favor by force of arms while Southerners anticipated British intervention to ensure cotton supplies for English textile mills and, thereby, Southern independence. Both sides soon found that the war dramatically affected agriculture and farm life. The Union blockade of the Atlantic and Gulf coasts and Mississippi River prevented Northern farmers from shipping pork, corn, butter, wheat, oats, lard, and other commodities to Southern consumers who began to experience food shortages by early 1862.

WAR AND SOCIETY:
SOUTHERN AGRICULTURE

The Union blockade of the Mississippi River prevented Texas cattle from reaching Confederate markets, particularly New Orleans, and, thereby, cutting supplies of beef for soldiers and civilians. During the first two years of the war, many planters continued to raise cotton because they believed the conflict would increase prices. Confederate leaders, however, urged farmers and planters to increase corn, hog, and vegetable production to feed soldiers and

civilians. Although many planters raised less cotton, tobacco, rice, and sugar cane, by 1863, Confederate food
shortages became critical.

Southern agricultural production declined because
many farmers and their sons enlisted or were drafted into
the army. Confederate women now assumed many farm
jobs but they often could not handle tasks that demanded
considerable physical labor, such as plowing and harvesting grain. Moreover, Confederate ironworks concentrated on weapons and stopped making farm equipment,
and agricultural production declined as a result of inadequate planting and cultivating, and limited availability
of harvesting implements. The Confederate armies often
impressed slaves to build fortifications, or they were captured or ran away to nearby Union forces. The loss of
slave labor further hindered agricultural production. Slave
men and women also became increasingly reluctant to
work in anticipation of their freedom after President
Abraham Lincoln announced the Emancipation Proclamation, that became effective January 1, 1863.

The movement of farm and rural people to the cities
worsened the agricultural and food problem. Northern
forces drove an estimated 400,000 pro-Southerners from
Kentucky, Missouri, and Tennessee, thereby increasing
the demands for food on Southern farmers. Moreover,
the Southern railroad system proved inadequate to transport agricultural products to the cities or the moving
armies. By 1863, Confederate soldiers received only
twenty-five percent of their allotted meat rations, and
their horses had weakened due to insufficient grain and
hay. Bread riots occurred in Atlanta, Richmond, and Petersburg, among other cities.

As food became scarce, agricultural prices increased
rapidly. Soon inflated food prices became a major problem. Worthless Confederate paper money drove inflation. By 1862 many Confederate farmers refused to
accept it as payment for their commodities, and they began to hoard food, all to the detriment of the soldiers
and civilian population. Confederate farmers located near
Union markets or advancing armies frequently traded
across enemy lines because Northern buyers paid with paper money based on gold. The cost of goods that farmers needed also increased rapidly. In some areas farm
implements and clothing increased two thousand percent.

The Confederate government attempted to control
inflation by regulating farm prices, particularly those paid
by agents who purchased agricultural commodities, such
as meat, grain, and hay. Farmers, however, complained
that Confederate purchasing agents or impressment officers paid prices below those offered on the open market and with nearly worthless paper money, which
Confederate creditors often refused to accept for the
payment of farmers' bills. Impressment agents often left

Confederate farmers with too few horses, mules, cattle,
hogs, and forage to remain viable farm operations. Confederate and Union armies also took livestock, grain, hay,
and foodstuffs from Southern farmers as they passed
through an area and tore down fences for firewood. During the last year of the war, foraging Confederate troops
pillaged southern farms as wantonly as Union raiders.

WAR AND SOCIETY: NORTHERN AGRICULTURE

Northern farmers did not experience invasion and the loss
of property, crops, and livestock, except for Confederate
forays near Antietam in 1862 and Gettysburg in 1863.
Although farmers suffered a temporary loss of Southern
markets when the war began, the Union army quickly
provided a steady and lucrative market for them. An extensive railroad system carried agricultural commodities
from the farms to food processors, the army, and urban
consumers. Farmers increased production of commodities needed by soldiers. Some farmers began to specialize in the production of wheat, corn, hay, horses, and
dairy and beef cattle. Border state and Northern farmers,
particularly in Connecticut, increased tobacco production
to cover the loss of Southern supplies. Wood and flax
production increased, stimulated by high prices, and textile manufacturers wanting to offset the loss of Southern
cotton, although Union troops captured considerable cotton stores.

The North had a larger population, and enlistments
and draft inductions to the army proved less draining to
agricultural labor. Approximately half of Northern farm
families sent men to the army. Immigrants often took
their places as hired labor with no loss of production resulting. Many Northern farm women replaced husbands
and sons in the fields, and high wartime prices enabled
farmers to purchase agricultural implements, such as
reapers, mowers, horse rakes, and planters, that their
wives operated to ease and speed their work. Rapid technological adoption helped expand production and reduced the need for hired labor.

AGRICULTURE, WAR, AND PUBLIC POLICY

The Union Congress passed three important acts in 1862
that affected all farmers after the Civil War. Southerners had opposed this legislation because it threatened to
open the West to the creation of non-slave states, thereby
reducing Southern political power in Congress, or because they believed the acts would prove costly, bureaucratic, and increase the power of the federal government
at the expense of the states. On May 15, President Abraham Lincoln signed the bill that created the United States
Department of Agriculture, which became the most important scientific agency devoted to improving agriculture during the late nineteenth century.

The act authorized the department to acquire, test, and distribute new seeds and plants, conduct practical and scientific experiments, collect agricultural statistics and other information beneficial to farmers, and publish its findings in an annual report. Congress also approved the Homestead Act, which Lincoln signed on May 20. It authorized the federal government to provide 160 acres of pubic domain free to any head of a household, male or female, twenty-one years of age or older who was a citizen or who had filed for citizenship and who would live on it for five years and make improvements. On July 2, Lincoln also signed the Morrill Land-Grant College Act. It authorized the creation of state colleges where agriculture and mechanical arts would be taught to improve farm life.

AGRICULTURE AND THE LEGACY OF WAR

When the war ended in 1865, Southern farmers confronted a host of problems that would take years to solve. In areas of Virginia, Georgia, Tennessee, Mississippi, Louisiana, and the Carolinas where the armies had moved or fought, houses, barns, and fences lay in ruin, fields stood abandoned, livestock had been killed or captured, and farm equipment was worn out or destroyed. The slave labor force that had tended the fields and livestock had been freed. The emancipation of four million slaves brought significant capital and credit losses to their owners and the necessity to convert slave-based farm and plantation operations to free or hired labor after the war. Some 260,000 Confederate soldiers, mostly farmers, had been killed. In contrast, Northern farmers used high wartime prices to pay debts, buy new equipment, and purchase land. For them the Civil War brought prosperity.

After the Civil War, American agriculture experienced rapid technological change. In the North, the Corn Belt spread west across the Midwest. Farmers moved onto the Great Plains, many taking advantage of the Homestead Act. They increasingly specialized with a single crop, and farmers gave less attention to self-sufficiency and more to surplus production for the market economy. Specialized agricultural production tied farmers to bankers, railroads, and businessmen in ways that often caused discontent and encouraged agricultural organization and protest. In the South, farmers primarily remained reliant on cotton, but the sharecropping system held many farmers in a state of poverty and near peonage. Thus, the Civil War contributed to the transformation of American agriculture and American society: Western migration expanded; Northern farmers became more commercial and capitalistic; and in the South, decades of economic decline followed the end of slavery and the new system of sharecropping.

BIBLIOGRAPHY

Gates, Paul Wallace. *The Farmer's Age: Agriculture, 1815–1860*. New York: Holt, Rinehart, and Winston, 1960.

Gates, Paul Wallace. *Agriculture and the Civil War*. New York: Knopf, 1965.

Hudson, John C. *Making the Corn Belt: A Geographical History of Middle-Western Agriculture*. Bloomington: Indiana University Press, 1994.

Hurt, R. Douglas. *American Agriculture: A Brief History*. Revised edition. West Lafayette, IN: Purdue University Press, 2002.

R. Douglas Hurt

See also: **Sharecropping and Tenant Farming.**

FINANCING THE WAR

The scale and scope of the Civil War created unprecedented financial demands on both the Union and the Confederacy, whose governments spent a combined total of more than $3.4 billion for the war effort. These expenditures dwarfed those of the antebellum period: The federal government never spent more than $75 million per year in the 1850s. Each side faced a fundamental question: How would it pay the staggering sums needed to raise, equip, and supply its armed forces? Each had three basic options: extracting resources through taxes, tariffs, or outright confiscation; borrowing money by issuing bonds, interest-bearing notes, and other financial instruments; and inflating the money supply with fiat currency.

The Union used all three options but borrowed most of the money it needed. Borrowing did not alleviate the financial hardships of war—Northerners paid extraordinarily high taxes, and a general increase in prices resulted in declining real wages. The suffering of Northern families, however, paled in comparison to that of Confederate households. Lacking the financial resources of the North, the Confederacy had little choice but to rely upon new issues of paper currency. The resulting inflationary spiral made it increasingly difficult for the Rebels to sustain their cause.

THE UNION

The Union borrowed to pay for the bulk of its wartime expenses. Under the leadership of Treasury Secretary Salmon P. Chase, the national debt skyrocketed from $90.6 million in 1861 to almost $2.8 billion in 1866. The Union sold government bonds through two novel methods. Financier Jay Cooke, the brother of one of Chase's political associates, used massive publicity campaigns to sell hundreds of millions of dollars worth of bonds to ordinary citizens. These bond sales helped, but Chase also needed to tap the resources of banks, which had operated successfully for decades as state-chartered institutions that issued their own notes. When government demands threatened to overwhelm the state-chartered banks, the Republicans created a national banking network in 1863. Under this system, the federal government itself chartered banks. In exchange for the right to issue federal bank notes, banks had to buy large sums of government debt. This system, in essence, guaranteed that bankers would buy government bonds.

To ensure that the federal government could pay the interest on its mushrooming debt, Congress authorized a series of new taxes in 1861 and 1862. The federal government had traditionally relied on tariffs for the bulk of its revenue, but tariff revenues, despite sizeable increases in rates, could not keep pace with wartime demands. In August 1861, the government authorized its first income tax, which was eventually expanded to all incomes over $600. Income taxes provided the federal government $55 million in revenue during the course of the war, but a comprehensive series of excise taxes on certain goods and licenses proved much more important. The Internal Revenue Act of 1862, in the words of Republican politician James G. Blaine, was "one of the most searching, thorough, comprehensive systems of taxation ever devised by any government" (Hummel, p. 222). Taxing almost every type of good imaginable—from liquor and tobacco to iron and steel to butchered meat—federal excise taxes raised hundreds of millions of dollars. By the end of the war, Northern citizens paid higher taxes per capita than citizens of any other nation.

In periods of crisis, though, the Union had trouble raising money. Investors shunned bonds, and taxes could not provide an immediate infusion of revenue. The Union found itself in precisely such a situation in the winter of 1861–62, when a series of military reverses and the possibility of war with Britain threatened the solvency of both the nation's banking system and the treasury department. To overcome this crisis, the federal government issued its own paper money, known as *greenbacks*. To make sure that greenbacks circulated as currency, Congress made them legal tender; individuals, businesses, and the government had to accept all greenbacks for payment. The federal government eventually issued $450 million in greenbacks. The fiat money helped stabilize the economy, but it also contributed to sustained inflation. Northern prices rose 80 percent during the war, which led to a substantial drop in real wages for most workers.

THE CONFEDERACY

The northern inflation rate was tame compared to the 9,000 percent increase in prices the Confederacy suf-

fered. This extraordinarily high rate of inflation highlighted a central problem for the Confederacy: It was fighting a fundamentally modern war without the ability to pay for it. The Confederacy had far fewer banks than the Union and thus relatively little in the way of specie that could be used to pay investors in government bonds. The Union blockade and capture of key southern ports left Southerners without the ability to collect revenue from import or export taxes. Cotton, which many Confederates had regarded as a great potential source of revenue and collateral, provided little help as the South found itself increasingly isolated from foreign markets. Confederates exported two million bales of cotton between 1861 and 1865, a far cry from the more than 17 million bales the South had exported during the previous four years.

The Confederacy's solution to the problem was to print money to pay for government expenses. Secretary of Treasury Christopher Memminger recognized the dangers of this method, but a variety of taxes and bond issues had failed to raise sufficient funds. Despite aggressive measures—including a 10 percent tax-in-kind, paid in crops, livestock, and goods rather than in cash—taxation covered less than 7 percent of the Confederate government's income. Borrowing at home and abroad provided another 25 percent. Paper money covered the rest. Between 1861 and January 1864, the Confederacy's money supply increased elevenfold, and more dramatic increases occurred thereafter.

Confederate inflation essentially operated as a highly regressive tax that fell most heavily on ordinary households, which had great difficulty surviving as the prices of food and clothing grew at a far higher rate than wages and income. Southerners often blamed speculators for rapidly rising prices, fueling the sentiment that the conflict was, as the saying went, "a rich man's war and a poor man's fight." The Confederacy's inflationary spiral undoubtedly contributed to the increasing rates of desertion that plagued Rebel armies in the last year of the war.

The end of the Civil War hardly resolved the nation's financial problems. Greenbacks remained in circulation but were without the backing of either gold or silver. In subsequent decades, the nation and Congress tried to deal with major issues related to money, including the size of the nation's money supply and a bimetallic standard based on gold and silver. The North emerged from the war in a relatively strong financial position. The postwar South, on the other hand, found itself with a worthless currency of Confederate dollars, a paucity of banks, and an enormous debt. The Civil War and its postwar effects had created the conditions that began to transform the nation's currency and its financial institutions.

BIBLIOGRAPHY

Ball, Douglass B. *Financial Failure and Confederate Defeat.* Champaign: University of Illinois Press, 1991.

Hummel, Jeffrey Rogers. *Emancipating Slaves, Enslaving Free Men: A History of the American Civil War.* Chicago and La Salle, IL: Open Court, 1996.

Lerner, Eugene M. "Money, Prices, and Wages in the Confederacy, 1861–65." In *The Economic Impact of the American Civil War,* edited by Ralph Andreano. Cambridge, MA: Schenkman, 1967.

Paludan, Phillip Shaw. *A People's Contest: The Union and the Civil War, 1861–1865,* 2d edition. Lawrence: University of Kansas Press, 1996.

Surdam, David. G. *Northern Naval Superiority and the Economics of the American Civil War.* Columbia: University of South Carolina Press, 2001.

John Majewski

See also: **Business and Finance; Economic Change and Industrialization.**

FOOD SHORTAGES

The shortage of food during the Civil War affected many Southerners on the homefront. Although some parts of the South enjoyed an abundance of foodstuffs, other parts of the Confederacy experienced severe deprivation. As the war continued and conditions grew worse, Southerners' winter of discontent turned into years of unhappiness and sacrifice. Southerners consumed milk, corn, butter, meal, and an occasional piece of meat. Tea, sugar, and coffee were rare commodities for them.

Agriculture suffered as farms and plantations were neglected when men left home to fulfill their military obligations to the Confederacy. The inability of families to cultivate and harvest crops was a constant reminder of how their world had been turned upside down by the war. The long and brutal conflict tested the endurance of men, women, and children, not least in terms of how they coped with and reacted to the scarcity of food.

As poverty spread across the region, white Southerners turned to their neighbors, friends, and families for help. In response to the lack of food, desperate citizens rioted in several towns and cities. The most memorable of the food uprisings occurred in Richmond, Virginia, in April 1863, when dozens of angry women took to the streets in search of provisions. The exigencies of the conflict forced record numbers of women to seek employment in an effort to stave off starvation. The food crisis behind the lines caused numerous families to accept handouts in the form of public or private assistance and to barter for the basic necessities of life.

The Union blockade of Southern ports added to the shortages in the South. Those affected by the blockade were convinced that it was a deliberate scheme by the federal government to compel the Confederate nation to surrender. Making a bad situation worse was the common practice of food hoarding by speculators, who hoped to reap huge profits by selling items at exorbitant prices. Those who hoarded food and other supplies earned the scorn of their fellow Southerners. With the plantation economy in shambles and inflation out of control, the price of many food items was beyond the reach of ordinary citizens. An example of the runaway inflation was the increase in the price of flour in Richmond, from $20 a barrel in January 1863 to $250, fourteen months later.

Civilians' criticism of the Jefferson Davis government coincided with the difficulty of procuring food. The mismanagement of the South's nearly 9,000 miles of railroad track was symptomatic of the Confederate government's inability to meet the expectations of the people. The rail transportation system was bedeviled by short lines and the South's limited ability to do repair work on trains and tracks, which were often ruined by Union soldiers. As Union soldiers invaded the South, its inhabitants were helpless to prevent them from taking chickens, sheep, turkeys, pigs, hogs, calves and other property. Foraging, however, was not limited to Northern troops. As the war dragged on, the basic need to survive forced Confederate soldiers to engage in the practice as well.

Provisions for slaves on plantations were also in short supply. The common staples of a slave's diet were mush, peanuts, potatoes, and cornbread. Although malnutrition had become a common phenomenon in this agricultural land, the elderly among the slave population were the most vulnerable to death by starvation. Hardship on the homefront was a reality shared and endured by both white and black Southerners. Wartime food shortages, however, took a greater toll on whites than on blacks, for blacks had been accustomed to subsisting on less. Though facing a mountain of obstacles, Southerners proved to the rest of the country that the human spirit had the power to persevere in the face of extreme adversity.

Confederate soldiers also experienced major food shortages, especially in the latter two years of the war. Much of this was due to food spoilage, inadequate or disrupted supply lines, bad weather, the destruction of crops, and Union occupation of food-producing areas of the South. The Confederate Subsistence Department contracted with Southern farmers to supply food to Southern soldiers, but that department of the government was poorly organized. By 1864, soldiers' rations had been drastically reduced. Military fare often consisted of dried meat, hardtack, corn, and potatoes. Hungry soldiers suffered from night blindness, dysentery, depression, and lethargy. Many became experts at foraging for food and learning to deal with hunger. Confederate soldiers defending Vicksburg faced near-starvation in July 1863; the Army of Northern Virginia was starving as it retreated from Gettysburg. Lee's famished army marching toward Appomattox, with some soldiers not eating for days and others scrounging for corn kernels intended for horses, has become a well-known emblem of the Confederate Army's devastation.

Food shortages had an enormous impact on the Civil War, reducing the ability of the South to wage war. Desperate families on the homefront begged their men to abandon the cause and come home. The wars of the twentieth century have applied the lessons learned from the South in the Civil War. In what is known as "total war," which treats civilians as combatants, warring nations have used military means to undermine civilian morale through starvation and deprivation.

BIBLIOGRAPHY

Davis, William C. *A Taste for War: The Culinary History of the Blue and the Gray.* Mechanicsburg, PA: Stackpole Books, 2003.

Gates, Paul W. *Agriculture and the Civil War.* New York: Knopf, 1965.

Marten, James. *Civil War America: Voices from the Home Front.* Santa Barbara, CA: ABC-CLIO, 2003.

Taylor, Robert A. *Rebel Storehouse: Florida in the Confederate Economy.* Tuscaloosa: University Press of Alabama, 1995.

Leonne M. Hudson

See also: **Blockade, Civil War.**

FREEDMEN'S BUREAU

The Freedmen's Bureau, officially known as the Bureau of Refugees, Freedmen, and Abandoned Lands, was established on March 3, 1865. The agency, a part of the War Department, owed its very being to the Union's Civil War victory. Absent the war's consequences, particularly emancipation, the federal government would have had no reason to establish such an extraordinary organization that had the potential to insert itself into state, local, and individual affairs as it tried to guide white and black Southerners in their transition from a slave society to a free society. Because the agency was a departure from past experience, it was the product of compromise. Political restraint meant that the Freedmen's Bureau never had the resources or the power to accomplish what Congress demanded of it or what the freedpeople expected of it.

LABOR, LAND, AND EDUCATION

Circumstances shaped the Bureau into an organization that was part labor regulator, part social service agency, part peacekeeper, and part civil rights advocate for the freed slaves. Bureau commander Major General Oliver Otis Howard supervised officers, agents, education officials, and medical men who carried the Bureau's presence down to the local level. Not all were ideal missionaries of Northern ideals, but the majority of these men were committed to securing the fruits of Union victory, including the economic rights and civil rights of the former slaves. Approximately 2,441 men served as officers and agents of the Bureau during its lifetime, but at any given time there were never sufficient numbers on duty to blanket the South with their presence. At the end of 1865, there were only 799 Bureau men, including clerks; by the end of 1868, Bureau personnel rosters carried a total of 901, with over a third being clerks.

Bureau officials brought relief to white and black Southerners left destitute by the war and subsequent poor harvests. The Bureau never considered itself a charitable organization; most of its personnel, reflecting ideas of the time, believed that prolonged charity damaged the character of its recipients. Bureau men were primarily missionaries for a Northern-style free labor system based on written contracts that would allow the agency to supervise the fledgling work arrangements. Former slaves were disappointed the Bureau did not act as an agent of land redistribution, and some freedpeople felt betrayed when the agency returned property, on which they had settled, to white claimants. The majority of freedpeople, however, accepted the need to work and appreciated the Bureau's assistance especially when their employers mistreated them. While many Southern white employers considered the process to be no more than Yankee meddling in their personal affairs, others believed the work documents might impose some degree of labor discipline on their former slaves. White employers eventually used labor arrangements to oppress black workers, but that was not the Bureau's intention.

Complementary to a free labor system that taught the freedpeople the virtues of hard work by experience was an educational system that would instill similar virtues in the classroom. The Bureau acted as a coordinator of the efforts of freedpeople and Northern charitable associations to found schools, but also provided some funding to assist them in securing buildings, books, and teachers. The Bureau also attempted to protect schools and teachers from white violence, a problem that also troubled Bureau personnel. Officers and agents found themselves ostracized, threatened, and attacked by whites; a few officers and agents were murdered.

From the outset, white Southerners knew the Bureau was a temporary organization authorized by law to exist for only one year from the end of the Civil War. While Congress voted to continue the agency on July 16,

Students and teachers in front of a Freedmen's Bureau school in Beaufort, South Carolina, ca. 1865. © CORBIS

1866, it did so over President Andrew Johnson's objections, which confirmed in the minds of many white Southerners that the agency lacked the support of its commander in chief. Such circumstances did not nurture respect for the agency among white Southerners, who constantly tested its power and, more often than not, found it wanting. Ultimately, the Bureau never had sufficient power to protect the freedpeople from whites who feared black education, economic independence, and political activity.

Overworked agents and officers relied primarily on arbitration to settle difficulties between whites and blacks, acted as the freedpeople's "next friend" when they had to take their cases to civil or criminal court, and interceded with the military authorities when situations required the use of military force. In 1868 the Bureau began to reduce its presence in the South and in January 1869 restricted itself to education and assisting black veterans in obtaining their bounties. Congress terminated the Bureau at the end of June 1872. Its termination, along with the end of Reconstruction in 1877, greatly slowed the social revolution in the South begun during the Civil War. The black struggle for economic advancement and educational equality would continue,

however, as black demands for civil rights rose after World War I and World War II.

BIBLIOGRAPHY

Bentley, George R. *A History of the Freedmen's Bureau.* New York: Octagon Books, 1970.

Cimbala, Paul A., and Randall M. Miller, eds. *The Freedmen's Bureau and Reconstruction: Reconsiderations.* New York: Fordham University Press, 1999.

Cimbala, Paul. *Under the Guardianship of the Nation: The Freedmen's Bureau and the Reconstruction of Georgia, 1865–1870.* Athens, GA: University of Georgia Press, 2003.

Cimbala, Paul. *The Freedmen's Bureau: Reconstructing the American South After the Civil War.* Melbourne, FL: Krieger Publishing Company, 2004.

Crouch, Barry A. *The Freedmen's Bureau and Black Texans.* Austin: University of Texas Press, 1992.

Finley, Randy. *From Slavery to Uncertain Freedom: The Freedmen's Bureau in Arkansas, 1865–1869.* Fayetteville: University of Arkansas Press, 1996.

McFeely, William S. *Yankee Stepfather: General O. O. Howard and the Freedmen.* New Haven, CT: Yale University Press, 1968.

Nieman, Donald G. *To Set the Law in Motion: The Freedmen's Bureau and the Legal Rights of Blacks, 1865–1868.* Millwood, NY: KTO Press, 1979.

Oubre, Claude F. *Forty Acres and a Mule: The Freedmen's Bureau and Black Landownership.* Baton Rouge: Louisiana State University Press, 1978.

Paul A. Cimbala

See also: **African Americans (Freed People); Education; Johnson, Andrew; Occupation of the South; Reconstruction.**

GETTYSBURG ADDRESS

On November 19, 1863, President Abraham Lincoln spoke at the dedication of the national cemetery at Gettysburg, Pennsylvania. The orator of the day was Edward Everett, a famed speaker, former senator, and candidate for vice president in 1860. Lincoln received a late invitation to make "a few appropriate remarks." Lincoln's brief Gettysburg address became a cornerstone of American expression of the nation's ideals, mission, and patriotism.

On the first three days of July 1863, the Army of Northern Virginia, commanded by General Robert E. Lee, had fought the Army of the Potomac, the principal northern army, to which General George G. Meade had been assigned command only four days earlier. In early May, Lee had won a smashing victory at Chancellorsville, Virginia, over a Union force approximately twice as large, then had boldly determined to carry the war to the enemy by invading Pennsylvania. Drawn into an offensive battle at Gettysburg, Lee attacked both wings of the Union army before launching an attack on the center in the third day of fighting. That assault, led by Major General George E. Pickett, had approached success before Union forces rallied. The three-day battle cost the North 17,684 men killed and wounded; the South lost 22,638. The failure of Pickett's charge, sometimes labeled the high water mark of the Confederacy, compelled Lee to withdraw from Pennsylvania. However, Meade failed to conduct the vigorous pursuit that Lincoln wanted.

On July 7, Lincoln had spoken to a crowd assembled at the White House to celebrate the twin Union victories at Gettysburg and at Vicksburg, Mississippi, the key to control of the Mississippi River, which had surrendered on July 4. Lincoln gave an awkward speech: "How long ago is it?—eighty-odd years—since on the Fourth of July for the first time in the history of the world a nation by its representatives, assembled and declared as a self-evident truth that 'all men are created equal.'" Later, after rambling, Lincoln confessed that he was not prepared to make a speech "worthy of the occasion." He had, nonetheless, expressed the central theme of the Gettysburg Address, which he refined and strengthened for delivery at the cemetery.

Fiction created a legend that Lincoln wrote his speech on the back of an envelope while on the train to Gettysburg. In fact he had already written two complete drafts, later presented to his two secretaries. Another legend exists that Lincoln was sadly disappointed in the speech, especially after it drew strong criticism in newspapers. Such criticism appeared only in Democratic papers; hostile editors savaged the speech not because they thought it weak but because they recognized its strength. Republican editors and others knew immediately that Lincoln's speech was masterful.

In some 271 words, 202 of them having one syllable, Lincoln captured the meaning of the war, transforming "eighty-odd years" into the sonorous "four score and seven," using imagery of birth, death, and resurrection to move from what "our fathers brought forth . . . a new nation, conceived in Liberty" and dedication to the principle that "all men are created equal" to the war itself. At the cemetery, said Lincoln, lay those "who here gave their lives that that nation might live." Lincoln paid honor to the Union dead, not praising their officers, not celebrating their victory, but claiming their sacrifice for the principles of the Declaration of Independence. At the same time, he emphasized that these men had died to preserve the nation, although the war previously had been fought for the Union. Subtly, Lincoln transformed a Union of states into a national union. That nation stood for "a new birth of freedom" based on "government of the people, by the people, for the people." Lincoln unified past, present, and future into an evocation of American mission. Today, the words of the Gettysburg Address and Lincoln's Second Inaugural Address are enshrined in the Lincoln Memorial in Washington, D.C.

BIBLIOGRAPHY

Kumhardt, Philip B., Jr. *A New Birth of Freedom: Lincoln at Gettysburg.* Boston: Little, Brown, 1983.

Warren, Louis A. *Lincoln's Gettysburg Declaration: "A New Birth of Freedom."* Fort Wayne, IN: Lincoln National Life Foundation, 1964.

Willis, Garry. *Lincoln at Gettysburg: The Words that Remade America.* New York: Simon & Schuster, 1992.

John Y. Simon

See also: **Lincoln, Abraham; Memorials and Monuments.**

GRANT, ULYSSES S.

(b. April 27, 1822; d. July 23, 1885) General; eighteenth president of the United States (1869–1877).

Ulysses S. Grant was born at Point Pleasant, Ohio, and became an officer in the U.S. Army after graduating from West Point in 1843. He was appointed by Abraham Lincoln in 1864 as commander in chief of the Union armies, and served as president of the United States from 1868 to 1876.

Grant's father was a tanner, an occupation his son was loath to take up. He was eager for a West Point education, and his father was also enthusiastic about it, especially after he showed some promise in mathematics and an interest in engineering during his early education. Civil engineers were in great demand, and Jesse Grant petitioned his congressman, Thomas Hamer, on his son's behalf.

At first, West Point was a disappointment. Grant found himself unexpectedly on the losing end of a class battle. He was an outsider. His parents were working people, and his classmates' were not—and they let him know it. Only later, living in such close proximity to his fellow cadets and under the difficult regimen of military orders, did Grant begin to revel in the camaraderie of the place and soften toward army life.

Grant graduated from West Point in 1843 and fought in the war with Mexico (1846–1848). He took part in most of the important battles, gaining valuable experience as an officer and serving with many of the men who would later become his allies and enemies. On leave in August 1848, Grant married Julia Dent, the sister of his West Point roommate.

But trouble followed. Separated from his wife and children by his military assignment and terribly lonely, Grant indulged his latent thirst for alcohol, and he soon attracted the unfavorable notice of his commanding officer. The details of what happened next are murky, but Grant resigned his commission in 1854. He was working in his father's leather shop in Galena, Illinois, when the nation's regional tensions over slavery exploded and the Civil War began.

A soldier at heart, Grant volunteered to serve in the Union army and was commissioned colonel of the 21st Illinois Volunteers. In 1861, he was promoted to brigadier general of volunteers and reassigned to Cairo, Illinois, a small river town in the southernmost part of the state. Not longer after, Grant engineered the first notable Union victories of the war, the capture of Fort Henry and Fort Donelson, in Tennessee. For this, President Lincoln made him a major general of the volunteer forces with which he served.

More victories followed. While other generals demurred, Grant favored direct action, even at the cost of greater casualties. In him, the North had found a commander willing to fight an ugly war on its own terms. In 1862 and 1863, after repeated frustrations, Grant employed ground forces and Union gunboats to take Vicksburg, Mississippi, by siege, cutting the Confederacy in half. In 1864, President Lincoln made him commander in chief of the Union armies and an act of Congress raised him to the rank of lieutenant general, a long-dormant rank.

So positioned, Grant was free to prosecute the war on his own terms. He surrounded himself with brilliant generals such as William Sherman, George Thomas, and Philip Sheridan. With considerable strategic skill, he directed the bloody and brutal wilderness campaign against the forces of Robert E. Lee. In 1865, he contrived to cut Lee's army off at Appomattox, Virginia, effectively ending the war. A year later, Grant was named full general.

In the chaos and divisiveness that followed the Civil War, the country turned to Grant for leadership. As it had once with George Washington and Andrew Jackson, the nation looked to its wartime leader to guide it through a difficult peace. Grant was perfect for the part. No American since George Washington had risen to such high rank within the military. Grant had defeated the Confederacy and rescued the Union. He was a hero. Grant served as secretary of war under President Andrew Johnson in 1867 and in 1868 was elected president.

Grant served two turbulent terms as president. His inexperience in politics was troublesome enough, but his tendency to remain doggedly loyal to his friends, regardless of their misdeeds, and his tendency to trust and admire the wealthy proved disastrous and aggravated an already difficult national moment. Scandals blossomed. Grant's friends deceived him for their own gain and escaped unscathed through Grant's tireless beneficence. In the legislature, the demands of big business ruled the day. Worse, much of the country was bitterly divided, in large part over Grant's decision to pursue the harsh Reconstruction plan advocated by Andrew Johnson and Abraham Lincoln's political opponents within the Republican Party. It was the disastrous continuation of a disastrous policy. A former combatant, Grant was all too-willing to view the conquered South as enemy territory, its inhabitants as adversaries. Still, much of the trouble with, indeed the ultimate failure of, Grant's reconstruction policies can be explained by the president's inability to act decisively in the face of rapidly developing circumstances. A see-saw policy of determination and resolution followed by apparent timidity and uncertainty served only to increase the nation's sense of confusion. Grant would strike hard in one instance, waver the next. To many observers in the North, Grant's reconstruction seemed feckless and ill-planned; to many enduring it in the South, it seemed reckless, arbitrary, even malicious. There, a great and abiding bitterness took shape and spread. It is unclear, as of this writing, if the wound created by that bitterness has entirely healed.

At the end of his second term, Grant retired to New York. Bankrupted by ill-advised business investments, he set about writing his memoirs to provide for his family. He died on July 23, 1885, of throat cancer. Among the mourners who attended his funeral were thousands of the

Ulysses S. Grant.

soldiers he had led so brilliantly during his nation's moment of greatest need.

BIBLIOGRAPHY

Carpenter, John. *Ulysses S. Grant.* New York: Twayne, 1970.

Scaturro, Frank. *President Grant Reconsidered.* Lanham, MD: University Press of America, 1998.

Simpson, Brooks D. *Ulysses S. Grant: Triumph over Adversity, 1822–1865.* Boston: Houghton Mifflin, 2000.

Laura M. Miller

See also: Reconstruction.

GREELEY, HORACE

(b. February 3, 1811; d. November 29, 1872) American journalist, editor, and political leader.

Newspaper editor Horace Greeley abhorred war. Greeley was one of the most widely read and best known Americans of his day. His life spanned the War of 1812, the Mexican War, and the American Civil War. The

Horace Greeley.

founding editor of the *New York Tribune* was an inveterate talker and writer who played a major role in transforming American liberty into American freedom in the years before 1860. Greeley's political language, inspired by the European republican revolutionaries of 1830 and 1848, transformed propertied liberty under the law into equal freedom for all, grounded in God's moral law. Freedom meant both rights guaranteed under the Constitution and the natural rights of all to land, association, and peace. He believed that war threatened both liberty and freedom in a republic.

The War of 1812 shaped Greeley's youth. Born in Amherst, New Hampshire, Greeley grew up in Vermont and New York and rose to eminence as a journeyman printer, then became founding editor of the *New Yorker* (1834) and finally the *New York Tribune* (1841). As a young man, Greeley listened to opponents of "Mr. Madison's War" and to Fourth of July speeches by Revolutionary War veterans. Greeley entered politics hating Andrew Jackson, Martin Van Buren and other "corrupt" Democrats, suspecting that Freemasons were taking over the country, and admiring Kentucky Senator Henry Clay. In time, he became a protectionist Whig (an anti-Democrat who favored higher tariffs to protect American industries) and then helped form and name the Republican Party in 1854. In New York, Greeley also be-

came a lifelong Universalist who believed that all people, not an elite, deserved Christ's salvation.

During the 1840s, Greeley campaigned vigorously for Whig candidates, both at the polls and in his newspaper. After the economic depression of 1837, he urged young unemployed men of eastern cities to take their families and "go West" to find land and employment; thousands did so. In 1840, he helped elect William Henry Harrison to the presidency. For a time, Greeley was a follower of French associationist Charles Fourier, both at Brook Farm near Boston and at the North American Phalanx in Red Bank, New Jersey (organizations large enough to support their own industries and social needs). Greeley was also Henry Thoreau's literary agent in New York for fifteen years. He gave Margaret Fuller her start as a literary editor and invited her to stay for a year in his home. He also became an opponent of slavery, but not an abolitionist.

Greeley opposed the Mexican War both because of his pacifist leanings (Greeley wanted to dismantle the U.S. army and navy) and because he believed territorial gains might extend slavery to the American West. In 1849, he supported the Free Soil Party's campaign against slavery in the territories. He also became a major spokesman for organized labor, especially printers, and for women's rights, but not suffrage.

Aside from serving out an unexpired term in Congress in 1849, Greeley never held elected office. But the weekly edition of his *Tribune* became the Bible of farmers and plain folk across the expanding country. He hired a group of militant young writers to staff the newspaper—Charles A. Dana, George Ripley, Margaret Fuller, Karl Marx (who survived in London for a decade on his *Tribune* articles), and Adam Gurovsky. He sharply opposed the Compromise of 1850, the Kansas Nebraska Act of 1854, the Dred Scott decision, and all other attempts to maintain slavery. In 1860, he helped nominate Lincoln by throwing the votes he had amassed for another candidate to the rail-splitter, largely in order to defeat Greeley's archenemy and former ally, William Seward of New York.

In 1861, Greeley opposed the Civil War and urged Lincoln to let the "erring sisters" of the Confederacy depart from the Union in peace. But once war came, he was staunchly supportive, hoping that it would become a war not simply to maintain the Union, but for the emancipation of the slaves. Some blamed Greeley and the *Tribune* for prematurely encouraging a Union defeat at Bull Run by running daily headlines urging "On to Richmond!" before federal troops were prepared. Greeley subsequently helped inspire Lincoln's Emancipation Proclamation with his widely read "Prayer of Twenty Million." He then tried to negotiate an end to the war with both foreign and Confederate representatives, much to Lincoln's chagrin.

After the war, Greeley urged amnesty and charity toward the South. He published a two volume history of the Civil War entitled *The American Conflict*. Subscriptions to his paper fell off, however, after Greeley helped put up bail money to free Jefferson Davis from prison in 1867. In 1872, Greeley ran for U.S. president as a candidate of both the Liberal Republican and Democratic Parties against Republican Ulysses S. Grant. He lost badly, and died shortly thereafter.

Horace Greeley hated war as much as he hated slavery. He was not a socialist, but a bourgeois utopian that cherished peaceful community where men and women were equally free to labor and prosper. He felt war threatened that prosperity and that freedom.

BIBLIOGRAPHY

Fahrney, Ralph Ray. *Horace Greeley and the* Tribune *in the Civil War*. Cedar Rapids, IA: Torch Press, 1936.

Greeley, Horace. *The American Conflict: A History of the Great Rebellion in the United States of America, 1860–1864*, 2 vols. Hartford, CT: O. D. Case & Co., 1864–1866.

Kirkland, Edward Chase, ed. *The Peacemakers of 1864*. New York: Macmillan, 1927.

Lunde, Erik S. *Horace Greeley*. Boston: Twayne, 1981.

Maihafer, Harry J. *The General and the Journalists: Ulysses S. Grant, Horace Greeley, and Charles Dana*. Washington DC and London: Brassey's, 1998.

Schulze, Suzanne. *Horace Greeley: A Bio-Bibliography*. New York: Greenwood Press, 1992.

Robert C. Williams

See also: **Emancipation Proclamation; Lincoln, Abraham; Newspapers and Magazines.**

GUADALUPE HIDALGO, TREATY OF

On February 2, 1848, representatives of the United States and Mexico signed the Treaty of Guadalupe Hidalgo, ending the war between those two countries that had begun two years earlier. This document ceded to the United States almost half of Mexico's national territory in exchange for a payment of fifteen million dollars. The discovery of gold in California a few weeks before the treaty was signed led to a massive western migration that changed the future of the country.

The Treaty of Guadalupe Hidalgo contained provisions promising to protect the civil rights of the more than one hundred thousand Mexicans who lived in the conquered territories. Their lands and ways of life, however, came under attack by the new settlers, and the treaty guarantees were largely ignored. This violation of the treaty fueled decades of conflict, especially over land. Furthermore, the acquisition of new territories intensified conflicts between northern and southern politicians over the extension of slavery. The Compromise of 1850, the Fugitive Slave Law, and the violence surrounding the idea of popular sovereignty, all of which were instrumental in bringing about the Civil War, all resulted from the incorporation of these new territories.

The war between the United States and Mexico broke out in May 1846. Though the causes of this conflict were many, the most important was the spirit of expansionism called manifest destiny. Thousands of Anglo-Americans believed that it was God's will that they should move west across the entire North American continent, occupying lands of Mexicans and Indians and casting their inhabitants aside in the process. For many, manifest destiny had an economic dimension, justifying a more efficient use of natural resources by the industrious Anglo-Americans. Mixed in with this economic motive was an attitude of racial superiority. As one American writer wrote, "The Mexicans are *Aboriginal Indians,* and they must share the destiny of their race."

Two articles in the treaty promised to protect the private property and provide eventual U.S. citizenship to those living on the land, but these provisions were often disregarded. In California, thousands of gold-rush migrants encroached on "Californio" land grants and demanded that something be done to free up the land so they could claim it. The result was the passage by Congress of the California Land Claims Act of 1851, which set up a three-person commission to adjudicate Mexican land grants in California. Eventually the commission confirmed most of the grants brought before it, but many Mexican landholders lost their land, for only the wealthy could afford the lengthy litigation process. The conflict over the land claims continued until the beginning of the twentieth century, leaving a bitter legacy that many have not forgotten. In the eyes of Mexico and the millions of Hispanos, Tejanos, and Chicanos now living in the United States, the promises made to them were ignored.

With the signing of the Treaty of Guadalupe Hidalgo, the U. S. government had vast lands open for westward expansion. One of the most difficult issues that emerged was the determination of whether these lands would be open to slavery. In 1846, foreseeing this problem, Congressman David Wilmot of Pennsylvania presented what became known as the Wilmot Proviso, urging that Congress prohibit the expansion of slavery into whatever territory the United States might acquire from the war. That bill did not pass, but the issue it raised exacerbated an enormous debate over the future of the American West. Many northerners were opposed to opening the land to slavery, feeling that it should be "free soil." They did not want to compete with slave labor or see southern states expand their power.

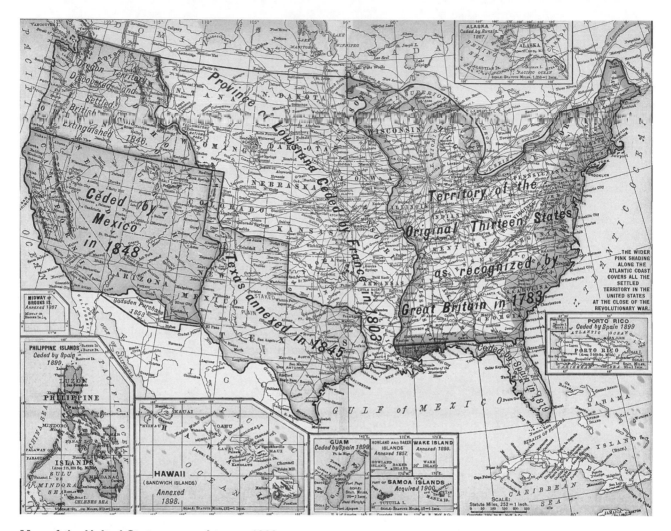

Map of the United States expansion, ca. 1900. © BETTMANN/CORBIS

Two years after the war ended, California petitioned for statehood, and the Senate had to grapple with the question of whether that state would be slave or free. The result of that debate was the Compromise of 1850. For the next decade, the U.S. government was in conflict over the issue of the expansion of slavery into the western lands. The Treaty of Guadalupe Hidalgo ending the War with Mexico fostered the internal war over slavery, which ultimately led to the outbreak of the Civil War.

BIBLIOGRAPHY

del Castillo, Richard. *The Treaty of Guadalupe Hidalgo: A Legacy of Conflict.* Norman: University of Oklahoma Press, 1990.

Merk, Frederick. *Manifest Destiny and Mission in American History, a Reinterpretation.* New York: Knopf, 1963.

Pletcher, David M. *The Diplomacy of Annexation: Texas, Oregon, and the Mexican War.* Columbia: University of Missouri Press, 1973.

Internet Resource

"Treaty of Guadalupe Hidalgo." Avalon Project at Yale Law School. Available from <http://www.yale.edu/lawweb/avalon/diplomacy/mexico/guadhida.htm>.

Richard Griswold del Castillo

See also: **Age of Westward Expansion; Compromise of 1850; Polk, James K.**

HOMESTEAD ACT

The Homestead Act of 1862 was one of three public-land acts advocated by the Republican Party and passed during the Civil War. Like the other two, the Land Grant Act and the Pacific Railway Act, this act had to await the secession of the Southern states before it could be enacted. Destined to draw large numbers of settlers to the West, an area that had proven itself resistant to slavery, the act was seen by the South as antithetical to its best interest.

The Homestead Act provided for free grants of up to 160 acres of contiguous, surveyed, unreserved public lands to bona fide settlers. To be eligible, an applicant had to be the head of a family or twenty-one years of age and a U.S. citizen, or an alien who had filed for citizenship. Women could qualify under the head-of-household provision. All applicants had to live on the homestead for five years and make certain improvements to gain title to the land.

Reflecting the passions of the time, however, the act initially disqualified a large segment of the American public from homesteading eligibility: those who "had borne arms against the United States Government or given aid and comfort to its enemies." This, of course, included nearly everyone in the Confederacy. On the other hand, it granted the favor of an age waiver to Union soldiers and sailors under the age of twenty-one.

The Homestead Act reflected the entrepreneurial, opportunity-promoting, and optimistic views of the new Republican Party, which stressed the importance of landownership. "I am in favor of cutting up the wild lands into parcels, so that every poor man may have a home," said Abraham Lincoln of the homestead proposal in 1861. Lincoln had earlier shared with Congress his belief that such settlement represented a "higher and more enduring interest" than simply selling the public lands to raise revenue. He attached sufficient enough importance to the act that he detailed its operation to Congress in his annual messages of 1863 and 1864.

From enactment until the 1930s, when homesteading virtually ended, some 250 million acres were claimed as homesteads. By nearly any measure, however, the Homestead Act fell short of its promises and expectations. It suffered from several inherent fallacies. Most Western land was not suited to the intensive agriculture envisioned by such limited-size grants, and rainfall was often inadequate for farming. The act required improvements and envisioned self-sustaining farms but did not

Homestead Act settlers outside a farmhouse in Custer Country, Nebraska, ca. 1870–1899. © BETTMANN/CORBIS

provide for operating capital; much of the better land had already been, and would continue to be, incorporated into farms, ranches, railroad land grants, and other claims. Land speculators and corporations took much of the land to advance their own interests.

The Homestead Act was historically significant nevertheless. Once the Civil War removed the South as an obstacle to opening the West, the act beckoned to settlers and enhanced the image of the West as a place of opportunity and adventure. It spawned numerous other homesteading measures, some offering up to 640 acres, during the next half-century. Its nod to women was startlingly progressive and portentous. Not to be overlooked, amendments to the act eased service members' procedures for getting land and applying their service time toward the residency requirement. These benefits were part of the federal government's practice, which extended through both world wars and the Cold War, of rewarding its military personnel with bonuses, grants, and other favors.

BIBLIOGRAPHY

Gates, Paul W. *History of Public Land Law Development.* Washington, DC: Government Printing Office, 1968.

Lindgren, H. Elaine. *Land in Her Own Name: Women as Homesteaders in North Dakota.* Norman: University of Oklahoma Press, 1996.

Robbins, Roy M. *Our Landed Heritage: The Public Domain, 1776–1936.* Lincoln: University of Nebraska Press, 1962.

Stanford J. Layton

See also: **Age of Westward Expansion; Farming.**

HUMOR, POLITICAL

Humor and politics, when combined, can be a powerful force. During a war, this intersection can serve several purposes: it can offer relief from serious and disturbing events; boost morale and patriotism in the civilian population; and ridicule the inhumanity, hypocrisy, vanity, stupidity, and other foibles that may be involved in the war. The war with Mexico and the Civil War provided an impetus for humor, and much of the comedy accurately mirrored the sentiments of the people.

THE MEXICAN WAR

Using a combination of caricature and captions, many of the Mexican War's political cartoons unsparingly ridiculed the enemy. A lithograph caricatured Mexican commander Santa Anna, accentuating his oversized head as he glared at the American forces. Another celebrated American optimism and hauteur by showing a man stepping across the Rio Grande River and with an enormous pair of scissors—one blade representing the regular army under General Zachary Taylor and the other blade the volunteers—preparing to cut a figure representing Mexico in two.

Humor was more rarely used to oppose American involvement in the Mexican War, but what there was of it generally shared the North's contention that the South was using the war as an opportunity to expand slavery. James Russell Lowell, who opposed the war for this reason, wrote *The Biglow Papers, First Series* (1846–1848), using versified letters in Yankee dialect from a New England farmer as his chief satiric weapon.

THE CIVIL WAR: NORTHERN HUMOR

The political humor of the Civil War era was extensive and increased the demand for cartoon illustrations. The illustrated weeklies that emerged in the 1850s and early 1860s, including *Harper's Weekly,* the *New York Illustrated News,* and *Southern Punch,* produced numerous cartoons soon after the war began. German-born Thomas Nast, the principal cartoonist of the era who was a loyal Republican and ardent champion of the Union, launched his career as an illustrator for *Harper's Weekly* in 1862, producing about sixty drawings during the course of the war. Nast's satiric illustrations, which savagely attacked the Confederacy and helped advance the Union cause, prompted Lincoln to praise him as the North's "best recruiting sergeant" (Vinson, p. 5). Nast's typical wartime drawings—such as "The War in the Border States," a portrait of a mother and her children grieving over a Union soldier husband-father killed by a Confederate sniper—derided the South and were more often bitter and searing than amusing. One of Nast's more satiric pieces, "Aid and Comfort to the Enemy," caricatured Confederate leaders, the beneficiaries of an irresponsible Northern press that often revealed too much about the Union army's war plans, thereby alerting the enemy's troops and giving the South an advantage.

In 1864, Nast temporarily shifted his attention to promoting President Lincoln's reelection by attacking Lincoln's political enemies, principally the promoters of the Copperhead peace movement. In "How Copperheads Obtain Their Votes," Nast depicted two Copperheads in a graveyard at night copying the name of a dead Union soldier onto a Democratic ballot. His cartoons helped Lincoln's reelection campaign in 1864 and promoted

Political cartoon caricaturing President Andrew Jackson, who is seen kicking a bureau full of miniature black men down a flight of stairs, in reference to his veto of the Freedmen's Bureau Bill. © BETTMANN/CORBIS

Grant's first bid for the presidency in 1868 as well as his reelection in 1872. Regarding Grant as the savior of the Union and as absolutely honest, Nast portrayed him in one cartoon as a bulldog guarding the public treasury.

Although Nast was the Union's major political humorist, other cartoonists contributed to the North's propaganda effort. A Currier and Ives lithograph disparaged the South's efforts to recruit troops, showing a recruitment office where disreputable men were being forced into the army. Notable in this drawing were a shabbily clad man being coerced to volunteer at bayonet point and a drunkard sitting against a wall while a dog urinated on him. Popular literary comedian David Ross Locke used the lecture circuit and newspaper columns to berate the Confederacy. Locke wrote his self-deprecating columns as Petroleum V. Nasby, a Confederate sympathizer living in the North. They took the form of letters characterized by misspellings, mispronunciations, and mangled grammar, starkly exposing Nasby's bigotry, cowardice, and opposition to freeing slaves.

THE CIVIL WAR: SOUTHERN HUMOR

The war caused ink and paper shortages in the South, and many engravers and lithographers were forced into producing currency, stamps, and other documents, but the Confederacy still used humor to promote its war effort, although much of it was inferior to Union humor. Adalbert J. Volke, a German-born Baltimore dentist, captured the sentiments and bolstered the morale of the Southerners, particularly in his mocking caricatures of Lincoln as a jester-puppeteer who managed the war poorly and in his depiction of Northern draft dodgers buying the services of substitutes. The engravings featured in the South's leading humor magazine *Southern Punch* not only mocked Lincoln as the Prince of Darkness abducting the Goddess of Liberty and General Grant as the "the master of ceremonies and and author of the dance of death" for a gala ball in Richmond (Piacentino, p. 258) but also disparaged Richmond extortionists and speculators who bought up scarce supplies of flour, sugar, clothing, and other basic necessities and resold them at exorbitant prices.

On the literary front, Charles Henry Smith, known as Bill Arp, the "mouthpiece of the southerner people" (Parker, p. 67), wrote dialect letters, many accurately reflecting the sentiments of Southerners on topics ranging from draft evaders, the behavior of Union combatants, and Lincoln—or as Arp called him, Abe Linkhorn.

AFTER THE CIVIL WAR

The Civil War disrupted society not only during the conflict but for years to come. The greed and corruption of politicians and new industrial leaders were, to a degree, a measure of the long-term social effects of the war. Nast waged his greatest assault against the greed and corruption of New York City's William Marcy "Boss" Tweed and Tammany Hall in this period, significantly enhancing his fame as a cartoonist. One of Nast's most famous and frequently reprinted cartoons graphically depicted a tiger destroying innocent, defenseless women representing the republic, and another showed Tweed and members of his ring standing in a circle, each pointing an accusing finger at the man standing next to him. Although Tweed admitted he did not care what the newspapers said about him because his constituents could not read, Nast's drawings contributed to his political demise.

Ephemeral and topical, negative and acerbic, hostile and satiric, intended to sway public opinion and to influence government actions, nineteenth-century American political humor, particularly the editorial cartoon, emerged as a formidable force during the turbulent years of the Civil War and the political instability of its aftermath. Of the cartoonists of the period, Thomas Nast—champion of the Union, maker of presidents, and despoiler of Boss Tweed—became the most effective purveyor of American political sentiment. Political humor had firmly established itself in American popular culture and political life.

BIBLIOGRAPHY

Anderson, George McCullough, ed. *The Work of Adalbert Johann Volck, 1828–1912.* Baltimore, MD: Privately printed by George McCullough Anderson, 1970.

Inge, M. Thomas and Dennis Hall, eds. *The Greenwood Guide to American Popular Culture.* Westport, CT: Greenwood, 2002.

Nevins, Allan, and Frank Weitenkampf. *A Century of Political Cartoons: Caricature in the United States from 1800 to 1900.* New York: Octagon, 1975.

Parker, David B. *Alias Bill Arp: Charles Henry Smith and the South's "Goodly Heritage."* Athens: University of Georgia Press, 1991.

Piacentino, Edward J. "Confederate Disciples of Momus." In *Studies in American Humor* 4, no. 4 New Series (1985–1986): 249–261.

Reilly, Bernard F., Jr. *American Political Prints, 1776–1876: A Catalog of the Collections in the Library of Congress.* Boston, MA: G.K. Hall, 1991.

Smith, Kristin M. *The Lines Are Drawn: Political Cartoons of the Civil War.* Athens, GA: Hill Street, 1999.

Vinson, J. Chad. *Thomas Nast: Political Cartoonist.* Athens: University of Georgia Press, 1967.

Edward Piacentino

See also: **Newspapers and Magazines.**

IMMIGRANTS AND IMMIGRATION

American wars have provided both opportunities and difficulties for immigrants. On the one hand, conflict has given immigrants a chance to demonstrate their loyalty to the United States. On the other hand, immigrants have faced problems when hostilities arise between the United States and their native country or when, for various reasons, American citizens suspect that their immigrant neighbors do not fully support the military effort.

In the nineteenth century America's first major immigrant groups, the Irish and the Germans, faced this dilemma. The Irish arrived in large numbers after the end of the War of 1812. The Great Potato Famine of 1845 to 1849 brought the number of Irish in the United States to 1.6 million by 1860. These Irish were overwhelmingly Catholic and often poor. They lived in the worst neighborhoods, did the least desirable work, and were overrepresented in prison, insane asylums, and poorhouse populations. Large-scale German immigration began with the failed 1848 revolutions in Europe. By 1860, Germans numbered about 1.3 million. Although not as poor or socially disruptive as the Irish, many of them harbored radical political tendencies that made many Americans nervous. A number of Americans responded negatively to Irish, German, and other immigrants. In the 1850s some organized secret fraternal organizations and then a political party, the American Party, more commonly known as the Know Nothings. Its members called for extending the naturalization waiting-period from five to twenty-one years.

The Irish first faced the challenge of the disruptive effects of war when the United States fought Mexico in 1846. Mexico was a Catholic country, and some critics wondered if the Irish would support such a war. When about fifty Irish soldiers already in the regular army (along with another ninety soldiers from eleven other countries) deserted to the Mexican army and formed the San Patricio (St. Patrick) Battalion, many Irish in the United States were shocked and felt vulnerable to accusations of being unpatriotic. Irish and Irish American politicians tried to distract attention from the "traitorous" San Patricios with the performance of loyal Irish units and prominent generals such as General Stephen Kearney. The Mexican war left a mixed impression of immigrant loyalty in American conflicts.

CIVIL WAR

The Civil War gave another chance for immigrants to prove themselves. Both the Union and Confederate au-

Immigrants arriving in New York City in the early 1890s. AP/WIDE WORLD PHOTOS

thorities recruited foreign units into their ranks. Irish and German companies were prominent in both armies, but other immigrants including the British, Italian, Spanish, Mexican, and Polish also served in "foreign legions." These units generally had a reputation for tough fighting but also for high desertion rates. The actions of recent immigrants on the home front also challenged their efforts to gain acceptance as patriotic citizens. In particular, the New York City draft riots of 1863 destroyed the trustworthiness of the Irish in many Americans' eyes. In the Confederacy, it was the Germans who raised native ire because many favored the abolition of slavery. In Texas, Confederates executed a number of Germans whom they suspected of being "traitors."

Despite their disputed record in the Civil War, immigrant advocates spent the postwar decades defending the loyalty of ethnic soldiers. According to their story, they had fought as hard as native soldiers and had proved their loyalty to the United States. Using veterans' magazines and memoirs, immigrant soldiers managed to recreate their record into a wholly positive one. The latter half of the nineteenth century, however, saw an influx of new immigrants who, again, would be seen as foreign and suspect. The new migrants did not come primarily from western and northern Europe but rather, in growing numbers, from southern and eastern Europe and Asia. Italians, Poles, Russians (predominantly Jewish), Mexicans, and Chinese flooded the United States between 1865 and 1920. These new groups tended to live in ghettoes and retained their distinctive languages and cultures. The presence of large numbers of foreigners in American cities who, unlike the Irish for example, were dark-skinned or Asian and did not speak English, worried many natives. As a result of this influx, the government began to restrict immigration. In 1882 the U.S. Congress prohibited Chinese immigration, the first foreigners to be targeted in this manner.

IMPERIALISM

The call of imperialists, such as the British writer Rudyard Kipling, for the advanced nations to take up the

"White Man's burden" to civilize "backward" peoples only increased racial tensions. The propaganda of the Spanish American War in 1898 was virulently anti-Hispanic. The resulting takeover of the colonies of Cuba and the Philippines after the U.S. victory over Spain only increased the use of racist justifications for government policies. As an imperial power, the United States began to emphasize the need for national unity by condemning what President Woodrow Wilson described as "hyphenated Americanism." This attitude reached its height in the anti-German hysteria of World War I and the immigration acts of 1921 and 1924. In this legislation the federal government established national quota systems to preserve the racial composition of the country, discriminating particularly against southern and eastern European and Asian immigrants.

Though a nation of immigrants since the initial settlement, the United States has always dealt with complex issues surrounding immigrants. Their presence has created a strong nation of enormous diversity but also fostered negative responses from those who preceded them, as well as tensions among various immigrant groups as they vie for their place in this country. Americans at war have tended to be intolerant toward immigrants. War has often brought out the best in American society; but it has also revealed the nativist tendencies in American culture. Although wartime patriotic feelings serve the nation by binding the people in a common cause, those same feelings have legitimated persecution of immigrants.

BIBLIOGRAPHY

De Leon, Arnoldo. *They Called Them Greasers: Anglo Attitudes toward Mexicans in Texas, 1821–1900.* Austin: University of Texas Press, 1983.

Bodnar, John. *The Transplanted: A History of Immigrants in Urban America.* Bloomington: Indiana University Press, 1985.

Chang, Iris. *The Chinese in America: A Narrative History.* New York: Penguin/Viking, 2003.

Gleeson, David T. *The Irish in the South, 1815–1877.* Chapel Hill: University of North Carolina Press, 2001.

Goldscheider, Calvin, and Goldstein, Sidney. *Jewish Americans: Three Generations in a Jewish Community.* Englewood Cliffs, NJ: Prentice Hall, 1968.

Horsman, Reginald. *Race and Manifest Destiny: The Origins of American Anglo-Saxonism.* Cambridge, MA: Harvard University Press, 1981.

Kenny, Kevin. *The American Irish.* New York: Pearson-Longman, 2000.

David T. Gleeson

See also: **Farming; New York City Draft Riots; Railroads; Urbanization.**

INDIAN REMOVAL AND RESPONSE

The incursion of European imperial powers into North America initiated an almost relentless assault on American Indian territorial claims and prompted military conflicts that continued until near the end of the nineteenth century. Most of the American Indian wars began with increased tensions caused by European or American encroachment onto tribal territories; the hostilities usually resulted in disastrous defeats for the tribes and the confiscation of their land.

REVOLUTIONARY ERA

A widespread pattern of encroachment, unrest, war, and dispossession prevailed throughout the colonial and revolutionary periods. After the Revolutionary War, the Continental Congress informed American Indian tribes that the United States had acquired dominion over their people and lands. The westward movement of settlers across the Appalachians and Alleghenies into American Indian country antagonized tribes along the United States' western frontier. In an attempt to foster peace with its American Indian neighbors, the Continental Congress negotiated a series of treaties with various tribes, ceding land to the United States. In 1787 Congress passed the Northwest Ordinance, which provided an orderly process for the organization, survey, and sale of land between the Ohio and Mississippi rivers. The legislation promised that the United States would recognize the rights of the American Indian tribes of the region and treat them with "utmost good faith."

During George Washington's presidency, Henry Knox, the secretary of war, implemented a policy in which the United States recognized the sovereignty of the tribes and paid for tribal cessions. Knox also instituted a "civilization program" designed to prepare American Indian people for their assimilation. Native political and spiritual leaders rejected this indoctrination and forged alliances to confront the expanding influence of Anglo-American culture and the predatory encroachments of American settlers. The United States responded to these uprisings with military force and used the wars that resulted to seize tribal land.

FORCED REMOVAL AND THE "TRAIL OF TEARS" (1803–1842)

In 1803, Thomas Jefferson's administration concluded the Louisiana Purchase and began encouraging tribes in the East to surrender their land and migrate to the newly acquired territory. While most tribes rejected Jefferson's entreaties, between 1808 and 1820 a few thousand Cherokees moved westward beyond the Mississippi River. In the War of 1812, the United States destroyed

★★★

WOUNDED KNEE

The Wounded Knee Massacre in 1890 effectively ended Native American resistance to the encroachment of white invaders on the North American continent.

Toward the end of the nineteenth century, most Native Americans knew that the Wasichu, or invading whites of European heritage, were too powerful to defeat by conventional means. By the 1880s Native tribes were largely sequestered on reservations managed by the Indian Bureau of the United States government. Some Plains tribes followed traditional nomadic ways and were dealt with—confined to reservations or wiped out—as they came into contact or conflict with government interests.

A millennial religious movement, The Ghost Dance, spread among the remaining Plains tribes, beginning with a Paiute holy man named Wovoka. The Ghost Dance was believed to have the power to defeat the foreign invaders, bring back the buffalo, and restore the Sioux nation. Unlike most Sioux rituals, it was practiced by women as well as men, and was unaccompanied by music. It consisted of slow dancing and chanting, often

for days. Adherents believed that while they were dancing, they would be taken up while new earth, plants, and animals covered the invading Wasichu. They would be returned to an earth that was free of the depredations of the white invaders.

As with many Native American rituals, The Ghost Dance was pronounced illegal by the American government. Its practice was forbidden. Still, a few Sioux continued to practice the ritual. Indian Bureau agents blamed Sitting Bull for the movement, and he was killed in the course of a bungled arrest attempt on December 15. The Sioux who had followed Sitting Bull and Crazy Horse, and the practitioners of the outlawed millennial religion, sought to escape arrest, death, or a forced march to a reservation by fleeing south through the Dakota Badlands. These people, about 300 men, women, and children, were massacred by American Army troops—members of the Seventh Cavalry that had once been led by George Custer—on the snow-covered banks of Wounded Knee Creek (Cankpe Opi Wakpala) on December 19, 1890.

---

two major Native American forces and eliminated the possibility of successful American Indian resistance in the East. In the Old Northwest, the United States crushed a major pan-American Indian uprising at the Battle of the Thames (1813) and killed Tecumseh, the leader of the Native resistance. In the South, American forces put down a nativist Creek revolt at Horseshoe Bend (1814). After the battle, General Andrew Jackson forced the Creeks to surrender over twenty million acres of their national territory. Soon after the war, Jackson urged President James Monroe to abandon the policy of recognizing American Indian title and sovereignty and adopt Jefferson's idea of relocating eastern tribes. From that point forward, the southern states, led by Georgia, began pushing the federal government to remove the tribes. In 1828 Jackson was elected president; in 1830, Congress passed the Indian Removal Act, which authorized the president to negotiate cession and removal treaties with the Indian nations in the East.

The state of Georgia had moved to extend its jurisdiction over the Cherokee Nation even before the adoption of the Removal Act. The Cherokees filed suit to enjoin Georgia's attempt to expropriate their land. Al-

though the United States Supreme Court declared that the Cherokees comprised a sovereign nation possessing a right to their territory in *Worcester v. Georgia* (1832), Jackson and Congress refused to enforce the decision. In 1835 a dissident faction of Cherokees signed a treaty (New Echota) in which they putatively ceded their nation's lands and pledged that their people would remove to the "Indian Territory" Congress had established west of the Mississippi River. In 1838 the U.S. Army rounded up almost all the Cherokees and marched them along the "Trail of Tears" to their new home.

One nation, the Seminoles, opposed removal by force. In 1835 their warriors began attacking settlements and plantations in Florida. The United States sent troops to put down the uprising and resorted to ruthless tactics to subjugate the Seminoles, including the capture of Seminole leader Osceola under a flag of truce. Finally, in 1842, the United States Army captured all but a few hundred Seminoles and relocated them to the Indian Territory.

Along with expelling all five of the major Southeastern nations, the United States also removed most of the remaining American Indians in the North. Although

Yellow Bird, a Miniconjou Sioux medicine man, laying dead on the Wounded Knee battlefield, 1861.

tribal representatives had ceded their territory in Illinois to the United States, many of the Sauk and Fox tribes, led by a warrior named Black Hawk, refused to recognize the legitimacy of the removal agreement. When Black Hawk's followers moved back onto land ceded under the treaty, white settlers called for assistance. In 1831 to 1832, United States troops and Illinois volunteers defeated Black Hawk's forces and forced the Sauks and Foxes out of the state. In 1843 the United States War Department estimated that it had removed almost 90,000 American Indians to the West. Many more died on their journey west. It is estimated that over 4,000 (as many as a quarter) of the Cherokees, for instance, died on the "Trail of Tears."

WAR AND RESERVATIONS (1843–1865)

Even before the completion of the Removal, thousands of Euro-Americans began moving westward across the Mississippi in search of a new life or cheap land. The acquisition of western lands from Mexico in 1848 at the

end of the Mexican-American War, and the discovery of gold in California in 1848, along with other valuable ores throughout the West, prompted thousands of Americans to journey across the continent on the Oregon, Santa Fe, Mormon, and Bozeman trails. While most Native Americans maintained peaceful relations with the migrants, many American Indians became embittered by the seemingly endless streams of white people who traversed their lands and killed their game. Animosities between whites and American Indians spread over the West, and the period between 1850 and 1890 was marked by scores of conflicts between Native Americans on one side and the United States Army, or civilian militias, on the other.

In the 1850s the United States government moved to protect its citizens and its railroad interests. The government established forts throughout the West and along the overland trails and used them as strategic locations to conduct operations against hostile tribes. The federal strategy was to defeat a tribe, force it to cede territory, and isolate tribal members onto a "reservation," a portion of land reserved to the tribe. For example, in 1854 federal troops killed or captured over 100 Brule Sioux at the Battle of Blue Water and forced them to sign a treaty at Fort Pierre. American forces also defeated Cheyenne warriors at Solomon Fork in Kansas in 1857 and engaged various groups of Kiowas, Comanches, Apaches, and Navajos in ~~~~~~~~~~~ and Texas and New Mexico between 1855 and 1861. In California, the U.S. Army and groups of marauding miners destroyed American Indian resistance to trespasses into their territory. In the Oregon and Washington territories, a general American Indian rebellion of over a dozen tribes threatened federal control over the region. In several wars between 1855 and 1858, the U.S. Army defeated the recalcitrant tribes and moved them to reservations. In all, according to federal military records, the Army fought 160 actions against American Indians between 1848 and 1860, suffered close to 500 casualties, and killed, wounded, or captured almost 700 Native people.

Conflict between the United States and the American Indian tribes did not abate during the Civil War. In 1862 the Santee Sioux attacked settlements and forts in Minnesota. After killing perhaps as many as 800 whites, they were put down by a combined force of army regulars and state militia. A military commission sentenced 303 of the Sioux to death; President Abraham Lincoln stayed all but thirty-eight of the executions. The United States ordered the remainder of the tribe to a reservation in the Dakotas. In 1864 a major conflict broke out between white miners and Arapaho and Cheyenne Indians in eastern Colorado. Colorado militia under Major Chivington attacked an American Indian encampment at Sand Creek and massacred over 200 American Indians, most of them women and children. In 1868, over one hundred of those who escaped the Sand Creek attack, including their leader Black Kettle, were slaughtered at the Washita River by federal troops under Colonel George A. Custer. The United States also defeated the Navajos in 1864 and forced 8,000 of their people to take the "Long Walk" across New Mexico to a reservation. Federal troops also sent the Utes, Bannocks, Northern Shoshones, and Northern Paiutes to reservations during the Civil War. The Civil War also pulled the nations living in the American Indian Territory into the conflict; after the war, the Cherokees, Creeks, Chickasaws, Choctaws, and Seminoles were forced to surrender territory and free their slaves as the price of renewing peaceful relations with the United States.

FINAL SUBJUGATION (1866–1890)
After the Civil War, the United States Army campaigned relentlessly to extinguish the American Indian military threat in the West. In 1871 Congress ended its policy of treating with the American Indian nations. By 1875 the army had eliminated Kiowa and Comanche resistance in the southern Plains in the Red River War. When gold was discovered in the Black Hills of the Dakota Territory, thousands of miners flooded into the sacred American Indian land. In 1875 the Sioux left the reservation they had been forced to occupy in the Fort Laramie Treaty of 1868. When the United States ordered them back, large groups of warriors gathered in Montana under the leadership of several prominent leaders, including Sitting Bull and Crazy Horse. Custer's Seventh Cavalry located and attacked the American Indian encampment at the Little Bighorn River in 1876. The American Indian force killed Custer and annihilated his troops. By 1881, however, the United States had forced them back to their reservations. Crazy Horse and Sitting Bull were subsequently killed by American Indian reservation police. In 1890 the Seventh Cavalry massacred over 200 Sioux men, women, and children who were participating in a religious ritual, Wovoka's Ghost Dance, at Wounded Knee, South Dakota. Wounded Knee was the last major conflict between the Plains tribes and the United States Army.

The United States also stamped out American Indian resistance in the Pacific Northwest. In 1877 the federal government ordered the Nez Perce to surrender their lands and move to a reservation. Chief Joseph, the leader of the Nez Perce, led his people on a dramatic 1,700 mile campaign toward Canada before they were captured and temporarily relocated to the American Indian Territory. In the Southwest, after ten years of sporadic warfare under the leadership of Cochise, Victorio, and Geronimo, the diminished and demoralized Apaches surrendered and retired to a reservation.

LEGACY
According to federal records, between 1866 and 1890 the United States Army engaged in 1,040 combat actions against American Indian opponents. In that time, the army experienced some 2,000 casualties and killed over 4,000 American Indians, wounded close to 1,300, and captured over 10,000 more. With the military subjugation of the western American Indians, federal policy makers, at the prompting of Christian philanthropists, moved to abolish the tribal form of government, communal landholding, and American Indian culture. In the Dawes Severalty Act of 1887, Congress established a process to divide tribal lands into homestead tracts and allot them to individual heads of households. In many cases, American Indians were defrauded out of their allotments and left destitute. In encouraging assimilation, the federal government also forced many American Indian children to attend boarding schools, like the Carlisle Indian School, designed to erase the child's tribal influence and inculcate Anglo-American mores.

By the end of the nineteenth century, the collective populations of the American Indian nations had been reduced by perhaps as much as 90 percent since the arrival of Europeans to North America. The American Indian nations had been forced to surrender almost all of their land, and most Native Americans had been forced onto reservations where they typically lived in poverty without any of the rights possessed by white Americans of the time. Not until 1934 would American Indians be offered the opportunity to become citizens of this country and receive full voting rights. They still struggle with poverty, poor health, and land ownership.

BIBLIOGRAPHY

Dowd, Gregory Evans. *A Spirited Resistance: The North American Indian Struggle for Unity, 1745–1815*. Baltimore, MD: Johns Hopkins University Press, 1992.

Garrison, Tim Alan. *The Legal Ideology of Removal: The Southern Judiciary and the Sovereignty of Native American Nations*. Athens: University of Georgia, 2002.

Jackson, Donald, ed. *Black Hawk: An Autobiography*. Urbana and Chicago: University of Illinois Press, 1955.

Jennings, Francis. *The Invasion of America: Indians, Colonialism, and the Cant of Conquest*. Chapel Hill: University of North Carolina Press, 1975.

Leach, Douglas Edward. *The Northern Colonial Frontier, 1607–1763*. New York: Holt, Rinehart and Winston, 1966.

Prucha, Francis Paul. *The Great Father: The United States Government and the American Indians*. Lincoln: University of Nebraska Press, 1984.

Robinson, W. Stitt. *The Southern Colonial Frontier, 1607–1763*. Albuquerque: University of New Mexico Press, 1979.

Trennert, Robert A., Jr. *Alternative to Extinction: Federal Indian Policy and the Beginnings of the Reservation System, 1846–1851*. Philadelphia, PA: Temple University Press, 1975.

Utley, Robert M. *Frontiersmen in Blue: The United States Army and the Indian, 1848–1865*. New York: Macmillan, 1967.

Utley, Robert M. *Frontier Regulars: The United States Army and the Indians, 1866–1891*. New York: Macmillan, 1973.

Washburn, Wilcomb E., ed. *Handbook of North American Indians: Volume 4, History of Indian-White Relations*. Washington, D.C.: Smithsonian Institution, 1988.

Wilson, James. *The Earth Shall Weep: A History of Native America*. New York: Grove Press, 1998.

Tim Alan Garrison

See also: **Dawes Severalty Act; Transcontinental Railroad.**

JACKSON, THOMAS J. (STONEWALL)

(b. January 21, 1824; d. May 10, 1863) Confederate general.

Thomas Jackson was one of the South's most important generals in the Civil War, a man who became an icon of the Southern fighting spirit and the "Lost Cause."

Born in what is now West Virginia, Jackson was only two years old when his father, an attorney, contracted typhoid fever and died. Now a widow, Jackson's mother, Julia, was saddled with the family's considerable debt. In 1830, she married Blake Woodson, a shabby genteel man with numerous children scattered across the country, who was fifteen years her senior. Refined and charming in public, in private he was a hard man who detested Julia's children. They were soon sent away to live with various relatives.

Despite a less than rigorous early education, Jackson was admitted to West Point in 1842, but only after his congressman's first choice for an appointment had failed there. Academy life proved difficult for Jackson. His classmates, keenly aware of his modest upbringing, ridiculed him as "Tom Fool" and, because he was older than many of the other entering cadets, as "Old Tom." Still, he was a hard worker, and he learned the workings of the academy better than almost anyone else, developing a sense of discipline and self-containment that served him well during the difficult and dangerous years ahead. He finished his entire junior year without earning even one demerit, at an institution where demerits were passed out with a liberality bordering on zeal. When he graduated in 1846, he ranked seventeenth out of fifty-nine men in his class.

After serving with distinction in the War with Mexico (1846–1848), Jackson was offered and accepted a teaching position at the Virginia Military Institute. In 1852, he resigned his army commission, but he returned to active service at the outbreak of the Civil War. After a short stint at Harpers Ferry, Jackson was made a Confederate brigadier general. During the first Battle of Bull Run in the summer of 1861, Jackson earned his well-known nickname by standing pat against surging Union forces. Jackson's fame quickly spread (his division shared the nom de guerre "Stonewall," the only Confederate division to adopt such a name as its official designation), and he was subsequently promoted to divisional command.

Success bred further success. Jackson led brilliantly during the so-called Shenandoah Valley campaign of

Lieutenant General Thomas Jonathan "Stonewall" Jackson.

soldier to a position of authority, and, when questioned about his decision, replied that the man, being widely disliked, would have no reason to offer biased or inaccurate reports. If anything, however, these quirks of character served only to increase Jackson's celebrity.

It was at the height of this fame that the unexpected occurred. On May 2, 1863, during the Battle of Chancellorsville, Jackson's forces outflanked Union forces and forced them to withdraw. It was a great victory, perhaps Jackson's best. Then came darkness and, with it, misadventure. Returning from reconnaissance, he and his party had the misfortune of being mistaken by his own men for enemy riders. Jackson was struck three times, leading to the amputation of an arm. Eight days later, on May 10, 1863, Thomas Jackson died. It was a grievous blow to the Confederate cause and the entire Southern nation mourned his loss.

Of this masterful strategist and leader, no less a figure than Robert E. Lee later wrote, "He has lost his left arm; but I have lost my right arm." Jackson is widely admired in the South even today as a strategist and gentleman, the very picture of Southern fortitude and character.

BIBLIOGRAPHY

Farwell, Byron. *Stonewall: A Biography of General Thomas J. Jackson.* New York: W.W. Norton, 1992.

Krick, Robert K. *Stonewall Jackson at Cedar Mountain.* Chapel Hill: University of North Carolina Press, 1990.

Robertson, James I. *Stonewall Jackson: The Man, the Soldier, the Legend.* New York: Macmillan, 1997.

Tate, Allen. *Stonewall Jackson, The Good Soldier.* Nashville, TN: J. S. Sanders & Company, 1991.

Laura M. Miller

See also: **Lee, Robert E; Lost Cause.**

early 1862, using tactics that are still studied today. Employing surprise maneuvers and rapid marching, he was able to overcome Union forces that vastly outnumbered his own Confederate troops and claim victory. By doing so, he and Robert E. Lee were able to save the Shenandoah Valley at that point and keep Union troops from threatening the Confederate capital at Richmond. He fought effectively at Fredericksburg, Antietam, and the second Battle of Bull Run.

Jackson seems to have been that rare type of commander who was both respected and trusted by his superiors and also loved by the soldiers who served under him. That he was capable of unusual and inexplicable behavior is beyond dispute. His supposed passion for sucking on lemons has been overstated to the point of absurdity, and yet there was something of the eccentric in him. His penchant for responding with apparent non-sequiturs and verbal filler to both good news and bad is widely reported. Stalwartly religious, Jackson regretted fighting on Sunday, and always waited until Monday to post correspondence. He once promoted an unpopular

JOHNSON, ANDREW

(b. December 29, 1808; d. July 31, 1875) Seventeenth president of the United States (1865–1869); first chief executive to be impeached.

Andrew Johnson, a native of Raleigh, North Carolina, grew up in impoverished circumstances. In 1826, he and his family moved to Greeneville, Tennessee, where he opened a tailor shop. It was his wife, Eliza McCardle, whom he married the following year, who taught him to read and write. He took an interest in politics and proved an effective stump speaker. Beginning in 1828, he held public offices, including alderman, mayor, state representative, state senator, and U.S. congressman. He was elected governor of Tennessee in 1853 and four years later was elected to the U.S. Senate. Although he defended slavery, he supported the Union and refused to leave the Senate when the Civil War broke out in 1861.

Lincoln initially rewarded Johnson's loyalty by appointing him military governor of Tennessee after federal forces occupied Nashville in February 1862. During the next two years, Johnson actively supported most of Lincoln's wartime policies, including emancipation, and made at least one well-received speaking tour of the North. Lincoln chose him as his running mate for the 1864 campaign as an affirmation of the sectional unity promoted by the Republican Party's National Union platform.

Lincoln's assassination thrust Johnson into a role he was ill-prepared to play, despite his previous experience. Johnson was a stump speaker with a quick temper and strong prejudices, including a clear bias against any expansion of federal power. As president, he began well, putting aside his own initial demands for postwar vengeance against the South to issue plans for amnesty and political reconstruction that mirrored those developed by Lincoln. Controversy ignited because he did not consult with Congress but relied instead on white Southern leaders to establish loyal governments and comply with federal initiatives such as the Thirteenth Amendment. When some of the Southern conventions, and the provisional governors he had appointed, ignored his requests concerning the endorsement of emancipation and the repudiation of secession and the Confederate debt, Johnson angered congressional leaders, especially the Republicans, by not quashing their defiance. Instead, he issued pardons liberally, insisted that federal reconstruction was not needed because the South had never left the Union, and declared Reconstruction officially over in April 1866.

Congress counterattacked, beginning in December 1865 with a refusal to seat the new members from the South. In early 1866, Congress overrode Johnson's vetoes of bills to protect civil rights and continue the Freedmen's Bureau, both of which he opposed as unwarranted assertions of federal power. Congress also passed the Fourteenth Amendment, prompting Johnson to undertake a speaking tour to persuade Northern voters to replace the radical Republicans who opposed him. Instead of being defeated, radical Republicans won two-thirds of the seats in Congress. They passed the Reconstruction Acts in 1867, placing ten of the eleven former Confederate states under military rule (Tennessee was excluded because it had already ratified the Fourteenth Amendment). Many Southern leaders were subsequently removed, and new state conventions adopted constitutions and reforms that were more amenable to Republican leaders.

Andrew Johnson.

Johnson attempted to use his authority as commander in chief to limit Reconstruction. When Secretary of War Edwin M. Stanton refused his orders, Johnson dismissed him in deliberate defiance of the Tenure of Office Act, which, like the Reconstruction Acts, Congress had passed over his veto in 1867. The House of Representatives impeached Johnson on eleven counts, the most damaging of which focused on the Tenure of Office Act. Tried by the Senate, he was acquitted by a margin of one when seven Republicans voted against a conviction. His victory proved hollow, however, because he retained almost no control over Reconstruction other than the power to issue pardons. This he continued to do through December 25, 1868, when he extended executive clemency to all former Confederates.

No faction seriously considered nominating Johnson for the presidential race in 1868, despite accomplishments that included the acquisition of Alaska, and he retired to his home in Greeneville, Tennessee. He campaigned unsuccessfully for the United States Senate and the House of Representatives in 1869 and 1872 respectively, and served one term as senator, starting in 1875. Not fully recovered from an attack of Asiatic cholera two years earlier, he suffered a stroke and died at his daughter's home in Elizabethton, Tennessee, on July 31, 1875.

BIBLIOGRAPHY

Bergeron, Paul H.; Graf, LeRoy P.; and Haskins, Ralph W., eds. *The Papers of Andrew Johnson.* Knoxville: University of Tennessee Press, 1967–2000.

McCaslin, Richard B., comp. *Andrew Johnson: A Bibliography.* Westport, CT: Greenwood, 1992.

McKitrick, Eric L. *Andrew Johnson and Reconstruction.* Chicago: University of Chicago Press, 1960.

Trefousse, Hans L. *Andrew Johnson: A Biography.* New York: Norton, 1989.

Winston, Robert W. *Andrew Johnson, Plebeian and Patriot.* New York: Henry Holt, 1928.

Richard B. McCaslin

See also: **Constitutional Amendments and Changes; Lincoln, Abraham; Reconstruction.**

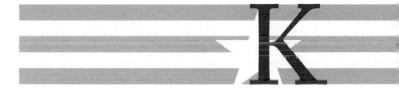

KANSAS NEBRASKA ACT

The Kansas Nebraska-act of 1854 both grew out of and contributed to the sectional crisis of the 1850s that ultimately led to war in 1861. This crisis pitted supporters of the extension of the slavery against those who sought slavery's restriction. Following the Compromise of 1850, which left extremists of North and South without grounds for anti and proslavery agitation, most Americans proclaimed an end—"a finality"—to the conflict over the extension of slavery. Reality was somewhat more troubling. There was never a majority in Congress in 1850 that favored a comprehensive settlement of the slavery extension issue. Both the Whig and Democratic parties suffered from sharp internal differences over the meaning of the Compromise. By the 1852 presidential election, the two-party system was fragmented and weakened. The Democrats won a convincing victory in the electoral college, essentially ending the political viability of the Whig Party; but Franklin Pierce, the newly elected president, won the popular vote by only 1.6 percent of three million votes cast. More ominously, as measured against the number of eligible voters, turnout sank to its lowest level since 1836.

Pierce quickly proved himself to be an inept president, unable to resuscitate Democratic unity. In the absence of effective political leadership, Senator Stephen A. Douglas, representing the "Young America" wing of the Democratic Party, took it upon himself to reassert his party's basic political tenets and, in the bargain, reinvigorate the democracy. To that end, his Kansas Nebraska bill, which sought to organize the lands west of Iowa and Missouri, combined the ideas of westward expansion, internal improvements (including a transcontinental railroad), and popular sovereignty. Douglas, in need of Southerners' support and believing that the Compromise of 1850 embraced a policy of government nonintervention into the practice of slavery in the territories, wrote the principle of popular sovereignty into the bill. Popular sovereignty meant that people living in the territories could determine if their territory would allow the presence of slaves or whether the area would be reserved for free labor. The bill thus repealed the Missouri Compromise (1820) and its ban on slavery north of the latitude 36°30'.

Douglas was excoriated by Northerners for repealing this ban on slavery extension. Many party members believed popular sovereignty was consistent with the

Democrats' commitment to nonintervention, limited government, and local self-governance. But, joined as it was to the repeal of the Missouri Compromise, popular sovereignty, in the eyes of Northern Democrats and Whigs, was not a reaffirmation of Democratic principles but a provocative and hostile initiative that increased the power of slavery.

Worse, although the people of Kansas were free to regulate their domestic institutions in their own way, the act failed to state when citizens could decide the status of slavery in their territory. This contributed to a real sense of urgency, on the part of both Northerners and Southerners, to settle the territory with "right-minded settlers" and thus seize political control of it. Subsequent to the act, widespread voting irregularities in Kansas gave way to armed conflict between free- and slave-state settlers. Rival governments were established at Topeka (free) and Lecompton (proslavery). "Bleeding Kansas" proved to a majority of Northerners and many Southerners that popular sovereignty was not an acceptable middle ground between the sectional extremes of slavery restriction and extension. Politically it destroyed the ascendancy of the Democrats in the North: in the off-year elections following the passage of the act, the party was able to save only twenty-five of ninety-one free-state seats it had won in 1852. The effect, not the intent, of the act was to upset the balance of power within the Democratic Party and thus weaken a powerful voice of nationalism in a period of growing sectional animosity. The act also contributed to the end of the Whig Party and to the rise of the Republican Party, which based its appeal on repealing the Kansas Nebraska act and halting the spread of slavery unleashed by that act. The extension of slavery proved to be a major cause of the outbreak of war in 1861.

BIBLIOGRAPHY

Johannsen, Robert W. *Stephen A. Douglas*. New York: Oxford University Press, 1973.

Malin, James C. *The Nebraska Question, 1852–1854*. Lawrence: University Press of Kansas, 1953.

Morrison, Michael A. *Slavery and the American West: The Eclipse of Manifest Destiny and the American Civil War*. Chapel Hill: University of North Carolina Press, 1997.

Potter, David M. *The Impending Crisis, 1848–1861*. New York: Harper and Row, 1976.

Rawley, James A. *Race and Politics: "Bleeding Kansas" and the Coming of the Civil War*. Philadelphia: Lippincott, 1969.

Michael A. Morrison

See also: **Age of Westward Expansion; Compromise of 1850.**

KU KLUX KLAN

The Civil War ended the institution of slavery. Despite the Constitutional protections of the Fourteenth and Fifteenth Amendments, peace ushered in a new struggle that would affect American society and culture for over 100 years. In the South, the war to defend slavery was transformed into a conflict to repress free blacks through custom, law, intimidation, and violence. In one sense the Civil War continued but in a different form.

The Ku Klux Klan (KKK) emerged in 1866 from the Pulaski, Tennessee, law office of Judge Thomas M. Jones as a social movement responding to the Thirteenth Amendment's legislated end of slavery after the defeat of the Confederacy. Six former Rebel soldiers changed the Greek word "kuklos" ("circle or band") to "Ku Klux," adding the redundant "Klan." Based on fraternity rituals, the Klansmen disguised themselves as spirits to torment the free black population.

Under Reconstruction, the Southern Republican Party gained political momentum as the Fourteenth and Fifteenth Amendments granted and enforced male blacks the right to vote. Angry former Confederates, disqualified from political office, resented "carpetbaggers," "scalawags," and Radical Republicans, whom they believed prevented white Southerners from retaining their proper social status. When the Freedman's Bureau granted blacks land and assistance, Black Codes echoed the antebellum period, continuing to keep the blacks disenfranchised, poor, and unable to rise in social status.

In the beginning, the Klan resembled an umbrella organization for many anti-African-American groups. Former Confederate General Nathan Bedford Forrest in Tennessee organized one of the first in 1866 (eventually becoming the first Imperial Wizard) and men united in their hatred and fears of the black population answered his call. By January of 1868, the name "Ku Klux Klan" began to become more widely adopted. Employing secret signals, complicated codes, and following a military style manual, the KKK gained momentum. Assemblages of camps and dens ranged from thirty to forty thousand men in each Southern state; there were estimated to be 500,000 Klansmen in the entire South.

The Reconstruction Acts of March 1867 prepared former Rebel states for return to the fold of the Union, reorganizing state governments in 1868. Despite President Johnson's unconditional pardon of former Confederates, Southern whites resented the ratification of the Fourteenth Amendment. Enraged, and unable to discern that the blacks only wished to achieve equality before the law, whites determined for themselves that the black population meant to dominate the native white Southern population. Capitalizing on the fear that blacks would rise against the whites, the KKK set out to scare and to stop a black extension of power through thousands of acts of intimidation and of violence. Whites too, who were deemed to be enabling or collaborating with blacks, similarly were made targets. From Radical Republicans to clergy to teachers, neither black nor white were spared. The KKK also was known to abuse those from within their own organization whom they deemed to have committed treason against the Klan. Violence escalated as civil authorities ignored, participated in, or were intimidated by Klan activities.

Mounted, hooded (many seeming to possess long moustaches and beards) and clothed in white robes, members of the Klan generally drew members from the lower white classes. Literally casting issues in black or white, with only one race or one form of politics viewed as all good or all evil, the Klan was able to muster broad appeal. Yet, the power to continue these abuses rested in the hands of the Southern elite, who directed the marginalized classes in the new cause.

Often preceding attacks with written warnings setting precise times to vacate or disband and clearly delineating punishments for decided offenses, the KKK utilized a system of surprise, appearing at night to disarm, terrorize, whip, lynch or murder chosen targets. The KKK also burned black schools and verbally and physically abused and killed their white schoolteachers. Perpetrators viewed themselves as protecting the Southern way of life, much as they had fought for it during the Civil War.

Ultimately, Congress began to act. The Enforcement Acts of May 31, 1870 and February 28, 1871 allowed the president to use military force and extended Federal control to elections. Further, Republicans pushed through Congress the Ku Klux Act on April 20, 1871, which enforced the Fourteenth Amendment. Deciding after Congressional hearings that the form Reconstruction had assumed in the South had allowed for the creation of the Klan, rules against Southern Democrats were relaxed. Federal arrests and prosecutions against the Klan began in earnest in 1871. As a result, the first wave of Klansmen disappeared in 1873 and Reconstruction ended in 1877.

In the early 20th century the KKK revived in response to efforts by blacks and whites to end segregation, the so-called "Jim Crow" laws, that had reduced many former slaves to poverty and dependency. In 1915, William Joseph Simmons led fifteen men to the top of Atlanta's Stone Mountain with an American flag, a burning cross, and a Bible (opened to the Twelfth Chapter of Romans) and pledged to the Knights of the Ku Klux Klan. Delineated in a revised fifty-four-page manual of

Hooded Ku Klux Klansmen from the late nineteenth century. GREENHAVEN PRESS, INC.

the original rituals (entitled and copyrighted as the "Kloran"), Simmons set the structure of a new centralized second KKK. Comprised of domains, realms, provinces, and local klaverns, it rode the rising wave of nativism that preceded and then increased after World War I. Between 1920 and 1925 membership peaked to around five million members in forty-five states. Capitalizing on the fears of white men and women at the margins of society, whose employment and social status was threatened by the tides of immigrants and returning soldiers from Europe, the Klan aimed its furious propaganda at African-Americans, Catholics, Jews, Communist labor organizers, and emigrating masses.

Utilizing films such as *The Face at Your Window*, newspapers like *The Searchlight*, and lecturers who spoke of "100 percent Americanism," protecting white women, and upholding Protestantism, appeals of recruiters (kleagles) were answered in the cities, where competition for housing, jobs, and authority was strongest. It found its base in all regions of the country where influxes of African-Americans and immigrants competed for work. Enduring internal schisms and publicly printed unmaskings, weathering legislative scrutiny incurred by increasing violence, and entering into politics with vigor (strengthened by the women's right to suffrage, and therefore increased participation in the Klan), the 1928 Presidential campaign of New York Governor and Catholic Al Smith signaled its demise. Ironically, the Klan claimed to protect the Constitutional rights of Americans, while simultaneously being anti-freedom of religion, anti-freedom of speech, and anti-equality under the law. With a dwindling influence and membership, and in some cases becoming outnumbered by minority populations, by 1944 the Klan was gone.

However, as returning soldiers and new waves of minorities moved north to compete for work, Atlanta hosted the revival of the Klan on Stone Mountain on May 9, 1946. Drawing from traditional sources, the revived Klan found its voice after the May 1954 Supreme Court decision of *Brown vs. the Board of Education*. The ensuing Civil Rights movement increased Klan activity and membership. By 1965, Congress began to investigate the Klan. Despite FBI infiltration, the Klan continued to publish their newspaper *The Fiery Cross* and to support segregationists like George Wallace. In the end, its failure to at-

tract a larger following came from owing legal fees, FBI successes, and the inability of the Klan to effect racial, social, and political change.

No longer centralized, and hurt by the retribution of the Southern Poverty Law Center, which in 1979 began suing leaders for subordinates' violence, the Klan still can be found in many regions of the country where restricted economic circumstances among whites make the quest for white supremacy attractive.

BIBLIOGRAPHY

Jackson, Kenneth T. *The Ku Klux Klan in the City, 1915–1930*. Chicago: Ivan R. Dee, 1992.

Tourgee, Albion Winegar. *The Invisible Empire*. Baton Rouge & London: Louisiana State University Press, 1989.

Trelease, Allen W. *White Terror: The Ku Klux Klan Conspiracy and Southern Reconstruction*. Baton Rouge & London: Louisiana State University Press, 1971.

Sarah Hilgendorff List

See also: **Reconstruction.**

LABOR AND LABOR MOVEMENTS

By the time of the Civil War, most American workers were wage earning employees, rather than independent farmers or business owners. Although only a minority of these workers belonged to unions, organized labor movements had powerful effects on American economy and politics throughout this period. Especially for agricultural workers in the South, but also for Northern workers, the Civil War and its aftermath served as an important turning point in the history of American labor and business-labor relations.

BEFORE THE CIVIL WAR

During the antebellum era, most Americans worked on farms. In the North and the Southern upcountry, men tended to work with grain production and larger animals, while women oversaw poultry, dairying, and gardening, as well as sewing and housework. On the plantations of the Southern low country, most of the work was performed by African-American slaves. By 1860, most slaves were occupied with the work of planting and harvesting cotton, the nation's number one export.

Even as millions of people continued to be occupied with agricultural work, more Americans came to be employed in services and industry. Among the first manifestations of the industrial revolution in the United States were early textile mills, such as those built in Lowell, Massachusetts. By the 1820s, hundreds of young women from New England farm families had moved to Lowell, where they ran the machines that turned raw cotton into finished textiles. In the years that followed, more textile mills and other factories were built in the North. By the 1850s, many of the workers in these factories were the men, women, and children of immigrant families from Ireland.

Industrialization, which pushed many kinds of manufacturing out of small workshops and into mechanized factories, threatened the livelihoods of skilled artisans. During the 1820s and 1830s, artisans in Northern cities formed General Trades' Unions, which resisted wage cuts and fought for a 10-hour workday and public schools. The high point of organized labor activism before the Civil War was during the period from 1834 to 1836, when there were major strikes by male and female workers in New York, Philadelphia, Lowell, and other cities and towns in the North.

WAR WORKERS, 1861–1865

The Civil War demanded the labor of hundreds of thousands of Americans, who served as soldiers on the front lines and worked in military industries on the home front. Over the course of the war, three million men left farms and factories to serve as soldiers in the Northern and Southern armies. Hundreds of thousands more worked for government-run supply operations, military contractors and subcontractors in the private sector, and soldiers' aid organizations. In the end, few working adults in the North and South failed to contribute directly or indirectly to the mobilization for the Civil War.

In the North, where inflation caused prices to double by 1864, many workers suffered because their wages did not rise as fast as the cost of living. Workers responded to this problem by forming new organizations and demanding change. The thousands of seamstresses who were employed making soldiers' uniforms petitioned President Lincoln and the War Department to raise wages at government-run clothing plants. Other workers carried out strikes, which became increasingly common during the second half of the war. Some strikes by workers in military industries, such as one 1864 strike by employees of the North's largest cannon manufacturer, were ended forcibly by troops. The Civil War experience led more Northern workers to join unions for they saw themselves as having distinctly different interests from their employers.

REVOLUTIONARY CHANGE IN THE POST-EMANCIPATION SOUTH

Between 1863 and 1865, nearly four million African Americans in the South were freed. For them, the Civil War was a revolutionary event. Because former slaves refused to return to working in gangs on large plantations, families now farmed on smaller plots of rented or sharecropped land. Free from the direct coercion of slavery, many former slaves chose to work fewer hours; mothers and children now performed less heavy labor in the fields. Despite these changes in the organization of work and the lives of workers in the South, however, many African Americans found themselves trapped in poverty by debts owed to landlords and merchants.

Many poor white farmers in the South, who turned to cotton production in the postbellum years, also found themselves trapped in a cycle of long-term tenancy and debt. Because state laws protected the property rights of landlords and merchants and because world cotton prices stayed low, most tenant farmers stayed poor. By the 1880s, many black and white farmers in the South (like their counterparts in the West) were attracted to the programs of the Farmers' Alliance, which encouraged cooperation among small farmers to free them from debt. During the early 1890s, many Farmers' Alliance members voted for the People's Party (Populists), an important third party movement that represented the interests of small farmers, farm workers, and factory workers.

ORGANIZED LABOR IN LATE NINETEENTH CENTURY AMERICA

In the post-Civil War North, as more workers moved to cities and worked in factories, open conflict between labor and business became more common and more violent. The most important labor organization in the early Reconstruction period was the National Labor Union (NLU), created in 1866, which fought for the 8-hour day and tried to organize workers' cooperatives. Although the NLU fell apart by 1873, many former NLU members worked during the 1870s to support the Greenback party, which argued that the Republicans' plan for returning to the gold standard was good for rich bankers but bad for most farmers and workers.

The twenty-year period after the national centennial in 1876 witnessed the most violent labor-business conflicts in American history. In 1877, after railroad workers around the country used strikes to protest wage cuts, over 100 people were killed in clashes between workers, police, and soldiers in Pittsburgh, Chicago, and other cities. Other bloody labor-business conflicts during this period, each of which left at least ten people dead, included disputes associated with strikes and lockouts at the large factories of the McCormick Harvester Company (Chicago, 1886), Carnegie Steel (Homestead, Pennsylvania, 1892), and the Pullman Company (Chicago, 1894).

In the latter decades of the nineteenth century, hundreds of thousands of immigrants came annually to this country, seeking job opportunities and a better life from what they had known at home. Many immigrants, especially Catholics, were not welcome in existing labor organizations; in other cases, labor disputes arose over misunderstandings between newly arrived immigrant workers and those who considered themselves true Americans. Some immigrants, such as German workers, formed their own labor unions.

The two largest national labor organizations during the late nineteenth century, the Knights of Labor (KOL) and American Federation of Labor (AFL), had distinct programs and strategies. The KOL, which started as a secret society of Philadelphia workers in 1869, was organized by workers into mutual aid societies and cooperatives. By 1886, when it was led by Terence Powderly and counted 700,000 members, the KOL had become an inclusive national organization that welcomed women and African Americans as well as socialists and trade unionists. By this time, the KOL had entered the field of electoral politics and succeeded in winning dozens of local elections across the country. But in the late 1880s, the power of KOL declined sharply due to poor leadership decisions and counterattacks by employers. By 1890, the biggest national labor organization was the AFL, founded in 1886 by Samuel Gompers. A less diverse organization than the KOL, the AFL stayed out of electoral politics and concentrated on improving wages and working conditions for members of craft unions. It would continue to be the most important national labor organization in the United States into the twentieth century.

From the cotton South to the industrial North, the Civil War and the three decades that followed proved to be the most dramatic period in the history of American labor. While historians do not credit the Civil War with making America an industrialized society, that war nevertheless remains a watershed marking the transformation of the United States. In general terms, prior to the war the nation was divided between a planter economy based on slavery in the South and a Northern economy based on agriculture and small manufacturing enterprises. The period after the Civil War saw not only the end of slavery, but the rise of influential new labor organizations across the country and business-labor disputes of unprecedented violence. These key developments of the late nineteenth century defined the history of American labor until the years of the Great Depression and New Deal in the 1930s, which would redefine the relationship between American workers, employers, and government.

BIBLIOGRAPHY
Laurie, Bruce. *Artisans into Workers: Labor in Nineteenth-Century America.* New York: Hill and Wang, 1989.

Licht, Walter. *Industrializing America: The Nineteenth Century.* Baltimore, MD: Johns Hopkins University Press, 1995.

Montgomery, David. *Beyond Equality: Labor and the Radical Republicans, 1862–1872.* New York: Knopf, 1967.

Palladino, Grace. *Another Civil War: Labor, Capital, and the State in the Anthracite Regions of Pennsylvania, 1840–68.* Urbana: University of Illinois Press, 1990.

Reidy, Joseph P. *From Slavery to Agrarian Capitalism in the Cotton Plantation South: Central Georgia, 1800–1880.* Chapel Hill: University of North Carolina Press, 1992.

Voss, Kim. *The Making of American Exceptionalism: The Knights of Labor and Class Formation in the Nineteenth Century.* Ithaca, NY: Cornell University Press, 1993.

Mark R. Wilson

See also: **Economic Change and Industrialization.**

LEE, ROBERT E.
(b. January 19, 1807; d. October 12, 1870) Leading Confederate General during the Civil War.

Robert E. Lee was the most notable Confederate commander of the Civil War, and a figure of mythic proportions. Son of "Light-Horse Harry" Lee, a

General Robert E. Lee

Revolutionary War hero who had fallen into financial and personal disgrace, Lee was born at the family plantation named Stratford, in the tidewater region of Virginia. When Lee was four, his father fled the country, plunging his family into impoverished dependence on relatives. In 1829, Lee graduated West Point with a perfect conduct record (and a reputation as the most handsome man in the army) and embarked on a long career as an army engineer. In 1831, he married Mary Custis, daughter of George Washington's adopted son, George Washington Parke Custis, and moved to the Custis plantation at Arlington, near Washington, D.C.

In 1861, at the apex of a distinguished army career, including service in the Mexican War and a tour as superintendent of West Point, Lee was offered the most important command in the Union army after the lower South seceded. Instead, choosing to align himself with his state and his slaveholding class, Lee resigned his commission to ally his fortunes with the Confederacy. At first his military record was undistinguished, particularly when he mishandled Confederate forces in West Virginia, and lost that state to the Union. Confederate President Jefferson Davis still valued him, and made Lee his military advisor. When General Joseph E. Johnston was badly injured in battle in June 1862, Davis placed Lee in charge of the Army of Northern Virginia.

Reorganizing the Confederate army, Lee skillfully beat back the offensive of General George McClellan during the Peninsula Campaign, and went on to a year-long series of victories, albeit at the loss of irreplaceable troops and material. Indeed, his military leadership was sometimes marked by unconventional audacity. With the exception of a draw at Antietam in September 1862, his army won every battle until the stunning defeat at Gettysburg in July 1863. There, having grown contemptuous of his opponents and perhaps too prideful of his own forces, as well as ignoring the enemy's solid defensive position, Lee fell into haphazard attacks, ending with the slaughter of Major General George E. Pickett's division.

Falling back to Virginia, Lee waged a tenacious defensive struggle, blocking General Ulysses S. Grant's relentless attacks during the Wilderness Campaign of May and June, 1864. Driven into a line of trenches south of Richmond, the Confederate capital, Lee's army gradually wore out during a prolonged siege. The Army of Northern Virginia finally crumbled in early April 1865, after Lee abandoned his Petersburg defenses and Richmond and fled eastward. Finally, surrounded by Union troops, Lee surrendered at Appomattox Courthouse on April 9, 1865.

After the war, Lee went on to become president of Washington College (later renamed Washington and Lee College) in Lexington, Virginia, where he also played a vital, behind-the-scenes role in the rebirth of conservative white rule in his state. During this period, and even more after his death, Lee became the chief symbol of the nobility of the Lost Cause.

Ever since the Civil War, historians have debated General Lee's military leadership, particularly in contrast to Grant. At the moment of his surrender, Lee began the narrative that the Union had won only because of superior material resources. While it is true that the Union had had far better resources, it also had talented generals and tenacious soldiers of its own, and so material inferiority was only part of the explanation for Confederate defeat. Lee squandered his limited resources through willingness to commit his army to bloody battles. He believed that only by defeating the Union army on the battlefield could the South gain independence. However, one could also argue that the South needed only to keep from losing the war until horrified Northern public opinion turned against it and elected a government that would allow Southern independence. This nearly happened in

the Union elections of 1864, but the aggressive tactics of Grant, and, even more importantly, defeats of other Confederate generals led Southern popular opinion to wear out first, even while Lee continued to hold off Grant. Lee's focus on defending Virginia and winning victories in the eastern theatre proved insufficient in a far vaster conflict. Yet Lee's determined leadership doubtless enabled the South to hold out for as long as it did.

After the war, Lee also gained wide national admiration as the perfect Christian general, the calm stoic gentleman always doing his duty for a cause that he supposedly did not support—the defense of slavery. In fact, Lee was at the core of the pro-slavery leadership cadre of the Confederacy. The values of that class, white supremacy included, now seem less attractive to most Americans, and therefore Lee's reputation as the ideal American is fading somewhat. Nevertheless, as the naming of the college in Lexington symbolizes, the great hero of the Revolution, Washington, and Lee's romanticized heroism in defeat have been linked as icons of honor that are used to define American character and national identity.

BIBLIOGRAPHY

Connelly, Thomas L. *The Marble Man: Robert E. Lee and His Image in American Society.* New York: Knopf, 1977.

Fellman, Michael. *The Making of Robert E. Lee.* New York: Random House, 2000.

Freeman, Douglas Southall. *R. E. Lee: A Biography.* 4 vols. New York: Scribners, 1934–36.

Michael D. Fellman

See also: **Lost Cause.**

LINCOLN, ABRAHAM

(b. February 12, 1809; d. April 15, 1865) Sixteenth president of the United States (1861–1865).

Abraham Lincoln's life was lived under the shadow of war. During his lifetime he would witness three major American wars: the War of 1812, the War with Mexico (1846–1848), and the Civil War (1861–1865).

Born in Kentucky to impoverished parents, Lincoln migrated with his family to Indiana and then to Illinois, where he left his father's farm in 1831 to settle in New Salem, Illinois, and try his hand unsuccessfully at business. In 1832, the Sac and Fox chieftain, Black Hawk, attempted to resettle his followers on lands near Rock Island, Illinois, which they had previously vacated by treaty. Governor John Reynolds called out the Illinois militia, and New Salem's militia company was sworn into state service on April 28, 1832, with Lincoln elected as captain for thirty days' service. He re-enlisted two more times in other units, and was finally mustered out on July 10, 1832, near Black River, Wisconsin, without having seen action.

The Black Hawk War would prove to be Lincoln's only direct experience of soldiering. In 1836, after years of private study, he was licensed as a lawyer—a profession in which he had considerable success. He aligned himself politically with the American Whig party, and endorsed the Whigs' ideological suspicion of the military, a suspicion aggravated by the popularity of General Andrew Jackson, the victor of the Battle of New Orleans (1815), as the figurehead of the rival Democratic Party. When Lincoln was elected to Congress in 1847 as the only Whig in Illinois's congressional delegation, he joined with Whig representatives from other states to criticize President James K. Polk's conduct of the War with Mexico.

In 1856 Lincoln joined the then-new Republican Party and two years later he ran unsuccessfully for the Senate against Stephen A. Douglas, engaging in a series of debates on slavery that attracted wide attention. As he rose to national prominence and became president in 1860 as the Republican candidate, he was increasingly forced to confront the likelihood of conflict over the slavery issue. That likelihood became a reality after the slaveholding states of the South formed the Confederate States of America and opened fire on the United States garrison in Fort Sumter. From that point onward, the Civil War demanded that Lincoln devote his energies to precisely the military affairs he liked least.

Lincoln had no experience in developing strategic doctrine, and the program of self-education he set for himself by reading textbooks in military science never raised his sights above conventional, and sometimes deeply-flawed, notions of strategy. On a few occasions, he even suggested taking field command of the armies; May 9–10, 1862, he personally participated in an amphibious expedition that captured Norfolk, Virginia. However, his real genius lay along the lines where political and military issues met, and as the constitutionally mandated commander-in-chief of the United States army and navy, he turned his attention to four major areas of war-related policy-making.

LEGAL STATUS OF THE WAR

Lincoln maintained that the secession of the Confederate states was a constitutional and legal nullity. The federal Union, as shaped by the Constitution, did not allow individual states to unilaterally withdraw from the Union. Once the Confederate forces attacked Fort Sumter April 12–14, 1861, Lincoln issued a proclamation, calling on

Abraham Lincoln, four days before he was assassinated.

the states for 75,000 militia to suppress what he described (using the words of the Militia Act of 1792) as "combinations too powerful to be suppressed by the ordinary course of judicial proceedings." Hence, Lincoln regarded the Civil War, from the viewpoint of law, strictly as a local insurrection, rather than a declared war between two sovereign and equal nations.

This, however, posed serious problems in international law. Captured Confederates could, as insurrectionists, be indicted as traitors and executed under civil law; but in practice, both Union and Confederate armies treated captives as prisoners of war, organized prisoner-of-war camps and exchange policies, and in general behaved as though a normal state of belligerent war existed, rather than a civil insurrection. Much more important was the legal problem that emerged when Lincoln sought to impose a naval blockade on the Confederacy. On April 19, 1861, Lincoln announced the imposition of a complete "efficient" blockade of the Confederacy's ports "in pursuance of the laws of the United States and of the law of nations," which authorized capturing ships attempting to run the blockade, under whatever flag, and turning them over to admiralty courts for sale as prizes of war. However, according to the Paris Convention of 1856 (the first attempt by nations, in the aftermath of the Crimean War, to establish mutually-agreed-upon codes to govern international war) full blockades could only be imposed between sovereign belligerent nations—which was exactly what Lincoln denied that the Confederacy was.

This was a calculated risk. On May 13, 1861, the British government took advantage of the contradiction and extended recognition of belligerent rights to the Confederacy; and in 1863 the United States Supreme Court, ruling on a major suit known as *Prize Cases,* came within one vote of striking down Lincoln's blockade proclamation as unconstitutional. But the efficiency of a blockade in choking off supplies to the Confederacy was, in Lincoln's mind, worth the risk.

MILITARY PERSONNEL

The United States Army had only 16,000 men on its rolls in 1861, and only four of general officer rank. Lincoln sought to deal with the rebellion by calling on the states for the use of their militia alongside the regular army. But the state militias were clearly unequal to the task of serious campaigning, and in May Lincoln issued a call for 42,000 so-called volunteers. The use of volunteers rather than militia as a supplement to the regular army was first resorted to in the War with Mexico, and involved the organization and enlistment by the states of soldiers who were then mustered into federal service.

The army's senior major general, Winfield Scott, was unwilling to parcel out the regular army's cadre of professional officers to lead the volunteer units. This, together with the comparatively small number of experienced former officers who returned to military service for the war, forced the commissioning of officers at all ranks who had little experience or who had conflicting political convictions. This created embarrassing confrontations for Lincoln, especially with Major General John Charles Fremont, whom he cashiered for imposing sweeping martial law decrees (including slave emancipation) in politically sensitive areas; and with Major General George McClellan, the commander of the Army of the Potomac, whom he cashiered for failing to press military opportunities against the Confederates. Not until 1864, when he offered the post of general-in-chief to Major General Ulysses Simpson Grant, did Lincoln find a senior commander sufficiently competent to bring the war to a successful close. By that point, conscription had been added as a means of swelling recruitment for the Union armies.

POWERS OF THE COMMANDER-IN-CHIEF

Although the Constitution designates the president as the commander-in-chief of the armed forces in time of war, there was little jurisprudence or precedent to provide a clear picture of what Lincoln's war powers as commander-in-chief actually were. In 1861 the arrest of a Confederate recruiter, John Merryman, in Maryland provoked U.S. Chief Justice Roger B. Taney to issue a writ of habeas corpus so that Merryman could be tried in a civil court rather than held in military detention. Citing the Constitution's allowance for suspension of the writ in times of insurrection, Lincoln had authorized military arrests such as that of Merryman "for the public safety." The difficulty was that the Constitution did not specify exactly who had the power to suspend the writ—the President, Congress, or the courts—and Taney categorically denied that Lincoln possessed the authority, commander-in-chief or not. Lincoln ignored Taney, and Congress later endorsed Lincoln's action.

A far larger difficulty loomed over whether Lincoln's war powers authorized him to deal with what he believed was the root cause of the war, slavery. The litigation over Merryman and the blockade taught Lincoln that any effort to use those powers to decree the emancipation of the South's slaves would be challenged in the federal courts. But by mid-1862, the progress of the war was so discouraging that Lincoln determined to risk the issue of an Emancipation Proclamation, which went into effect on January 1, 1863, on the strength of "military necessity." The question of the legality of the Proclamation was never put to the test, as Congress approved a constitutional amendment banning slavery in January, 1865, and its ratification lifted emancipation above court scrutiny.

RECONSTRUCTION

Lincoln began working on plans to reintegrate a defeated Confederacy into the union in 1862, appointing military governors for those portions of the Confederacy occupied by Union troops. The record of the military governors, however, was uneven, so Lincoln turned in 1863 to fostering the organization of civilian loyalist regimes as the new governments of the conquered Southern states. Congress refused to recognize the legitimacy of the representatives these regimes sent to Washington, and by 1865, Lincoln was gradually returning to the idea of using military governors to oversee the political reconstruction of the South.

Although Lincoln refused to discuss any peace terms short of national reunification, by the last year of the war he was willing to sanction three separate peace initiatives. He would not, however, modify his insistence on emancipation and the restoration of federal authority as conditions for peace. In his second inaugural address (on March 4, 1865), Lincoln declared his hope that the Civil War could come to its close "with malice toward none, with charity for all." But this hope was cut short by his death only six weeks later from an assassin's bullet. The subsequent reconstruction of the defeated Confederacy was politically confused and ineffectively managed by Lincoln's successors.

BIBLIOGRAPHY

Bruce, Robert V. *Lincoln and the Tools of War.* Indianapolis, IN: Bobbs Merrill, 1956.

Davis, William C. *Lincoln's Men: How President Lincoln Became Father to an Army and a Nation.* New York: Free Press, 1999.

Hattaway, Herman, and Jones, Archer. "Lincoln as Military Strategist." *Civil War History* 26 (1980): 293–303.

Hendrick, Burton J. *Lincoln's War Cabinet.* Boston: Little, Brown, 1946.

Lowry, Thomas P. *Don't Shoot That Boy! Abraham Lincoln and Military Justice.* Mason City, IA: Savas, 1999.

MacCartney, Clarence Edward. *Lincoln and His Generals.* Philadelphia: Dorrance and Co., 1925.

MacCartney, Clarence Edward. *Mr. Lincoln's Admirals.* New York: Funk & Wagnalls, 1956.

Prokopowicz, Gerald J. "Military Fantasies." In *The Lincoln Enigma: The Changing Faces of an American Icon,* edited by Gabor S. Boritt. New York: Oxford University Press, 2001.

Williams, Kenneth P. *Lincoln Finds a General: A Military Study of the Civil War.* 5 vols. New York: Macmillan, 1949–59.

Williams, T. Harry. *Lincoln and His Generals.* New York: Knopf, 1952.

Allen C. Guelzo

See also: Emancipation Proclamation; Lincoln, Mary Todd.

Mary Todd Lincoln. © BETTMANN/CORBIS

LINCOLN, MARY TODD

(b. December 13, 1818, d. July 16, 1882) Responsible for major renovations of the White House as First Lady during the Civil War, 1861–1865.

Mary Todd was a proud member of a wealthy Kentucky family whose members on both her paternal and maternal sides had fought in the American Revolution and the War of 1812. Intelligent and charming, though quick-tempered, she attended school for twelve years in Lexington before moving to Springfield, Illinois, to live with her married sister Elizabeth Todd Edwards in 1837. There she met Abraham Lincoln, who was at the time an aspiring Whig politician and ambitious lawyer.

In November 1842 Mary Todd and Abraham Lincoln married, and by 1853 they were the parents of four sons, three of whom would predecease their mother. During her years as a married woman and mother in Springfield, Mary Lincoln enthusiastically supported her husband's political career, especially in the 1850s, when Lincoln lost two elections to the United States Senate.

Unlike many women of her generation, she studied politics and served as her husband's counselor and occasional clerk. For example, in 1850 she spent a good part of her summer writing patronage letters for Lincoln, who wanted to be appointed Commissioner of Land. Mary Lincoln also assisted her husband by graciously entertaining prominent Illinois politicians, and she was especially well known for her strawberry parties, to which she invited the elite of Springfield. She made sure that the enlarged Lincoln home was a suitable expression of Lincoln's growing importance. By 1860, when Lincoln heard in the Springfield telegraph office that he had been elected president, he hurried home to tell his wife and principal supporter that "we" are elected.

In the White House, the energetic Mary Lincoln began another campaign. She was convinced that the President's Mansion was not just a place where the Lincoln family, consisting of Robert (a Harvard student during most of the war), Willie, and Tad, lived with their parents. Rather, during the devastating war that began six weeks after the Lincolns moved in, she felt the White House must display the power and authority of the government. Accordingly, Mary Lincoln began her renovations of what had been a shabby interior, filled with broken furniture and soiled upholstery. With the good taste that marked her style in clothes, she purchased wallpaper in Paris, rugs in Philadelphia, crystal, and a new set of state china in New York. But she overspent the allotted budget and thus embarrassed her husband and his Republican administration.

As had been the case in Springfield, Mary Lincoln used her entertainments (the receptions, dinners, and evening parties) as important events where politicians and diplomats could exchange important wartime information unofficially. Mary Lincoln also participated in the traditional obligations of Union women who served as nurses for the wounded. Her visits to hospitals in Washington included spending time with soldiers, writing their letters home to their mothers, and carrying food and flowers to cheer them. Sometimes the president went with her; sometimes she and the boys went alone. Mary Lincoln was also one of the few women in Washington to raise money for the so-called "contraband," or former Virginia slaves, who concentrated in the Capitol as the Army of the Potomac moved into northern Virginia.

This First Lady's experience was intimately involved with the Civil War, as she and her husband followed the four-year pendulum of Union victories and defeats. The death of Mary Lincoln's son Willie in the White House in 1862 from typhoid fever, followed by her husband's assassination in April 1865 (as the Civil War was ending) made Mary a part of the tragedies that other Americans experienced.

After her husband's assassination and after finding it financially impossible to keep a house in Chicago, Mary Lincoln had no permanent residence. She and Thomas (Tad), the youngest of the four Lincoln sons, traveled to Europe, returning in 1871. That same year Tad died, and Mary Lincoln was bereft. Her aberrant behavior (she had become a spiritualist, and shopped far too often) led her son Robert to place her in an insane asylum. But she was not insane, and after incarceration for three months, she was released. Worried that her son would continue to threaten her freedom, she moved to Pau, France. There she lived independently until health problems made it impossible to live alone. She died in 1882 in her sister's home in Springfield.

BIBLIOGRAPHY

Baker, Jean H. *Mary Todd Lincoln: A Biography.* New York: Norton, 1987.

Turner, Justin, and Turner, Linda Levitt. *Mary Todd Lincoln: Her Life and Letters.* New York: Knopf, 1972.

Jean Harvey Baker

See also: **Lincoln, Abraham.**

LITERATURE

The Civil War, and the ideological passions that led to armed hostility, dominate American war literature of the nineteenth century. Yet for all the drama of this great national conflict, the major writers of the nineteenth century American literary establishment tended to avoid direct treatment of the Civil War and the divisive issues such as race and slavery that produced it. The most well-known writer to address the war was the poet Walt Whitman, most famously in *Drum-Taps,* a volume of poems published in 1865. The novelist Herman Melville also published poems and commentary on the war in *Battle Pieces* in 1866. However, in great measure it was the amateurs and other writers on the margins of literary acceptance, including women and blacks, who struggled to comprehend their national upheaval through writing. In fact, the literature of the Civil War was emancipating for these two groups. Many women writers, most famously Harriet Beecher Stowe and Louisa May Alcott, used the metaphor of a "civil war" to characterize class, race, and gender tensions within American life.

Much of the writing of the Civil War appeared in publications designed for popular consumption, such as weeklies and news magazines. These periodicals featured fiction, sensational novels and romances, and children's adventure tales, poems, songs, and histories. In addition, letters and journals intended for private audiences have been made available through the efforts of Civil War researchers.

Although no one prevailing tone can be identified in such a large body of literature, certain patterns do emerge. Early in the war writers tended to invoke abstract and ideological concerns such as nationhood; later, as the enormous cost in human life became apparent, individual experiences of the war became a prominent theme. The growth of American literary movements of the later nineteenth century—local color, realism, and naturalism—can be traced in large part to the war's bloody impact on American consciousness.

ANTEBELLUM LITERATURE

Few could have anticipated that the war would completely reconfigure the American literary scene. The antebellum literary tradition saw a general flourishing of fiction as well as the formalization of certain expectations of war literature, such as patriotic poems and songs, during the Mexican-American War of 1846–1848. But even as American literature thrived in the first decades of the nineteenth century, most writers remained silent about slavery, with the exception of a number of Southern writers during the 1820s and 1830s who produced what were called plantation novels, essentially defenses of the institution of slavery.

During the 1850s the abolitionist movement and legal landmarks like the passage of the Fugitive Slave Act and the Dred Scott decision dominated the political scene. More writers began overtly criticizing slavery. In his tale "Benito Cereno" and poems like "Misgivings," Melville revealed his conviction that the natural rights enshrined in the Declaration of Independence and the U.S. Constitution applied to blacks as well as whites and that the persistence of institutionalized slavery exposed a profound moral weakness in the American character. Henry David Thoreau bitterly attacked slavery in his essays and speeches. The 1859 raid by John Brown on Harpers Ferry, West Virginia, drew even more impassioned, quasi-religious rhetoric from Thoreau in defense of John Brown, and inspired Louisa May Alcott to pen the poem "With a Rose, that Bloomed on the Day of John Brown's Martyrdom" for the abolitionist journal *The Liberator*.

However, one work of fiction—Harriet Beecher Stowe's *Uncle Tom's Cabin* (1852)—looms over all other writing of the antebellum years. The influence of this novel on American society was so great that, when Stowe visited the White House, President Abraham Lincoln is said to have called her the "little woman who wrote the book that started this great war." The novel, originating in Stowe's anger over passage of the Fugitive Slave Act of 1850, was published in serial form in the *National Era* from 1851 to 1852 and then in book form in 1852. Historians have noted the immediate impact on public opinion of Stowe's sentimental novel, especially in the North. In the South, even long after the war was over, some writers, such as Thomas Dixon in his 1902 novel *The Leopard's Spots,* continued to bitterly attack *Uncle Tom's Cabin*.

CIVIL WAR LITERATURE: THE FIRST PHASE
The literature of the Civil War years moved through distinct phases. At the beginning of hostilities, both Northern and Southern writers tended to frame the conflict in nationalistic, rigidly ideological terms designed to unite various factions within the borders of the two warring nations. As works of propaganda, these writings typically demonized soldiers of the opposing side, most obviously in Southern depictions of Northerners as "Yankee" rapists and looters. Much of the literature of the early war years was a call to arms, appealing to the patriotic ardor of young men on both sides. Although the tone of Whitman's poetry would later soften in response to his nursing of wounded soldiers in hospitals, he began by presenting readers with images of heroic Northern manhood marching to battle in poems such as "Eighteen Sixty-One" and "Beat! Beat! Drums!"

Many stories and poems also urged women to contribute to the war effort not only through service on the home front but also by actively encouraging men to fight and, if need be, by enduring the sacrifice of losing their men for a greater cause. Other literature explored the racial issues of the war, with Northern works exploring the implications of emancipation and Southern works often depicting slaves as remaining loyal to their white masters. After black soldiers began fighting for the Union, the *Atlantic Monthly* published in 1864 Alcott's "The Brothers," about the death at Fort Wagner of a former slave turned soldier.

CIVIL WAR LITERATURE: THE SECOND PHASE
As the war continued and its staggering human costs became more apparent, the focus of popular war literature narrowed to the individual soldier's experience of war. Although not brutally graphic in its depictions, this literature acknowledged—sometimes in sentimental fashion—the realities of wartime death and suffering. Poems that dramatized a dying soldier's last thoughts of home and the women left behind were prevalent, expanding upon a genre established during the Mexican-American War. Whitman, whose brother George was wounded at Fredericksburg, Virginia, and who served as a volunteer nurse's assistant during much of the war, paid tribute to the quiet bravery of those wounded men he saw suffering (and in many cases dying) in the hospitals in *Memoranda during the War*. His *Specimen Days* featured realistic portrayals of battle. He also depicted the loyalty of men under fire in poems such as "As I Lay with My Head in Your Lap Camerado" and the human toll of war in poems such as "The Wound Dresser." Alcott fictionalized her wartime experience as a nurse in her *Hospital Sketches*, published in 1863.

Some works also began to discuss, at least implicitly, the war's disastrous emotional and economic toll on individual women, who faced the loss of loved ones and uncertain new financial and domestic realities. Whether in the North or South, the uncertainty of the times and the growing awareness that the conflict was to be long and brutal dictated the tone of these works, and often compelled writers to state positions they might have avoided earlier. In the South, the diarist Mary Boykin Chesnut, who began keeping her wartime diary in 1861 and moved with her husband from state to state as the war progressed, spoke of her dislike of slavery and her personal distress over the long casualty lists that resulted from increasingly bloody battles. Beecher Stowe advocated immediate emancipation in the January 1863 issue of the *Atlantic Monthly* and urged grieving women in her 1865 essay "The Chimney Corner" to turn to the service professions, such as nursing, for employment in the postwar nation. This focus on the importance of the individual in and after battle can best be understood as an artistic reaction to the impersonal mass slaughter of modern warfare.

POSTWAR LITERARY MOVEMENTS

Reader interest in the war remained high for a few years after 1865. A large number of war histories, commemorations of President Lincoln such as Whitman's famous poems "O Captain! My Captain!" and "When Lilacs Last in the Dooryard Bloomed," and sensational war novels heavily reliant on action and melodrama appeared in the immediate postwar period, from the mid- to late 1860s through the early 1870s. Even in well-known novels that were not directly about the war, such as Alcott's *Little Women* (1868), the conflict loomed large in the narrative. In Alcott's novel, for example, the women of the March family must maintain their household while Mr. March is away at war with the Union army. However, during most of the 1870s, popular interest in literature of the war dropped dramatically.

The war did nonetheless have a lasting effect on literature. Increasing urbanization and modernization were leading to a more complex way of life. Realist writers attempted to record as accurately as possible regional and class differences, and local-color literature, a variant of realism, aimed to preserve in print the unique character of various locales before industrial modernization could consume all such distinctiveness. For example, the novel *The Country of Pointed Firs* (1896), by the New England writer Sarah Orne Jewett, captured the rapidly disappearing traditional way of life in rural Maine.

Yet the Civil War is not the focus of the preeminent texts of the American realism movement (Mark Twain's *Huckleberry Finn* and Henry James's *The Bostonians*, to name just two). James, who did not fight in the Civil War because of a back injury, is representative of the American realists who either avoided the subject of the war altogether or who, in the three stories he did write about the war ("Poor Richard," "The Story of a Year," and "A Most Extraordinary Case"), depicted men who did not fight. Acknowledged as the dean of American realism, William Dean Howells avoided the subject of the Civil War because he had no direct experience of the South, slavery, or the war and did not desire to write about something he did not know.

As industrialism continued to alter American society toward the end of the century, realism contributed to the growth of literary naturalism. Naturalism emphasized the tyrannical impact of economics and environment on human existence. In the naturalist view, human free will was an illusion; environment and nature determined characters' actions, and notions of social reform seemed hopelessly quaint. Naturalist literature did not really take up the subject of the Civil War until the appearance in 1895

of *The Red Badge of Courage,* a novel by Stephen Crane about the horrors and confusion of battle as experienced by its youthful protagonist, Henry Fleming. The publication of Crane's novel is arguably the defining moment of the literature of the postwar period. Crane, who was born after the Civil War (in 1871), based his novel's vivid battle scenes not on lived experience but on his reading of war histories published during the postwar years. The novel became a bestseller and influenced later generations of authors who presented individualized, graphic accounts of warfare. The twentieth-century writer Ernest Hemingway said of *The Red Badge of Courage* that no Civil War literature existed until its publication.

The Civil War appeared as the subject of a large number of literary works during the twentieth century, the most famous being Margaret Mitchell's *Gone with the Wind*, published in 1936.

BIBLIOGRAPHY

Aaron, Daniel. *The Unwritten War*. London: Oxford University Press, 1973.

Fahs, Alice. *The Imagined Civil War: Popular Literature of the North and South, 1861–1865*. Chapel Hill: University of North Carolina Press, 2001.

Limon, John. *Writing After War: American War Fiction from Realism to Postmodernism*. New York: Oxford University Press, 1994.

Lundberg, David. "American Literature of War: The Civil War, World War I, and World War II." *American Quarterly* 36 (1989).

Wilson, Edmund. *Patriotic Gore*. New York: Oxford University Press, 1962.

Young, Elizabeth. *Disarming the Nation: Women's Writing and the American Civil War*. Chicago: University of Chicago Press, 1999.

Philip L. Simpson

See also: **Chesnut, Mary Boykin;** *Uncle Tom's Cabin*; **Whitman, Walt.**

LOST CAUSE

As a way to ease the trauma of the Confederate defeat in the Civil War and the resulting Union occupation, many white Southerners sought to justify the cause for which they and their loved ones had fought. Led by figures such as Father Abram Ryan, the "poet-priest of the Confederacy," and groups such as ladies' memorial associations dedicated to creating and maintaining Confederate cemeteries, supporters of the "Lost Cause," as they called it, sought to preserve the memory of their dead.

From the beginning, the commemoration of the Confederacy had religious overtones that developed into a type of civil religion. Just as with any religion, the Lost Cause had its own elaborate ceremonies (parades and memorials), icons (statues of Confederate soldiers), and "saints," especially its "Blessed Trinity" (Generals Robert E. Lee and Thomas "Stonewall" Jackson and Confederate President Jefferson Davis). Confederate cemeteries became places of pilgrimage on various feast days of the Confederacy, which included Robert E. Lee's birthday and the anniversary of Thomas "Stonewall" Jackson's death. Clergy played a central role in all the events and were key people in transforming historical commemorations into religious spectacles.

The Confederate dead were also honored because they had fought for what many white Southerners insisted was a just cause: states' rights, not slavery. Thus, while the Lost Cause began as a way to memorialize the fallen, it quickly developed a political side. The Southern Historical Society (SHS), founded in 1869, used its *Southern Historical Society Papers* to justify the Confederate effort. Its members were avowedly "unreconstructed" (that is, opposed to the federal government's "Radical Reconstruction" program giving rights to former slaves) and firmly against any reconciliation with the "accursed Yankees."

The SHS, however, did not have broad support. As the federal government began to retreat from reconstruction after 1873, unabashed hostility to everything Yankee seemed anachronistic to many Southerners, particularly those who called for a New South dedicated to economic development in partnership with Northern business. The prophets of this New South ideology, however, realized that they could not just dismiss the Lost Cause. For example, New South proponent General John B. Gordon, "the hero of Appomattox," used his Confederate record to win elections. He became the first president of the newly organized United Confederate Veterans (UCV) in 1889 and remained in that position until his death in 1904. The UCV organized annual reunions throughout the South which brought together thousands of veterans. The reunions became major events with various southern towns vying to hold them. Through its magazine, *The Confederate Veteran,* the UCV emphasized the experience of the average soldier, but it also continued the SHS position of denying that slavery was the cause of the war. Unlike the older organization, the UCV embraced reconciliation with the North and made some contacts with its Union counterpart, the Grand Army of the Republic. By the mid-1890s, over 75 percent of the South's counties boasted UCV groups. The UCV helped many white Southerners embrace their future and simultaneously vindicate their past.

A new organization formed out of, but not totally replacing, the ladies' memorial associations joined the UCV in remembering and justifying the Confederacy. The United Daughters of the Confederacy (UDC), organized in 1894, became the carrier of the Confederate torch as veterans began to die. The spectacular growth of the UCV and the UDC led to a new spate of Confederate memorializing, except that, unlike the memorials of the 1860s and 1870s, the new monuments and events were as often on the town square as in a cemetery. Because of UDC pressure, the ceremonies also began to recognize the role of civilians, particularly women, in the Confederate effort. By 1910, women of the UDC had become the preservers of the Confederate tradition.

Nonetheless, the southern-born Woodrow Wilson's election to the presidency in 1912, followed by the United States's entry into the First World War in 1917, dramatically decreased the Lost Cause's importance. Memories of the Civil War had faded, and Wilson's victory marked the South's ultimate return to the nation. The rise of Jim Crow and the disfranchisement of African Americans by the turn of the century also decreased the overarching need for white unity so well displayed on Confederate memorial days. The UDC kept the traditions alive, but they had lost their potency. The South did not need the political or religious power of the Lost Cause anymore. The recent revival of the concept in the 1990s, particularly in connection with the display of the Confederate battle flag, has had more to do with the contemporary political, economic, and cultural trends than with the Civil War or the trauma it caused.

BIBLIOGRAPHY

Ayers, Edward L. *The Promise of the New South: Life After Reconstruction.* New York: Oxford University Press, 1992.

Cox, Karen L. *Dixie's Daughters: The United Daughters of the Confederacy and the Preservation of Confederate Culture.* Gainesville: University Press of Florida, 2003.

Foster, Gaines. *Ghosts of the Confederacy: Defeat, the Lost Cause, and the Emergence of the New South, 1865–1913.* New York: Oxford University Press, 1987.

Horwitz, Tony. *Confederates in the Attic: Dispatches from the Unfinished Civil War.* New York: Pantheon Books, 1998.

Poole, W. Scott. *Never Surrender: Confederate Memory and Conservatism in the South Carolina Upcountry.* Athens: University of Georgia Press, 2004.

Wilson, Charles Reagan. *Baptized in Blood: The Religion of the Lost Cause, 1865–1920.* Athens: University of Georgia Press, 1980.

David T. Gleeson

See also: Jackson, Thomas J. (Stonewall); Lee, Robert E.

MANIFEST DESTINY

The mid-1840s were years of extraordinary territorial growth for the United States, a period in which the national domain increased by 1.2 million square miles, a gain of more than sixty percent. In 1845, the United States annexed Texas and the following year reached a settlement with Great Britain for control of the Pacific Northwest. Mexico's opposition to the annexation of Texas led to the Mexican War (1846–1848), which resulted in the U.S. acquisition of California and the American Southwest through the Treaty of Guadalupe Hidalgo. So rapid and dramatic was the process of territorial expansion that it came to be seen as an inexorable process, prompting many Americans to insist that their nation had a "manifest destiny" to dominate the continent.

Yet the expansionist agenda was never promoted by a clearly defined movement, nor did it enjoy broad bipartisan support. Some champions of Manifest Destiny favored rapid expansion and the bold pursuit of U.S. territorial claims, even at the risk of war with other nations. Others, no less committed to the long-term goal of a U.S. empire, opposed the use of force to achieve that end, believing that contiguous lands would voluntarily join the Union in order to obtain the benefits of republican rule.

For all its brash rhetoric, American expansionism was driven by economic and geopolitical anxieties. Troubled by creeping urbanization and a rising tide of immigrants from Europe, expansionists viewed Manifest Destiny as a way to attain the Jeffersonian ideal by providing new lands and unlimited economic opportunities for future generations. Southerners anxious to add slave states to the Union were among the most ardent supporters of the crusade for more territory, and American commercial interests saw expansion as a way to gain access to lucrative foreign markets. Manifest Destiny was also a response to American suspicions of British interference in the western hemisphere, a fear that had grown more acute as the United States began to define its strategic and economic interests in terms that extended beyond its own borders.

In the 1850s, preoccupied with the increasingly bitter sectional conflict over slavery, many Americans rejected Manifest Destiny. Although Southern extremists sponsored filibuster expeditions into Latin America with the objective of gaining new lands into which to extend slavery, the expansionist movement faded from the national agenda in the years prior to the outbreak of the Civil War. Instead, Americans argued over the settlement of those western lands and whether they would include or exclude slavery. That problem was not fully resolved until the Civil War and the Thirteenth Amendment put an end to slavery in the nation.

Ironically, Manifest Destiny proved to be a mixed blessing for U.S. society and culture. On one hand, it appeared to confirm a religious conviction that the United States had a divine mission to spread its institutions across the continent, thus contributing to the nation's sense of itself as an exceptional society with a mission to play in the world. On the other hand, it became divisive because it was associated with the spread of slavery, an institution many believed to be incompatible with American ideals. Thus, rather than uniting the nation, it further divided North and South and became a factor leading to the Civil War.

Sam W. Haynes

See also: **Age of Westward Expansion.**

MEDICINE AND HEALTH

When the Civil War began in April 1861, American medicine was approaching what Union Surgeon General William Hammond called "the end of the medical Middle Ages." The Civil War was the last great armed conflict in the world fought without knowledge of the germ theory, which would in subsequent wars allow doctors to understand the cause and prevention of disease. Yet the war, despite its unparalleled death and destruction, revolutionized American medicine and improved medical care and public health in the postwar era.

ANTEBELLUM MEDICINE AND HEALTH

Before the Civil War began, most Americans were skeptical of doctors' ability to heal them. Inadequate medical training accounts for some of this skepticism. In sharp contrast to today's high academic entrance standards, admission to medical school was based only on students' ability to pay tuition. Medical school curriculum consisted of a series of lectures delivered by the schools' professors. These lectures were repeated during the students' second year of study because it was assumed that students would learn more the second time around.

Public hospitals were rare in antebellum America. Only large cities like Boston, New York, and New Orleans offered sick people the option of hospital treatment. Few hospitals meant that most doctors received no clinical or surgical experience before they earned their medical degrees. Most Americans believed that family members, rather than doctors, were best suited to restore

their loved ones' health. Thus, many mid-nineteenth-century Americans avoided hospital treatment and viewed hospitals as being primarily for poor people who had no family to care for them.

Two distinct schools of medical thought existed in antebellum America: those who advocated a scientific approach to healing and those who advanced unorthodox medical practices. Advocates of scientific medicine believed that excess bodily fluids caused sickness by pushing the body out of its natural balance. Recovery required that these fluids be expelled from the body through bleeding, blistering, purging, and vomiting. Because these procedures were often painful, many Americans sought relief in other medical treatments such as phrenology, mesmerism, homeopathy and hydropathy.

THE CIVIL WAR

The Civil War, with its 620,000 deaths and ten million cases of disease, pushed scientifically-based medical care to the forefront of American society. When the war began, neither the Union nor the Confederacy was prepared to handle the large number of sick and wounded soldiers. Efficient medical care demanded that both the Union and Confederate governments create medical departments to accompany their armies. In April 1861, the scanty resources of both medical departments consisted of less than one hundred doctors, few ambulances, and no military hospitals.

In the spring of 1861, the lack of medical preparedness reached crisis proportions. Gathered in crowded training camps to drill and prepare for war, many Union and Confederate soldiers were exposed to childhood diseases (mainly mumps and measles) for the first time in their lives. Although these diseases were rarely fatal, they incapacitated thousands of soldiers at a time, necessitating the erection of large hospitals.

Civil War hospitals fell into two categories: field hospitals and general hospitals. Army doctors erected field hospitals near camps and battlefields. Designed for mobility and short-term care, field hospitals were located in tents or civilian buildings like churches, schools, or farm houses. Soldiers needing protracted medical care received treatment at more permanent general hospitals. Built in the "pavilion" style, each ward held about sixty patients and was detached on three sides from the main corridor, allowing patients to receive plenty of fresh air. Most general hospitals also contained kitchens, laundries, operating rooms, ice houses and morgues.

Diseases such as dysentery, diarrhea, typhoid fever, and malaria were the principal killers of Civil War soldiers. Poor hygiene and sanitation in army camps added to the rapid spread of disease. Although ideas concerning the importance of clean drinking water and the proper

Dr. John J. Craven, medical director of the Depertment of the South and physician who later attended Jefferson Davis, performing a battlefield operation. © CORBIS

diopooal of human waoto woro in thoir infanoy, oomo doc-tors and nurses saw the connection between unsanitary conditions and disease transmission. To aid in the clean-up of army camps, the United States government created the U.S. Sanitary Commission in June 1861. Directed by Frederick Law Olmsted, this commission worked to im-prove camp sanitation and preached the virtues of clean water, good food, and fresh air. Yet despite the Sanitary Commission's efforts, approximately 390,000 soldiers died from disease during the Civil War—twice the num-ber of those killed by bullets.

Second to disease as a cause of death, battlefield in-juries killed approximately 200,000 soldiers. Transport-ing wounded soldiers to field hospitals was problematic during the war's first year because musicians, cooks, and other noncombatants detailed as stretcher-bearers often fled during battle, stranding the wounded on the field for hours. The creation of a trained ambulance corps for the Army of the Potomac in August 1862 solved this prob-lem by efficiently delivering the wounded to field hospi-tals. The Confederates adopted a similar strategy, and the Civil War ambulance corps became the American model for battlefield evacuation through World War I.

Army doctors performed a large number of Civil War surgeries at field hospitals. Because many wounds consisted of gunshots to arms and legs, amputation was the most common procedure. Surgery during the Civil War was risky because the importance of sterilization was unknown until 1867. Surgeons rarely washed their hands or knives and used the same dirty sponges and clamps for many patients. As a result, post-operative infections pro-duced extremely high death rates.

Before amputation, most patients received anesthesia—chloroform or ether—which was sprinkled on a cloth and held over the patient's nose and mouth. After the sur-geon removed the limb, he clamped the arteries and tied them off with oiled silk. Most surgeons could amputate a limb in two or three minutes.

Field hospitals were not equipped for long-term pa-tient care. For this purpose, sick and wounded soldiers were transported to general hospitals located near supply and railroad depots. At the war's outset, both sides filled hospital positions with soldiers taken from the ranks. As wounds and sickness depleted each army's strength, gov-ernmental and military authorities moved to replace sol-diers with civilian hospital workers.

WOMEN AND CIVIL WAR MEDICAL CARE
Northern and Southern women made their most vital contribution to the war effort as hospital workers. Before

the war, few people recognized the importance of nurses. Florence Nightingale's work on behalf of British troops during the Crimean War changed attitudes, but it took the Civil War to professionalize American nursing and to foster acceptance of women as nurses. To serve their respective countries, women overcame many obstacles including familial objections and prejudice from doctors.

Northern women often found their way to general hospitals through Dorothea Dix, whom President Abraham Lincoln named Superintendent of Female Nurses in June 1861. A pre-war reformer, Dix worked with the U.S. Sanitary Commission and demanded that nursing applicants be at least thirty years old and plainly clothed. Approximately 3,200 women served as Union army nurses during the war.

Because the Confederacy did not have a sanitary commission or a centralized nursing agency, Southern women applied directly to general hospital administrators for positions. In September 1862, manpower shortages forced the Confederate Congress to officially authorize the employment of female nurses, and thousands of women, both white and black, served as nurses, cooks, and laundresses in Confederate general hospitals.

Medical care during the Civil War served to modernize and professionalize American medicine. Women's work advanced the professional status of nursing in the United States, and after the war, several nursing schools were created. Based on the pavilion plan, public hospitals were constructed across the country, and many Americans received medical treatment there instead of in the home. Mobile field hospitals and permanent general hospitals, an innovation of the Civil War, provided the framework for modern military medicine. Because army doctors recorded and studied their patients' progress, scientifically-based medical care slowly overcame the popularity of less orthodox medical practices. Most importantly, the success from enhanced hygienic practices during the Civil War stimulated the sanitary movement in American cities, improving the health of postwar Americans.

BIBLIOGRAPHY

Adams, George Worthington. *Doctors in Blue: The Medical History of the Union Army in the Civil War.* New York: Schuman, 1952.

Bollet, Alfred Jay. *Civil War Medicine: Challenges and Triumphs.* Tucson, AZ: Galen Press, 2002.

Brooks, Stewart. *Civil War Medicine.* Springfield, IL: C. C. Thomas, 1966.

Cunningham, H. H. *Doctors in Gray: The Confederate Medical Service.* Baton Rouge: Louisiana State University Press, 1958.

McPherson, James M. *Ordeal By Fire: The Civil War and Reconstruction,* 2d edition. New York: McGraw-Hill, 1992.

Nancy Schurr

See also: **Dix, Dorothea; United States Sanitary Commission.**

MEMORIAL (DECORATION) DAY

Memorial Day was the first American holiday created to commemorate dead soldiers. The carnage of the Civil War demanded some ritual of remembrance, and the cemetery provided the place for the ritual of grave decoration. Women began to decorate soldiers' graves during the war, and this practice developed into Memorial Day and Confederate Memorial Day. In 1966 Congress officially recognized Waterloo, New York, as the town that held the first Memorial Day on May 5, 1866.

The annual holiday was created in 1868 by a Union veterans' organization, the Grand Army of the Republic (GAR). Gen. John Logan, commander-in-chief of the GAR, designated May 30 as Memorial Day and ordered all posts to decorate the graves of their fallen comrades. The idea of Memorial Day spread quickly, as the GAR made the observance obligatory for each member and lobbied for official recognition of the holiday. Congress made Memorial Day a federal holiday in 1876, and by the 1880s most states outside the former Confederacy had legalized it.

Local GAR posts sponsored Memorial Day exercises in cemeteries across the nation, including the national cemeteries established in the former Confederacy. The featured rituals were speeches by distinguished veterans, who recalled the sacrifices and heroism of the dead, and decoration of the soldiers' graves with flowers woven into wreaths by members of the Women's Relief Corps. The ceremonies might also feature the dedication of a monument to the dead, and concluded with the playing of taps and a twenty-one-gun salute.

After Reconstruction ended in the late 1870s, Memorial Day attendance began to decline. The GAR added military parades to attract crowds and condemned the desecration of its sacred holiday by civilians who seemed more interested in recreation and sports than commemorating dead soldiers. In this it found common cause with Confederate veterans, and the former foes turned to each other for recognition of their valor and to recapture the camaraderie of battle. A series of Blue and Gray reunions occurred in the late nineteenth century, often held on Memorial Day, but this reconciliation was clearly for white veterans only. In the North African Americans had to join segregated GAR posts, and in the South white and black GAR posts held separate holiday exercises.

By the end of the century, diverse groups of Americans had embraced Memorial Day, but it meant different things to different people. Immigrants honored their

Memorial Day parade. © BETTMANN/CORBIS

BIBLIOGRAPHY

Blight, David W. *Race and Reunion: The Civil War in American Memory.* Cambridge, MA: Harvard University Press, Belknap Press, 2001.

Litwicki, Ellen M. *America's Public Holidays, 1865–1920.* Washington, DC: Smithsonian Institution Press, 2000.

O'Leary, Cecilia Elizabeth. *To Die For: The Paradox of American Patriotism.* Princeton, NJ: Princeton University Press, 1999.

Warner, W. Lloyd. *American Life: Dream and Reality.* Chicago: University of Chicago Press, 1953.

Ellen M. Litwicki

See also: Civil War Veterans.

MEN ON THE HOMEFRONT, CIVIL WAR

Despite the modern image of the patriotic volunteer in the Civil War, not all men fought for the Union or the Confederacy. Between 1861 and 1865 thousands of eligible men refused to serve. Some were draft dodgers and others were conscientious objectors. Still others purchased substitutes to fight for them. There were also thousands of deserters from the armies of the North and South who tried to melt into the general population.

Eligible men who did not serve risked being perceived as cowardly or unpatriotic. In a rousing letter to Kentuckians in 1861, one writer said that it was a time when "the workshop, the office, the counting-house and the field may well be abandoned for the solemn duty that is upon us . . . while the noble ship pitches and rolls under the lashings of the waves . . . the man who, at such an hour, will not work at the pump, is either a maniac or a monster." Senator Stephen A. Douglas echoed this opinion, stating, "There can be no neutrals in this war, only patriots or traitors."

Some men who lived in border states that were split in their loyalties, such as Kansas and Missouri, suffered violence. Men who were suspected of being loyal to the Union cause were hunted down by gangs of Southern loyalists called "bushwhackers." Union loyalists called "jayhawkers" wreaked havoc on Confederate supporters. Some men actually joined the army to avoid being attacked.

One occupation that was exempt from military service was the expressman. These couriers worked for express companies that delivered letters and packages. The express was the only way for prisoners to receive clothing and supplies from their loved ones across the Mason-Dixon line. The expressmen also carried the coffins of

countrymen who had fought in the Civil War with expressions of ethnic and American loyalty. Politicians promoted their own policies. For example, President Theodore Roosevelt used his 1902 address at the GAR's Arlington National Cemetery exercises to justify the American conquest of the Philippines. Many Americans without any ties to the Civil War dead decorated the graves of dead relatives on Memorial Day, which became popularly known as Decoration Day. The GAR campaigned against this new name, however, arguing that it did not properly reflect the holiday's purpose of memorializing dead soldiers and veterans. Most poignantly, as white veterans of North and South reconciled, it was left to their black comrades to remind Americans on Memorial Day that the Union army had fought for freedom for African Americans.

soldiers who had died on the battlefield to families who could afford to have the bodies shipped home.

When the war began, thousands of men on both sides immediately volunteered to join the army. As time passed, this initial surge proved insufficient to fill the ranks. The Confederacy enacted the first draft act in U.S. history in April 1862. The Enrollment Act of 1863, issued by President Abraham Lincoln, provided that a mandatory draft of men ages 20 to 45 would be held to create a sizable army. There was a loophole, however, in both draft acts; men who could afford to pay an exorbitant exemption fee of $300 were excused from serving. Among those who did not fight in the war, choosing instead to focus on their careers, were the future magnates James Mellon, John D. Rockefeller, Jay Gould, and J. P. Morgan.

In the North, the draft was met by protests and riots in several cities due to the perceived unfairness of the situation. The most serious of these riots took place in New York City, where laborers, particularly Irish immigrants, were angry at the prospect of having to serve in the army while wealthy men avoided the draft entirely. On July 13 and 14, 1863, they rioted, causing great damage and resulting in some 100 deaths.

Some men who stayed on the homefront were involved in keeping the wartime economy going. The railroads still ran. Factories churned out uniforms and rifles. Saloons and other businesses stayed open, whether run by the original proprietor or by a relative or friend. Newspapermen followed the war on a daily basis. Photographers took keepsake photos of soldiers on their way off to war and as the troops stopped in a town or city.

Some front men were draft dodgers; others were conscientious objectors. Thousands of deserters hid until the war was over, or sometimes dared to return home at the risk of being arrested. Others on the homefront included many of the 400,000 men who were wounded during the war and returned home disabled or sick.

BIBLIOGRAPHY

Bernstein, Iver. *The New York City Draft Riots: Their Significance for American Society and Politics in the Age of the Civil War.* New York: Oxford University Press. 1990.

Cashin, Joan E., ed. *The War Was You and Me: Civilians in the American Civil War.* Princeton, NJ: Princeton University Press. 2002.

Damon, Duane. *When This Cruel War is Over: The Civil War Home Front.* Minneapolis, MN: Lerner, 1996.

Ellis, Edward Robb. *The Epic of New York City.* New York: Kodansha, 1997.

Murdock, Eugene C. *Patriotism Limited 1862–1865: The Civil War Draft and the Bounty System.* Kent, OH: Kent State University Press. 1967.

Stevens, Joseph E. *1863: The Rebirth of a Nation.* New York: Bantam, 1999.

Richard Panchyk

See also: New York City Draft Riots.

MOBILIZATION FOR WAR

Raising an American army has traditionally been complicated by competing political ideologies, the fear of a strong standing army, a reliance on citizen-soldiers, and wartime dissent. From the nation's inception in the late eighteenth century through the Cold War years (1946–1991), America's defenses consisted of state militia forces (later called the National Guard) and a small regular (federal) army—the latter expanded by citizen-soldiers who joined as volunteers and only when necessary as draftees. This two-army tradition of militias and professionals grew out of the colonies' early use of militia forces, the new nation's intense debate over the power of the federal government, and the growing concern that a permanent force of trained soldiers could threaten the liberty of the people. During America's wars, patriotic fervor as well as varying degrees of political dissent converged with each mobilization effort.

THE MEXICAN WAR

The Mexican War (1846–1848) was no exception. Years of tension stemming from the Texas Revolution and Texas's subsequent declaration of independence from Mexico resurfaced with a boundary dispute and the 1845 admission of Texas into the United States. This was far more than a quarrel over land. President James K. Polk's insistence that Mexico acknowledge the boundary Texas claimed had more to do with the president's desire (and the desire of many other imperialists in the United States) to spread what they thought of as America's superior cultural, political, and economic institutions from sea to sea. A war with Mexico had the potential to add vast lands, from Texas to California, and to extend American commerce to countries across the Pacific. Although most Americans generally supported the idea of expansion westward, others (particularly abolitionists and the northern Whig and the Free Soil political parties) resisted the spread of slavery into any newly acquired lands. Anti-imperialists and pacifists—a small minority of Americans—stood firm against Manifest Destiny, most of them objecting to an attitude they considered presumptuous for violating other peoples' right of self-determination.

When war with Mexico began in May 1846, the country's longstanding tradition of maintaining a small regular army brought the United States to the conflict with a force of only about 8,600 men. Polk quickly expanded the military after Congress authorized a regular (federal) army of 15,500 men and an enlistment of over 50,000 one-year (or duration) volunteers. Also called into service were 1,390 three month militiamen, a call up which soon expanded to 11,211 six-month militiamen. However, a fierce public debate over the war forced the government to restrict its military efforts. Mobilization was not easy; Northern opposition to the war forced the government to recruit in other regions. The American military victory over Mexico came in 1848 and involved the combined forces of the regular U.S. army, 12,000 militiamen from the Gulf states, and 73,000 volunteers who came primarily from the Southern and Midwestern states. Irish and German immigrants composed some forty-seven percent of the army's recruits during the 1840s, so undoubtedly immigrants made up a significant part of the American regular army during the war. Like native-born enlistees, they were lured into the military by a sense of adventure, a feeling of patriotism for their (adopted) country, and the anticipation of upward mobility.

THE CIVIL WAR: VOLUNTEERS AND DRAFTEES

Mobilizing for war became even more complex during the American Civil War (1861–1865), which was brought about by continued political and economic conflict between the North and the South and exacerbated by conflict over whether slavery would expand westward. Despite the South's rallying cry of states' rights, the Confederacy implemented a national draft before the Union did, on April 16, 1862. In response to increasing casualties, a decreasing number of volunteers, and the expiration of one-year enlistments, the South declared all white males between the ages of eighteen and thirty-five eligible for the draft. Facing conscription, many men volunteered in order to have some say in which unit they joined. However, a draft-age man was allowed to hire someone to take his place, and substitutes soon charged top dollar (some over $5,000) to take up arms. Of the 120,000 Confederate draftees, 70,000 found substitutes. Although Southern lawmakers later eliminated the substitution option, the new draft system allowed for so many exemptions (particularly for the wealthier classes), that fifty percent of would-be draftees stayed out of service.

Attempts to mobilize men in the North resulted in similar problems. President Abraham Lincoln asked Congress for 300,000 three-year volunteers. At the start of the conflict, enlistment of young men eager to fight for the cause and drawn by patriotism, the spirit of adventure, or the promise of a steady paycheck allowed the North to attract a good supply of soldiers. The threat of a possible draft also helped bring volunteers, especially among men who would rather join on their own terms than be forced into the army. Initially, 421,000 volunteers and 87,500 militiamen answered the call. The North's early use of volunteer and militia forces permitted the Union to honor the deeply held beliefs of the founding fathers that a small standing federal army be enlarged in time of crisis by citizen-soldiers.

However, as one bloody battle followed another and casualties mounted, an acute manpower shortage left the North no alternative but to institute a draft. The March 3, 1863, Enrollment Act (also called the Conscription Act) made all able-bodied male citizens between twenty-one and forty-five eligible for conscription. This included native-born citizens, naturalized citizens, and immigrants who had declared their intention of becoming citizens. Problems with the Northern draft also quickly became apparent due to special exemptions allowing men to hire substitutes or pay $300 to purchase exemptions.

The federalized draft system caused much controversy, further divided Republicans and Democrats, and led to widespread draft resistance, including riots. Peace Democrats saw the draft exemption rules as class based and argued that commutations would cost a worker one year's pay. They vehemently challenged exemptions that allowed the upper class to escape military service while the lower classes died in what was often called a rich man's war and a poor man's fight. Resistance to the Union draft took on a number of forms, including creating fictitious identities, going into hiding, and open violence. More than 161,000 men evaded the draft.

Armed draft resistance led to bloodshed and even murder as a growing number of working class Democrats from both native-born and immigrant groups mixed their resentment of the draft with anger over prolonged economic hardships and lingering feelings of exploitation by their Republican bosses. Many from the working class also feared that freed African Americans would compete with them for jobs, especially after the Emancipation Proclamation of January 1863, which freed slaves in the Confederate states. Draft resistance and riots took place in Illinois, Indiana, Iowa, Massachusetts, Michigan, Minnesota, New Hampshire, New York, Ohio, Vermont, and Wisconsin. The worst draft riot occurred in New York City and began on July 13, 1863, after the first name was drawn from the conscription wheel. The riot lasted five days and included beatings, looting, vandalism, arson, and murder. The frustration of the rioters was directed at not only upper class Republicans but also at New York's African-American population.

The Northern drafts were far from effective. Of the 522,187 men examined, 315,509 received exemptions for medical or other reasons, and many of those who could afford to pay their way out of service did so. Of 206,678 "draftees," 86,724 paid their way out of service and 73,607 found substitutes. Only 46,347 men who served in the Civil War—about six percent—came directly from the conscription system. To attract more volunteers, the government resorted to bounties, payments to entice men to enlist, which eventually cost the government some $700 million. Most of those who served in the Union army came from the lower classes and were brought into the war as draftees, bounty enlistees, volunteers, or substitutes. Irish and German immigrants made up about twenty-four percent of the soldiers and African Americans represented ten percent. Several hundred women also served in the Union Army, however, most women who joined the war effort did so in non-combatant roles.

POST-CIVIL WAR PERIOD

America's rapid demobilization at the close of the Civil War was in keeping with its prewar ideology: The country returned to a small standing army. By 1876, the regular forces were made up of about 27,500 men, and most of them were scattered on the Western frontier. Increased settlement, dramatically accelerated by railroad construction, brought over two million settlers to the West and further disturbed the land and game that sustained the Indian way of life. Government policy forced tribes to live on reservations, often on uninhabitable lands, and treaties with the Indians were commonly invalidated when white fortune hunters found gold and silver on Indian lands. Skirmishes in the Great Plains increased sharply as Indians reacted to this encroachment. Territorial militiamen and volunteers joined the fight, but in many cases they made the situation even more contentious by their cruel treatment of Indian tribes.

Before the close of the nineteenth century, the United States fought the Spanish-American War and the Philippine Insurrection. Both conflicts forced the nation to rethink its military practices. By the early twentieth century, America was fully industrialized and involved in global trade and international affairs. As an emerging world power, military leaders argued that reform was not only recommended, it was necessary. Although leaders could agree on many aspects of military modernization, they debated America's mobilization practices, especially the use of volunteers and militiamen in combination with a small regular army. Some reformers argued for universal military training, which would require all able-bodied young men to practice as soldiers. Others called for maintaining a larger federal army of professionally trained soldiers. In the end, the tradition of expanding the military only in time of crisis was maintained. Mobilization continued to bring together citizen-soldiers in the form of draftees, volunteers, and the National Guard to assist the

regular army. Not until the late twentieth century did the United States break the tradition, forming and maintaining a large professional trained army and stationing it throughout the world.

BIBLIOGRAPHY
Chambers, John Whiteclay, II. *To Raise an Army: The Draft Comes to Modern America.* New York: Free Press, 1987.
Ford, Nancy Gentile. *Issues of War and Peace.* Westport, CT: Greenwood, 2002.
Millett, Allan R., and Maslowski, Peter. *For the Common Defense: A Military History of the United States.* New York: Free Press, 1984.
Weigley, Russell F. *The American Way of War: The History of United States Military Strategy and Policy.* Bloomington: University of Indiana Press, 1977.

Nancy Gentile Ford

See also: **New York City Draft Riots.**

MUSIC, CIVIL WAR

Music played a major role in the Civil War, making it perhaps the most musical of all U.S. military conflicts. More songs were written, adapted, sung, and remembered from the Civil War than from any other U.S. war: Estimates suggest that around 9,000 new songs were printed in the North and as many as 750 in the South. The young but vigorous sheet music industry of the mid-nineteenth century capitalized on the event, and the popularity of both religious tunes and minstrel melodies provided affecting music for many purposes, including inspiring crowds at political rallies, recruiting soldiers, accompanying marching and fighting, and comforting soldiers' families at home. Music helped shape attitudes and mark regional identities, and the potentially subversive qualities of some songs were recognized by military leaders, including the Union commander General Benjamin Butler, who tried to destroy all copies of the Southern song "The Bonnie Blue Flag" upon the North's capture of New Orleans in April 1862 (he also fined the publisher and threatened a $24 fine for anyone caught singing or whistling the melody). Like the war itself, which was a war of brother against brother, some of the songs claimed by one side had pedigrees rooted in the other.

SLAVE AND ABOLITIONIST MUSIC

Slaves on Southern plantations produced many types of music, although most modern knowledge of it comes not from musical notation but in the less reliable form of accounts written by white listeners who were unfamiliar with African musical traditions. Frederick Douglass wrote in his autobiography that slaves were "generally expected to sing as well as to work," and that some masters used singing as a way of monitoring their slaves' locations and moods. He also explained how slaves cloaked the real meaning of some songs—meanings such as frustration at the injustices of slavery or a desire to be free—by adopting biblical topics. When a group of slaves fled to Fortress Monroe, Virginia, after the start of the Civil War, their song "Let My People Go" was heard and described by Reverend Lewis Lockwood, and it was quickly published and circulated in a Northern abolitionist newspaper, marking the beginning of the printed spiritual and demonstrating one type of African-American music and sentiment to a white, Northern audience. In many slave states, drumming by slaves was banned, and in 1845 Georgia passed a law prohibiting slaves from performing loud instruments out of fear that it might provide a source of communication for uprisings and resistance. Yet slaves danced and sang to the accompaniment of percussive objects like sticks and hands, and aspects of their speech (a mocking dialect) and preferred instruments, such as the tambourine, bones, and banjo, were absorbed into the minstrel show traditions that arose in the 1840s. The first printed collection of slave songs, *Slave Songs of the United States*, appeared shortly after the war, in 1867.

Abolitionist sentiments were expressed in song by the Hutchinson Family Singers of New Hampshire, who used their popularity in the 1840s to advance a number of causes, including women's rights, utopian communities, and temperance, as well as fierce opposition to slavery. They appeared with Frederick Douglass at a Boston antislavery rally in 1843, and a year later their song "Get Off the Track!" was used at events like the New England Anti-Slavery Convention held in Salem, Massachusetts. In their song "Get off the Track!" a train engine called Liberty was headed down the track, building a full head of steam, and proslavery forces needed to get out of the way or risk disaster. Ironically, the original melody, Daniel Emmett's "Old Dan Tucker," had been a popular song on the minstrel stage; blackface minstrelsy, a form of entertainment based on degrading stereotypes of African Americans, originated in the North, where it enjoyed great popularity, a reminder that abolitionist goals were not necessarily synonymous with the desire for racial equality.

CIVIL WAR MUSIC

The speed with which sheet music could be produced and distributed allowed it to take on a journalistic function during the Civil War. On April 15, 1861, three days after the bombardment of Fort Sumter and the military start of the conflict, George Root, a Union sympathizer whose works rivaled those of Stephen Foster in contem-

porary popularity, responded with the song, "The First Gun Is Fired! May God Protect the Right." The Baltimore riots of April, 1861, where a prosecessionist mob attacked Union troops, inspired James Ryder Randall to write a poem, "Maryland! My Maryland," urging fellow Marylanders (Randall was born in Baltimore but had moved to Louisiana) to resist what he labeled the "tyrant's chain" held by the federal government. Quickly printed in newspapers, Randall's poem—which included phrases like "Northern scum"—was fitted to the German song "O Tannenbaum" and published as sheet music in October. Northern parodies countered with descriptions of Southerners as "rebel thieves" and "traitors."

The histories of "The Battle Hymn of the Republic" and "Dixie" reflect how closely the combatants were related. Daniel Emmett, an Ohio-born Union sympathizer, premiered "Dixie" in New York City, and the melody for "The Battle Hymn of the Republic," called "Glory, Glory Hallelujah," was a Georgia camp revival song credited to the Virginia native William Steffe. In November 1861, abolitionist Julia Ward Howe was reviewing federal troops and witnessed a surprise Confederate attack; during the retreat, she heard some soldiers singing Steffe's revival tune. Later that night, she wrote a poem that fit the tune and that became "The Battle Hymn of the Republic." The words were printed on the front page of the February 1862 issue of the *Atlantic Monthly* and Howe was paid $4 for it. The song reveals a strong religious character, especially in its fifth stanza, where she parallels the goals of Christianity and the federal government:

> In the beauty of the lilies Christ was born across
>   the sea,
> With a glory in his bosom that transfigures you and
>   me;
> As he died to make men holy, let us die to make
>   men free,
> While God is marching on!

The First Arkansas, an African-American unit, had new words in the old minstrel dialect written by a white captain:

> Oh! we're de bully soldiers of de "First of
>   Arkansas";
> We are fightin' for de Union, we are fightin' for de
>   law;
> We can hit a rebel furder dan a white man eber
>   saw;
> As we go marching on.

Emmett's "Dixie" was originally written as a walka-round, or finale for a minstrel show in New York City. When it was first heard in New Orleans, its attractiveness to Southern audiences led to unauthorized publications that appeared in print before Emmett's authorized version. It became the unofficial anthem of the Confederate

States of America—neither side had an official national anthem during the Civil War, (the "Star-Spangled Banner" was not adopted until 1931)—and it was played at Jefferson Davis's inauguration in Montgomery, Alabama. Perhaps no other song was rewritten as often during the Civil War; among the resettings were Southern versions expressing confidence in the Confederacy's military prowess, a Michigan call to arms bemoaning how the South had torn "our good old flag asunder," and a Republican salute to Lincoln's candidacy in the 1860 election. When he was serenaded by bands right after the South's surrender, President Lincoln requested that they play "Dixie," calling it "one of the best tunes I have ever heard," but by 1865 the song was too strongly attached to Confederate ideals to be comfortably reintegrated by the entire nation.

BIBLIOGRAPHY

Cockrell, Dale. *Excelsior: Journals of the Hutchinson Family Singers, 1842–1846.* Stuyvesant, NY: Pendragon, 1989.

Crawford, Richard. *The Civil War Songbook: Complete Original Sheet Music for Thirty-Seven Songs.* New York: Dover, 1977.

Crawford, Richard. *An Introduction to American Music.* New York: Norton, 2001.

Douglass, Frederick. *Life and Times of Frederick Douglass: His Early Life as a Slave, His Escape from Bondage, and His Complete History.* New York: Collier Books, 1962.

Harwell, Richard B. *Confederate Music.* Chapel Hill: University of North Carolina Press, 1950.

Heaps, Willard A., and Heaps, Porter W. *The Singing Sixties: The Spirit of Civil War Days Drawn from the Music of the Times.* Norman: University of Oklahoma Press, 1960.

Lawrence, Vera Brodsky. *Music for Patriots, Politicians, and Presidents: Harmonies and Discords of the First Hundred Years.* New York: Macmillan, 1975.

Wiley, Bell Irvin. *The Life of Johnny Reb: The Common Soldier of the Confederacy.* Indianapolis: Bobbs-Merrill, 1943.

Wiley, Bell Irvin. *The Life of Billy Yank: The Common Soldier of the Union.* Indianapolis: Bobbs-Merrill, 1952.

Internet Resources

Newsom, Jon. "The American Brass Band Movement: A Historical Overview." Available from <http://memory.loc.gov/ammem/cwmhtml/cwmpres01.html.>.

"'We'll Sing to Abe Our Song!': Sheet Music about Lincoln, Emancipation, and the Civil War." Alfred Whital Stern Collection of Lincolniana, Library of Congress. Available from <http://memory.loc.gov/ammem/scsmhtml/scsmhome.html>.

Neil W. Lerner

NEW YORK CITY DRAFT RIOTS

The most destructive urban violence in U.S. history occurred in New York City during four days of draft riots, July 13 to July 16, 1863. In the midst of the Civil War, tens of thousands of mainly foreign-born (mostly Irish) workers poured onto the streets to protest the new draft law that made them, not the wealthy, likely to be conscripted into the army. Rioters attacked the city's draft headquarters, defied police, looted stores, and sought out African-American victims to hang from the lampposts. During those four days, New York City became a battlefield.

In general, most wage workers in the North supported the Union and Abraham Lincoln's policies in the war. However, they were increasingly disturbed by what they considered to be inequities in the conscription, or draft, laws. They were especially antagonized by a new draft provision that allowed anyone with $300 to buy his way out of the army. Because most workers in New York City and elsewhere—black and white alike—earned only about $500 a year, they had little hope of escaping the military.

Resentment about the coming drawing of names for enlistment had been festering during the spring and early summer. Although the Union recorded victories at Gettysburg and Vicksburg, the growing list of dead and injured soldiers only pointed up the desperate need for new recruits.

With the drawing of names about to begin, mobs poured into the streets and headed for draft headquarters. They set fire to the building. From there, the wildness ran unchecked. The rioters burned bridges, tore down telegraph lines, stole weapons from munitions plants, and put up barricades of defense around their own neighborhoods. But the worst violence was directed against African Americans. If caught on the streets, they were sometimes lynched on the spot, their bodies then burned and mutilated and carried through the streets. An orphan asylum housing African-American children was destroyed. White women who were known to have married black men were sought out and killed.

Ironically, African Americans lived and worked in the same neighborhoods as the foreign immigrants and suffered from the same poverty. But the war had caused new concerns for the white workers. They feared that the emancipation of slaves would bring an influx of blacks into the city who would compete for jobs. Actually, em-

Print of the *Provost Guard Attacking the Rioters.* During the New York Draft Riots in July of 1863, tens of thousands of mainly foreign-born workers poured into the streets to protest a new draft law. © BETTMANN/CORBIS

ployers had previously brought in African Americans as strikebreakers during this period. White immigrants, desperately poor and living in economic slavery themselves, became violent at the thought of losing more ground to blacks.

The violence and destruction in New York City continued for four days until July 16, when the battle-weary Seventh New York Regiment was called to return from Gettysburg. As the final hours of the rioting erupted into a frenzy, soldiers chased the looters through the streets and finally into the tenements, where some jumped to their deaths.

In all, about 119 people died in the draft riots; a number were killed by U.S. troops. At least twelve African Americans died. They were either lynched by rioters or drowned in the river trying to escape their tormentors. The number of injured was estimated at 1,000 and property damage as high as $2 million.

After all the violence and destruction, the draft went on as planned, quietly enforced in August. However, this time there was a heavy military presence to enforce it. In addition, political boss William M. Tweed administered a county loan ordinance that paid a $300 draft waiver for the poor. The New York City Draft Riots reveal the smoldering class and racial tensions that existed both North and South, far from the actual battlefields. War had exacerbated these tensions into a bloody domestic conflict.

BIBLIOGRAPHY

Bernstein, Iver. *The New York City Draft Riots: Their Significance for American Society and Politics in the Age of the Civil War.* New York: Oxford University Press, 1996.

Hayes, Susan. "The Great Draft Riots." *Scholastic Update* 131 (1998): 18–21.

Katz, William Loren. "The New York City Draft Riots of 1863." *New York Amsterdam News* 94 (2003): 15–20.

Corinne J. Naden and Rose Blue

See also: **Mobilization for War; Urbanization; Violence.**

NEWSPAPERS AND MAGAZINES

For most of the nineteenth century, newspapers in the United States were heavily partisan. Newspaper editors sat on party central committees, and they tailored their matter to promote a party line. Most of their news was copied directly out of other partisan newspapers, which editors exchanged for free through the mail. A typical editor with 500 or 800 subscribers might exchange with as many as a hundred other newspapers throughout the country, passing on bits of information and opinion from all of them and hoping that they too copied items from his or her paper. This party press system was remarkably open ended. Items could enter from any point, although they had to fit within the boundaries set by the agendas of the major political parties.

One issue that the major parties tried to keep out of the papers was slavery. Because they relied on votes from the South, political parties saw no benefit in even discussing slavery and took sometimes violent action to show their disdain for abolitionism. Canny agitators such as William Lloyd Garrison, editor of the *Liberator* and the best known of the abolitionists, turned this to their advantage. Garrison found that party editors—especially in the South—were eager to exchange newspapers with him so they could copy items they found outrageous. He in turn could show how important his newspaper was by publicizing how often it was copied. He exchanged with as many as 400 publications.

By demonizing its discussion, the party press system helped polarize the nation over the slavery issue. In the South, leading fire-eaters, such as Robert Barnwell Rhett of South Carolina, used their newspapers to feed proslavery news items into the national system. Rhett owned the *Charleston Mercury,* a Democratic newspaper that his son edited.

In the fifteen years before the Civil War, new technologies began to change the press. The telegraph allowed for news to be transmitted instantaneously and created a system of buying and selling news quite different from the traditional sharing of news in the party press. The telegraph also helped centralize the news system in New York City, home to powerful papers like Horace Greeley's *Tribune* and James Gordon Bennett's *Herald.* The popularity of photography, which was introduced in 1839, helped promote engraved illustrations in newspapers and newsweeklies such as *Harper's* and *Leslie's.* By the mid-1850s, the telegraph and illustrations allowed the entire nation to instantly and simultaneously know and imagine current events. John Brown's face, spread by the illustrated press during the troubles in Kansas, would spring to everyone's mind when the telegraph transmitted news of his Harper's Ferry Raid.

During the Civil War, both the Northern and Southern press played a central role in carrying news and opinion. The news kept people informed. The opinion, which produced a surprising amount of dissent, allowed governments to claim legitimacy by maintaining the habits and appearances of party competition. This was true in both the North and the South but was more pronounced in the North. In the South, print culture was less developed, with fewer newspapers and magazines having smaller circulations, penetrating to a smaller proportion of the population, and featuring less diversity in content and opinion. The Confederate government was also quicker to regulate the press, although Southern editors tended to be more uniform in their loyalty to their government. In the North, a vigorous copperhead press continually challenged the Lincoln administration. Occasionally the government took action against it, and often as elections approached opposition newspapers would be visited by mobs that included soldiers on leave. But the spectacle of interparty conflict remained an important confirmation that the government was legitimate.

Military secrecy was a major concern during the Civil War. No U.S. war has ever produced more eyewitness newspaper accounts—not just accounts from newspaper correspondents who traveled with the armies but also from ordinary soldiers, whose letters home were published in both local newspapers and national weeklies. Inevitably, generals blamed the press for leaking important details to the enemy, and some, including William T. Sherman, developed a real animosity to the correspondents in camp. To counter this hostility, correspondents often trumpeted the virtues of the generals whose armies they accompanied, helping to create cults of personality. Meanwhile, governments North and South took steps to control the telegraph system and censor reports from the armies. This vigorous control of military information contrasts starkly with the period's permissive attitude toward opposition politics.

The Civil War accelerated changes in the news system. The special correspondents of the period, known as the bohemian brigade, are often considered the first professional reporters. The circulation of illustrated papers expanded rapidly. Photographers such as Mathew Brady accompanied the armies, partly to document the war in photographs they hoped to sell later and partly to make money by taking portraits of soldiers for the soldiers to send home. Because of the long exposure times required for photographs then, the images that survive tend to be of posed soldiers, landscapes, and corpses.

After the war, some of the period's changes were incorporated into the news system. The inverted pyramid style, in which the main points of an article are made in the opening paragraph, was adopted from the style of military dispatches. The telegraph system, consolidated under Western Union, allowed the Associated Press to establish a national monopoly as a news provider. The war also reaffirmed the dominance of New York City as the national distributor of news, as well as the powerful position of the largest New York dailies.

BIBLIOGRAPHY

Andrews, J. Cutler. *The North Reports the Civil War*. Pittsburgh: University of Pittsburgh Press, 1955.

Andrews, J. Cutler. *The South Reports the Civil War*. Princeton, NJ: Princeton University Press, 1970.

Blondheim, Menahem. "Public Sentiment Is Everything: The Union's Public Communications Strategy and the Bogus Proclamation of 1864." *Journal of American History* 89 vol. 3 (December 2002): 869–899.

Brown, Joshua. *Beyond the Lines: Pictorial Reporting, Everyday Life, and the Crisis of Gilded Age America*. Berkeley: University of California Press, 2002.

Marszalek, John F. *Sherman's Other War: The General and the Civil War Press*. Memphis: Memphis State University Press, 1981.

Starr, Louis Morris. *Bohemian Brigade: Civil War Newsmen in Action*. New York: Knopf, 1954.

John Nerone

See also: **Greeley, Horace; Humor, Political; Photography, Civil War.**

OCCUPATION OF THE SOUTH

The only Americans, other than American Indians, who ever experienced extended, large-scale enemy occupation were the people of the Confederate South. The "enemy" was the U.S. army, which set forth in 1861 to conquer the Confederacy and force the seceded states back into the Union. Over the next four years, the Union army occupied large sections of the Confederacy, especially in Virginia, Tennessee, and Arkansas, along the Mississippi River, and on the Atlantic coast. Many important Southern cities were captured, including Nashville, New Orleans, and Atlanta. Union troops in the invaded regions eventually numbered over half a million.

When the Civil War began, Northerners, including President Abraham Lincoln, believed that most Southerners were not "Rebels" at heart, but instead had been deceived into supporting secession by scheming politicians. The initial Union policy toward citizens of the occupied regions was therefore conciliatory, aimed at bringing the "misguided" to their senses and winning them back to the Union. Army officers took pains to ensure that the citizens were not abused by troops and that their property (including slaves) was protected. Soon, however, it became clear that Northern assumptions were wrong and that conciliation was fruitless. Most whites in the Confederacy were, in fact, devout secessionists, and in the invaded regions they demonstrated their Confederate patriotism and their hatred of the enemy by insulting Union troops, spying on them, and engaging in guerrilla warfare.

In 1862, the occupiers abandoned conciliation and began moving toward a harsh policy, which included imprisoning active secessionists and confiscating or destroying their property. Among the first commanders to crack down was Benjamin Butler in New Orleans. Fed up with the behavior of the women there (who were even more outspoken than the men), Butler decreed that any woman who insulted a Union soldier would be dealt with as a common prostitute.

The new policy was motivated in part by the desire to punish the obstinate Rebels. But it was also intended to help win a war that was turning out to be longer and harder than Northerners had anticipated by depriving the Confederacy of resources and destroying the morale of its people. The Union general who best exemplified the harsh policy was William T. Sherman, who led his army on a notoriously destructive march to the sea through Georgia and the Carolinas in 1864 through 1865. Sherman's men, however, actually exercised a good deal of

Hastily built Union camp for the 2nd Massachusetts Infantry Regiment, during the occupation of Atlanta, ca. 1864. © CORBIS

restraint, as did other Union troops; physical assaults by soldiers on unarmed citizens during the war were rare.

Hand in hand with the destruction of Southern resources under the harsh policy went the emancipation of the slaves. The slaves themselves took the first steps toward liberation, many of them fleeing to the Union invaders even when the conciliatory policy prevailed. The desire of the slaves to be free and to aid the Union helped move President Lincoln toward emancipation. The Emancipation Proclamation of January 1, 1863, which Lincoln justified as a measure to weaken the Confederacy's war effort, declared free all slaves in the rebellious territories. As the influx of runaway slaves increased, the army set up camps to house, feed, and educate them. Many freed slaves worked as wage laborers on plantations seized by the army. On the South Carolina and Georgia coast, the army undertook an experiment in which freed people were given land to farm on their own.

Slaves were not the only people in the South who took advantage of the Union invasion. Some Southern whites who remained loyal to the Union seized the opportunity to take revenge on their secessionist oppressors. Some poor whites defied the aristocrats who had long dominated Southern society. Like the freedom-seeking slaves, these insurgent Unionists and poor whites were aided by the Northern invaders.

After the war ended in 1865, the U.S. army occupied the entire South, but with a reduced force. Demobilization left fewer than forty thousand troops in the former Confederate states in 1866, and the number continued to decline thereafter. During Reconstruction (1865–1877), army officers and troops in the South were called on repeatedly, mostly for political purposes. They were assigned a major role in the restoration and readmission of the Southern states (accomplished by 1870 under Congress's Reconstruction Acts); and they were frequently employed to protect black voters and their white Republican allies from violence at the hands of ex-Confederates, particularly Ku Klux Klan terrorism. With the overthrow of the last Republican-dominated Southern state regime by the ex-Confederates in 1877, Reconstruction ended and with it the army's role in the South.

The military occupation of the South that began in 1861 had profound consequences, some short-lived, others long-lasting. The suffering and destruction were enormous, but the suffering abated with the war's end and the destruction was soon repaired. The liberation of the slaves, however, changed the nation in ways that continue to affect every American deeply, while the memory of those years of invasion and occupation helped shape a distinctive Southern mentality that endures to this day.

BIBLIOGRAPHY

Ash, Stephen V. *When the Yankees Came: Conflict and Chaos in the Occupied South, 1861 1865*. Chapel Hill and London: University of North Carolina Press, 1995.

Grimsley, Mark. *The Hard Hand of War: Union Military Policy Toward Southern Civilians, 1861–1865*. Cambridge, UK: Cambridge University Press, 1995.

Sefton, James E. *The United States Army and Reconstruction, 1865–1877*. Baton Rouge: Louisiana State University Press, 1967.

Stephen V. Ash

See also: **Ku Klux Klan; Reconstruction; Sherman's March to the Sea.**

PEACE MOVEMENTS

Efforts to retain and regain peace during the Civil War (1861–1865) were uniformly unsuccessful. The earliest of these efforts took place in Washington in the winter of 1860–1861 as the outbreak of war threatened. Kentucky Senator John J. Crittenden drafted a series of initiatives, including an irrevocable constitutional amendment protecting slavery, protection of slavery south of the Missouri Compromise line, and compensation to owners for fugitive slaves. The Republican Party immediately rejected these proposals. Shortly thereafter, a peace convention of Unionists from the upper South met to try to find an alternative plan to prevent war. The convention adopted a modified form of the Crittenden plan that both the Republicans and the newly formed Confederate States of America rejected.

The initial organization of purely voluntary armies by both governments and the overwhelming martial spirit in both sections temporarily silenced peace advocates after April 1861. Individual pacifists, especially the Quakers, announced their opposition to the war on moral and religious grounds and were allowed to avoid participation in the bloodshed. Peace advocates became more outspoken when the Confederacy imposed conscription in 1862 and the Union did so in 1863, and when Abraham Lincoln announced his Preliminary Emancipation Proclamation in September 1862. By 1863 one wing of the Democratic Party had become advocates of an armistice to end the fighting, and they expected peace negotiations would follow. Their most active spokesperson was Clement L. Vallandigham, a gubernatorial candidate in Ohio. Although there was substantial support for this policy in the North—particularly among farmers in the lower Midwest—peace candidates lost most of the major political races in the North in 1863.

Peace movements began to appear openly in the Confederacy in the summer of 1863. These movements appeared to be motivated by the economic challenges facing lower-class whites and a decline in morale that developed after major Confederate defeats at Vicksburg and Gettysburg in early July. The most significant of these efforts took place in North Carolina and was headed by newspaperman William W. Holden. More than 100 public meetings were held throughout the state, and participants demanded that the administration of Jefferson Davis, president of the Confederacy, seek an armistice and negotiate a peace. As a result of this popular clamor, three peace candidates were elected to the Confederate Congress from North Carolina.

By 1864 revulsion against the heavy losses suffered by both armies led to renewed efforts to end the hostilities. On the Union side, secret groups called the Sons of Liberty and Knights of the Golden Circle formed in the Midwest. They called for an end to the fighting and supported the Peace Democrats. The Peace Democrats controlled their party's national convention in August and called for an armistice and a convention of states. Although the Democratic presidential candidate, George M. McClellan, repudiated the peace plank, many Democrats supported the party platform throughout the campaign.

In the Confederacy, public disillusionment with the Davis administration also created an organized opposition. Clandestine groups—particularly among yeoman farmers in the Appalachian Mountains—worked to end the war and to bring about reunion. Among these organizations were the Peace Party in Alabama and the Heroes of America in Virginia and North Carolina. William Holden ran for governor of North Carolina in 1864 as an avowed peace candidate but was soundly defeated.

As the military defeat of the Confederacy became more obvious in the winter of 1864–1865, several individuals and groups in the South sought to end the fighting. Legislators in Virginia, Georgia, and North Carolina introduced initiatives calling for an end to the fighting, but these were defeated by a majority of members. Senator William A. Graham of North Carolina reported that some members of the Confederate Senate were encouraging the states of Virginia and North Carolina to withdraw their troops from the Confederate army. In February 1865 President Lincoln and his secretary of state, William H. Seward, agreed to meet Confederate representatives at Hampton Roads, Virginia. The three Confederate officials—Vice President Alexander Stephens, Senator Robert M. T. Hunter of Virginia, and Davis's assistant secretary of war, John A. Campbell—sought an armistice and a joint foreign policy initiative by the two governments. Lincoln rejected the Confederate overtures, and peace came only with the surrender of the Confederate armies in April.

The Civil War peace movements failed for two major reasons. First, the majority of people in both sections rejected compromise on the key issues of reunification and slavery. Second, both Jefferson Davis and Abraham Lincoln, and their advisors, refused to consider any peace terms other than those unacceptable to the other. Thus, the peace movements of the Civil War never had a chance to succeed.

BIBLIOGRAPHY

Auman, William T. and David B. Scarboro. "The Heroes of America in Civil War North Carolina." *North Carolina Historical Review*, LVIII (Autumn 1981), 327–363.

Curran, Thomas F. "Pacifists, Peace Democrats, and the Politics of Perfection in the Civil War Era," *Journal of Church and State*, XXXVIII (Summer 1996), 486–506.

Junk, Cheryl Fradette. "Good Soldiers of Christ: A Case Study of North Carolina Quaker Resistance to the Civil War." *Southern Friend*, XV (Spring 1993), 21–57.

Gordon B. McKinney

See also: **Davis, Jefferson; Lincoln, Abraham; Peace Movements.**

PHOTOGRAPHY, CIVIL WAR

"Reportage," wrote Civil War photographic historian Will Stapp, "was understood to be one of the most significant potentials—and goals—of photography at the very beginning of its history." The photographic coverage of the American Civil War, which was conducted only two decades after the invention of Louis-Jacques-Mandé Daguerre's photographic process in 1839, became direct inspiration for the more comprehensive photojournalism that has followed. Although actual combat and scenes of action could not be captured until faster film and smaller cameras evolved, the coverage of the Civil War was the first systematic attempt to document a conflict in its entirety.

THE AUDIENCE FOR PHOTOGRAPHY

Concurrent with the interest in capturing the war through photography grew the desire to circulate those images. Photographers, including the famous Civil War chronicler Mathew B. Brady, envisioned a popular appetite for images of the war. A sense of historical mission, as well as the profit motive, encouraged Brady and others to make the expensive investment necessary to cover the war. Brady estimated that he spent over $100,000 on his documentation. His project was a financial failure, however, and he ended up bankrupt, forced to sell his collection of negatives and daguerreotypes.

Photographs could not be reproduced in the pages of the press until publishers began to use the half-tone process in the early 1890s. Therefore Civil War photographs reached the public either as original images—in gallery shows, as *cartes de visite* (small visiting card-size portraits), and as stereocards—or transformed into engravings or lithographic illustrations for newspapers and magazines.

Photographers chose which type of photograph to produce depending on the audience for the image. To take pictures of celebrities for duplication, photographers either

Civil War casualties in a photograph by Mathew B. Brady. Brady organized a troop of photographers to follow troops in the field during the Civil War. In 1862, Brady displayed his images of the dead from the battle of Antietam, shocking the public, most of whom had never before witnessed the carnage of battle.

used large glass plates for large prints or smaller ones for *cartes de visites*. Many photographers preferred reproducible stereographs when covering news events; the illusion of depth as well as the presumed photographic fidelity gave viewers the sense that they were almost eyewitnesses. For portraits of soldiers going off to war, tintypes were the cheapest and the easiest to produce. Photographers both North and South churned them out by the hundreds.

Small tintypes and *cartes de visite* of loved ones were cherished both by men in the field and families back home.

PHOTOGRAPHERS

Perhaps as many as 400 photographers—300 in the North and 100 in the South—received special passes from the Union and Confederate military authorities to photograph the troops. In the Confederacy, supplies were always a problem. There was an interest in images from the front, but money and materials were lacking. Indeed, most photographers North and South dealt in the inexpensive tintype and *carte de visite* images; they set up shop near the encampments and waited for lines to form.

The military for the most part welcomed photographers. General Ulysses S. Grant not only approved photographers' access, he owned many Brady studio images. Other units also accepted photography as the document of record: Andrew J. Russell photographed many bridge spans, pontoons, and other engineering feats of the Union forces, and George Barnard, a well-known former daguerreotypist, documented General Sherman's campaign in 1863, when he was attached to the Military Division of the Mississippi.

Mathew Brady has become synonymous with Civil War photography, but his was hardly the only photographic studio engaged in documenting the war, even if he was the best known and perhaps the most gifted photographer of the era. By the time the war broke out, he was firmly ensconced as the principal photographer to American presidents and celebrities, but he was going blind and it is likely that he personally made very few of the thousands of Civil War pictures that are credited to him. Others who worked for him took the photographs, including Alexander Gardner, who managed Brady's Washington studio, and Timothy O'Sullivan, George Barnard, James Gibson, and David Woodbury. Brady's insistence on taking the credit for the images of his salaried photographers sufficiently alienated him from his employees that Gardner, O'Sullivan, Barnard, Gibson, and Woodbury left in 1863 to set up a rival studio.

TECHNOLOGY AND IMPACT

At times during the Civil War, Brady had as many as nineteen teams of operators covering the various fronts, equipped with 16 x 20, 8 x 10, and stereograph cameras. Each team brought into the field a horse-drawn darkroom in which the glass plates were carefully prepared and then rushed to the camera, which would have been set up close by the wagon. The glass plate was exposed in the camera for three to twenty seconds and then developed immediately. Depending on the humidity, the entire process took from ten to twenty minutes.

Camera technology dictated that photographs of the war had to be of preambles and aftermaths, usually staged portraits of men before battle and reproductions of the carnage and destruction after the fighting. A relatively small number of people actually saw photographs of the war, but those who attended the shows in Mathew Brady's galleries in New York and Washington, D.C. were stunned. The photographs of Antietam, for example, taken by Alexander Gardner, captured the ignominious sprawl of the dead. As the first of that war's images of the carnage, they received greater contemporary attention than any taken later in the conflict. They were exhibited and simultaneously offered for sale at Brady's gallery, and they were reproduced as wood engravings in *Harper's Weekly*. Articles about them appeared in the *New York Times* and *Atlantic Monthly*.

In its review of the exhibit, the *New York Times* wrote, "Mr. Brady has done something to bring home to us the terrible reality and ernestness [sic] of war. If he has not brought bodies and laid them in our door-yards and along streets, he has done something very like it." According to the reporter, visitors crowded the gallery in "hushed, reverend [sic] groups . . . bending down to look in the pale faces of the dead, chained by the strange spell that dwells in dead men's eyes. . . . We would scarce choose to be in the gallery when one of the women bending over them should recognize a husband, a son, or a brother in the still, lifeless lines of bodies that lie ready for the gaping trenches." For the first time, although not for the last, the photographs of war challenged the established convention that death in battle was noble and glorious.

Since the Civil War, visual images have been a major factor in influencing Americans' reactions to war.

Susan Moeller

See also: **Newspapers and Magazines.**

POLITICAL PARTIES

Political parties played an important role in nineteenth-century America and ultimately had an impact on the secession of the Southern states and the Civil War (1861–1865). The Democratic Party emerged under the leadership of President Andrew Jackson, who proclaimed himself a man of the people. Opposition to him arose in the form of the Whig Party, which formed in the 1830s and lasted until the 1850s. Whigs resisted the growth of presidential power, promoted internal improvements and the creation of a national bank, and opposed territorial expansion. But neither party held to a rigid set of policies.

Civil War-era Americans viewed political parties as devices to protect and preserve the freedoms promised in America's founding documents. The failure of the existing parties to address perceived threats to these values in the 1850s led to a partisan realignment. The ensuing Civil War and Reconstruction shaped the identities of Republicans and Democrats for decades to come.

THE COMING OF WAR

In 1852, the national conventions of the Whig and Democratic parties endorsed the Compromise of 1850 as the final solution to the divisive question of slavery in the United States. Neither party addressed the tremendous increase in foreign immigration, which in half a dozen years had added significantly to the Roman Catholic portion of a hitherto overwhelmingly Protestant country. In the minds of many Americans, the existing parties were avoiding important issues. The result was factionalism within the existing parties and attempts to found new parties. Anti-immigrant nativists formed the American Party. Responding to the Kansas Nebraska Act of 1854, which overturned the Missouri Compromise on slavery, antislavery extensionists formed the Republican Party. As a result of the formation of the new parties, the Whig Party ceased to function, and although the Democratic Party continued it divided into factions, its southern wing increasing in strength and its northern wing losing many native-born Protestant voters.

In the late 1850s, the Republican Party broadened its appeal beyond the slavery issue. It gradually edged out the American Party as an opponent to the Democrats in the North but remained sectional. This alarmed some Southerners, who saw secession as the best way to combat the Republican threat. President James Buchanan, however, insisted that the Democrats' policies of strict construction of the Constitution and limited government could preserve the Union. In 1860, Southern and Northern Democrats failed to agree on the protection of slavery and ran separate candidates for the presidency. Some former Whigs and American Party members created a Constitutional Union Party to contest both the Republicans and the Democrats. The Republicans' concentrated strength in Northern states that had many electoral votes enabled Abraham Lincoln to win the presidency with only 39 percent of the popular vote, precipitating the secession of seven Southern states. Four other states joined the Confederacy following the April 1861 bombardment of Fort Sumter in and Lincoln's call for volunteers to suppress the rebellion.

THE CIVIL WAR AND POLITICAL PARTIES

At first, most people in the North and South greeted the war as the type of calamity that required mutual support and cooperation, not partisanship, within communities. In the first Northern elections after the war started, partisans in many states worked together to forge Union slates to fill local or state offices. The Republicans were still claiming the name Union Party during Lincoln's reelection campaign in 1864. Most Democrats had long since become disillusioned, however. A faction of radical Republicans believed that the government needed to maximize its power to prosecute the war efficiently and

resolve sectional differences permanently. They favored emancipation of slaves, confiscation of rebel property, the conscription of soldiers, and modernizing the North's banks, manufacturing, and railroads—positions that were anathema to most Democrats. Moderate Republicans preferred crafting policy in ways that answered Democrats' charges that Republicans intended to elevate African Americans and cared nothing for the wartime suffering of white Northerners—protecting the slave property of loyal individuals, for example, or reviewing draft quotas and procedures.

Democrats, too, factionalized. Peace Democrats (called Copperheads by Republicans) believed the Confederates were unbeatable on the field of battle but would return to the Union of their own accord if the Union faithfully protected constitutional rights. This strategy was well-suited to rebuilding the Democratic Party in the South after the war. Other Democrats believed that advocating peace smacked of defeatism and might destroy the party's legitimacy in the eyes of Northern voters. They supported the war but sharply criticized the Lincoln administration's conduct of it. The Democrats thus articulated popular wartime discontents, compelling Republicans to justify and sometimes moderate their policies. United at the beginning of the war, Northerners dissolved into hostile political factions because of the war.

Partisan activity no longer occurred only at election time. Some Republicans formed Union Leagues to help the war effort (and hector Democrats) year round; some Democrats joined the Order of American Knights to oppose the Union Leagues. Partisanship led to charges of disloyalty. Rumors of Copperhead plots to liberate Confederate prisoners of war circulated among Republicans in the Midwest. Churches, schools, and businesses, never politicized before, became in some communities places of political confrontation between supporters and opponents of the war. Off-duty soldiers sometimes attacked Democratic newspaper offices that published what the soldiers considered disloyal articles. Women took more interest in politics than they had previously and showed increasing sophistication in their arguments on political topics. Turnout in elections was high. Some states allowed soldiers to cast absentee ballots; commanders furloughed others home to vote. Soldiers favored the Republicans by a much larger proportion than did the civilian population, reflecting in many cases deep and abiding anger against the Peace Democrats. Negative views of the opposing party helped cement party identification for a generation to come.

The Confederacy, unlike the Union, had no acknowledged political parties. Like Lincoln, however, President Jefferson Davis sought to centralize the conduct of the war and resorted to measures like impressment of property, conscription, and heavy taxation to carry on the war. Professing support for the Southern cause but insisting that such measures threatened individual and states' rights, critics, including his own vice president, lambasted Davis on a daily basis. Without parties, the choices at election time lacked clarity and turnout was low. Those tired of the war responded as best they could, sometimes by avoiding military service and secreting property.

THE LEGACY OF WAR

Andrew Johnson, who succeeded to the presidency upon Lincoln's assassination in 1865, had been a lifelong Democrat who hoped to base reunification on the creation of a National Union Party embracing political moderates North and South. Republicans feared that the president's desire to accommodate white Southerners would undermine the freedom of the former slaves and set the stage for renewed sectional clashes. Republicans waved what was referred to as the bloody shirt of Civil War remembrance to reinforce the existing parties. Although the enactment of black suffrage in Southern states introduced the Republican Party there, with African-American voters flocking to the party that had freed them, many white southerners refused to accept the party's legitimacy. A long campaign of violence and intimidation brought conservative Democrats to power in every Southern state by 1877. These redeemers, as they were called, limited African-American voting and set the stage for what would later become a solidly Democratic South.

The legacy of the Civil War would thus shape the political identity of the political parties for the next hundred years. Memories of the war known as the Lost Cause sustained the Southern wing of the Democratic Party, which strongly supported states' rights and Jim Crow segregation laws. The Republican Party, on the other hand, identified itself as the Party of Lincoln, which had ended the institution of slavery. These identities, forged in the Civil War, would be recast by the Great Depression (1929–1941) and Franklin Delano Roosevelt's New Deal (1933–1944).

BIBLIOGRAPHY

Altschuler, Glenn C., and Blumin, Stuart M. *Rude Republic: Americans and Their Politics in the Nineteenth Century.* Princeton, NJ: Princeton University Press, 2000.

Frank, Joseph Allan. *With Ballot and Bayonet: The Political Socialization of American Civil War Soldiers.* Athens: University of Georgia Press, 1998.

McKitrick, Eric. "Party Politics and the Union and Confederate War Efforts." In *The American Party Systems: Stages of Political Development,* edited by William N. Chambers and Walter Dean Burnham. New York: Oxford University Press, 1967.

Neely, Mark E., Jr. *The Union Divided: Party Conflict in the Civil War North.* Cambridge, MA: Harvard University Press, 2002.

Rable, George C. *The Confederate Republic: A Revolution against Politics.* Chapel Hill: University of North Carolina Press, 1994.

Smith, John ?? ?????????? ???????? ???????, ????–????. Stanford, CA: Stanford University Press, 1991.

Smith, Adam I. P. "Beyond Politics: Patriotism and Partisanship on the Northern Home Front." In *An Uncommon Time: The Civil War and the Northern Home Front,* edited by Paul A. Cimbala and Randall M. Miller. New York: Fordham University Press, 2002.

Phyllis F. Field

See also: Elections, Presidential: The Civil War; Lincoln, Abraham; Reconstruction.

POLK, JAMES K.
(b. November 2, 1795; d. June 15, 1849) Member of House of Representatives, including speaker of the House; eleventh president of the United States (1845–1849).

James Knox Polk was born November 2, 1795, in North Carolina and raised in Tennessee. He graduated from the University of North Carolina in 1818, practiced law, and was elected to the Tennessee Assembly in 1823. Polk's political career ascended with his serving seven terms in the U.S. House of Representatives (1825–1839), including four years as Speaker of the House (1835–1839). After leaving Congress, he served as governor of Tennessee (1839–1841). Polk was elected president of the United States, serving from 1845 to 1849. A life-long devotee of Thomas Jefferson's political creed and a loyal son of Andrew Jackson's democracy movement, Polk holds a unique place in American history as the first "dark horse" candidate for president, the first former Speaker of the House of Representatives to serve as president, and the first commander in chief to lead the nation in a foreign war.

The issue of the nation's expansion gave a serious cast to the otherwise boisterous presidential contest of 1844. The threat of war with Britain over Oregon and with Mexico over Texas framed the political discourse of the campaign. Polk was elected by less than a majority of the voters and the narrowest of popular pluralities, proving that the American electorate was divided almost evenly between expansion and consolidation, between free trade and protection, between tolerance of immigrants and native xenophobia, and between agrarian rule and market revolution.

Despite his narrow win, Polk took the presidential oath with a determination to personally direct the administration of the general government. Pledged to serve but a single term, he accomplished all four of the major goals he set for his presidency: reduction of tariffs, creation of an independent Treasury divorced from the banking industry, institution of a republican government in the Oregon Country, and the acquisition of Upper California from Mexico. In the course of meeting his objectives, he also led the nation into war with Mexico in the defense of Texas annexation.

From the Mexican point of view, the United States had no right to annex lands west of the Sabine River, and, as promised, Mexico broke diplomatic relations with the United States shortly after Polk's inauguration. Polk sought to restore amicable ties, but Mexican leaders would not accept the loss of their eastern province, fearing that demonstrating weakness in the Texas question would encourage other provincial uprisings and result in a further loss of centralized control by the military. Recovery of Texas would not be required; occasional war along the Rio Grande would suffice to keep the Texas claim alive and civil authority intact. For his part, Polk did not wish to pursue a long-term border war defending Texas's right of self-determination. Convinced that Mexico intended to move its army into Texas, Polk sent Zachary Taylor and his troops to the Rio Grande. On April 24, 1846, a Mexican force of sixteen hundred crossed the river and captured an American patrol of sixty dragoons.

Within a week of learning that the Mexican and American armies had clashed, the British cabinet decided to settle the Oregon boundary dispute and sent instructions to their minister in Washington to agree to a partition at the forty-ninth parallel. Some of Polk's advisors, Secretary of State James Buchanan included, had feared that the British would fight over their control of the Oregon Country and that the United States might find itself engaged on two fronts, a land war in Mexico and a maritime struggle with the British navy. Although militarily the United States stood unprepared for either, President Polk calculated correctly that Britain would not go to war over its commercial interests in Oregon, Texas, or Mexico. Polk's diplomatic successes in settling the Oregon question and his military strategy for winning the war in Mexico, however, failed to bring political consensus at home, for Whig opposition blamed him for giving up half of Oregon and charged him with fighting an immoral war in Mexico.

Polk made every effort to resolve the Texas issue through diplomacy and offered to purchase Mexico's northern provinces, not because he believed in Manifest Destiny but because he knew that the agrarian republic

James K. Polk, in an engraving by John Sartain after a painting by T. Sully, Jr.

could not close its borders and so prevent emigration. The Texas-Oregon pattern of occupant rule was replicated in New Mexico and Upper California, and neither the government in Mexico nor that in Washington could contain the migration. Successive generations of independent farmers would find their own rich soil or go begging into wage dependency.

Polk's expansion policies postponed the end of the agrarian republic but did not resolve the problems of a Union divided by incompatible economic, religious, and racial interests. In four tumultuous years he accomplished his goals, and true to his word he declined all interest in a second term. Although blessed with a strong constitution, "Young Hickory" fell victim to cholera and died at his home in Nashville on June 15, 1849, just three short months into his retirement.

Wayne Cutler

See also: **Texas, Republic of.**

POOR RELIEF, 1816–1900

Before the Civil War, most poor relief efforts in the United States had their roots in traditional English poor laws dating from the late sixteenth century. These efforts were primarily guided by these laws, and relief was performed primarily at the state and local levels of government.

These state laws, along with the U.S. Constitution's Tenth Amendment ["The powers not delegated to the United States by the Constitution, nor prohibited by it to the states, are reserved to the states respectively, or to the people"] meant that responsibility for providing relief for the poor rested not on any federal authority, nor even explicitly on state governments, but rather on local ones or more commonly, on private charities or individuals themselves. The poor relied mainly on individual philanthropy, local public and private institutions (primarily churches during this period), and their own extended families. This localized social safety net was highly personal for the poor at this time, as the relief network was localized and familiar, with the relationships between those in need and those providing assistance being most critical in determining the quality, duration, and effectiveness of such assistance.

During the Civil War the capability for local assistance had all but disappeared as resources in cities and towns, especially in the South, were often stretched to the breaking point. There was little, if any, help available for the destitute. As the war continued to claim casualties, both actual lives and disabling injuries, many politicians in Washington, D.C. began pushing for military pensions for their constituents. American military pensions had first been granted to veterans of the Revolutionary War to recognize their service and contributions, but the Civil War Pension Acts that arose from that war went far beyond any earlier measures, and they caused lasting changes in the American social fabric.

The Union Congress passed the first Civil War Pension Act in 1862, and by the end of the war Pension Acts were passed that granted aid not only to those veterans permanently disabled by wounds received in battle, but also for widows and dependent children of soldiers who had died while in federal service. Long after the war ended Pension Acts continued to be passed, becoming more and more liberal with respect to who was eligible to receive pensions. Before the last Pension Act referring to Civil War veterans was passed, even old age was considered a viable disability. By 1883 the Pension Bureau had become one of the largest agencies of the federal government, dispensing nearly $100 million, almost one-fourth of the country's annual revenues.

For Southern veterans the outcome was less promising. The federal government refused to pay pensions to soldiers who had served in the Confederacy, so the burden of providing relief for these veterans fell on the individual Southern states. In 1867, Alabama and North Carolina were the first Southern states to award pensions. It was 1879 before Georgia became the first Southern state to award a pension to widows. Although most Southern states eventually adopted some form of pension program, such payments were never remotely on a par with those received by Union veterans. Eventually, at the close of the nineteenth century, the federal government extended veterans benefits to all soldiers of both sides, but for many Southerners this was too late.

In 1890 the federal government extended pension eligibility to any veteran who, for any reason, was unable to support himself by manual labor. This helped to transform the traditional pension for military disability into an old-age pension meant to reward veterans and relieve them of poverty.

The Civil War and its relief measures fostered a systematic public policy for dealing with poor relief. The stigma that had long been attached to receiving aid was greatly reduced; the federal government had assumed a role that had earlier been deemed a state or local role; and a new sense of social accountability for veterans as well as the poor and the elderly had been instilled in the country. It set the tone so that even those not associated with military service would later benefit from the effects of the Civil War Pension Acts.

David Sloan and Michael W. Hail

BIBLIOGRAPHY

Bremner, Robert H. *From the Depths: The Discovery of Poverty in the United States.* New York: University Press, 1964.

Fitzpatrick, Michael F. "Payback for Broken Soldiers." *Civil War Times.* (December, 2002) 38–.

Lens, Sidney. *America's Enduring Paradox: A History of the Richest Nation's Union War.* New York: Thomas Y. Crowell Company, 1971

Lowell, Josephine Shaw. *Public Relief and Private Charity.* (1884). Reprinted New York: Arno Press & The New York Times, 1971.

See also: **Civil War Veterans.**

PRISONS AND PRISONERS OF WAR, 1816–1900

Soldiers fear captivity. Regardless of international rules agreed to by participating nations, few universal laws govern the behavior of captors. Captivity denies civil rights

Rations being issued at Andersonville Prison, Georgia, in 1864.

to an individual by the physical constraint imposed by the captor and confirms the reality of failure in an assigned mission. Hostile and punitive captivity not only threatens a soldier's mental well-being during a conflict, but can cause deep institutional and personal distress among those who survive the experience.

By the nineteenth century, laws and policies regulating POW treatment among European and American armies leaned toward the Golden Rule: the mutual usefulness of providing humane treatment for the enemy's soldiers with the reasonable expectation of the same for one's own, tempered by military necessity.

During the War of 1812, an extraordinary number of American naval personnel, privateers for the most part, were captured and taken as POWs by British forces. About 14,000 men of a total seafaring manpower pool of approximately 100,000 were held captive for months to years. On April 20, 1815, 263 Americans left the British Dartmoor prison; a few days later 5,193 freed prisoners followed with a large white flag that depicted the goddess of liberty sorrowing over the tomb of their dead compatriots with the legend, "Columbia weeps and will remember!" During the Mexican-American War (1846-1848), few American soldiers fell into Mexican hands; for those who did, treatment was fair and humane.

During the Civil War (1861-1865), Union and Confederate forces were unprepared for the enormous numbers of POWs, which eventually reached 211,400 Union POWs in the South and 220,000 Confederates in the North. Exchanges took place regularly according to the Dix-Hill Cartel until 1864, when Union General Ulysses S. Grant, ordered a halt because of Confederate mistreatment of black Union soldiers and the belief that Confederate parolees were returning to their units. That decision cost thousands of lives on both sides. Thereafter, the South was glutted with huge numbers of starving Union prisoners it could not support. Civil War POWs on both sides endured the ordeal of being quarantined in stockades, converted armories, or former fairgrounds. By the autumn of 1864, nearly 14,000 Union prisoners had died at the infamous prison camp Andersonville. Thousands of Confederate prisoners suffered and died at prison camps at Elmira, New York, and Rock Island, Illinois.

When the Civil War broke out, there were still no written international statutes concerning the conduct of war and the humane treatment of prisoners, binding belligerents to reasonable behavior. Francis Lieber, a Prussian German immigrant who soldiered against Napoleon and who had a keen understanding of war and captivity, produced the first comprehensive code for the rules of war. This code could be used by any government anywhere and was the first recognized published legal code pertaining to issues concerning POW treatment. President Abraham Lincoln issued it on July 3, 1863, through the War Department, ordering the document delivered to every field commander in the Union and Confederate armies. Still in force today, *General Order 100, The Rules of Land Warfare* rests on the firm moral foundation that an enemy is a fellow human being with dignity and lawful natural rights. If these rights are violated, the offender can be brought to trial. After the Civil War, Confederate Captain Henry Wirz, Interior Commandant of Camp Sumter, Georgia (Andersonville), was tried, convicted, and executed for murder; however, some historians have argued that the miseries of Andersonville were the fault of the system, not the individuals.

Prisoners of war have rarely changed the course of history; wars have been won or lost not because of them but in spite of them. Although the technology of warfare has changed, the horrors of captivity have not. For the individual soldier thrown into the uncertain life of a POW, victory becomes a daily commitment to survival through the development and maintenance of the will to live. To meet their physical needs, prisoners have been forced to secure food by any and all means. But there is also strong and powerful evidence suggesting that POWs' will to live stems from a deep well of religious, ethical, and moral faith. Freedom becomes an ever-present dream of the faces of home and family. Memoirs and letters by soldiers who were imprisoned have had a strong impact on how Americans view war.

BIBLIOGRAPHY

Doyle, Robert C. *Voices from Captivity: Interpreting the American POW Narrative.* Lawrence: University of Kansas Press, 1994.

Doyle, Robert C. *A Prisoner's Duty: Great Escapes in U. S. Military History.* Annapolis, MD: United States Naval Institute Press, 1997.

Futch, Ovid L. *History of Andersonville Prison.* Gainesville: University of Florida Press, 1968.

Hesseltine, William Best. *Civil War Prisons: A Study in War Psychology* (1930). Columbus: Ohio State University Press, 1998.

Marvel, William. *Andersonville: The Last Depot.* Chapel Hill: University of North Carolina Press, 1994.

Speer, Lonnie. *Portals to Hell: Military Prisons of the Civil War.* Harrisburg, PA: Stackpole, 1997.

U.S. War Department. *War of the Rebellion: A Compilation of the Official Records of the Union and Confederate Armies.* Washington, DC: U.S. Government Printing Office, 1880–1901.

Robert C. Doyle

See also: **Grant, Ulysses S.**

RAILROADS

The transportation revolution helped America become a modern nation. In 1815 most Americans lived as subsistence farmers. They either made, raised, grew, or bartered for everything their families needed. High transportation costs made commercial farming (growing crops for sale) unprofitable for most farmers. New York's Erie Canal, completed in 1825, and then railroads, changed Americans' lives. By 1850 canals and railroads had reduced transportation costs by 95 percent. Farmers were now able to grow all the crops they could produce and sell them for cash. They could now buy items they previously had to make themselves. Factory-made cloth replaced the homespun clothing that had been produced after hours of labor by farm wives and daughters. Farmers in the North bought newly invented farm machinery to increase their crop production so they could make more money. They became consumers in America's industrial revolution.

Railroads were ideally suited for America's vast size. They ran all day, every day, and covered greater distances by more direct routes than did transportation by roads, canals or riverboats. America had 3,000 miles of track in 1840, 10,000 in 1850, and 30,000 in 1860. With 5 percent of the world's population, the United States had 50 percent of the world's railroad miles in 1855. Railroads' far-flung operation presented unique management problems that led to the development of modern management practices.

Railroads also introduced speed to business practices. Indeed, railroads started what Americans today call "standard" time. Before 1883, every town measured noon by when the sun stood directly overhead. This greatly complicated the setting of timetables and increased the danger of accidents. So the railroads adopted "railroad time" based on the concept, used earlier by some British railroads, of time zones in which the minute hand remains the same throughout the zone. The United States adopted railroad time as its official time with the Standard Time Act of 1918.

Railroads were still an emerging technology at the beginning of the Civil War. None had bridged the Ohio River or the Hudson River south of Albany. They ran on thirteen different gauges, the distance between the rails. It was not until 1886 that all railroads finally converted to the four-foot, eight-and-a-half-inch "standard" gauge. Local laws often required railroads to locate train stations at city limits in order to prevent fires and reduce unpleasant noise and smoke. This meant that passengers and freight had to be unloaded, carried through the city to the next station, and reloaded. Many railroads refused to allow their cars to travel on other rail lines for fear that they would lose them. Rail companies also refused to pull other companies' cars for fear of the wear and tear on equipment. The pressure to keep up with higher volume during the Civil War, however, encouraged efficiency and fostered greater cooperation among Northern railroad companies. The war set the stage for an integrated 200,000-mile national rail system by 1900.

THE CIVIL WAR

Some historians call the Civil War the first modern war. It became a conflict increasingly driven by logistics, the practice of obtaining military supplies and distributing them as needed. Governments had to supply food and military supplies to armies fighting on several fronts and campaigning through thinly populated areas. Civil War armies rarely, with notable exceptions, provided their own food by taking supplies from local farmers, as armies did in earlier wars. Accurate rifled muskets greatly increased ammunition use and thus the need for renewed ordnance. Railroads carried wounded soldiers from battlefields to distant hospitals. Although railroad construction declined during the Civil War, railroads had an impact on the war's outcome.

Logistics requirements made the Civil War a railroad war. Every major battle took place within twenty miles of a railroad or river port. Union strategic planners deliberately targeted rail junctions, such as Manassas, Petersburg, Nashville, Chattanooga, Corinth, and Atlanta. Each side's skill in managing its railroads became an important factor in fighting the war and its ultimate outcome.

The Union received excellent service from Northern railroads. The government paid two cents per mile for carrying troops and a sliding scale for freight. High military traffic volume made the arrangement very profitable to the railroads. The profits, however, provided the money necessary to maintain tracks, locomotives, and railroad cars. Congress passed a law in February 1862 giving the president the authority to take control of the railroads during military emergencies. It also created the independent U.S. Military Railroad (USMRR) to repair or build tracks and to operate railroads in captured Confederate territory. By the end of the war, the USMRR was the largest railroad in the world, with 25,000 employees and 2,100 miles of track. Efficient Northern railroads gave Union armies an advantage of speed that offset the Confederacy's advantage of size.

Southern railroads were less advanced than Northern railroads, partly because of the seasonal nature of the South's agricultural production. Still, they formed an "imperfect skeleton" of a transportation system—or would have, had the Confederate government taken the necessary steps to organize it. Southern railroads used only two track gauges, the standard gauge or five-foot. The government sought to have the tracks of different railroads joined so as to form an integrated rail system with the capability to shift locomotives and cars to other tracks. However, although the Confederate Congress passed a law giving the Quartermaster General the power to take control of Southern railroads in time of emergency, it never enforced it. In spite of clear wartime need, railroads and the communities they served refused to join their tracks to other railroads.

The Confederate government also agreed to pay Southern railroads a two-cents-per-mile rate, but this did not cover the railroads' operating costs. Further, it paid with Confederate bonds that rapidly lost their value. Cash-starved railroads thus had no money with which to maintain their tracks and rolling stock. Finally, Confederate officers routinely disrupted railroad operations. As a result of the Confederacy's failure to organize its railroads, Southern railroad efficiency declined during the war. Its armies became immobile in a war of mobility.

The Confederacy proved very resourceful in using railroads despite these limitations. At the first battle, Bull Run, or Manassas, General Rene Beauregard shuttled soldiers by train from the Shenandoah Valley during the battle. These reinforcements helped to secure the Confederate victory. In 1862 General Braxton Bragg moved 30,000 soldiers from Mississippi to Chattanooga, Tennessee, to stop a Union advance. Its most famous movement occurred in September 1863, when 13,000 soldiers from General James Longstreet's corps traveled from Virginia to northwest Georgia. Half the soldiers arrived in time to play a significant role in the Confederate victory at Chickamauga. That half of Longstreet's force did not reach the battlefield in time, however, shows the shortcomings of Southern railroads.

In contrast to the South, the Union showed its railroading expertise after the battle of Chickamauga. It sent 23,000 soldiers from the 11th and 12th Corps, their artillery, horses and wagons, and other equipment 1,300 miles over eight railroads to reinforce its army in Chattanooga. The first infantry regiments reached the area five days after leaving Virginia. The last combat units arrived in fifteen days. They helped to secure eastern Tennessee for the Union. Chattanooga became General William Tecumseh Sherman's staging area for his Atlanta campaign in 1864. The Union and Confederacy proved the value of railroads in conducting modern war. Railroads provide an example of America's increasing expertise in logistics.

AFTER THE CIVIL WAR

In the decades following the Civil War, the United States chartered four transcontinental railroad lines. The first one was completed in May 1869, with the joining of the Central Pacific and Union Pacific Railroads at Promontory Point, Utah. All the railroad companies, benefiting from enormous financial support from federal and state governments in the form of generous land grants and loan agreements, brought great wealth to their investors and founders. These railroad lines fostered Western settlement by Euro-Americans, improved communication between people on the East and West coasts, and eased the transportation of manufactured and agricultural products. Tragically, the railroads hastened the demise of American Indians, their culture, and their way of life.

BIBLIOGRAPHY

Black, Robert C., III. *The Railroads of the Confederacy*. Chapel Hill: University of North Carolina Press, 1952.

Taylor, George Rogers. *The Transportation Revolution, 1815–1860*. New York: Holt, Rinehart, and Winston, 1951.

Turner, George Edgar. *Victory Rode the Rails*. New York: Bobbs-Merrill, 1953.

Weber, Thomas. *The Northern Railroads in the Civil War*. New York: King's Crown, 1952.

John E. Clark, Jr.

See also: **Age of Westward Expansion; Indian Removal and Response.**

RECONSTRUCTION

The aftermath of a long, hard war can be as arduous as the fighting itself. Such is the case with Reconstruction, one of the most volatile peacetime periods in American history. Rebel armies may have surrendered, but the Confederate people did not. The Republican Party in the North may have triumphed, but its power was not unrivaled. Black slaves may have gained their freedom, but they did not enjoy equality. The often violent political, social, and economic struggles that came to characterize Reconstruction should compel any student to consider it an extension of the Civil War. The effects of Reconstruction contributed to segregation (Jim Crow laws) and intense race conflict through most of the twentieth century. Reconstruction, like the Civil War, left a deep imprint on American society and culture.

Reconstruction scholarship exemplifies the period's restlessness. Historians have gone from condemning Reconstruction as a harsh form of punishment to praising it as a noble, albeit failed, experiment in racial justice. In

the early 2000s, scholars usually took the middle road, seeing Reconstruction as the product of countless participants whose motives reveal a complex mixture of idealism and self-interest.

Regardless of the various schools of thought, the general purpose of Reconstruction was twofold: The establishment of loyal governments in the former Confederacy, and the assimilation of over four million freed black slaves into American society. Achieving these objectives was no easy task. Republican politicians disagreed over means, while ex-Confederates in the South and Democrats in the North denounced the goals altogether. Power struggles between the president and Congress, between state and Federal authority, between whites and blacks, threatened to sabotage Reconstruction at every turn.

PRESIDENTIAL RECONSTRUCTION

An inchoate form of Reconstruction began shortly after the Civil War started. As Federal troops occupied Confederate territory, Unionists emerged to reorganize their states politically. On December 8, 1863, President Abraham Lincoln unveiled a more comprehensive plan for Reconstruction, the so-called Ten Percent Plan. Once ten percent of a rebellious state's prewar voting population had taken an oath of loyalty, then civil government could be restored. Radicals in Congress, however, considered Lincoln's plan too lenient and they insisted, via the Wade-Davis bill, that reorganization be contingent on the loyalty of no less than fifty percent of a state's electorate. Lincoln pocket-vetoed the Radical plan, and no definitive Reconstruction policy existed at the time of his assassination.

While the politicians wrangled over the scope of Reconstruction, southern blacks began to initiate their own reconstruction. Some freedmen volunteered their military services to the Union after emancipation. In 1865 many freed blacks sought to reunite their families or form their own churches. Aided by the Freedmen's Bureau, blacks throughout the South also pursued opportunities for education and land. For blacks, Reconstruction was a time of hope; behind them lay the shackles of slavery; before them lay the allure of citizenship and economic independence.

Under Andrew Johnson's presidency (1865–1869), Reconstruction took a less optimistic turn. Johnson always believed his Reconstruction policy was in keeping with Lincoln's concept of reunification, but where Lincoln was pragmatic, Johnson was dogmatic. An ardent foe of the southern planter class and slavery, Johnson was also a rigid states rights politician and white supremacist. In the summer of 1865, with Congress out of session, Johnson decided to effect Reconstruction on his own with a conciliatory plan. Ex-Confederates, save a select few,

U.S. CONSTITUTION

AMENDMENT XIII.

SECTION 1. Neither slavery nor involuntary servitude, except as a punishment for crime whereof the party shall have been duly convicted, shall exist within the United States, or any place subject to their jurisdiction.

AMENDMENT XIV.

SECTION 1. All persons born or naturalized in the United States and subject to the jurisdiction thereof, are citizens of the United States and of the State wherein they reside. No State shall make or enforce any law which shall abridge the privileges or immunities of citizens of the United States; nor shall any State deprive any person of life, liberty, or property, without due process of law; nor deny to any person within its jurisdiction the equal protection of the laws.

AMENDMENT XV.

SECTION 1. The right of citizens of the United States to vote shall not be denied or abridged by the United States or by any State on account of race, color, or previous condition of servitude.

CONGRESSIONAL RECONSTRUCTION

An enduring myth about Reconstruction is that Radical Republicans dominated the process. To be sure, the Radicals, most notably Pennsylvania Congressman Thaddeus Stevens, were dynamic personalities, but moderate Republicans, such as Illinois Senator Lyman Trumbull, exercised greater influence. The moderates shelved Radical demands to treat the South like a conquered territory and to seize and then redistribute plantation lands in behalf of the freedmen. Instead, they formulated what they thought were reasonable conditions for readmission. To counteract the Black Codes, Congress passed the Civil Rights Act (1866), which established racial equality before the law. When President Johnson vetoed this measure on the grounds that it overstepped the authority of the Federal government, Republicans were stunned.

Although Congress overrode the veto, members realized that lasting civil rights protection required a constitutional safeguard. The Fourteenth Amendment followed, which made the federal government, not the states, the final protector of a citizen's rights and due process of law. This amendment, which included other provisions that temporarily disfranchised certain Rebels and repudiated the Confederate war debt, became the centerpiece of the Congressional plan for Reconstruction in 1866; a state's readmission was contingent on ratification.

The Fourteenth Amendment triggered a bellicose response from the white South. Emboldened by President Johnson's defiance, every former Confederate state, except Tennessee, spurned the amendment as an affront to their sovereignty, their race, and their honor. Exacerbating the situation were summertime race riots in Memphis and New Orleans. To many observers, these events were indicative of a persistent sectional hostility. Consequently, in 1867 Congress gravitated toward a more forceful Reconstruction.

Convinced that only direct Federal intervention could properly reconstruct the South, Congress passed the first of four Reconstruction Acts in March 1867. These laws required the ten remaining Confederate states to reorganize their governments and rewrite their constitutions to include universal male suffrage; therefore, black men received the right the vote. To enforce these unprecedented measures, Congress placed the South under military jurisdiction, vesting army generals with discretionary powers to keep any ex-Confederate interference in check.

This extraordinary process of military Reconstruction did not go unchallenged. While white southerners protested, President Johnson embarked on a course of action that produced a dramatic showdown with Congress. Johnson exercised his authority as commander in chief to

received general amnesty in exchange for an oath of loyalty. Once pardoned, Johnson required the former Rebel states to merely ratify the Thirteenth Amendment abolishing slavery and to renounce their ordinances of secession. In a few states, such as Tennessee, Unionists controlled Reconstruction, but in most cases ex-Confederates seized political power and turned Reconstruction to their own ends. The new "Rebel" governments carried out Johnson's decrees, but they also elected former wartime leaders to Congress and organized militias comprised of rearmed Confederate soldiers. Moreover, they instigated an ominous program for race order, one embodied in Black Codes that were special laws designed to regulate the life and labor of the freedmen.

Many northerners were disappointed with Johnson's apparent mismanagement of Reconstruction. When Congress reconvened in December 1865, the Republican majority refused to seat the southern delegation and, instead, formed a Joint Committee on Reconstruction to consider alternatives to Johnson's approach. In effect, Congress assumed control over Reconstruction.

remove personnel whom he felt executed Reconstruction policy too aggressively. In response, claiming that Johnson was deliberately obstructing Reconstruction in violation of the law, Republicans in the U.S. House impeached the president in 1868. Johnson avoided conviction in the U.S. Senate by a single vote, but his trial ushered in an era of congressional supremacy.

Ultimately, the radicalism of Congressional Reconstruction proved too much for most northerners, many of whom were disturbed by the advent of black suffrage. The election of the popular Ulysses S. Grant to the presidency in 1868 signaled a return to moderation. By 1870, readmission of Southern states was complete and the Fifteenth Amendment, which forbade disfranchisement on matters of race, went into effect. Reconstruction appeared to be over.

RECONSTRUCTION IN THE SOUTH

Although each state experienced a unique Reconstruction, several general developments apply to them all. Politically, Reconstruction constituted a major realignment of power in the South. The new state governments initially bore the stamp of the Republican party. Grassroots political clubs (Union Leagues) arose to indoctrinate blacks into the party and mobilize them as voters. Eventually, in states where their numbers were large, such as Louisiana, Mississippi, and South Carolina, blacks achieved considerable political success. Sixteen blacks served in Congress, while the freedmen in South Carolina briefly commanded a majority in the state legislature. Despite their crucial participation, blacks never dominated the party or Reconstruction. Instead, northern whites, known as Carpetbaggers, and southern whites, pejoratively referred to as Scalawags, tended to dictate Reconstruction policy. In competing for leadership and taking black support for granted, however, white Republicans engaged in factional quarrels which undermined effective government.

Economically, Reconstruction produced a compromise between white landowners and black farm laborers, a system known as sharecropping. Blacks never received the proverbial "forty acres and mule," but they did display noticeable savvy in labor negotiations. In exchange for farming plantation land on the tenuous promise of receiving a share of the crop, blacks enjoyed unsupervised labor and obtained the use of a small, private plot of land. Unfortunately, bad harvests coupled with exploitative creditors reduced most black farmers to a vicious cycle of debt peonage.

Socially, Reconstruction inaugurated a revolution in race relations. The Republican administrations enacted a great deal of progressive legislation, most notably programs for public education open to both races, the first in southern history. Other significant racial reforms included black access to public transportation and the right of black men to sit on juries. Interestingly, with the exception of politics, both races voluntarily segregated themselves in most social settings. Schools, churches, saloons, and other gathering places remained all-white or all-black.

WHITE COUNTER-RECONSTRUCTION

For most white southerners, Reconstruction was little more than despotism. Repudiating the Republican administrations as illegitimate and insisting that blacks were unfit for citizenship, the ex-Confederate populace unleashed a campaign of counter-Reconstruction. The goals were simple (home rule and white supremacy) while the means took two forms: political and paramilitary. Politically, most southern whites marched under the banner of the Democratic party. In states where whites were in the majority, such as in Virginia, the Democrats were able to regain power legally at the polls. More often than not, however, counter-Reconstruction entailed substantial violence.

Paramilitary resistance was perhaps the most decisive factor in Reconstruction's demise. Disgruntled whites harassed freedmen throughout the post-war period, but following Congressional Reconstruction, southern violence became political as well as racial. The most notorious paramilitary challenge to Reconstruction was the Ku Klux Klan. A decentralized organization of Rebel vigilantes, the Klan conducted an erratic campaign of terror, roughly from 1867 to 1871. Indiscriminately attacking blacks and white Republicans, the Klan did much damage to Reconstruction at the grassroots level. While a few Republican governors managed to suppress the Klan with biracial militias, night-riding did not cease until Congress passed a series of Enforcement Acts that enabled President Grant to use the army against it. By 1872, the Klan was finally eradicated.

In the 1870s, southern paramilitary activity became more sophisticated. Ex-Confederate officers enrolled virtually every white man into new, extra-legal militias and then instilled the kind of discipline lacking in the Klan. Combining public intimidation with shocking acts of violence, organizations such as the White League in Louisiana and the Redshirts in South Carolina gave the Democratic Party a powerful edge at election time. President Grant tried to punish the worst abuses, but his application of force was inconsistent. In 1874, he used troops to thwart White League usurpation in New Orleans, but in 1875, the president ignored the widespread political violence in Mississippi that helped bring down the Republican administration in that state. By 1877, every southern state had been recaptured by the Democrats. The Rebels, more so than the Republicans, understood that the politics of Reconstruction was the politics of force.

THE END OF RECONSTRUCTION

Following the official readmission of southern states, the North's commitment to Reconstruction gradually waned. Given that southern black men had the right to vote, white northerners expected them to stand on their own. Other post-war issues began taking on greater importance, including industrialization and westward expansion. Problems arising from labor unrest, immigration, and American Indian warfare seemed more urgent than perpetuating the Reconstruction process. In 1873, the nation succumbed to a severe economic depression. In 1874, Democrats won control of the U.S. House, thereby breaking Republican control over Reconstruction policy. During these years, the U.S. Supreme Court interpreted the new Reconstruction amendments conservatively, returning national protection of citizens' rights to the states.

The traditional end of Reconstruction came with the so-called Compromise of 1877. During the presidential election of 1876, paramilitary fraud and violence left in dispute the electoral votes of three southern states. A bipartisan Federal investigation ruled in favor of the Republican candidate, Rutherford B. Hayes. The new president soon appeased the white South by permanently withdrawing the army. Political-economic stability, even under ex-Confederate leadership, had become preferable to ensuring social justice at the point of a bayonet. By 1900, the South may have lost the Civil War, but in certain respects, Confederates won the peace by disempowering black citizens through Jim Crow laws that legalized segregation and by laws barring blacks from voting.

In evaluating Reconstruction, the failures are more obvious than the successes. The Republicans failed to establish a viable two-party system and blacks failed to achieve equality. This outcome suggests that Reconstruction was too mild. Perhaps the Federal government should have confiscated land for the freedmen, or punished Confederate leaders for treason, or maintained indefinitely a standing army over the South. But America in the nineteenth century was a white man's country where property rights were sacrosanct and where notions of federalism (strong state's rights and a weak national government) still prevailed.

In the long run, however, Reconstruction should be viewed as a success. Blacks did exercise their freedom and, regardless of how that freedom is qualified, the post war world for black Americans was a more promising place than slavery. Furthermore, with the passage of the Thirteenth, Fourteenth, and Fifteenth amendments, the nation did "reconstruct" its constitution so as to reflect its highest ideals. The new amendments may have been trampled on for many years after Reconstruction, but they provided the legal foundation for the civil rights movement of the 1950s and 1960s.

BIBLIOGRAPHY

Benedict, Michael Les. *The Fruits of Victory: Alternatives in Restoring the Union, 1865–1877*. Philadelphia: Lippincott, 1975.

Foner, Eric. *Reconstruction: America's Unfinished Revolution, 1863–1877*. New York: Harper & Row, 1988.

Olsen, Otto H. ed. *Reconstruction and Redemption in the South.* Baton Rouge: Louisiana State University Press, 1980.

Perman, Michael; Franklin, John H., ed.; and Eisenstadt, Abraham S., ed. *Emancipation and Reconstruction, 1862–1879*. Arlington Heights, IL: Harlan Davidson, Inc., 1987.

Rable, George C. *But There Was No Peace: The Role of Violence in the Politics of Reconstruction*. Athens: The University of Georgia Press, 1984.

Simpson, Brooks D. *The Reconstruction Presidents*. Lawrence: University Press of Kansas, 1998.

Trefousse, Hans L. *Reconstruction: America's First Effort at Racial Democracy*. New York: Van Nostrand Reinhold, 1971.

Ben H. Severance

See also: **Constitutional Amendments and Changes; Education; Freedmen's Bureau; Grant, Ulysses S.; Johnson, Andrew; Ku Klux Klan; Occupation of the South.**

RECREATION AND SOCIAL LIFE

In antebellum America (1840–1860), recreational and social amusements tended to differ according to region, ethnicity, class, and gender. Rural communities frequently combined socializing with work such as quilting bees or barn raisings. Get-togethers were largely informal, with all who attended actively participating. In the cities, however, class defined leisure pursuits. The middle class frequented theaters, ice cream parlors, and restaurants. Home amusements, such as parlor games, dinner parties, and holiday celebrations, were also popular. The custom of calling and receiving visitors, once reserved for the upper class, had become a favorite social activity of middle-class women. The working class could also be found in theaters, but drinking in saloons was the most common form of socializing for working men. In the streets of working-class neighborhoods, children played, women visited, men smoked and drank, fire companies staged races, and militia and ethnic groups paraded. The upper class gathered at more exclusive places for socializing and recreation. Mountain and beach resorts, which were difficult to reach and therefore expensive, attracted elite families from across the country. The society and amusements of places such as Saratoga, New York, the Virginia springs, and Newport, Rhode Island, drew the upper class, as did the opportunity to escape from hot weather and improve their health. Plantation elites also spent their leisure time at barbeques, balls, horse races, and card and

Scene from the midway at the World's Columbian Exposition in Chicago during the summer of 1893. AP/WIDE
WORLD PHOTOS

dinner parties. Their slaves often spent their off times at religious gatherings that blended singing, shouting, and dancing, reaffirming their communal ties.

The Civil War and its accompanying urbanization and industrialization significantly altered the nature of society and the ways Americans spent their leisure time. During the war, many theaters and resorts closed or were used as hospitals. After the war, railroads made most of the resorts more accessible. The expense that had ensured the exclusivity of these places disappeared. Railroads also made travel to other sites across the country, such as Atlantic City, Niagara Falls, and Yellowstone Park, relatively easy and inexpensive. The movement of large numbers of people by train began to blur the regional distinctions that had previously characterized most recreational areas. More importantly, after the war leisure became a regular part of more and more Americans' lives in the form of the vacation, and new kinds of entertainment emerged to meet the insatiable appetite for pleasure. Parks, railroad excursions, beaches, scenic sites, and sporting events all offered pleasure-seekers respite from

ordinary life. Commercialized public amusements, such as dance halls, penny arcades, vaudeville theaters, and amusement parks—especially Coney Island—became increasingly popular after the war. At these new venues, male and female members of the working and sometimes middle class easily socialized with one another. Most of these commercial amusements, however, excluded African Americans. In response, African Americans established their own, yet similar, places of recreation, including mountain and seaside resorts, amusement parks and theaters, though they still regarded their churches as their primary place for socializing.

Postwar urbanization and expansion of the railroad networks also influenced the development of athletic activities and the increasing organization of sports. In response to accelerating industrialization, many people began to view sports as a necessary and safe outlet from the pressures of work. Baseball had become enormously popular among soldiers during the war, and it emerged as the nation's favorite team sport and the major spectator sport in the post-Civil War era. Rail expansion allowed teams to travel quickly to other cities and facilitated the development of professional national leagues. Between the Civil War and World War I, sports assumed an important role in American life for both men and women. Indeed, women in ever-increasing numbers played tennis, golf, basketball, and other sports, and participated in the cycling craze. Baseball, boxing, and football, however, remained the preserve of men. After the war, sports attracted a growing proportion of the general American public and became one of the main forms of recreation and entertainment

BIBLIOGRAPHY

Aron, Cindy S. *Working at Play: A History of Vacations in the United States.* New York: Oxford University Press, 1999.

Braden, Donna R. *Leisure and Entertainment in America.* Dearborn, MI: Henry Ford Museum and Greenfield Village, 1988.

Dulles, Foster Rhea. *A History of Recreation: America Learns to Play,* 2d edition. Englewood Cliffs, NJ: Prentice-Hall, 1965.

Nasaw, David. *Going Out: The Rise and Fall of Public Amusements.* Cambridge, MA: Harvard University Press, 1993.

Charlene M. Boyer Lewis

See also: **Urbanization.**

RED BADGE OF COURAGE

Stephen Crane's *The Red Badge of Courage*, published in 1895, is the story of Henry Fleming, a young, inexperienced small-town soldier who is coming of age during the Civil War battle at Chancellorsville. Fleming finds himself involved in a bewildering and petrifying landscape of war rather than the patriotic scenes of glory that he romanticized from the songs and tales of his youth. Mustering up the courage for a heroic rush into battle only to suffer a failure of nerves, he moves back and forth within himself between the desperation for a bold, visible statement of heroic manhood (a wound, or "red badge") and the crippling anxiety that engulfs him. Fleming eventually achieves his heroic charge as his fear gives way to a wild, mad frenzy of "sublime recklessness" in a brave resolution to run at a faltering flag.

The Red Badge of Courage is significant for a number of reasons. It greatly changed the conventions of the traditional war story because it constructs a new point of view, set almost exclusively on the battlefield without ever returning to life on the home front, offering comic relief, or providing other national or patriotic subplots that characterize more romantic war narratives. The language of the novel is minimal and sparse, more journalistic than the traditional grandeur that dominates war stories, con-

tributing to the reader's sense of the "reality" of battle. The looming feeling of anonymity and the animal-like descriptions of the characters suggest what becomes known as a "naturalist" vision of the universe in which the motives and actions of the characters are forces largely beyond their control. Within this worldview that Social Darwinists call "survival of the fittest," whatever high and moral reasons might motivate agency give way to the violent indifference to human suffering that is the central defining feature of nature, the world, and the self.

Although other works had in many ways anticipated naturalism, *The Red Badge of Courage* inaugurated what became a significant movement in American literature. It met with tremendous approval from both its American and British readerships and saw ten reprintings within its first year. Despite its revision of the mainstream portrait of military courage, the novel was published in a historical moment that was charged with a patriotic, militant imperialism. President Teddy Roosevelt, an avid admirer of the novel, saw its success as an occasion to revitalize an apathetic nation through vigorous military application.

The novel survives today as a masterpiece of American realism and a classic rite of passage from boyhood into adulthood. It is also another illustration of how war inspires literature and how literature transforms views of warfare. Crane's realism answers Cooper's romanticism and thus provides new cultural images that contributed to America's emergence as a world power.

BIBLIOGRAPHY

Bloom, Harold, ed. *Stephen Crane's the Red Badge of Courage (Modern Critical Interpretations).* New York: Chelsea House, 2000.

Cady, Edwin. *Stephen Crane,* rev. edition. Boston: Twayne, 1980.

Colvert, James B. *Stephen Crane.* New York: Harcourt, Brace, 1984.

Pizer, Donald, ed. *Critical Essays on Stephen Crane's "The Red Badge of Courage."* Boston: G. K. Hall, 1990.

Jonathan E. Vincent

See also: **Cooper, James Fenimore; Literature.**

REFUGEES

In 1863, the artist George Caleb Bingham captured the upheaval, uncertainty, and injustice that refugees faced during the Civil War in his painting *General Order 11*. This painting depicts civilians in four Missouri counties who refused to sign loyalty oaths to the Union and who were forced to vacate their homes and properties.

Whereas both the North and the South cavalierly believed that the war would end quickly and decisively, such was not the case. Instead, military tactics included banishing the residents of occupied areas to weaken the moral and tangible support that civilian communities provided to the military effort. Yet the governments in the North and South did not provide any comprehensive plan to ameliorate the condition of the refugees. And significantly, refugees tended to be women and children.

Nearly 500,000 civilians were displaced during the war. For example, in Alexandria, Virginia, approximately sixty-five percent of the townspeople vacated the area fearing for their lives. Diarist Elvira Scott, author of *Recollections of 92 Years, 1824–1916*, spent the war years exiled in St. Louis. Unlike many refugees, she was able to return to her home and reopen the family store. Some wealthy refugees fled to Europe, Canada, or the Caribbean, and many Southern refugees moved several times during the war to escape the invading Union army.

Life on the run was extremely difficult for refugees. The civilian population was totally unprepared for the hardships of war and occupation. In 1862 a typical victim, Elizabeth Meriwether, ex-slave and mother of ragtime musician John William "Blind" Boone, was forced to vacate her home in Memphis and gave birth to her third child on the roadside. Refugees often made poor decisions about where to go and what items to take with them. Many of them mourned over the loss of property and family heirlooms. To provide themselves with economic support, they often sold items of value including jewelry, silver, and china. Refugees were not always welcome in the areas to which they moved. Conflict over scarce resources was constant. Those in rural communities fared better than their urban counterparts in acquiring food. Families sometimes resorted to stealing to feed themselves and or their children.

African Americans and Native Americans also suffered during the war. Cherokees, Creeks, and Seminoles fled to Kansas from the Southeast because of their Union sympathies. Their arrival in Kansas was difficult; they found poor accommodations and little food. African-American slaves who escaped or were freed by the advancing Union army were considered "contraband of the war." Some joined Union forces to fight for the cause. Many African-American wives, with their families, followed husbands who had joined the Union army, creating difficulties for military operations. One of the best examples can be found at Fort Nelson, Kentucky. Food, clothing, and proper shelter for women and children became a concern for military leaders there. Other women, such as ex-slave Rachel Boone, took refuge with the Union army and found work as cooks.

On March 3, 1865, the War Department established the Bureau of Refugees, Freedmen, and Abandoned Lands, better known as the Freedmen's Bureau. It responded to the refugees' needs by providing food, clothing, and medicine, as well as by supporting educational endeavors and supervising the distribution of confiscated lands. But for the four years that the war raged, many lives, homes, and properties were devastated. Despite the improved conditions after the war, all refugees longed for the familiarity of their old lives.

BIBLIOGRAPHY

Bradbury, John F. Jr. "Buckwheat Cake Philanthropy: Refugees and the Union Army in the Ozarks." *Arkansas Historical Quarterly* 57 (Autumn 1998): 233–254.

Buker, George E. *Blockaders, Refugees, and Contrabands: Civil War on Florida's Gulf Coast, 1861–1865.* Tuscaloosa: University of Alabama Press, 1993.

Hague, Parthenia Antoinette. *A Blockaded Family: Life in Southern Alabama During the Civil War.* Lincoln: University of Nebraska Press, 1991.

Massey, Mary Elizabeth. *Refugee Life in the Confederacy* (1964). Reprint, with a new introduction by George C. Rable, Baton Rouge: Louisiana State University Press, 2001.

McGuire, Judith W. *Diary of a Southern Refugee During the War, by a Lady of Virginia.* Lincoln: University of Nebraska Press, 1995.

Warde, Mary Jane. "Now the Wolf Has Come: The Civilian Civil War in the Indian Territory." *The Chronicles of Oklahoma* 71 (Spring 1993): 64–87.

Delia C. Gillis

See also: **Freedmen's Bureau; Reconstruction.**

RELIGION, CIVIL WAR

Religion was central to the American Civil War experience. It gave Americans at war a vocabulary through which to understand life and death, a rationale for fighting (or not fighting) for one's country, a moral compass, and an institutional means of providing relief to soldiers in the field and people suffering on the homefront. Before the war, religious ideas informed the debates on slavery and the character and destiny of the Union. After the war, religious institutions and imperatives gave substance to African-American aspirations for freedom and autonomy; helped rebuild the defeated South and explain defeat to white Southerners; and spurred Northern interest in Reconstruction.

BACKGROUND

Although much variety existed among Americans regarding culture and class, the men who served in the armies, especially those who rallied to the flags in 1861 and stayed for the duration of the conflict, were remarkably homogeneous in their backgrounds and beliefs. In both North and South, they came largely from farms or small towns in which family and church formed the basic cement of community. If they were not ardent believers or churchgoers, they at least accepted the basic tenets of nineteenth-century American Protestantism. Theirs was a faith still deeply rooted in the Old Testament, with a God of judgment who demanded discipline and devotion from His people. The theme of America as a new Israel rang from pulpits and in public rhetoric with great force, invoked and adapted by Northerners and Southerners alike to their particular regions but no less powerful as an axiom of faith.

To be sure, the New Testament God of love and mercy gained much currency during the religious awakenings of the nineteenth century, but the prevailing tone of Protestantism was that God expected His children to follow His ways as prescribed in scripture. And it was a largely Protestant people who went to war in 1861. Later in the war, when African Americans, Irish, and Germans formed an increasingly large percentage of the Union forces, numbering collectively in the hundreds of thousands, greater religious variety marked the Northern armies. Although Catholics, Lutherans, Jews, and others did not subscribe to the dominant evangelical Protestant code, with its Calvinist thrust, they were not numerous enough to displace it.

The Protestant religion of the time, in both North and South, spoke directly to the way people were supposed to conduct themselves. It informed and reinforced the emerging Victorian code of courage, which demanded that men be brave and virtuous to honor family, community, and God, and it promised that their faith and good habits would be their armor. Such beliefs cast war as an ennobling experience, in which those who were right with God would prevail. It assumed that individual character counted and that virtue would be rewarded. The individual soldier's actions in battle and in camp thus would not only decide the contest but also inspire and save others. Such beliefs made parting from home less painful, for the men had a high purpose and their women trusted in them.

But war in fact proved different than war in imagination. In camp, men found vice, not virtue, in the form of gambling, drinking, swearing, and sometimes a shocking indifference to religious services and discipline. The religious societies and churches of the North and South tried to combat these evils with a prodigious output of Bibles, religious tracts, hymnbooks, and papers, and men hungry for anything to read grabbed at the materials. The Northern effort to reach the soldiers was more organized than the Southern one. The United States Christian Commission, established in 1861 by branches of the Young Men's Christian Association, provided reading materials and succor to Union soldiers and sailors. The Christian Commission allied with the American Bible Society and the American Tract Society to distribute almost 1.5 million Bibles, testaments, and scriptural chapbooks, over 1.3 million hymn and psalm books, more than 18 million religious weekly and monthly newspapers, and roughly 39 million pages of tracts. It also established lending libraries in the camps to facilitate reading.

Religious publishing houses in the South produced enough materials to get a Bible into the hands of any soldier wanting one, even though paper and printing facilities became scarce during the war. Southern religious tracts and papers stressed personal stories of redemption and moral discipline. Typical was the immensely popular *A Mother's Parting Words to Her Soldier Son,* by the Reverend Jeremiah Jeter, in which the mother called on her son to "uphold liberty and Christian valor" by acting honorably in all ways.

Both the Northern and Southern churches, and then governments, attempted to supply the armies with preachers and chaplains. Most Civil War chaplains on both sides were Methodist, reflecting the large percentage of Methodists in the churched population, but all the major religious groups had chaplains with the armies, although they were unevenly distributed and too few to meet all the needs of their coreligionists. At first, officers worried that ministers and the purveyors of religious literature stalking the camps would distract soldiers from the duty of war. But the chaplains and religious societies soon showed that they could help make the armies more effective because religious men were disciplined soldiers. Many officers on both sides came to recognize that organized religion brought order to the camps by emphasizing the need to submit to authority as the Protestant and Catholic emphasis on submission to God's will demanded. Also, a Christian army was believed to be less likely to dissipate its energies in brawling, boozing, and malingering, and it was thought that a Christian soldier would not be afraid to die. The presence of chaplains also reassured those at home that their men would not lose their faith and morals while at war. Organized religion thus promised to bind homefront and camp and to make the troops fight harder.

It is difficult to measure the extent to which soldiers accepted the logic of submission, the preaching of the ministers, the advice in the religious tracts, and the prayers from home, for few soldiers' diaries and letters offer any sustained reflections on their spiritual or moral development. The most visible evidence of religious concerns is the wave of revivals that swept across both armies

Religious services in a Union camp. Photograph by Mathew B. Brady, 1863. LANDOV

from 1862 on. The Army of Northern Virginia erupted with widely reported revivals in 1862, 1863, and 1864, which contributed to the postwar myth that Southern armies were more Christian than Northern ones and to the later deification of Robert E. Lee and Thomas "Stonewall" Jackson as exemplars of piety and nobility. Revivals in Northern armies got less notice but counted tens of thousands of converts each year. Among victor and vanquished alike, revivals broke out most effusively after bloody battles, suggesting that what happened in battle had spiritual consequences. Faced with the horror of a war that was unimaginable in the Victorian code of courage, soldiers sought a way to regain control and to give meaning to life and death.

Religion came to matter more as the war dragged on. Death proved anything but noble in a war where disease, mass slaughter, protracted suffering from fatal wounds, and anonymous burial challenged the Victorian code of death's noble, gentle embrace. Dismembered and disemboweled bodies, left rotting on fields after battle, proved no temples of God. The governments responded by acknowledging and dignifying death through religious

ritual. The Union made a special effort, through the U.S. Sanitary Commission, a quasipublic agency, to identify and reinter the bodies of soldiers buried in mass graves and with the consecration of national cemeteries such as the ones at Gettysburg and Arlington. The reinterment effort also further bound the soldier and his family to the nation, for it nationalized death and linked the nation to sacrament. In popular culture, especially in the North, new ideas about heaven as a home where family would be reunited gained currency. In the South, pilgrimages to the gravesites of "Stonewall" Jackson and other Christian heroes during and after the war—and later in the century the profusion of memorials and statues in the public squares across from the main churches and county courthouses—fused together the idea of the Confederacy as a Christian effort and the departed warriors as soldiers in Christ.

During the war, both the Union and Confederate governments claimed the mantle of redeemer nation and emphasized the Christian duty of soldiers and civilians by establishing national fast days, using religious symbols in public places, having ministers bless the troops, and uttering public prayers. The Confederacy was perhaps more vigorous and self-conscious in doing so because it had to create a national identity distinct from the North's. It moved quickly to place the Confederacy in the chain of Christian history as the true heir of Israel and the Founding Fathers of the United States. In their currency and coinage, both sides proclaimed themselves God's chosen people. Beneath George Washington's image on the Confederacy's national seal were the words *Deo Vindice* (God will avenge), and the United States government added "In God We Trust" to its money, where the assertion remains.

RELIGION AND THE POLITICS OF SLAVERY

Religion and religious leaders figured prominently first in the politics that led to the war and later in the interpretation of its meaning. Abolitionists in the North had long made the moral argument for emancipation and challenged churches to come out against slavery. Before the war, however, Northern churches were not of one mind on how to deal with the slavery question, and some congregations splintered over the issue. Southern churchmen were more unified in their stand, using pulpit and print to defend slavery and "Southern rights." In the hothouse of sectional politics and amid angry arguments over biblical literalism and church missions in the 1840s and 1850s, the slavery question caused the Baptist, Methodist, and Presbyterian churches to divide into Northern and Southern branches. The rupture of the three dominant denominations left the United States with few national institutions and contributed to secession.

The war caused many northern Protestants to see ending slavery as central to the salvation of the Union. Protestant ministers from several denominations organized petition campaigns to lobby Lincoln and the Congress to make the war for Union also a war for freedom in order to ensure America's claim to be a redeemer nation. Ministers explained Union defeats in 1861 and 1862 as God's judgment on the nation for failing to end the abomination of slavery, and they pointed to Union military successes after emancipation became Union policy as proof of God's favor. The blood baptism of war, they insisted, also required citizens to sacrifice for the national good and made support for the government's war effort almost a moral obligation. Thus resistance to the draft, hoarding goods, organizing dissent, and other acts that were considered unpatriotic became sins in the new civic religion. Some Protestant churches brooked no dissent on the war effort, driving out supporters of compromise with the South and even supporters of the Democratic Party. Churches thus radicalized the Union war effort. They also hastened slavery's demise by providing teachers and other support to help prepare African Americans in Union-occupied areas of the South for freedom.

RELIGION ON THE HOMEFRONT

Faith played an important role in providing strength to the men and women on the homefront who kept their houses, farmed their land, ran their businesses, and raised their children. People who experienced the deaths of loved ones turned to their faith to help them deal with their sufferings and sorrow. Religious beliefs became their mainstay in facing the horrors and tragedies of war and the daily struggles they confronted in order to survive. Many churches, especially in the South, were now empty as preachers left to minister to soldiers on the battlefront. Lacking formal religious services, men and women on the homefront read their Bibles, said their prayers, and sometimes gathered together to share the strength of their faith to help them endure the tragedies of war.

After the war, Northern churches continued to send resources (Bibles, tracts, and financial support) and missionaries to the South. They saw the region as ripe for their religious message and in need of assistance in building churches and Sunday schools. Most freedpeople voluntarily left biracial churches by 1867 or spurned Northern white efforts to establish churches for them after the war, preferring instead to form all-black churches. The African Methodist Episcopal and African Methodist Episcopal Zion churches, both independent black denominations, made a major effort to attract former slaves into their churches, with some success. Many freedpeople, however, preferred to form their own Baptist congregations wherein they had more control over their particular religious needs and ministers. Still, the connections between Northern churches and Southern black ones helped the freedpeople construct and supply church buildings and establish and run schools.

The North emerged from the war emboldened in the conceit that it was the true instrument of God's will. Radical Republicans especially draped themselves in this belief when they made the case for entrusting the federal government with new powers to ensure the reconstruction and redemption of the South. Lincoln's assassination on Good Friday 1865 offered a martyr to the Union cause that Republicans traded on for years. The postwar deification of Lincoln proved a powerful political symbol for Republicans and a reminder of the people's religious obligation to stand by the nation.

At the same time, Southern ministers blamed Southern reverses and the sufferings of war on moral laxity and corruption at home (e.g., hoarding of goods, refusal to serve in the army) and, after major military defeats in 1863 and 1864, on Southerners' failure to be good masters to their slaves. Only through spiritual renewal might the South be saved, they warned. In such arguments lay the South's postwar explanation for defeat. Southern white ministers—along with many politicians—insisted that God had not abandoned the South; rather, the argument went, God had chastised Southerners for their moral failings and lack of will. Southerners thus remained a chosen people who like the Israelites of the Old Testament needed to be humbled by defeat and exile as the prelude to building the true church and nation.

The war had significant effects on American religion, which in turn helped shape American society and culture. In making possible the liberation of African Americans in the South, it allowed Southern blacks to create their own churches. It also left the three largest white denominations divided in politics and organization for decades (the Baptists remain divided). Yet even though the war did not much change the dominant American religious belief, it deepened the millennial strains within it. It also reinforced Americans' idea that they had a special place in history as God's chosen people. This belief would contribute to the ways Americans remembered the Civil War, enshrined the nation, and justified their involvement in subsequent wars.

BIBLIOGRAPHY

Chesebrough, David B. *God Ordained This War: Sermons on the Sectional Crisis, 1830–1865*. Columbia: University of South Carolina Press, 1991.

Faust, Drew Gilpin. "Christian Soldiers: The Meaning of Revivalism in the Confederate Army." *Journal of Southern History* 53 (1987): 63–90.

Faust, Drew Gilpin. *The Creation of Confederate Nationalism: Ideology and Identity in the Civil War South*. Baton Rouge: Louisiana State University Press, 1988.

Genovese, Eugene D. *A Consuming Fire: The Fall of the Confederacy in the Mind of the White Christian South*. Athens: University of Georgia Press, 1998.

Goen, C. C. *Broken Churches, Broken Nation: Denominational Schisms and the Coming of the Civil War*. Macon, GA: Mercer University Press, 1985.

McPherson, James M. *For Cause and Comrades: Why Men Fought in the Civil War*. New York: Oxford University Press, 1997.

Miller, Randall M.; Stout, Harry S.; and Wilson, Charles Reagan, eds. *Religion and the American Civil War*. New York: Oxford University Press, 1998.

Mitchell, Reid. *Civil War Soldiers: Their Expectations and their Experiences*. New York: Viking, 1988.

Moorhead, James H. *American Apocalypse: Yankee Protestants and the American Civil War, 1860–1869*. New Haven, CT: Yale University Press, 1978.

Shattuck, Gardiner H., Jr. *A Shield and Hiding Place: The Religious Life of the Civil War Armies*. Macon, GA: Mercer University Press, 1987.

Woodworth, Stephen E. *While God Is Marching On: The Religious World of Civil War Soldiers*. Lawrence: University Press of Kansas, 2001.

Randall M. Miller

See also: **Reconstruction**.

SECESSION

The secession of seven Southern states in 1860 to 1861 set in motion the train of events that led to the American Civil War. The war ultimately cost 620,000 lives, precipitated the internal collapse of slavery, prompted President Lincoln's Emancipation Proclamation, changed the Constitution, and transformed the American union of states into a nation. The destruction of slavery was arguably the greatest social revolution in American history, and it removed the most glaring contradiction to the ideals of the Founding Fathers. Union victory ensured the inviolability of the Union and supremacy of the federal government. Secession, in short, inaugurated the most transforming crisis in American history. More than any other single event, the Civil War defined modern America.

SECESSIONIST THEORY

As early as the 1820s, some southerners raised secession as a last resort to defend slavery and southern rights. The notion that any state could voluntarily leave the Union was based on the state compact theory of the Constitution, articulated first in the Virginia and Kentucky Resolutions of 1798 and 1799. The states existed before the Constitution, this argument ran, came together to create the national government, and therefore were ultimately superior to it. This theory was the basis for nullification and secession, neither of which are mentioned in the Constitution. Southerners sometimes voiced an abstract commitment to the ideal of states' rights, but most regional spokesmen understood it as a means through which they might protect slavery. As the South's share of population, and thus its political power, shrank within the Union, the drastic step of secession became more attractive and likely as the last gamble of an increasingly out numbered minority.

GROWTH OF SECESSIONISM

Prior to the 1850s, the actual threat to slavery remained slight, although southerners watched closely the steady growth of abolitionism in the North. The turning point in the sectional conflict (and ultimately the real beginning of widespread support for secession) was the birth and rapid success of the free soil Republican Party. Increasingly dominant in the North after 1856, Republicans threatened slavery because of their commitment to its non-extension. Most southerners believed that slavery needed to expand in order to survive—to preserve its economic viability by finding productive ways to use slaves, to maintain racial control amidst a growing slave population, and to add slave states to preserve the South's political power within the national government. Finally, the success of Republicanism, for southerners, represented an insult to their equality within the Union. If their slave-based way of life were not allowed to expand, most southerners considered it an insult to their standing as good Americans and good Christians. In addition to the threats posed by the concept of free soil, more and more Republicans actually were abolitionists and, although still a minority, they gained rapidly in New England. Thus, by the late 1850s a large number of southern whites considered a Republican president unacceptable.

The most important event that preceded the much-anticipated election of 1860 was the confused raid led by abolitionist John Brown at Harpers Ferry, Virginia (now part of West Virginia). Apparently planning to start a regional slave rebellion, Brown and his followers seized the federal arsenal in the small town in October 1859. Brown was quickly captured, convicted by the state of Virginia for inciting slave rebellion, and hanged. Although most northerners condemned his violent methods, Brown became something of a martyr and symbolic victim of southern arrogance and violence. For their part, southerners often failed to distinguish Brown from Republicans or northerners generally. The Harpers Ferry raid panicked southerners, heightened tensions across the country, and invigorated secessionists who preached disunion if a Republican was elected in 1860.

Throughout the 1860 presidential campaign, southerners debated potential responses to a Republican victory. By October, Abraham Lincoln seemed certain to win after he carried crucial early elections in Pennsylvania, Illinois, and Ohio. The bottom line for Southerners, as always, was how best to protect slavery and the southern way of life based on the peculiar institution. Immediate secessionists called for southern states to leave the Union as soon as Lincoln's election was certain. Others counseled a more moderate course, possibly a cooperative movement in which states would withdraw as a group.

DISUNION

Secessionists moved quickly in November and December 1860 to capitalize on the public outrage over Lincoln's victory and to maintain the momentum toward disunion. The popular mood across the lower South where slavery was so widespread favored immediate secession, and local "vigilance committees," Minute Men clubs, and volunteer militia units pressured and intimidated Unionists. Leaders in South Carolina acted first. Following the procedure used for nullification in 1832, a

special election was held for delegates to a special convention that would decide the state's course of action. On December 20, the South Carolina convention unanimously approved an Ordinance of Secession, declaring "the union now subsisting between South Carolina and other States under the name of the United States of America is hereby dissolved." Six other states in the deep South followed South Carolina out of the Union early in 1861. Everywhere, secessionists emphasized the dangers of a Republican administration hostile to slavery's growth and future within the Union; spokesmen painted a bleak picture of potential slave rebellions, racial warfare, and the violation of southern women. With their homes and women threatened, leaders invoked the language of honor and masculinity when they called on southern men to support immediate secession—a "bold and manly move," as hundreds of editors and politicians phrased it. Or, as Mississippi's Governor John Pettus declared: "Can we hesitate! when one bold resolve, bravely executed, makes powerless the aggressor, and one united effort makes safe our homes?"

Among scholars the popularity of secession remains in dispute. In nearly all southern states, convention delegates rejected proposals to submit secession to a popular vote, prompting some historians to conclude that they feared being rejected by the masses. On the other hand, Southern Democrats preached secession throughout the 1860 presidential campaign, and their candidate, John Breckinridge, received nearly two-thirds of the vote in the lower South. Immediate secession candidates controlled the conventions in each of the first seven states to leave the Union.

The remaining eight slave states rejected secession before Lincoln took office. Only after the surrender of Fort Sumter and the President's subsequent call for volunteers to ensure "the existence of our National Union, and the perpetuity of popular government" did four more states (Virginia, North Carolina, Tennessee, and Arkansas) secede and join the Confederacy. The Republicans' refusal to accept secession signaled the beginning of civil war.

BIBLIOGRAPHY

Barney, William L. *The Secessionist Impulse: Alabama and Mississippi in 1860.* Princeton, NJ: Princeton University Press, 1974.

Channing, Steven A. *Crisis of Fear: Secession in South Carolina.* New York: Simon and Schuster, 1970.

Crofts, Daniel W. *Reluctant Confederates: Upper South Unionists in the Secession Crisis.* Chapel Hill: University of North Carolina Press, 1989.

Ford, Lacy K. *Origins of Southern Radicalism: The South Carolina Upcountry, 1800–1860.* New York: Oxford University Press, 1988.

Olsen, Christopher. *Political Culture and Secession in Mississippi: Masculinity, Honor, and the Antiparty Tradition, 1830–1860.* New York: Oxford University Press, 2000.

Thornton, J. Mills, III. *Politics and Power in a Slave Society: Alabama, 1800–1860.* Baton Rouge: Louisiana State University Press, 1977.

Christopher J. Olsen

See also: Confederate States of America; Lincoln, Abraham.

SEGREGATION, RACIAL, 1816–1900

In some instances war has increased American consciousness about the nation's ideals and identity, and the public's awareness of its failings to live up to the principles it professes. The War for Independence, for example, made plain the contradiction between the practice of slavery and struggle for liberty. Although independence resulted in the abolition of slavery in the North, the institution continued in half the nation after that war and racism existed in all sections of the country. One of the ironies of American history is that gains made by blacks in the Revolutionary War were lost by a later generation. One of the tragedies of that same history is that the Civil War, which fundamentally altered American society and culture by ending slavery, did not destroy the underlying racism that would produce more than a century of segregation following that war.

Racial segregation existed in America long before laws and biases enacted a physical separation. Dependent upon one another for colonial survival, fears of insurrection by a growing slave population created insurmountable boundaries between blacks and whites. Blacks who served in the Revolutionary War expected freedom or rising class status. Yet in the 1820s, as the country struggled to meet President Thomas Jefferson's ideal of equality, many states withdrew blacks' rights and curtailed civic participation. Although slavery nearly had been eradicated in the North by 1830, strong racial bias in non-slave holding states enforced segregation in public spaces, transportation, education, distinct residential housing, medical care, even in death.

Although traditional belief systems throughout the colonies taught white superiority, blacks served in military units side by side with whites during the colonial wars, the Revolutionary War, and the War of 1812. But by August 25, 1862, with a decision made to use the sizeable black populations for service in Civil War regiments, segregated units such as the 54th Massachusetts Infantry and 35th United States Colored Troops were the order of the day. Ultimately, the Bureau of Colored Troops in

the War Department would oversee 178,892 Union soldiers in the Army and over 10,000 black sailors and pilots in the Federal Navy. In occupied territories, U.S. generals utilized the black population for skilled labor, as scouts and spies, cooks, nurses, and gravediggers. After the war, four black regiments remained in federal service. (Their number was reduced to two in 1869.)

With the Thirteenth Amendment signaling the end of slavery, in March 1865 Congress designated the Bureau of Freedmen, Refugees, and Abandoned Lands (known as the Freedmen's Bureau) as an arm of the War Department to help displaced blacks make the transition from slave to wage earners and property owners. Under Reconstruction, Radical Republicans and the Union League grappled against Southern Democrats and the Ku Klux Klan (KKK) for control; primarily black militias raised in efforts to support and protect freedmen's advocates heightened the animosity.

JIM CROW

As the Southern white vote splintered between political parties, harnessing the newly emerging black vote became critical for success. Adhering to the previously unnamed system of "Jim Crow" (separate facilities for blacks and whites) and further determined to disenfranchise the blacks, Southerners enacted "Black Codes" to prevent blacks from accumulating wealth or acquiring education. Thus, racial segregation began in earnest as freed Southern blacks moved towards cities across the country, only to find their access restricted. In the South, the KKK did its part to keep freed men and women from escalating in social rank and economic status, and local residence requirements directed towards tenant farmers ensured that blacks would not be moving into white zones any time soon.

Racial segregation existed at this time through custom and practice (*de facto* segregation), and both races mostly accepted their places. Modes of transportation proffered varying expectations of separation (including classes), with streetcars being not as firmly enforced, railroad cars more so, and steamships strictly separated.

The Federal Civil Rights Act of 1875 expressly prohibited racial segregation, and it was against Federal law from 1875 to 1883. Then, in 1883, the Supreme Court heard seven civil rights cases and lay precedent towards establishing "separate but equal" as the law of the land. In 1896, Homer Plessy, an octoroon (a person of one-eighth black ancestry) in Louisiana, challenged a statute by refusing to leave a white railroad car, and he was arrested and convicted for his crime. In deciding *Plessy v. Ferguson*, the Court failed to overturn the conviction, holding that separate but equal had become universally recognized (therefore not violating the Fourteenth

Amendment), and stating that integrating transportation or education would upset the existing local customs that defined social relations between the races. The lone dissenting judge opined that segregation violated the Constitution, but soon discrimination and violence against blacks were again on the rise. Between 1887 and 1892, nine Southern states passed Jim Crow laws marking the passage into *de jure* segregation. By 1899, the Supreme Court routinely upheld rulings on statues permitting segregation.

Ensuing Jim Crow laws treated blacks harshly and focused energies on lowering their status in society. No longer were differing classes within the races tolerated; rather all blacks were perceived to hold the same human worth, which was very little. The result of such legislation and direction had a lasting impact on American cities, as marginalized blacks, vying for jobs against whites and immigrants, set their own social, political, and economic structures, with fraternal orders, housing, education, and financial ventures following color lines.

Increasingly populated Western states had similar tensions among people of different races. Working in mines or on the transcontinental railroad, Mexicans, Chinese, blacks, and white immigrants competed for jobs. Mexicans (absorbed by the annexation of Texas and lands won in the Mexican-American War), displaced Native Americans, and emigrating Chinese and Japanese pooled with waves of European immigrants and white pioneers to claim land and work on the frontier.

Additionally, the Federal government warred against, displaced, and cordoned off Native American populations throughout the West. Poorly paid and deprived of amenities provided to whites, the Chinese faced prejudice in many forms. In California, whites alarmed at the large number of Chinese passing through Angel Island passed the 1882 Chinese Exclusion Act, following with segregation legislation. In addition, as the cattle and mining industries thrived and expanded, Mexicans were moved off traditional homesteads. The Hispanic American Alliance formed in 1894 to aid the displaced.

Adding to the crisis, in 1898, the "Buffalo Soldiers," who fought Native Americans on the Plains, helped win the Spanish-American War, which delivered eight million people of varying races unto the authority of the United States. Throughout America tides of nativism began to surge. Anti-immigration and segregation legislation separated races, religions, and cultures into enclaves; it would be nearly sixty years before segregation began to be outlawed and dismantled.

BIBLIOGRAPHY

Hale, Grace Elizabeth. *Making Whiteness: The Culture of Segregation in the South, 1890–1940.* New York: Pantheon Books, 1998.

Lofgren, Charles A. *The Plessy Case: A Legal–Historical Interpretation.* New York: Oxford University Press, 1987.

Rabinowitz, Howard N. *Race Relations in the Urban South, 1856–1890.* New York: Oxford University Press, 1978.

Woodward, C. Vann. *The Strange Career of Jim Crow: A Commemorative Edition.* New York: Oxford University Press, 2002.

Sarah Hilgendorff List

See also: **African Americans (Freed People); Freedmen's Bureau; Ku Klux Klan, Sharecropping and Tenant Farming.**

SHARECROPPING AND TENANT FARMING

The close of the Civil War ushered in profound changes in the character of American society. The North emerged from the war at the forefront of the process of recasting the national identity. In spite of the men it had lost, the North had been secure from the ravages of war and both the industrial and agricultural sectors of its economy had enjoyed unprecedented growth during the conflict. In sharp contrast to Northern prosperity, the South emerged from the war devastated.

Fundamental to Southern recovery was the need to get people back to work, which was no simple task in a region where brutal warfare had forcibly emancipated the slaves, its primary labor force prior to the Civil War. Many freedpeople celebrated the destruction of the slave system by abandoning farms and plantations by the thousands, exercising their newfound freedom by traveling across the South in search of loved ones they had been separated from or merely tasting their liberty. Their absence from the farms nonetheless greatly inhibited efforts at economic recovery. They wanted and had been promised the land necessary to sustain an independent existence, but white Southerners refused to give up land they considered their own, and even many of their Northern supporters seemed unwilling to accept massive seizures of Southern property to benefit the freedpeople. Among the greatest dilemmas in the post-war South was the existence of African Americans who were free but still without the tools necessary to ensure economic independence.

Ordinary white farmers also faced a severe challenge in the wake of the Confederate defeat. Although many commentators outside the South, inspired by abolitionist rhetoric, spoke of a South composed of rich planters, slaves and poor whites, reality proved to be more complicated. Recent research suggests that far from being fabulously rich or desperately poor, the majority group of whites in the South were independent yeomen farmers, often referred to as the plain folk. The residual effects of defeat proved catastrophic to this category of Southerners. Their high rate of participation in the Confederate Army meant that scores of farms had been neglected, thousands of soldiers never returned home, leaving their families to descend from a comfortable, nearly self-sufficient lifestyle to impoverishment. Expected to pay back taxes that had accumulated while they fought for the Confederacy and confronted with new higher land taxes imposed by the Reconstruction governments, many once-proud white farmers faced the possibility that their land would be forfeited.

A solution to the South's economic crisis emerged in the form of a system of sharecropping and tenant farming that included both poor whites and freedpeople. Initially received with hope by thousands of poorer Southerners as well as by large landowners, the program seemed to offer the freedpeople an interest in the land they farmed. It would keep them on the plantations and also allow whites with small or no farms to rent land or secure credit and continue farming their own property.

The agreement between landlord and tenant seemed simple. Large landowners subdivided their holdings into parcels that sharecroppers farmed for a share of the crop, usually half the harvest. Tenant farmers, who usually owned some equipment or resources that placed them in a stronger bargaining position than sharecroppers, rented the land, maintaining control of the crop until "settling up" time, when landlords received their payment. Tenant farmers typically enjoyed a higher social status than sharecroppers, and were subject to less control by the landlord.

Cotton dominated the post-Civil War era, fueling an emerging industrial economy that had been deprived of a reliable source of the fiber during the war. Landlords demanded that their sharecroppers and tenants plant only cash crops—in other words, cotton—which soon resulted in overproduction and falling prices. Rather than seeking to adjust agricultural practices to accommodate the changing circumstances, landlords encouraged increasingly desperate farmers to plant even more cotton in a futile effort to improve their situation. Tenant farming and sharecropping, which began in hope, soon became bywords for despair.

The details of the annual contract added to the misery of Southern farmers. Although most sharecropping and tenant arrangements included some form of housing, farmers were otherwise expected to provide their own food, clothing, and other essentials. Little thought was initially given to how a former slave or an impoverished Confederate veteran would obtain such supplies. Eventually, merchants, along with financially sound landlords, advanced credit, placing a lien on the farmers' half of the crop. Facilitated by the expansion of the railroads across the South, merchants—many of them recently arrived Northerners, others local people—provided essentials, or "furnish," to farmers, often at exorbitant rates. At the end of the season, the farmer delivered half the crop to the landlord and then used the rest to settle up with the merchant. As the late nineteenth century progressed, sharecroppers and tenants increasingly found that the return on their crop did not equal the line of credit advanced by the merchant, ensuring an ever-widening cycle of poverty.

Through the first decades of the twentieth century, sharecropping and tenancy trapped increasing numbers of poor white and, even more acutely, black Southerners in sustained desperation. It would take another war to offer thousands of Southerners the opportunity to break free from the cycle of poverty they generated. Born of poor planning in the aftermath of a brutal war and the end of slavery, sharecropping and tenancy shaped the character of the South, creating in the popular mind a caricature of Southerners that still remains.

BIBLIOGRAPHY

Hagood, Margaret J. *Mothers of the South: Portraiture of the White Tenant Farm Woman*. Chapel Hill: University of North Carolina Press, 1939.

Nieman, Donald G., ed. *From Slavery to Sharecropping: White Land and Black Labor in the Rural South, 1865–1900*. New York: Garland, 1994.

Royce, Edward C. *The Origins of Southern Sharecropping*. Philadelphia: Temple University Press, 1993.

Shaw, Nate. *All God's Dangers: The Life of Nate Shaw*. New York: Vintage, 1984.

Harold D. Woodman. *New South, New Law: The Legal Foundations of Credit and Labor Relations in the Postbellum Agricultural South*. Baton Rouge: Louisiana State University Press, 1995.

Woodward, C. Vann. *The Origins of the New South, 1877–1913*. Baton Rouge: Louisiana State University Press, 1951.

Samuel C. Hyde, Jr.

See also: Civil War and Industrial and Technological Advances; Economic Change and Industrialization; Farming.

SHERMAN'S MARCH TO THE SEA

After his capture of Atlanta on September 2, 1864, Union General William T. Sherman undertook a military campaign that helped end the Civil War and establish his historical reputation. He sent one part of his triumphant army under General George H. Thomas to defeat John Bell Hood's Confederate forces in Tennessee and himself took 62,000 men to bring the war home to a twenty- to sixty-mile-wide section of Georgia between

William Sherman's March to the Sea. In November, 1864, Sherman began a march from Atlanta to Savannah, Georgia, carving a sixty-mile-wide swath of destruction. His goal was to use destruction to convince Southerners to stop fighting and return to the Union © BETTMANN/CORBIS

Atlanta and Savannah. From November 15 to December 21, 1864, Sherman used a war of destruction to try to convince Southerners to stop the fighting and return to the Union. He promised them a hard war if they kept resisting but a soft peace if they quit.

Sherman divided his 62,000-man force into two wings and marched them along separate paths through Georgia. He feinted toward Macon and Augusta but bypassed those cities. His two wings came together only at the war capital of Milledgeville and finally again near Savannah. There were scarcely 8,000 Confederate soldiers in his path, and he so thoroughly confused them that their opposition was negligible.

Upon departure, Sherman's soldiers had with them twenty days' rations and a herd of 3,000 cattle. Otherwise they lived off the countryside, Sherman having used census figures to determine that there was enough food in his line of march to feed his army. Each wing traveled about fifteen miles per day, throwing foragers (called bummers) out in all directions to bring in supplies for the marching troops. Sherman prohibited useless destruction, but his men did take or destroy much material that was not needed for the army's survival. Whenever his troops arrived in an area, thousands of slaves left their bondage,

eventually following the army to the coast, creating further chaos for white Georgians.

Sherman did not practice total war in the modern sense of the term. He brought the harshness of war to the civilian populace, but he did so to avoid further bloody conflict. He wanted to end the fighting as quickly as possible, and he believed that an attack on the Southern psyche through property destruction was the best way—the quickest and least bloody way—to accomplish this end.

White Southerners, however, did not see it that way. White Southern civilians were shocked and frightened at what they experienced in Georgia or heard about from a distance. Although Confederate General Joseph Wheeler's cavalry, Southern army deserters, fugitive slaves, and looting civilians did their share of damage, white Southerners blamed Sherman exclusively and considered him brutish for his brand of warfare. Blacks, on the other hand, viewed him as a deliverer.

Sherman's march to the sea helped bring the war to an end more quickly, and it played an important role in later white Southern attitudes. The pro-Confederate Lost Cause view of the Civil War places great reliance on castigating Sherman and his soldiers as villains, in contrast to the saintliness it attributes to Robert E. Lee and the heroism it attributes to the Confederate soldiers. Sherman's greatest influence on white Southerners was not merely the physical destruction he caused, but also the psychological scar he left behind.

BIBLIOGRAPHY

Bailey, Anne. *War and Ruin: William T. Sherman and the Savannah Campaign.* Wilmington, DE: Scholarly Resources, 2003.

Glatthaar, Joseph T. *The March to the Sea and Beyond: Sherman's Troops in the Savannah and Carolina's Campaign.* New York: New York University Press, 1985.

Kennett, Lee. *Marching through Georgia: The Story of Soldiers and Civilians during Sherman's Campaign.* New York: HarperCollins, 1995.

Marszalek, John F. *Sherman: A Soldier's Passion for Order.* New York: Free Press, 1993.

John F. Marszalek

See also: **Confederate States of America; Lost Cause.**

SLAVERY

Understanding the origins, justification, and economy of slavery is crucial to understanding American society, the coming of the Civil War, and the effect of that war on American culture and identity. Chattel slavery has existed throughout world history, and U.S. slavery grew out of older European and African forms of enslavement. Yet slavery in the United States was distinctive for two important reasons. First, there have been relatively few true slave societies (as opposed to societies with slaves) in world history: ancient Greece, ancient Rome, Brazil, the Caribbean and the United States. Second, among these only the last three were based on race. Thus the slave system in place in the United States from about the mid-seventeenth century until the war's end was one of only three societies in world history to be a race-based slave society.

HOW SLAVERY WAS JUSTIFIED
Slavery began in what would become the United States with the importation of twenty enslaved Africans into Virginia in 1619. Given the universality of slavery, its legitimacy was rarely questioned or explained. By the 1660s, English settlers clearly believed that enslavement was a normal, if unfortunate, position in society for which Africans and their descendants were perfectly and naturally suited. However, racism—far from being the original justification for American slavery—emerged over time. In the early seventeenth century, English colonists used a longstanding rationale for enslavement: Africans

were not Christian. Because enslaved Africans sometimes converted to Christianity in order to be freed, this definition created a good deal of fluidity in early Virginia. Some Africans were enslaved, but others were not. Some slaves were freed for exemplary service, whereas others were enslaved for life. Some even enjoyed social mobility, becoming not only free but landowners and slaveholders.

In the mid-seventeenth century, Virginia's lawmakers passed laws that shifted the reason for enslavement from heathenism to Africanness, and they made enslavement lifelong. These laws connecting enslavement with place of origin provided the legal foundation for ideas about race that persist today by associating a degraded status (enslavement) with descent. By the end of the seventeenth century the linkage of Africanness or blackness with deserved enslavement was solid. Racism gained more weight over the eighteenth century as the growing trend toward rationalism sought to catalogue the world and its people.

The spread of Enlightenment thought during the eighteenth century changed this view of slavery. The Enlightenment's insistence on human rights and equality inspired an age of revolution in the late eighteenth century; the American Revolution, the French Revolution and the Haitian Revolution were all inspired in part by these ideals. In the 1740s, a spiritual movement swept the American colonies. The Great Awakening preached the importance of a direct experience of God's love, the value of expressing spiritual rapture, and the equal worth of all souls before God. In addition, the slow rise of industrial capitalism in the late eighteenth and early nineteenth centuries in the North caused some to question slavery's devaluation of competition, its degradation of work, and the absence of wages as incentive.

For all these reasons, a small minority of Americans began to question the validity of slavery; and by the late eighteenth century, a group of Philadelphians had formed the world's first antislavery society. Upon its heels followed organizations in New York, Boston, Baltimore and other cities throughout the North. Among this first generation of abolitionists it was commonplace for elite white men to form organizations that excluded white women and all black persons. Women's and black organizations were formed in the late eighteenth and early nineteenth centuries, and by about 1830, these groups came together in a second-generation abolitionist movement. The first generation had fought (successfully) for an end to the African slave trade, which ceased in 1808, and for the gradual abolition of slavery in the North. The second generation distinguished itself by working interracially in societies that included both women and men, and demanding immediate abolition; the most radical also promoted rights for black Americans.

Though abolitionists remained few in number, they were a vocal group that made it difficult for slaveholders (and to a certain extent, non-slaveholders) to unthinkingly accept the legitimacy of slavery. Increasingly, slaveholders had to explain what before had scarcely been questioned. Slowly the idea that slavery was a natural but unfortunate status died out, and the idea of paternalism took its place.

Paternalism idealized slavery as a family-like institution, which had a protective (if demanding) father-figure at the head of the household and many dependents (a wife, children, and slaves) below him. In exchange for care, protection and support, paternalists expected obedience and deference; some even hoped for love. They preferred to think of themselves as kind custodians of a childlike and dependent race rather than as cruel oppressors of their fellow men. Paternalism was also a method of control: It was the kid glove over the iron fist of violence that enforced the Old South's social order. For when slaveholders' provision of food and clothing, medical care, time off for holidays and the occasional frolic failed to garner the submission they expected, most used the lash without hesitation.

HOW THE SYSTEM BROUGHT WEALTH TO THE UNITED STATES

Racial slavery brought great wealth to the nation. The skills of West Africans in rice cultivation made South Carolina's planters among the richest in the Americas, and Louisiana's sugar barons were not far behind them. But it was King Cotton that brought the greatest profits. In 1793, Eli Whitney invented the cotton gin, an instrument that separated seed from the cotton lint that could be used to make thread and cloth. Cotton could now be processed sixty times faster than before, and production boomed. Not only did cotton become the nation's first-ranked export, but its dollar value was greater than that of all other American exports combined. Cotton was key to social mobility in the Old South, and slaves were key to cotton. Just as the non-landowner often aspired to landownership and then to the ownership of larger tracts of land, so the non-slaveholder hoped one day to own a few slaves, and perhaps in time to become the master of many.

Throughout the colonial period, slavery could be found in every colony. The profits from cotton, sugar, tobacco, and rice fed many parts of southern society. The slave trade needed slave traders, landlords to house slaves being transported to market, cook-shops to feed them, doctors to inspect them and treat their illnesses, insurance agents to insure their lives, and notaries public to notarize sales. Southern cities and states profited from slave sales, which they taxed.

Northern businesses and farms also counted on slavery for some of their revenues. Northern insurance companies, too, insured the lives of slaves in the market, and northern as well as southern banks collected interest on loans granted to slave traders to procure their initial shipments of slaves. The textile mills of the North would have ground to a halt without the constant supply of slave-grown cotton that went into the factory-made cloth and clothing. Many of the earliest contributions to elite northern universities came from those who made their money buying and selling human chattels. Northern farmers sold food crops to feed the slaves of the Caribbean, and barrels to hold the sugar they produced.

WHY MOST WHITE SOUTHERNERS EMBRACED SLAVERY

Most southern whites did not own slaves. In some places as few as one-quarter of all landowners owned slaves, in others no more than half did; and in mountainous areas, where plantations could not thrive, hardly any were slaveholders. In spite of this, many supported slavery. By the antebellum period, feelings of contempt and hatred for blacks were widespread among white southerners. Underlying the belief in white supremacy was the assumed existence of a common white identity, an identity that gained much of its essence from the existence of black slavery. The nineteenth century exhibited the full development of racist thought in everything from limericks, ephemera, and minstrel shows to politics and the law. Common whites, though subjugated to and held in contempt by slaveholding whites, nonetheless overwhelmingly supported slavery, for though they may have resented elite whites, they despised enslaved blacks more.

Black slavery also provided an economic and social "mudsill," as slaveholder, Governor and Senator James Henry Hammond put it in a famous speech he made in 1858—a drudge class at the bottom of society that elevated whites and freed them from the worst work. By the antebellum period, few white southerners could imagine any method of farming that would approach the level of agricultural production possible through forced labor. Ambitious whites sought to improve their financial situation by climbing through the ranks of slaveownership. In this way, slavery provided the most basic tool for social and economic mobility in the South as well as opportunities for whites in the supporting trades of slave trader, overseer, preacher, and doctor. Only in the mountainous regions of the South did support for slavery and slaveholding flag.

LAWS REGULATING SLAVE BEHAVIOR AND THE TREATMENT OF SLAVES

Southern law enshrined racist beliefs; indeed, even before racist beliefs were widespread and consistent in

Slaves picking cotton in the field.

southern society, the law led the way in giving slavery a racial basis and then separating enslaved blacks from the rest of society. The behavior of slaves was strictly controlled: They were barred from learning to read and write, working in printing offices, drinking, gathering after dark, bearing arms, gathering in large numbers, traveling without a pass, or running away (whether permanently or temporarily). Slaves lacked legal personhood; consequently, they could not testify against whites (but only against blacks), and crimes against their persons were treated as trespasses against their owners. The law also restricted the actions of whites in regard to slaves: It did not permit them to help slaves run away, sell them alcohol, teach them to read or write, or intermarry with them. Laws also limited and governed the conditions of manumission and taxation.

FAMILY, COMMUNITY, SURVIVAL

Thus dramatically separated from much of the rest of American society, enslaved Americans lived largely in a world unto themselves—though it was a world profoundly shaped by the European and American Indian cultures around and within slave society. By the early nineteenth century, most slaves in the United States had been born on American soil, not in Africa. These native-born blacks had known only slavery, as had their parents and perhaps even their grandparents. Thus, syncretism occurred through which enslaved people became a new people, a people with a very strong identity as such. At the same time, enslaved communities were rife with conflict between women and men, between those with power or property that others lacked, between the faithful and the secular—all the ordinary conflicts that can erupt between individuals.

During the Great Awakening, U.S. slaves converted to Christianity in large numbers, drawn to the Old Testament's message of sympathy for the downtrodden and deliverance from oppression and suffering. Afro-Christianity continued to be an important source of spiritual strength and social rejuvenation for generations. Alongside, and sometimes overlapping, this faith were social and healing practices that mixed African traditions with Christianity and to a much lesser degree, Islam. In Louisiana, this mixture was often formalized as Voudoun, whereas throughout the rest of the South, it remained informal. Whatever its form, spirituality offered courage and hope to the enslaved.

For almost all American slaves, the family was a source of both sustenance and suffering. Only a minority lived in nuclear families; many couples were separated either by the sale of the husband or wife in the slave market or by living "abroad" from one another—living on different farms. Enslaved families adapted to the vicissitudes forced upon them. Extended family relationships were vital and compensated, in part, for missing family members, who were remembered in naming practices and oral culture.

SLAVERY AND THE CIVIL WAR

In writing the U.S. Constitution, slavery was one topic among many that delegates to the Constitutional Congress had to address. After some debate, they decided to count each slave as three-fifths of a person in determining population for apportionment of state representation in Congress, to eliminate the external slave trade in 1808, and to impose a fugitive slave law that required that runaway slaves be returned to their owners. Thus, slavery was included in the Constitution. However, many northern states passed laws to begin the process of gradually emancipating slaves. Many northern slaveholders sold their slaves to the South where slavery was extremely profitable.

Because of the extra representation their states gained from counting three-fifths of slaveholders' human property, slavery gave southern elites disproportionate power in Congress. This power extended into other branches of government: Until the Civil War, southern slaveholders dominated the presidency and the Supreme Court, and most northerners who occupied those offices were pro-slavery as well.

During the 1850s, as the question of the expansion of slavery into new western territories was debated in Congress and on the streets, the perspective of many formerly neutral northerners began to shift. Increasingly, they came to see slaveholders as a "slave power" whose influence was spreading—not only within the traditional realm of the nation's political sphere, but into the West and even into the North, to the great consternation of growing numbers of northerners. Not to be mistaken for a conflict over the morality of slavery itself, the Civil War was the culmination of mounting tensions between southerners who believed each new state had the right to decide whether or not it would allow slavery and northerners who were increasingly resentful of the extending reach of the slave power.

During the years of the Civil War, the institution of slavery slowly fell apart. As the Union army advanced into parts of the Confederacy, many slaveholders fled into the Confederate interior. In coastal South Carolina, the land abandoned by planters was quickly claimed by those who had worked it for generations. After the war's end, landowners and Union officials found the task of prying the land away from the freedpeople difficult.

From the beginning of war onward, slaves ran away by the thousands. After a few years of war and flight, the Union army desperately needed a uniform policy for either sending the "contrabands of war" back to their owners (a policy objected to by many as aiding the enemy) or keeping them and using them in the army. A reluctant Abraham Lincoln was increasingly convinced of the need to arm these fugitives as well as the free blacks of the North clamoring for inclusion, and in 1863 he announced the Emancipation Proclamation, in part to satisfy the military need for men. The Proclamation freed enslaved people in the Confederacy, and paved the way for a general emancipation at the end of the war in 1865.

Slavery was at the heart of the issues that led to the outbreak of Civil War in April 1861. Whereas a probable majority of Americans accepted the existence of slavery in southern states, many opposed its expansion into new states and territories. And among slaveholding societies, the United States was unique in going to war to resolve the question of slavery and of how the nation would define itself. The end of the Civil War and the passage of the Thirteenth Amendment to the Constitution in 1865 resolved that question forever.

Stephanie M. H. Camp

See also: **Abolitionists; African Americans (Freed People); Compromise of 1850; Douglass, Frederick; Emancipation Proclamation; Farming: Occupation of the South; Tubman, Harriet; Uncle Tom's Cabin.**

STANTON, ELIZABETH CADY

(b. November 12, 1815; d. October 16, 1902) Women's rights activist and leader in the Abolitionist movement.

Elizabeth Cady Stanton supported the Civil War to end slavery and to gain equal rights not only for Blacks but also for women. While the war resulted in liberation for slaves, it did not fundamentally change the status of women. The struggle for women's rights would continue long after the war ended.

Stanton was born to a prominent family in Johnstown, New York, on November 12, 1815. Her family's status allowed her the benefit of a sound education. Access to her father's law office made her aware, at an early age, of the injustices that women faced. By law and tradition, women were considered secondary to men and lost access to their property and wages once married. Women could not vote or hold public office. As Stanton matured, she became more aware of reform issues, especially through her wealthy cousin, Garritt Smith. He introduced her to the abolitionist Henry Stanton, and the two married in 1840.

At the World Anti-Slavery Convention in 1840, which the Stantons attended on their honeymoon, Elizabeth met Quaker minister and abolitionist Lucretia Mott. Though they were official delegates to the Convention, Mott and six other women could not participate because they were female. Mott and Stanton became friends and shared their concerns about the secondary status of women. But it was not until the Stantons moved to Seneca Falls, New York, that Elizabeth and Mott met again. They and three other women discussed the need to hold a convention that focused solely on women's rights.

From this discussion came the Seneca Falls Convention, which marks the beginning of the woman's rights movement. The Convention met July 19 and 20, 1848. Some 300 people from the area attended. Stanton penned the Declaration of Sentiments, modeled on the Declaration of Independence, that stated "that all men and women are created equal." In the document, Stanton demanded women's right to higher education and to professions then closed to them, more liberal divorce laws, property rights for married women, and women's suffrage. The Declaration became the rallying cry for women's struggle for equality during the next several decades.

After Seneca Falls, Stanton's participation in the woman's rights movement was primarily through her writings. Overwhelmed by the rearing of her seven children, she had little time to organize or attend annual woman's rights conventions. Her writings continued to insist that women needed the right to vote, that society needed more liberal divorce laws, and that married women had the right to their own wages and property. In 1851, she met Susan B. Anthony, thus beginning a lifelong collaboration and friendship.

During the Civil War, Stanton became involved in the Women's Loyal National League, uniting women to support the Union and push for the abolition of slavery. Woman's rights issues were put aside, though female activists believed their needs would be addressed at the war's end. Women gathered hundreds of thousands of signatures on petitions that demanded abolition through a constitutional amendment.

With the end of the Civil War and of slavery in 1865, Stanton convened the American Equal Rights Association in 1866 to promote universal suffrage. She re-

Elizabeth Cady Stanton. AP/WIDE WORLD PHOTOS

sponded vehemently to the passage of the Fourteenth (1868) and Fifteenth Amendments (1870) to the Constitution. She and Anthony were angered that the Fourteenth Amendment guaranteeing citizenship included the word "male." She opposed the Fifteenth Amendment because it gave African-American males the right to vote before women had that right. In 1869, women split over these issues and the direction of the woman's rights movement. Stanton and Anthony formed and led the National Woman Suffrage Association), which pursued a fairly radical agenda, including a federal amendment to ensure women's suffrage. Lucy Stone and others created the American Woman Suffrage Association, which followed a more conservative, state-by-state approach to gain women's suffrage. Not until 1890 did the two groups overlook their differences and unite into one organization, the National American Woman's Suffrage Association.

In the late 1860s, Stanton began to work actively for women's suffrage. She and Anthony lectured nationwide, and Stanton continued to write for several newspapers. But by 1880, she reduced her commitments, tired by the work and overwhelmed by arthritis and her increasing weight. For several years she worked on the multi-volume *History of Woman Suffrage* published in the 1880s. Stanton became more critical of the direction of the woman's rights effort as a younger group of women became involved. Increasingly frustrated with the conservative stance of ministers towards women's equality, she launched new projects, producing a two-volume *Woman's Bible* and her autobiography. Her health began to decline; her weight made it difficult for her to get around; and she was blind by 1899. Stanton died at her home in New York on October 16, 1902, well before the passage of the Nineteenth Amendment in 1920.

BIBLIOGRAPHY

Banner, Lois. *Elizabeth Cady Stanton: A Radical for Woman's Rights.* Boston: Little, Brown, 1980.

Griffith, Elisabeth. *In Her Own Right: The Life of Elizabeth Cady Stanton.* New York: Oxford University Press, 1984.

Lutz, Alma. *Created Equal: A Biography of Elizabeth Cady Stanton, 1815–1902.* New York: Day, 1940.

Sally G. McMillen

See also: **Abolitionists; Anthony, Susan B.; Woman's Rights Movement.**

STATE'S RIGHTS, THEORY OF

War has affected American society and culture in many ways. In particular the Civil War (1861–1865) was a conflict over a theory of government as well as a war to end slavery. The South ascribed to the theory that the states were supreme and that the national or federal government was created by the states. Under this theory the United States was more like a compact formed by independent countries, in which states retained the right to decide what national laws applied to them and even the right to withdraw from the compact. The victory of the North in the Civil War rejected, but has not removed, that theory from the mainstream of American society.

In 1787, during the debates over the Constitution, the issue of state's rights came to center stage. Though almost all agreed that the national government needed to be strengthened, many believed that the new central government being created in Philadelphia would threaten their liberties. They believed that their local and state governments would be most responsive to their needs and therefore wanted as many limitations as possible on the power of the national governments over the states.

The most vocal proponent of states rights during the early republic was Thomas Jefferson. He produced one of his most significant writings on this subject during the presidency of John Adams, when the fiercely contested Alien and Sedition Acts were used by the national government to restrict freedom of speech and dissent against Adams's policies. Many saw this as unconstitutional. In the Kentucky Resolves, Jefferson attacked the Constitu-

tionality of these acts on several counts, especially the national government's infringement on state's rights. Excluded from the final draft, however, was the word "nullification." This is the idea that a state should have the power to declare a federal law they believed to be unconstitutional, "null" and void within their own borders.

The theory of "nullification" was later used during a regional conflict over tariffs—the tariffs would be beneficial to the North but detrimental to the South. The South protested these tariffs as being unconstitutional. One of the most ardent defenders of state's rights, John Calhoun, wrote "Exposition and Protest," which attacked the constitutionality of the tariffs and affirmed the idea of nullification. South Carolina acted on his idea and declared the tariffs unconstitutional and therefore null and void within the boundaries of South Carolina. Though the conflict was settled with a compromise, this was not a deterrent to the belief of many that nullification was the right of states.

After the war with Mexico in 1848, new issues faced the country involving the expansion of slavery. In 1850, Southern states called for a convention to be held in Nashville, Tennessee, to try and organize a united front on the question. But the convention failed. The states mistrusted each other and focused on their own concerns rather than on the greater interest of the South. The notion of state's rights greatly hampered the ability to compromise or to sacrifice for the good of the whole.

The flaws in the state's right theory became more evident during the Civil War. Though there was a national government for the Confederacy under Jefferson Davis, southern states were not about to give up their rights to that government—the very rights many believed the Confederacy was defending against the North. Davis had a difficult time getting individual states to think in terms of the good of the Confederacy. Many southern states objected to such necessary war measures as a draft and taxation, on the basis that they infringed on their rights as states.

The end of the war was a serious blow for the doctrine of state's rights in both the North and the South. The federal government asserted its authority over the rights of individual states. Citizens began to identify with the national government rather than with their local or state governments. Before the war it was common to refer to the United States as "are"; after the war it became the United States "is."

In particular, the Fourteenth Amendment to the Constitution established the principle that Americans are citizens of one nation and empowered the national government to uphold their rights. Although the issue of federalism—meaning which powers are better exercised by the federal or state governments—remains a vital part of American political culture, the principle of state's rights as understood by the South in the Civil War is no longer a central feature of the nation's politics.

Brian D. Stokes

See also: **Confederate States of America; Davis, Jefferson.**

SUPREME COURT, 1816–1900

As one of the three branches of our federal government, the Supreme Court played a significant role in events before, during, and after the Civil War. Several rulings from the 1850s to the 1890s had a profound impact on this nation. The Dred Scott decision heightened passions over slavery in the volatile decade leading up to the outbreak of war. The Court took an active part during the Civil War by adjudicating issues of civil rights. In the years that followed the war, the Court's rulings relating to the meaning of citizenship and the protection of civil liberties, especially in the Slaughterhouse cases and *Plessy v. Ferguson,* influenced the nation's stance on race and citizenship for decades to come.

Early in its history, the United States Supreme Court was preoccupied with establishing its legitimacy as a national institution and its power of judicial review. Following the War of 1812, however, with its status and popular support established, the Supreme Court under Chief Justice John Marshall began to play an important role in shaping the new nation. In a series of decisions such as *McCulloch v. Maryland* (1819) and *Gibbons v. Ogden* (1824), the Court set a pattern of favoring a strong central government and expansion of the nation westward by endorsing the federal government's efforts to regulate banking and commerce. These efforts reflected a strong popular culture of nationalism and protection of property rights that temporarily offset assertions of states' rights.

In 1835, Roger B. Taney became the Chief Justice of the Court, a change that gave the Supreme Court a key and controversial role in events leading up to the Civil War. Taney was a Jacksonian Democrat who favored states' rights. The growing crisis over slavery, with its strong basis in the states' rights issue, led Taney to attempt to settle the matter by authoring the most infamous decision in Supreme Court history, the Dred Scott decision. In this 1857 case, formally known as *Scott v. Sandford,* Taney and five fellow justices ruled that African Americans were not citizens of the United States but property protected by the Constitution. The justices further ruled that freed slaves could be enslaved again if they were found in a slave state. The public in the North re-

acted furiously to this decision. Many people thought that there was no longer any possibility of compromising on the issue of slavery, and the Court lost credibility as an institution, unable to exercise leadership as the nation surged to war.

At the beginning of the Civil War, the resignation of Southerners from the Court caused a change in its philosophy. Predictably, the Court moved from sympathy toward states' rights to sympathy with the cause of national unity. With this change came a tendency to be deferential to the president when he was perceived to be defending the nation against an external threat, a tendency that continues today. In the 1862 Prize Cases, the Court said that the president need not wait for a congressional declaration of war before repelling a sudden attack on the United States.

At the same time, the Court attempted to confront President Abraham Lincoln on civil liberties issues. In *Ex Parte Merryman,* when confronted with the issue of whether the president or Congress had the power under the Constitution to suspend the writ of habeas corpus, the Court ruled that Congress held the power. The detention of civilians by the military was unconstitutional. President Lincoln essentially ignored the ruling, and the Court was powerless to enforce it. In *Ex Parte Milligan,* however, the Court did not back off, holding that military courts could not try civilians when civilian courts were open and operating. Many Americans viewed these cases as a key to protecting civil liberties if a wartime president attempted to override them in the name of national security; the cases remain important today.

At the end of the Civil War, Congress, led by the Republican Party, overturned the prewar Dred Scott decision, abolishing slavery in the Thirteenth Amendment to the Constitution, and declaring in the Fourteenth Amendment that all persons born in the United States were citizens. Along with the Fifteenth Amendment, these constitutional changes were clearly meant to ensure that black Americans would have the same civil and political rights as whites. The Supreme Court, however, stalled that vision for decades.

In the 1873 Slaughterhouse Cases, the Supreme Court interpreted the Fourteenth Amendment's Privileges and Immunities Clause for the first time since the ratification of the amendment in 1870. The Privileges and Immunities Clause states that no state can enforce "any law which shall abridge the privileges or immunities of the citizens of the United States." At issue in the Slaughterhouse Cases, which involved restrictions affecting butchers, was whether states could infringe on the right to labor—in other words, to pursue a lawful trade. In a 5–4 vote, however, the Court narrowed the scope of this clause considerably, ruling that it did not protect the right to labor. Many people criticized this decision on the grounds that it undercut the federal government's ability to protect the newly-freed slaves from discriminatory treatment by the states.

This trend continued further in 1896 in the case of *Plessy v. Ferguson*, where the Supreme Court held that the Equal Protection Clause of the Fourteenth Amendment allowed segregation under the "separate but equal" principle. The State of Louisiana had a number of "Jim Crow" laws that sought to keep black Americans in an inferior social state. Among these was a law mandating that blacks and whites travel in different train cars. Black Americans sued to test this law and lost before the Supreme Court. The Court said that the Thirteenth Amendment abolished slavery, but not all distinctions based on race, and that the Fourteenth Amendment's Equal Protection Clause did not demand that the races be mixed. The Court stated that law could not alter long-standing customs of society, of which racial segregation was one.

BIBLIOGRAPHY

Hall, Kermit L. et al., editors. *The Oxford Companion to the Supreme Court of the United States.* New York: Oxford University Press, 1992.

McCloskey, Robert G. *The American Supreme Court.* Chicago: University of Chicago Press, 1960.

Margaret D. Stock

See also: Civil Liberties, Civil War; Constitutional Amendments and Changes; Reconstruction; Segregation, Racial, 1816–1900.

TEXAS, REPUBLIC OF

Modern Texas was originally part of a larger territory, Coahuila y Tejas—one of the states of Mexico, which became a nation in 1821 after gaining its independence from Spain. After Texas gained its independence from Mexico, the Republic of Texas (1836–1845) allowed slavery, and as a result its admission into the Union deepened the divisions between North and South that led to the Civil War. Texas' entry into the Union also fed American ambitions to expand U.S. control of the continent and led to the Mexican War (1846–1848), which resulted in the U.S. acquisition of California and territories in the Southwest.

COAHUILA Y TEJAS

In 1821, Spanish colonial administrators in Texas granted Moses Austin authority to colonize American settlers. Austin died shortly thereafter, and his son, Stephen, received permission from the new Mexican government to continue his father's work. By 1835, 13,500 families had legally immigrated to Texas from the United States; many also came illegally. Most were Southerners drawn by the promise of cheap land or fleeing the economic problems caused by the Panic of 1819. Slaveholders brought their slaves with them. Despite official prohibitions, loopholes allowed slavery to flourish in Texas.

In theory, Mexican policy mandated that immigrants become Mexican citizens, convert to Catholicism, and be persons of good character. The Mexican government allowed trial by jury, gave official status to both Spanish and English languages, and left considerable local powers to *empresarios* such as Stephen Austin who sponsored colonization efforts. In practice, American immigrants to Texas found lax governmental supervision, low taxes, and no serious effort to enforce official Catholicism. Some Mexican officials expressed concern at the area's growing Americanization and suggested curbing immigration.

American immigration to Texas occurred against a backdrop of chronic instability in Mexico. Military force often resolved political divisions between those favoring federalist and centralist approaches to governing the country. Frequent changes of government between 1821 and 1835 hampered good relations between Texas and the central government. During a period of centralist rule from 1829 to 1832, Mexican officials imposed tighter restrictions to prevent a drift toward greater economic ties with the United States. The Law of April 6, 1830, banned

The Republic of Texas

☐ Territory Claimed
by the Republic of Texas

╱ Modern State Bounderies

The Republic of Texas. GALE GROUP

on April 21, 1836. Texas General Sam Houston forced the Mexican leader to sign the Treaties of Velasco, recognizing Texas' independence and establishing the Rio Grande as its southern boundary. Mexican federalists overthrew Santa Anna and refused to recognize Texas, continuing to view the old Spanish boundary of the Nueces River as legitimate.

EFFORTS TO ANNEX THE TEXAS REPUBLIC

From its outset, the Republic of Texas sought to become part of the United States. Texans expressed overwhelming approval of annexation in a September 1836 referendum, but American political divisions over the issue of slavery delayed union. President Andrew Jackson's administration refused to recognize Texas' independence until March 1837. President Martin Van Buren's administration proved even less interested in annexing Texas. Both of the major American political parties, the Democrats and the Whigs, proved unwilling to disturb their delicate North-South coalitions with a debate over the admission of another slave state. As a result, alternative visions for the republic's future remained politically alive into 1844.

Sam Houston (president of the Republic of Texas, 1836–1838 and 1841–1844) and his political supporters favored joining the United States. Houston's opponents, led by Mirabeau Lamar (president, 1838–1841), proposed a grander future for Texas. Lamar advocated Indian expulsion, commercial and diplomatic relations with European powers, and the expansion of Texas to the Pacific. Lamar's schemes produced debt, inflation, and military disaster. When Houston returned to power in 1841, Texas faced a crippling economic situation and a rising threat from Mexico. Twice in 1842, Mexican military forces invaded and then withdrew. Houston devoted his second term to resolving Texas' untenable situation. He moved simultaneously on three different paths. First, he continued to press for annexation to the United States. Second, he flirted with the possibility of Texas becoming a British protectorate, which would probably have required the abolition of slavery but would have opened the door to British immigration, capital, and military protection. Third, Houston pursued reunification with Mexico on terms favorable to Texas. The wily Houston hoped British and Mexican interest would bait the American government into annexing Texas.

John Tyler's ascension to the American presidency offered hope for annexation. Tyler, a Southern Whig, feared that a British protectorate in Texas would prevent westward expansion of both the United States and slavery. Secret negotiations between Texas' representatives and U.S. Secretary of State John Calhoun produced an annexation treaty in February 1844. Calhoun warned the

new immigration, and trade restrictions and tariffs caused considerable resentment. A coup by General Antonio López de Santa Anna led to a return to federalist rule in 1833. Texans initiated efforts to obtain separate statehood, but Mexican officials refused to partition Coahuila y Tejas. As a federalist, Santa Anna generally accommodated Texans' concerns, lifting the 1830 immigration ban and continuing a policy of limited taxation.

Federalist reforms failed to improve Mexico's overall economic and political situation, and in 1835 Santa Anna seized dictatorial powers and shifted to a centralist approach. He abrogated the federalist Constitution of 1824. Federalists rebelled in Yucatán, Zacatecas, and Coahuila y Tejas. In Texas, Anglo settlers as well as *Tejanos* (Spanish and Mexican residents of Texas) took up arms and captured San Antonio de Bexar in late 1835. After brutally crushing the Zacatecas revolt, Santa Anna led a large Mexican army into Texas in early 1836. In March, the Mexicans defeated rebellious Texans at the Alamo and Goliad. However, Santa Anna suffered a decisive defeat at San Jacinto, near present-day Houston,

British government that meddling in Texas threatened American security interests since it threatened the westward expansion of slavery, making clear the proslavery motivations behind the annexation treaty. As a result, the treaty failed. The 1844 presidential election, however, became a referendum on expansion when the Democratic candidate, Tennessee governor James K. Polk, called for expansion in Oregon as well as Texas, balancing an additional slave state with a free state and thus mooting the slavery issue. Polk's election energized the lame duck Congress to move on Texas annexation. A joint resolution of Congress passed in February 1845, allowing for annexation if it was approved by Texas voters.

Under the joint resolution, Texas kept both its public lands and its debt. Texas voters could also divide the state into as many as four additional states. New states created north of the Missouri Compromise line (36°30' north latitude) would be free; slavery would be permitted in new states created to the south of the line. The international boundary dispute between Texas and Mexico fell to the United States government for resolution. On March 6, 1845, the Mexican government, upset with U.S. annexation of land Mexico had long claimed, broke diplomatic relations with the United States, setting the stage for the Mexican War. That October, Texas voters ratified the annexation agreement by 4,254 to 257. In December, Polk signed an act making Texas the twenty-eighth state. The following spring, Polk ordered American forces into the disputed region between the Nueces and Rio Grande, provoking war with Mexico.

The annexation of Texas represents a critical event not only in the path to war with Mexico but also in the developing sectional crisis within the United States. By making war with Mexico all but inevitable, annexation fueled U.S. expansion and brought on debates about slavery in newly conquered territories. The mechanics of annexation alarmed many Northerners, who found confirmation of a slave-power conspiracy determined to expand the institution and dominate the federal government. Northern opposition to annexation and the Mexican war conversely confirmed many Southerners' suspicions that the North hoped to curb the South's political power, limiting and ultimately abolishing slavery. These issues would ultimately lead to the outbreak of the Civil War in 1861.

BIBLIOGRAPHY

Calvert, Robert A.; DeLeón, Arnoldo; and Cantrell, Gregg. *The History of Texas*, 3d edition. Wheeling, IL: Harlan Davidson, 2002.

Campbell, Randolph B. *An Empire for Slavery: The Peculiar Institution in Texas, 1821–1865*. Baton Rouge: Louisiana State University Press, 1989.

Cantrell, Gregg. *Stephen F. Austin: Empresario of Texas*. New Haven, CT: Yale University Press, 1999.

Freehling, William W. *The Road to Disunion: Secessionists at Bay, 1776–1854*. New York: Oxford University Press, 1990.

Richardson, Rupert; Anderson, Adrian; Wintz, Cary D.; and Wallace, Ernest. *Texas: The Lone Star State*, 8th ed. Upper Saddle River, NJ: Prentice Hall, 2001.

Ricky Dobbs

See also: **Alamo; Guadelupe Hidalgo, Treaty of.**

TUBMAN, HARRIET

(b. ca. 1820; d. March 10, 1913) Former slave and conductor on the Underground Railroad, Civil War nurse and spy.

Harriet Tubman, heroine of the Underground Railroad, personally escorted as many as seventy or eighty former slaves to freedom in the North after her own daring flight from slavery in 1849. Frederick Douglass, whose Rochester, New York, home served as an Underground Railroad station, wrote to her in 1868, "Excepting John Brown—of sacred memory—I know of no one who has willingly encountered more perils and hardships to serve our enslaved people than you have" (Bradford, 1869). During the Civil War, she again risked her life in the antislavery cause by joining the Union Army in coastal South Carolina and Florida as a spy, scout, and nurse. Less well known but equally heroic was her postwar work, managing a small subsistence farm to support a large extended family in Auburn, New York. In her later years, she created a facility for the impoverished elderly in Auburn and found both private and church funding for it.

In 1844, while still a slave in Maryland, Harriet Tubman married John Tubman, a free black man. She had no children of her own, which was an advantage when she began to think of escape to the North, in 1849. When her legal owner, Edward Brodess, died, it seemed likely that she would be sold South and she decided to flee. She may have been helped initially by neighbors with antislavery sympathies—a white woman took her in and provided information leading to her next hiding place.

Tubman escaped alone to Philadelphia, where, aided by a strong abolitionist community, she found work and began to plan a return South for her family. John Tubman had remarried in 1851 and refused to join her. This personal blow may have intensified her belief that she had a mission to rescue her remaining kinfolk from slavery.

Harriet Tubman.

After the passage of the Fugitive Slave Act (1850), the Northern states were no longer safe havens for fugitive slaves and Tubman extended her route to Canada, guiding parties of up to ten or eleven to Saint Catharines, where a growing community of African Canadians welcomed newcomers to freedom.

Stories of the daring rescues by the "colored heroine" began to appear in the letters of her admiring abolitionist associate Thomas Garrett, a Quaker based in Wilmington, Delaware, who helped provide transportation, lodging, and funds for several thousand fugitives over his long Underground Railroad career.

In 1858 she met the antislavery crusader John Brown, then fresh from bloody guerrilla fighting against proslavery forces in the territory of Kansas. Knowing her skills, courage, and connections in the African-Canadian community, Brown sought her aid in recruiting former slaves as fighters for his forthcoming military action against slavery. She did not participate directly in the assault on the federal arsenal at Harpers Ferry, Virginia, in 1859 that led to Brown's death and martyrdom.

When the Civil War broke out, Tubman, along with other abolitionists, was disappointed in President Lincoln's failure to commit the Union to an explicitly anti-slavery policy. Nevertheless, in early 1862 she responded with enthusiasm when recruited by antislavery friends in Massachusetts to join the Union Army encampment in the federally occupied South Carolina Sea Islands. Although her assignment was ostensibly to perform humanitarian service work among the former slaves, she also served as a Union Army spy behind Confederate lines.

In South Carolina, Tubman recruited a small band of African-American men as spies and scouts, providing vital intelligence about Confederate capabilities and plans. She played a central role in the Combahee River Raid of June 1863, helping to destroy massive amounts of Confederate property and supplies.

Tubman's Civil War service also included the less glamorous but equally vital work of nursing. She nursed the wounded survivors of the 1863 assault on Fort Wagner by an African-American regiment from Massachusetts led by the abolitionist Robert Gould Shaw, who died in the battle. She also nursed Union troops in Florida who were suffering from dysentery, using a traditional root-based remedy.

Tubman was proud of her Civil War service, but because of her informal status (she was never officially enlisted) and gender she never received back pay, recognition as a veteran, or a veteran's pension, despite the repeated efforts of influential friends after the war, including Secretary of State William Seward. As an elderly woman, she was finally awarded a pension, but only as the widow of a veteran—her second husband.

At the war's end, Tubman returned to Auburn, New York, where she lived until her death. Immediately after the war, she raised funds for schools for the newly emancipated African Americans. Her major concern over the next fifteen years, however, was her own economic self-sufficiency and maintaining the home she shared with her elderly parents and an extended family of relatives and boarders. In her later years, she developed a new mission: raising funds for a home for the impoverished elderly. The Harriet Tubman Home opened under the auspices of the AME Zion church in 1908.

Rediscovered in the early twentieth century after many years of obscurity and poverty, Tubman again became an important symbol of heroic African-American womanhood. In the later twentieth century, the home evolved into a national shrine to Tubman's memory. She serves as an important symbol of slaves' intense desire for freedom and the bravery of those like her who risked their lives to achieve that freedom.

BIBLIOGRAPHY

Bradford, Sarah. *Scenes in the Life of Harriet Tubman.* Auburn, NY: W. J. Moses, 1869.

Cheney, Ednah. "Moses." *Freedmen's Record* 1 (March 1965): 34–38.

Conrad, Earl. *General Harriet Tubman*. Washington, DC: Associated Publishers, 1943.

Humez, Jean M. *Harriet Tubman: The Life and the Life Stories*. Madison: University of Wisconsin Press, 2003.

Larson, Kate Clifford. *Bound for the Promised Land: Harriet Tubman, Portrait of An American Hero*. New York: Ballantine, 2003.

Sanborn, Franklin B. "Harriet Tubman." (Boston) *Commonwealth*, July 17, 1863.

Jean M. Humez

See also: **Abolitionists; Douglass, Frederick.**

UNCLE TOM'S CABIN

Harriet Beecher Stowe wrote *Uncle Tom's Cabin* as a protest against the Compromise of 1850, specifically its Fugitive Slave Law, which required Northerners to abet the South in its retrieval of runaway slaves. Serialized in *The National Era* beginning in 1851 and published in book form on March 20, 1852, by John P. Jewett, Stowe's response to the incursion of slave law into free states took the United States by storm. The novel sold 50,000 copies in its first two months, 300,000 in its first year, and by early 1853, Americans and Britains had bought one million copies. The novel was such a phenomenon that when Abraham Lincoln met Stowe in 1852, he is said to have greeted her with these famous words: "So you're the little woman who wrote the book that started this great war!"

Many factors explain the enormous popularity of Stowe's abolitionist novel. *Uncle Tom's Cabin* combines a lively and accessible writing style with a portrait of antebellum American society that Northern readers, in particular, found convincing, thoughtful, and sympathetic. For example, Stowe's scenes of domestic life illustrated her culture's belief in the sanctity of family. Her representations of various regions in America evoked the nation's diverse geography, language, and thought. Perhaps most important, in linking the story of Uncle Tom's suffering with the life and death of Jesus Christ, Stowe had woven together slavery, the most controversial issue of the time, with Christianity, the culture's most profound belief system. Her political point was that Christianity and slavery were mutually exclusive. And, in choosing the vehicle of sentimental fiction, which appealed to readers' emotions through a series of unforgettable characters—Uncle Tom, Topsy, Eva, Legree—she succeeded beyond her wildest expectations.

Most Southerners would have none of this. Reviews of the novel indicate that Southern readers were outraged by Stowe's contention that slavery ravaged families, denigrated labor, and encouraged sexual indiscretion. They argued that she had misrepresented slavery and the South, insisting that Stowe's characterization was based on little, if not concocted, evidence. Censorship of the novel was unusual, although incidents of book burning in Virginia and Georgia did occur. A more typical response can be found in a set of more than twenty novels, known as "anti-Uncle Tom" novels, which represented happy slaves and their sensitive masters, who, unlike factory owners, fed, clothed, and cared for slaves in sickness and old age.

Harriet Beecher Stowe.

Nine years after *Uncle Tom's Cabin* was published, the Civil War began. War was not Stowe's solution to the problem of slavery. Sympathy was. At the novel's conclusion, she asked readers to "*feel right*" (p. 624). Once they did, Stowe believed that slavery would end. History, however, wrote a different ending. Stowe's son, Fred, fought, was wounded at Gettysburg in 1863, struggled with alcoholism, and disappeared sometime in 1871, never again to be heard of by his family. Stowe viewed the nation's conflict through a Christian framework: war became the necessary and final confrontation with the evils of slavery. In its indictment of those evils, *Uncle Tom's Cabin* laid the psychological groundwork for that struggle, and inaugurated a tradition of American reform literature that flourishes today.

BIBLIOGRAPHY

Gossett, Thomas F. *Uncle Tom's Cabin and American Culture.* Dallas, TX: Southern Methodist University Press, 1985.

Stowe, Harriet Beecher. *Uncle Tom's Cabin or, Life Among the Lowly* (1852). New York: Penguin, 1981, edited and with an introduction by Ann Douglas.

Weinstein Cindy, ed. *The Cambridge Companion to Harriet Beecher Stowe.* Cambridge, U.K.: Cambridge University Press, 2004.

Internet Resource

"Uncle Tom's Cabin and American Culture." Archive directed by Stephen Railton. University of Virginia, Department of English. Available from <http://www.iath.virginia.edu/utc>

Cindy Weinstein

See also: **Abolitionists; Slavery; Tubman, Harriet.**

UNITED STATES SANITARY COMMISSION

The United States Sanitary Commission (USSC), created in June of 1861, was the largest private war relief charity of the Civil War. Organized to coordinate Union homefront donations, assist in military hospitals, and advise the government on recruitment and medical issues, the men who founded the Commission expected it would provide a national stage for their ideas about class, society, and nation-building. Headed by Henry Whitney Bellows, Unitarian minister of All Souls' Church in New York; landscape architect Frederick Law Olmsted; and lawyer George Templeton Strong, the USSC approached the war less as a battle with the institution of slavery than as a contest for postwar political influence and social reform.

The idea of a centralized agency to coordinate homefront charity did not originate with Bellows or his colleagues. Rather, within days of the war's outbreak, a group of upper-class women in New York City, including Drs. Elizabeth Blackwell and Emily Blackwell, formed the Women's Central Relief Association (WCRA) to coordinate the volunteer efforts of homefront women and train female nurses. Seeing the possibilities inherent in a centralized war charity, Bellows stepped in to create a male-run organization, reducing the WCRA to a regional branch of the new Commission.

When the Civil War began, few Americans imagined a long or costly war; indeed, many believed Secretary of State William Seward's prediction that military conflict would be over in three months. Yet even a brief war required levels of material aid and support for recruitment that could overwhelm the meager War Department. Anxious to act on their politics and accustomed to handling the welfare needs of others, thousands of northern middle-class women responded to the war emergency by refocusing their charitable energies and creating soldiers' aid societies to produce uniforms, bandages, hospital clothing, and foodstuffs needed by departing regiments.

Commission leaders never anticipated that the greater part of their energies would be occupied with coaxing women to send their donations to the USSC. Having witnessed women's enthusiasm for early mobilization (and believing that charity was "instinctual" to women), they assumed easy compliance with their philanthropic structure. They failed to comprehend the extent to which the Sanitary Commission represented an incursion into the social prerogative middle-class women had acquired over philanthropy. Nor did they appreciate the realities of household labor and the sacrifices women made to meet demands for supplies. Worse still, by the middle of the war rumors of Sanitary Commission fraud and mishandling of supplies had spread throughout the North. Stories of widespread corruption, including the sale of goods women donated, led many on the homefront to conclude that the USSC was a mere money-making concern, igniting antebellum fears about concentrations of power. As women resisted USSC demands for their labor, they attempted to protect the meanings they attached to their patriotism and their benevolence. In cities and towns throughout the Union, they staged "Sanitary" fairs to raise money for soldiers' welfare, and sent their donations through alternate channels to hedge against misappropriation.

The Sanitary Commission continued its operations until the end of the war, bolstered by Union victories at the front and prodigious canvassing of the Northern homefront. After the war, it boasted of having distributed donations worth over $15 million. Generous with their praise for women's wartime labors, in personal correspondence USSC leaders expressed considerable frustration with the Commission experience. For their part, Northern women displayed ambivalence about the impact of their war work. Women leaders of Sanitary Commission branches were grateful for the opportunities they had for full-time involvement in the great conflict; a number went on to shape careers that utilized the organizational skills and personal contacts they had developed during the war.

For the vast majority of women, their labors in support of the Union left their lives little changed in terms of civil rights. Those who hoped that their participation would demonstrate their fitness for full citizenship were disappointed by their exclusion for suffrage rights in the Fourteenth and Fifteenth Amendments. Nonetheless, countless women took considerable pride in what they accomplished during the war and the real economic value they contributed to the Union.

BIBLIOGRAPHY

Attie, Jeanie. *Patriotic Toil: Northern Women and the American Civil War.* Ithaca, NY: Cornell University Press, 1998.

Fredrickson, George M. *The Inner Civil War: Northern Intellectuals and the Crisis of the Union.* New York: Harper Torchbooks, 1965.

Ginzberg, Lori D. *Women and the Work of Benevolence: Morality, Politics, and Class in the Nineteenth-Century United States.* New Haven, CT: Yale University Press, 1990.

Maxwell, William Quentin. *Lincoln's Fifth Wheel: The Political History of the United States Sanitary Commission.* New York: Longmans, Green, 1956.

Jeanie Attie

See also: **Civil Liberties, Civil War.**

URBANIZATION

Between 1815 and 1900 the nation fought wars that protected its independence, expanded its continental frontiers, and subdued Native Americans; it survived a bloody Civil War; and it won a "Splendid Little War" against Spain that created an empire that included Cuba and the Philippines. These wars, especially the Civil War and Spanish-American war, occurred while the United States was becoming an urban, industrial, and multicultural nation. By the end of the nineteenth century, industry and technology, such as steam-driven ships and the machine gun, had transformed warfare. To understand the impact of war upon American society and culture requires an understanding of the underlying changes, such as urbanization, that were modernizing the nation.

During the nineteenth century, cities in the United States grew significantly. Factors such as large scale immigration and rapid industrialization contributed to this process of urbanization. By the end of the century, instead of moving to frontier areas, Americans as well as immigrants settled in the country's larger cities. Between 1880 and 1900, the proportion of the urban population of the United States grew from 28 percent to 40 percent. Urbanization also brought with it important political, social, and cultural changes. In addition, the Civil War had an impact on the growth of American cities.

IMMIGRATION AND INDUSTRIALIZATION

The nineteenth century saw massive waves of immigrants arrive in the United States. The majority of these immigrants came from Europe, although there were also significant numbers from other countries such as China. Immigration was especially high in the second half of the century. Most immigrants settled in the largest American cities, thus promoting urbanization. Approximately 70 percent of immigrants lived in urban areas. All of the country's largest and fastest-growing cities had large immigrant populations. In 1890, for example, 80 percent of

A woman knitting in a New York City tenement in a photograph by Jacob Riis, ca. 1890. © CORBIS

the population in New York City was either foreign-born or first-generation children of immigrants. New York had more foreign-born residents than any city in the world. The large number of immigrants living in cities led to the development of immigrant neighborhoods and ethnic ghettos. Immigrant life was often very difficult. Immigrants were subject to a variety of types of exploitation and often remained poor. In 1860, 86 percent of New York City's paupers were foreign born. In response to the large number of immigrants in cities, nativist political movements emerged in the United States, reflecting growing hostilities toward foreigners. Immigrants were subject to discrimination and violence, as seen in the anti-Asian riots of western cities in the 1870s and 1880s. Anti-immigrant legislation also began to appear.

In addition to immigration, industrialization also contributed to urban growth. Many industries were lo-cated in cities, as urban areas possessed more workers and better transportation facilities. Led by the iron and steel industries, industrial production grew significantly in the post-Civil War period, doubling in the last two decades of the century. In Midwestern cities, meatpacking, flour milling, brewing, and production of farm machinery all contributed to industrialization and urbanization in cities such as Chicago. In the post-Civil War South, mill towns grew at a rapid rate as cotton mills became the symbol of the New South. Thus, by the late–1800s, more and more people moved to urban areas to find industrial jobs.

WAR AND URBANIZATION

The Civil War had a negative effect on a number of cities, especially those along the Mississippi River. The disruption of trade along the river hurt cities such as New Orleans and St. Louis. New Orleans was the fifth largest city in the country in 1860 but fell to fifteenth by 1910. Further to the north, St. Louis also suffered from reduced river commerce. Slow to innovate and believing its favorable position would always be an advantage, St. Louis fell behind Chicago in importance after the war.

In the North, draft riots occurred in a number of cities. The most significant of these draft riots took place in New York City in 1863. In particular, Irish immigrants in the city resented the draft, resulting in much violence and destruction, much of it aimed at New York's African American population. The immigrants resented the city's black population, who often worked for lower wages. Furthermore, the rioters also were upset that wealthy residents could purchase substitutes to fight for them. In response to the rioting, the federal government sent in troops to quell the violence.

SOCIAL, CULTURAL, AND POLITICAL CHANGES

One major problem associated with the rapid growth of cities in the nineteenth century was a housing shortage. By the time of the Civil War, large cities in the eastern United States had lost their open character as more people crowded into the cities. Population density grew dramatically, as urban residents moved into any space available, including basements, attics, and lofts. A defining characteristic of this housing problem was the presence of the tenement building. The term tenement came to be used to describe any residential building in a slum area. At first, the urban poor crowded into older buildings that had been divided into smaller units. During the 1850s and 1860s, many of these old buildings were torn down and replaced with new tenements with extremely small rooms that lacked heating and plumbing. These buildings could house hundreds of urban poor. Other problems included poor design, landlord neglect, and lack of governmental control. By the 1870s, the "dumb-bell" tenement appeared, which provided some light and ventilation. Whatever type of structure the urban poor lived in, problems such as disease, poor ventilation, and lack of basic services were common. As the number of tenements grew, slum areas such as New York's infamous Lower East Side appeared in all large cities.

In the 1870s and 1880s, the vaudeville house emerged as an important source of entertainment in cities, becoming the dominant form of theater in urban America. Earlier in the century, variety shows generally were seen as too risqué and seedy for most city dwellers. By the later part of the century, such shows had been "cleaned up" and transformed into mass entertainment acceptable to most people. The shows included comedy routines, gymnastic acts, and sentimental songs. While most plays and operas did not appeal to a wide range of people, the vaudeville acts were not aimed at a specific group or class.

Furthermore, vaudeville reflected many aspects of the urban experience, so city dwellers saw themselves in the show. Furthermore, the shows were often seen as more egalitarian, as they were inexpensive. There was no reserved seating at the "continuous shows," and spectators could move about the theater during the performance.

Another characteristic of the nineteenth-century city was the rise of the department store. Growing cities possessed an expanded retail market. Many urban residents sought a lifestyle of comfort and luxury, demanding goods that included furnishings, clothing, and toys. Department stores emerged that conveniently sold all these items. Women especially flocked to the downtown department stores on public transportation. They were attracted by the stores' great variety, convenient displays in large, impressive buildings, and constant advertising in the metropolitan press. Like the vaudeville house, the department store has often been described as egalitarian, as all customers were treated the same, service was first come, first serve, and all women were referred to as "ladies."

By the late-nineteenth century, a major development in urban politics was the emergence of political machines led by bosses. The growth of cities led to increased demands on local government for services. The political machines met this demand. By responding to the needs of urban dwellers through charity and patronage, bosses then built up a voting organization. These loyal voters then helped bosses and their machines to win elections. Once in office, politicians then distributed government spoils to their supporters. The most well-known of the political bosses was New York City's Boss Tweed and his Tammany Hall organization. Sometimes, the bosses and their machines acted illegally, breaking laws and resorting to bribes to win elections. However, they also built parks, schools, roads, and sewers, all to the advantage of urban residents. The machines also aided recent immigrants to the city, providing them with housing and jobs.

BIBLIOGRAPHY

Barth, Gunther. *City People: The Rise of Modern City Culture in Nineteenth-Century America.* Oxford, England: Oxford University Press, 1980.

Chudacoff, Howard; Smith, Judith E. *The Evolution of American Urban Society,* 5th edition. Upper Saddle River, NJ: Prentice Hall, 2000.

Glaab, Charles; and Brown, A. Theodore. *A History of Urban America,* 3d edition. New York: Macmillan, 1983.

Monkkonen, Eric. *America Becomes Urban: The Development of U.S. Cities and Towns, 1780–1980.* Berkeley: University of California Press, 1988.

Schuyler, David. *The New Urban Landscape: The Redefinition of City Form in Nineteenth-Century America.* Baltimore, MD: The Johns Hopkins University Press, 1986.

Ronald Young

VIOLENCE

Collective violence bracketed the Civil War and was important both to events leading up to the war and to its results.

In an upsurge of rioting in the mid-1830s, proslavery mobs predominated. Northern and Southern rioters attacked African Americans and abolitionists, attempting to silence the latter, but differences in sectional mob patterns laid the foundation for the coming struggles. Northern mobs commonly attacked property, and authorities checked them if they grew brutal or murderous; most of the people killed were rioters. Southern riots usually aimed at persons and were often sadistic or deadly, especially if the victims had been labeled abolitionists or insurrectionists. Authorities more often supported than controlled Southern mobs, so rioting became a communally sanctioned system of terror that quelled internal questioning of slavery.

In the 1850s, Catholic immigration and slavery were the primary explosive issues that resulted in violence. The 1850 Fugitive Slave Law, which required Northern authorities to aid in the capture of runaway slaves, led mobs to attempt rescues of captured slaves. Intensifying sectional furies led to the collapse of the Whig Party in 1854, and the American Party (1849–1856; often called the Know-Nothing Party) briefly replaced it and tried to defuse the issue of slavery by directing anger against Catholics and immigrants. This led to deadly election rioting between Know-Nothings and Democrats in the border and river cities of Baltimore, Washington, Louisville, St. Louis, and New Orleans.

The Kansas Nebraska Act of 1854 increased the level of social violence. Southern proslavery and Northern antislavery forces moved into the territory of Kansas, turning it into a battleground when, in a prelude to the Civil War, partisan bands on both sides carried out deadly raids. On May 21, 1856, a proslavery mob sacked the town of Lawrence, which was known as a hotbed of abolitionists. A few days later, in retaliation, John Brown led a small band that killed five proslavery men in an incident that became known as the Potawatomie Massacre. Because of the violent partisan conflict, Kansas became known as "Bleeding Kansas."

In May 1856, violence spilled onto the floor of Congress when South Carolina Representative Preston Brooks caned Massachusetts Senator Charles Sumner senseless at his Senate desk in response to Sumner's speech "The Crime against Kansas." The South reveled

United States Marines storming the engine house in Harpers Ferry, West Virginia, after it was captured by abolitionist John Brown. Brown planned to help runaway slaves and launch attacks on slave holders. He and a small band captured the federal armory and arsenal in Harpers Ferry, along with a weapons manufacturer, before the local militia, the Marines, and soldiers were dispatched. GETTY IMAGES

in the caning and in Brooks's claim that "it would not take much to have the throats of every abolitionist cut." Northerners recoiled at his demonstration of the South's violence against anyone who questioned slavery.

The start of the Civil War did not end mob violence. Insurrection panics continued in the South, draft riots erupted in the North, and guerilla bands devastated both the South and the border states. In 1865, peace brought renewed rioting against African Americans in the South, including insurrection scares and widespread urban mobs, the deadliest of which were in Memphis and New Orleans. The war's devastation and political uncertainties, the military occupation of the South, and the sudden transformation of chattel into free people fostered some violence on all sides, but the predominant pattern quickly became white mobbing to enforce the subordination of African Americans. Economic concerns and social subjugation motivated much of the antiblack violence, but the terror was primarily a political tactic to destroy all efforts to give African Americans full rights as citizens. Many groups were involved in this communally sanctioned terrorizing of blacks, but the best known is the Ku Klux Klan. Many able black leaders, and many whites

who promoted interracial cooperation, were murdered. Slavery-related violence before the war claimed more than 600 victims, but many thousands were murdered by mobs during Reconstruction, and countless thousands more were whipped, humiliated, brutalized, maimed, raped, robbed, and driven from their homes. With Southern whites securely in power, the number of African Americans killed by lynching rose steadily in the 1880s and 1890s, ensuring that African Americans had no pretensions to equal rights or the protection of law.

Mobbings over African-American issues were far from the only social violence in the decades surrounding the Civil War. Before the war, major ethnic, land, and urban riots occurred, and anti-Catholic mobs were numerous, especially in New England. Catholic-Protestant hostilities climaxed in Philadelphia in 1844. Mobs drove Mormons from their homes in Missouri and Illinois. The Mormons settled in Utah in 1847, where a decade later they perpetrated the nation's largest single mob murder at Mountain Meadows. Elsewhere in the West, vigilantes killed hundreds of victims. After the war, anti-Chinese riots and Indian wars and massacres showed the reach of American intolerance of other races. The great railroad strikes of 1877 initiated a half-century of violence, mostly against labor, giving the United States the world's deadliest industrial history, but the toll taken by this class rioting was still smaller than that of the nation's racial struggles.

Violence was part of American life in ways that went beyond fighting in wars. Violence increased as white Americans confronted other races and cultures, as they struggled and often fought over lands claimed by Indians and by Mexico in the West, as struggles became more common between workers and management, as whites in the South sought to maintain their supremacy over free African Americans, and as more deadly and accurate firearms were invented.

BIBLIOGRAPHY

Feldberg, Michael. *The Turbulent Era: Riot and Disorder in Jacksonian America.* New York: Oxford University Press, 1980.

Grimsted, David. *American Mobbing, 1828–1861: Toward Civil War.* New York: Oxford University Press, 1998.

Senkewicz, Richard M. *Vigilantes in Gold Rush San Francisco.* Stanford, CA: Stanford University Press, 1985.

Taft, Philip, and Ross, Philip, "American Labor Violence: Its Causes, Character, and Outcome." In *Violence in America: Historical and Comparative Perspectives,* edited by Hugh Davis Graham and Ted Robert Gurr. New York: New American Library, 1969.

Trelease, Allen W. *White Terror: The Ku Klux Klan Conspiracy and Southern Reconstruction.* New York: Harper & Row, 1971.

Tunnell, Ted. *Crucible of Reconstruction: War, Radicalism, and Race in Louisiana.* Baton Rouge: Louisiana State University Press, 1984.

Wright, George C. *Racial Violence in Kentucky, 1865–1940: Lynchings, Mob Rule, and "Legal Lynchings."* Baton Rouge: Louisiana State University Press, 1990.

David Grimsted

See also: **Indian Removal and Response; Ku Klux Klan; New York City Draft Riots.**

VISUAL ARTS, CIVIL WAR AND THE WEST

Artists have long been inspired to capture the heroism, tragedy, ideals, suffering, and destruction of war. Whether through painting and sculpture, or television and film, their images have a lasting impact on how people understand and remember war. The images of 19th-century artists who portrayed the Civil War and Indian Wars helped to create an American memory of those wars. Their art helped to shape American culture and identity.

Several prominent artists, including Edmonia Lewis and Winslow Homer, created paintings and sculptures that depicted the ideologies and realities that underpinned the Civil War. Violent conflicts in the West between Native American peoples, who desperately attempted to maintain their cultural integrity, and American settlers resulted from the nation's belief that its "manifest destiny" was to dominate the continent. Prominent artists who have depicted this cultural conflict include Oscar Howe, Frederic Remington, and Charles Russell.

THE CIVIL WAR IN ART

In 1867, two years after the Civil War ended, the sculptor Edmonia Lewis (ca. 1845–after 1909) created the sculpture, *Forever Free.* Lewis—part African American, part Native American—was particularly interested in the identity and oppression of African American people. *Forever Free* depicts an African American man, with a fragment of a recently-broken chain still shackled to his wrist, standing beside a kneeling African American woman. Although the American art establishment was male-dominated during the 19th century, Lewis represents an exception to the norm, as do other women who contributed to the visual culture of the Civil War era. For example, women were involved in the visual culture of the Civil War by sewing quilts used by soldiers.

Besides the highly refined sculpted imagery of Lewis, the Civil War was shown to American society through engravings published in newspapers. Artists traveled to battle sites and encampments to draw and paint the scenes first hand; subsequently, engravings were made from these originals. One of the most successful artists who depicted the Civil War for the Union was Winslow Homer (1836–1910). His depictions of the Civil War show the conflict in frank detail, and many of his renderings were published in the popular magazine *Harper's Bazaar.* The pictures show mundane scenes, as well as images of violence. Homer's engravings and paintings of the Civil War are often judged to be highly realistic and lacking sentimental qualities. However, his work certainly contains emotion; he was, in fact, consciously manipulating his subject matter for both emotional and didactic reasons. After the war ended, Homer created paintings that drew on his firsthand knowledge of the war. One painting, *Prisoners from the Front,* received international acclaim in 1866. In addition to Winslow Homer, several other artists depicted the Civil War in art, including Julian Scott and Thomas Nast (1840–1902), who painted scenes for the Union, and Conrad Wise Chapman (1842–1910), who painted scenes for the Confederacy.

Civil War imagery has remained important to the American public since the war ended. Numerous monu-

"The War for the Union—A Bayonet Charge," a lithograph by Winslow Homer, published in *Harpers Weekly,* **July 12, 1862.** AP/WIDE WORLD PHOTOS

ments were erected throughout the United States during the late 19th Century, attesting to America's need to commemorate the collective traumas of that war and celebrate the subsequent healing of the nation. One of the most important of these monuments is the Augustus St. Gaudens' relief sculpture depicting the Massachusetts 54th regiment of Black soldiers, led by Robert Gould Shaw, the son of a prominent Boston family, marching toward its destruction in the 1863 battle of Fort Wagner in South Carolina. St. Gaudens' monument captures the war's idealism, as blacks and whites fight for their freedom, as well as America's racial division, represented by black soldiers led by a white officer.

THE WEST IN ART

It is difficult to generalize about the imagery of violence between Native American peoples and the U.S. Government in the American West because uprisings occurred sporadically in many regions over an extended period of time. Although there was no clear beginning and no clear end to these conflicts, one event is often cited as a symbolic end of armed conflict between Native Americans and the U.S. Government: the Massacre at Wounded

Knee on December 29, 1890. The Massacre consisted of the killing of nearly 300 Lakota people by the U.S. Army. One artist who depicted this event is the Native American modernist Oscar Howe (1915–1983). Titled *Wounded Knee Massacre,* his painting shows a line of U.S. soldiers shooting at Lakota, whose bloodied bodies fall into an area that Howe evokes as an open grave.

Such violent conflicts between Lakota people and U.S. soldiers were easily recognized by the American people. Indeed, the Lakota warrior, with a full headdress of feathers, became the quintessential image of a Native American. One reason for this was the dramatic reinterpretation and display of the history as a clear narrative of conquest. Within this narrative, Native Americans were depicted as savage, and artists depicted U.S. soldiers as bringing civilization to them. During the 1860s and 1870s, huge paintings were created to illustrate this narrative. One painting by John Stevens consisted of a series of 36 individual images on a single canvas that was 222 feet long. The painting was viewed through a performance, in which the canvas was rolled across a specially constructed apparatus, lit from behind. As the scenes rolled past the audience, the artist narrated the events.

The best known artist of the West is Frederick Remington (1861–1909). Though Remington created both paintings and sculpture, his wide recognition is due to his mass-produced bronze sculptures. These bronzes depict images of a highly romanticized Western lifestyle. In Remington's art as a whole, the West appears as a region with continuous emotional activities, such as cowboys riding bucking broncos and Native Americans hunting bison. Many of Remington's paintings depict violent conflict between U.S. soldiers and Native Americans, clearly drawing on the narrative of conquest. Similar to Remington, the artist Charles M. Russell (1864–1926) also depicted scenes of the American West, showing conquest and stereotyped images of both Native Americans and cowboys. The West of Remington and Russell was a region almost devoid of women—both artists ignored women in nearly all of their art.

These images depicting the West have resounded in American culture in multiple ways. An organization founded in the 20th century, The Cowboy Artists of America, includes artists who imitate the style that Remington and other artists developed. Hollywood transformed this imagery into popular Western movies, and corporate America appropriates these images to sell products ranging from clothing to automobiles to cigarettes.

Imagery depicting the Civil War and the West has had an enormous impact on American culture. Some of the imagery depicting these conflicts dates from the 19th century, when the events occurred. However, the visual cultures of the Civil War and the West did not fade into obscurity, but rather influenced numerous later artists and molded the perceptions of America.

BIBLIOGRAPHY

Bassham, Ben L. *Conrad Wise Chapman: Artist and Soldier of the Confederacy.* Kent, OH: Kent State University Press, 1998.

Bell, John. "The Sioux War Panorama and American Mythic History." *Theatre Journal* 48, no. 3 (1996): 279–99.

Bonfield, Lynn. "Quilts for Civil War Soldiers from Peacham, Vermont." *Uncoverings* 22 (2001): 37–64.

Forsyth, Susan. *Representing the Massacre of American Indians at Wounded Knee, 1890–2000.* Lewiston, NY: E. Mellen Press, 2003.

Hassrick, Peter H. *Remington, Russell and the Language of Western Art.* Washington, DC: Trust for Museum Exhibitions, 2000.

Holzer, Harold, and Neely, Mark E., Jr. *Mine Eyes Have Seen the Glory: The Civil War in Art.* New York: Orion Books, 1993.

Howe, Oscar. *Oscar Howe: Artist.* Vermillion: University of South Dakota, 1974.

Nemerov, Alexander. *Frederic Remington and Turn-of-the-Century America.* New Haven: Yale University Press, 1995.

Savage, Kirk. *Standing Soldiers, Kneeling Slaves: Race, War, and Monument in Nineteenth-Century America.* Princeton, NJ: Princeton University Press, 1997.

Simpson, Marc. *Winslow Homer: Paintings of the Civil War.* San Francisco: Fine Arts Museums of San Francisco; Bedford Arts, 1988.

Titterton, Robert J. *Julian Scott: Artist of the Civil War and Native America.* Jefferson, NC: McFarland and Company, 1997.

Walker, Kara Elizabeth, and Berry, Ian. *Kara Walker: Narratives of a Negress.* Cambridge, MA: MIT Press, 2003.

Travis Nygard

WHITMAN, WALT

(b. May 31, 1819; d. March 26, 1892) American poet

Born in West Hills, New York to a large family of Quaker background and raised in Brooklyn, Walt Whitman was a journalist, wartime nurse, and poet whose poetry captured the pathos and spirituality of the ordinary soldier in the Civil War and reinforced the image of President Lincoln as a Christ like character.

Whitman left school at the age of eleven in order to help his struggling family, working in a law office and in the printing business and teaching school. Essentially self-taught, he was a voracious reader. In 1841, he moved to Manhattan and began to pursue journalism, contributing essays, poems, and short stories to a number of different newspapers. He edited the *Brooklyn Daily Eagle* from 1846 to 1848 and was a strong advocate of the United States' War with Mexico, which he saw as a means for achieving the nation's manifest destiny. Yet his support of the Free Soil Party, which opposed the expansion of slavery into western lands acquired from that war, cost him his editorship. Whitman then traveled to New Orleans where he edited the *New Orleans Crescent*. Upon returning to Brooklyn in 1850, he founded and edited a Free Soil newspaper, the *Brooklyn Weekly Freeman* which advocated the abolition of slavery.

Influenced by Ralph Waldo Emerson and Transcendentalism, Whitman in 1855 published his first edition of *Leaves of Grass,* a group of twelve lengthy, untitled poems. The critics were complimentary, but sales were slow, probably due to its free-verse form and frank expressions of sexuality. Over time, Whitman added more poems and produced five more editions of the work.

By 1860, Whitman was editing the *Brooklyn Times.* When the Civil War began, he supported the preservation of the Union and viewed the ensuing conflict as the ultimate test of America's willingness and ability to forge a national identity. Writing and engaging in political causes, he considered himself destined to play a significant role in the history of America. It was through his advocacy of the common man and soldier that he received fame.

In December 1862, Whitman left home seeking his brother George, who was listed among the missing soldiers after the battle at Fredericksburg, Virginia. After two weeks in the camp there, Whitman decided to volunteer as a nurse. Living in Washington, D.C. and working part-time as a copier in the Army Paymaster's Office,

Walt Whitman, in a photograph by Mathew B. Brady.

he wrote letters to newspapers and politicians on behalf of soldiers' needs. In January 1863, he received a commission from the U.S. Christian Commission to minister to the sick. Tending both Union and Confederate wounded soldiers, Whitman provided companionship for them and read to them, all the while taking notes on his time in the hospitals and camps to create a clear picture of soldiers' lives and document facts that he used in his editorials.

His health declined in late 1863. After recovering, he visited more camps in early 1864 and saw Northern prisoners who had been released. Their appearance horrified him. He again fell ill in June 1864, retired to Brooklyn, and in December resumed nursing in New York City. Whitman gave himself to the soldiers under his care and never let go of the experience of caring for the wounded, despite its depletion of his physical and psychological reserves. In twenty months, he estimated he made six hundred hospital visits and tended eighty to one hundred thousand soldiers.

To Whitman, the most important facet of the Civil War was the personal sacrifice it inspired. Casting his prose and poetry in the shadows of Jesus and Lincoln, Whitman portrayed the casualties of the common soldier, and even his own health, as noble sacrifices for a higher good. Like many in the North, Whitman was dev-

astated by Lincoln's assassination. However, he perceived it as the redemptive force the Nation needed to move forward. With slavery abolished, the war over, the and South in ruins, his poems "O Captain! My Captain!" and "When Lilacs Last in the Dooryard Bloom'd" enabled the nation to grieve for its fallen leader and sons.

Upon returning to Washington, in 1865 Whitman published *Drum Taps,* which he considered to be his finest piece of work. In 1871, he published three more books. Thanks to W. D. O'Connor's complimentary 1866 biography of him, Americans viewed Whitman as *The Good Gray Poet.*

A paralyzing stroke on January 23, 1873 necessitated his moving to Camden, New Jersey to live with his brother George. In 1876, the *Centennial Leaves of Grass, Memoranda During the War,* and *Two Rivulets* entered into his legacy of words inspired by America and its Civil War, followed in the 1880s by five other books. Throughout his last years, Whitman lectured on Lincoln. He died on March 26, 1890. His personal embodiment of the ideals and contradictions of the United States helped to solidify the world's perception of him as a consummate American poet, one heavily influenced by the Civil War.

BIBLIOGRAPHY

Allen, Gay Wilson. *The Solitary Singer: A Critical Biography of Walt Whitman.* Revised edition. Chicago: University of Chicago Press, 1985.

Callow, Phillip. *From Noon to Starry Night: A Life of Walt Whitman.* Chicago: Ivan R. Dee, 1992.

Kaplan, Justin. *Walt Whitman: A Life.* New York: Simon & Schuster, 1980.

Reynolds, David S. *Walt Whitman's America: A Cultural Biography.* New York: Knopf, 1995.

Zweig, Paul. *Walt Whitman: The Making of the Poet.* New York: Basic Books, 1984.

Sarah Hilgendorff List

See also: **Literature.**

WOMAN'S RIGHTS MOVEMENT

In mid-July, 1848, Elizabeth Cady Stanton, Lucretia Mott, Jane Hunt, and Martha Coffin Wright sat around a mahogany table in Mary Ann McClintock's parlor in Waterloo, New York, writing a Declaration of Sentiments calling for changes in American law and custom that would grant women rights that were equal to those of free, white men, rights denied to women for centuries.

Dr. Anna Shaw and Carrie Chapman Catt, founder of the League of Women Voters, leading fellow suffragettes down Fifth Avenue in New York City, 1915. AP/WIDE WORLD PHOTOS

EARLY REFORM EFFORTS

Sensitized to gender discrimination partly as a result of their participation in the abolitionist movement, they had a wide variety of complaints. They pointed out that being denied the right to vote, women had no voice in the passage of the laws they were expected to obey. They charged that married women had no right to control either their inherited property or their wages and that a mother's right to custody of her children was tenuous. They pointed out that women's access to employment was limited and that when they did work, they were frequently poorly paid (and certainly paid less than men).

Higher education and the ministry were closed to women, they complained. Women were held to a higher moral standard than men. Men, they charged, had attempted to destroy women's self-confidence and self-respect. For these reasons, they explained, women were "aggrieved" and "oppressed." Having been "deprived of their most sacred rights," they, like the founding fathers, demanded redress of their grievances.

Elizabeth Cady Stanton presented the Declaration of Sentiments to the first woman's rights convention, held in the Wesleyan Methodist Church in Seneca Falls, New York, on July 19 and 20, 1848. More than one hundred men and women signed the document, although the demand for woman's right to vote caused the greatest dissension. Similar conventions, petition campaigns, and public speaking tours during 1850s allowed woman's rights supporters to solicit popular support for their cause.

When the Civil War began in 1861, woman's rights advocates agreed to temporarily shift the focus of their reform efforts to winning the war and freeing the slaves. Toward that end, Stanton and Susan B. Anthony, who had joined the woman's rights movement in early 1850s, established the Woman's National Loyal League. Its members helped to collect over 400,000 signatures on anti-slavery petitions sent to Congress.

The war ended in 1865, and abolitionists were determined to secure the rights of emancipated slaves by guaranteeing their claim to citizenship and their right to vote through the fourteenth and fifteenth amendments. Woman's rights advocates supported those efforts but objected to the fact that the amendments said nothing about the rights of women. Some agreed with their abolitionist allies that it was the "Negro's hour" and were willing to wait to secure women's rights. Others like Stanton and Anthony were not willing to do so. In May 1866 Stanton and Anthony formed the American Equal Rights Association. Through that organization they campaigned to abolish both sex and race restrictions on rights from state constitutions.

CONSERVATIVES AND RADICALS

During the next three years, personal differences, combined with disagreements over priorities and strategy, further divided the leaders of the woman's rights movement. In 1869, Anthony and Stanton formed the National

Woman's Suffrage Association (NWSA). Lucy Stone, Henry Blackwell, and Julia Ward Howe formed the American Woman's Suffrage Association (AWSA). The NWSA was the more radical of the two. While the AWSA focused on getting the vote, the NWSA supported a broad reform agenda.

In order to promote that agenda, Stanton and Anthony collaborated with individuals who compromised the high moral tone of the original woman's rights movement. They accepted financial support from Francis Train, a man opposed to black suffrage, in order to pay for the publication of their newspaper, The Revolution. The NWSA also became associated with Victoria Woodhull, who ran for president of the United States in the election of 1872 on the platform of free love. The connection between Woodhull and the NWSA undermined whatever interest respectable, middle-class women might have had in the movement. The result was that while interest in woman's rights remained, neither the NWSA nor the AWSA flourished during the late 1870s and early 1880s.

By the late 1880s, memory of the Woodhull affair had diminished, grass roots support for woman's rights was growing, black women were organizing, and a new generation of woman's rights advocates was emerging. Individual states had passed laws expanding woman's rights to their own property and easier access to divorce. In 1890, the NWSA and the AWSA buried their differences and joined together to form the National American Woman's Suffrage Association (NAWSA). Under the leadership of Carrie Chapman Catt and Anna Howard Shaw, the NAWSA conducted the campaign that led, finally in 1920, to the passage of the nineteenth amendment to the Constitution granting women the right to vote. Their success attested to the dedication of generations of women and to the inspiration gained from the liberation of slaves and the struggle for equal rights.

BIBLIOGRAPHY

DuBois, Ellen Carol. *Feminism and Suffrage: The Emergence of an Independent Women's Movement in America, 1848–1869.* Ithaca: Cornell University Press, 1978.

Flexner, Eleanor. *Century of Struggle: The Woman's Rights Movement in the United States.* New York: Antheneum, 1972.

Terborg-Penn, Rosalyn. *African-American Women in the Struggle for the Vote, 1850–1920.* Bloomington: Indiana University Press, 1998.

Sylvia D. Hoffert

See also: **Abolition; Anthony, Susan B.; Constitutional Changes and Amendments; Douglass, Frederick; Stanton, Elizabeth Cady; Women on the Homefront.**

WOMEN ON THE HOMEFRONT

When the North and South mobilized for war in 1861, women on the homefront knew little of the four-year struggle that lay ahead. Imbued with a sense of patriotism, northern and southern women extended their domestic and maternal skills into new areas of work and civic involvement. Women also came to view the war years as a time of trial and hardship as mothers and wives struggled for their families' survival. Yet, regardless of their race, class, or regional identity, women met the challenges presented to them with strength and tenacity, and ultimately helped to shape the course of the conflict.

VOLUNTARY WORK

Women demonstrated their patriotism for their respective regions by participating in voluntary organizations. Northern women created associations to supply bandages, socks, food, medicine, and other necessities to soldiers. By April 1862, the U.S. government coordinated women's groups through the United States Sanitary Commission, which served as an umbrella organization for relief efforts and gave many women leadership opportunities. During her work with the Commission, Annie Wittenmyer rose through the ranks eventually to head the state agency in Iowa. Southern women organized their own associations to help aid the Confederacy. In their soldiers' aid societies and sewing circles, primarily established on the local level, women sewed uniforms, collected donations, and made food to send to troops. The Ladies Soldiers Aid Society of Natural Bridge, Virginia, established convalescent homes in local residences to care for ailing or wounded soldiers.

With women's energies focused on the war and family survival, few found time to concentrate on or had an interest in the woman's rights movement that had begun over a decade ago in the Northeast. To avoid seeming unpatriotic and in hopes of having their efforts rewarded after the war, activist women such as Elizabeth Cady Stanton, Lucretia Mott, and Susan B. Anthony concentrated on the abolition of slavery rather than woman's rights. In 1863, Anthony, Stanton, Ernestine Rose, and Lucy Stone organized the National Woman's Loyal League and sought signatures for a petition supporting the abolishment of slavery. Although the organization dissolved in 1864, their efforts helped move the focus of the war toward abolition. Moreover, the Loyal League trained women in organizational and campaigning skills that they later utilized in the female suffrage movement.

African-American women in the North also participated in the war effort while advancing the cause of freedom. Some black women collected donations for relief societies, gathered signatures on petitions protesting slav-

The Washington, D.C., camp of the 31st Pennsylvania Infantry Regiment in 1862. © MEDFORD HISTORICAL SOCIETY
COLLECTION/CORBIS

ery, and volunteered as teachers. The situation of "con-trabands" (the term given to runaway slaves) in Union camps drew concern from black female activists. In Washington, D.C., women formed the Contraband Relief Society to help provide clothing and food to the many former slaves flooding Union camps.

PAID EMPLOYMENT

The departure of men to the battlefront as well as economic difficulties due to the war caused some women to seek work outside the home, which led to a feminization of occupations traditionally reserved for men. Efforts to supply soldiers with weapons and clothing created jobs

for women in munitions factories, arsenals, and textile mills. The U.S. government also supplied jobs for young, single women, known as "Government Girls," who worked as clerks for a number of agencies. Southern women likewise sought paid positions with the Confederate and state governments. They served as seamstresses in the Confederate Clothing Bureau and printed currency in the Treasury Department while others worked as ordinance workers preparing ammunition.

Women increasingly turned to teaching as a way to supplement their family's income. Northern and southern schools hired female teachers long before the war began. After 1863, a few white and African-American women found jobs in areas of the South teaching in schools designed to educate former slaves. In the South, the absence of men on the home front combined with northern female teachers returning home when the war began caused a shortage of educators, and single, educated white women filled vacant positions.

Providing care for wounded and sick soldiers also created opportunities for paid employment. In the North, the Sanitary Commission assumed primary responsibility for the recruitment and placement of nurses. It appointed Dorothea Dix as "Superintendent of Nurses" to head these efforts. Fears over sexual impropriety between nurses and their male patients concerned Dix, and she responded by accepting only women who seemed plain in appearance and over thirty years of age. Nurses such as Clara Barton, who later founded the Red Cross, worked outside the strictures of the Commission and chose to go where hospitals and soldiers needed their services.

Organizing nurses in the South proved daunting as most hospital care depended on local or state efforts. Not until 1862 did the government allow women to work in official capacities as matrons, nurses, or orderlies in Confederate hospitals. Medical workers typically divided along class and racial lines with elite, white women taking on supervisory work and poor white or slave women relegated to menial tasks. Like those in the North, some southern women worked outside the parameters of the Confederate hospitals in "wayside hospitals" established in community buildings or homes.

HOME AND FAMILY LIFE

Women's home and family life changed considerably as fathers, husbands, and brothers left for war. In rural areas, white women took over managing the farm or plantation and continued their housework and cared for family members. Those from poorer families had little assistance in their farm labor and assumed care of financial matters as well as planting, cultivating, and harvesting the crops. Women from wealthy homes in the South assumed the responsibility of overseeing the plantation and relied on slaves to carry out the hard labor. In urban areas of the North and South, women ran their husbands' businesses, including keeping financial records, ordering supplies, and overseeing sales.

Those on the southern homefront knew firsthand the hardships that accompanied war since most military engagements took place in the region. The Union's naval blockade in 1861 cut much of the South off from both essential supplies and luxury goods. Roaming bands of both Union and Confederate deserters stole crops and livestock while Union officials confiscated food to supply the army. White women of the elite and poorer classes responded to material deprivations by turning to the home to produce necessities such as cloth. Without the presence of men in their homes, women found themselves in the role of protector against soldiers seeking to rob homes of valuables, food, and other items.

The war exacted large economic and emotional costs for both northern and southern women who struggled to provide for their families. During the war, patriotism upheld the ideal of female sacrifice. Nevertheless, economic hardships and food shortages brought many women to view the war as a burden. Poor women in the urban South, suffering from starvation and malnourishment, informally organized demonstrations to demand food for their families. The Bread Riots that erupted in cities like Richmond, Virginia, and Mobile, Alabama became public symbols of their discontent with the war. In the North, women of the working class also protested against what they saw as unfair conscription laws. In the 1863 Draft Riots in New York City, women participated in a six-day protest against draft policies that allowed those with financial means to avoid military service.

SLAVE WOMEN

The war caused dramatic changes in the work and family life of slave women. Many female slaves spent the duration of the war separated from their husbands, whom the Confederate army impressed to use as laborers on military-related projects. Slave women's workload in the fields and in the home increased as they attempted to fill their husband's duties in their absence. Shortages on the homefront especially disrupted the lives of slave women. Slave owners reduced the provisions such as food, medicine, and clothing that they allotted to slaves. As a result, bondwomen struggled to combat hunger and disease in their families. Moreover, responsibility for household production fell mainly to female slaves who spent many hours spinning, weaving, and making soap in addition to their demanding farm work.

Female slaves took advantage of the chaotic nature of the southern homefront and challenged their owner's authority. Some used subtle forms of resistance by slowing their work pace, damaging tools, or refusing to perform certain tasks. The presence of Union troops in or near southern communities brought hope for many slave women who escaped bondage with their children. Once behind Union lines, however, they confronted arduous conditions. Disorganization plagued Union camps as officials scrambled to accommodate the growing population of slave contraband. Many soldiers grew resentful toward black women since their presence taxed vital resources such as food and medical supplies. Freed women, however, found ways to support themselves and their families by working as laundresses and agricultural laborers for the Union army.

From one viewpoint, the Civil War provided women, rich and poor, white and black, northern and southern, avenues into new economic, social, and political activities. While the material and human costs of war challenged women's abilities, they provided for and protected the home and family in the absence of their male counterparts. Moreover, the skills women gained in voluntary and paid work helped to push the doors of opportunity wider for the generation of women to follow. Nevertheless, the majority found the war a sorrowful and physically challenging experience. Whatever feelings they embraced, most hoped or prayed for a quick resolution.

BIBLIOGRAPHY

Attie, Jeanie. *Patriotic Toil: Northern Women and the American Civil War*. Ithaca, NY: Cornell University Press, 1998.

Clinton, Catherine. *Tara Revisited: Women, War, and the Plantation Legend*. New York: Abbeville Press, 1995.

Faust, Drew Gilpin. *Mothers of Invention: Women of the Slaveholding South in the American Civil War*. Chapel Hill: University of North Carolina Press, 1996.

Leonard, Elizabeth. *Yankee Women: Gender Battles in the Civil War*. New York: Norton, 1994.

Rable, George. *Civil Wars: Women and the Crisis of Southern Nationalism*. Urbana: University of Illinois Press, 1989.

Schwalm, Leslie. *A Hard Fight for We: Women's Transition from Slavery to Freedom in South Carolina*. Urbana: University of Illinois Press, 1997.

Victoria E. Ott

See also: Abolition; Anthony, Susan B.; Davis, Varina Howell; Lincoln, Mary Todd; Slavery; Stanton, Elizabeth Cady; Tubman, Harriet; United States Sanitary Commission.

GLOSSARY

Abolitionist: In the United States, anyone who campaigned against the continued practice of slavery during the eighteenth and nineteenth centuries.

Allies: The nations, including Great Britain, France, and the United States, among others, aligned against the Central Powers during World War I and against the Axis during World War II.

American Anti-Slavery Society: Abolitionist organization found in 1833 by William Lloyd Garrison and Arthur Tappan. Frederick Douglass was one of the group's most prominent members.

Americanization Movement: During the early part of the twentieth century, a social trend, partly driven by fear, towards pressuring recent immigrants to adopt American styles, values, and language.

(Anti)Rent War: An uprising in New York state in which disgruntled tenants resisted attempts by local sheriffs to evict them. Governor Silas Wright involved the state militia in 1845, and the violent phase of the anti-rent movement came to an end.

Antisuffragist: Anyone who opposed the right of women to vote.

Baltimore Riots: On April 19, 1861, a pitched battle between a mob of secessionists and a group of Union soldiers on its way through Baltimore. Four soldiers and twelve civilians were killed. Scores more were wounded. The encounter is often considered to be the first blood drawn in the American Civil War.

Barbary Coast: Common name for the waterfront area of San Francisco, California, in the years following the Gold Rush of 1849, when the area was famous for prostitution, gambling, crime, and a surfeit of notorious characters.

Barbary States: From the sixteenth to the nineteenth century, collective name of the North African countries of Morocco, Tunisia, Algeria, and Tripoli, and used especially to denote a time and an area in which ocean piracy was common.

Bedouin: A desert nomad, especially an Arab in the Middle East or North Africa.

Berber: Of or belonging to any of a number of Muslim North African tribes. Also, the language of those tribes.

Berlin airlift: In 1948 and 1949, the massive air transport into post-war Berlin of food, fuel, and other necessities by the Allies in response to a Soviet blockade of the divided city. By the end of the operation, more than two million tons of goods had been delivered.

Berlin blockade: In 1948, an attempt by the Soviet Union to force the United States and its allies out of Berlin by blocking access to their occupied territories. Following the success of the Berlin airlift, however, the Soviets were forced to abandon their plan and reopen the borders in May 1949.

Berlin Wall: Constructed in 1961 by the East German government, a wall to separate West Berlin from East Berlin. Among the most visible symbols of the Cold War, the Berlin Wall kept East Germans from crossing over into the west until November 1989 when a series of bureaucratic miscommunications led the government of East Germany to once again begin issuing visas. The wall was soon demolished.

Bey: In the Ottoman Empire, a denotation of rank or superior status. A provincial governor there.

Black Codes: Laws passed by former Confederate states to restrict the personal freedoms of recently freed slaves. Among their many notorious proscriptions were the segregation of places of public access and restrictions on the right to own property.

British Crown: The monarchy of Great Britain and the United Kingdom.

Bumppo, Natty: The hero of the so-called Leatherstocking Tales by James Fenimore Cooper (1789–1851), Bumppo was a tracker, a trapper, and an all-around outdoorsman. A voluntary outcast from his own society, Bumppo lived among Native Americans and was known by several nicknames, among them Hawkeye, Pathfinder, Leatherstocking, and Deerslayer.

Carte De Visite: Literally, a visiting card. One's photographic likeness, printed on a card for use as proof of identity.

Central Powers: During World War I, Germany and its military allies, including Bulgaria and the Ottoman Empire.

Civil Rights Movement: In the United States, the popular movement among African Americans and their supporters during the 1950s and 1960s to secure equal treatment under the law and to defeat segregation and other forms of institutionalized racism.

Committee On Public Information: Established in 1917 during World War I, the Committee spread propaganda to help increase support for the war in the United States.

Communism: A political ideology in which property and industry belong to the citizenry, rather than to individuals.

Constitution: Established in 1787 at the constitutional convention in Philadelphia, the foundational document of the United States. Originally consisting of a preamble and seven articles, the Constitution has been amended twenty-seven times.

Defense Plant Corporation: Organized in 1940, a government agency responsible for overseeing the production and finance of the facilities utilized by private defense contractors and manufacturers.

Department of the Treasury: Established in 1789, an arm of the federal executive branch charged with minting currency, advising the President on fiscal matters, and collecting taxes. The treasury department also administers the Secret Service.

Détente: A period or state of relaxed tensions between two military powers.

Dey: During the reign of the Ottoman Empire, the title given to the governor of Algiers.

Don't Ask, Don't Tell: Adopted in 1993 during the administration of President Bill Clinton, a policy on homosexuals in the United States military in which commanders agree to not attempt to learn a soldier's sexual orientation ("don't ask") as long as the soldier does not volunteer it ("don't tell").

Dred Scott Case: In 1857, a case before the United States Supreme Court. Dred Scott, a slave, argued that since he had lived for four years in a free territory that he should be declared free. The court disagreed, declaring that Scott was property and therefore could not seek status as a citizen of the United States.

E-mail: A method of communication whereby correspondence is instantaneously transmitted from one computer to another. Also, a communication sent or received by this method.

Euro-American: A citizen of the United States of European descent.

Federal: Denotes a system of government in which several regions or states agree to defer certain rights and responsibilities to a centralized authority.

First Lady: The wife of the president of the United States or of one of its state governors.

Founding Fathers: A collective name for the men who signed the Declaration of Independence and who helped to compose the Constitution of the United States.

Freedpeople: Slaves freed after or during the American Civil War.

G.I.: In military parlance, general issue, or that provided by the United States military to its soldiers. By extension, a soldier in that military.

Gorbachev, Mikhail: Soviet political leader (b. 1931), responsible for many pro-democratic reforms and the liberalization of Soviet society, Gorbachev was instrumental in improving relations with the United States and in helping to end the Cold War. Gorbachev resigned in 1991.

Gross National Product (GNP): The accumulated value of goods and services produced by the citizenry of a country within a year. Often used as an indicator of a country's economic health.

Gulf War: From January to February 1991, a military conflict between Iraq and a United States-led coalition of more than thirty countries. The war erupted after Iraq invaded Kuwait, its oil-rich neighbor, on 2 August 1990. Hostilities came to an end on 28 February with the rout of Iraqi forces during a short-lived ground war.

Habeas Corpus: A legal writ issued to order the physical production of a detained person as well as appropriate evidence of the necessity of continued detention. Literally, you should have the body.

House of Representatives: In the United States, the lower house of Congress.

Image-Maker: An individual or organization employed to help create a positive public image for another individual or organization, especially in politics and the entertainment industry.

Indian Wars: Collective term for a number of violent clashes between Native Americans and Europeans or people of European descent at various times during American history.

Internet: A global network connecting computers for the purpose of information exchange and communication through a variety of specialized servers, such as e-mail, bulletin boards, and the World Wide Web of on-line sites, magazines, newspapers, stores, and entertainment venues.

Jamestown colony: Founded in 1607, the first English settlement in North America. Jamestown was named for King James I.

Kansas–Nebraska Act: A law passed by Congress in 1854 that created the western territories of Kansas and Nebraska. In the end, the Act, which legalized slavery in the new territories in defiance of the Missouri Compromise, led to the rise of the Republican party.

Know-Nothings: During the 1850s, nickname for members of the American Party, nativists who opposed the holding of public office by immigrants and Roman Catholics. The name derived from the party's notorious secrecy and its unwillingness to answer questions about its activities.

Lame Duck: An elected official serving out his or her term after having been defeated or having decided not to seek another term. A figure of powerlessness.

Lend-Lease Act: Legislation passed in 1941 by the Congress, the Lend-Lease Act gave the president the discretion to sell, lease, or lend supplies and necessities during wartime to countries believed to be vital to the security of the United States.

Lopez de Santa Anna: General of the Armies of Mexico, politician, dictator, and twice President. Santa Anna (1794–1876) had a remarkable, often brutal, capricious, and mystifying career in his various roles. His most infamous military achievement was the capture of the Alamo and the slaughter of Texas revolutionaries in 1836. In and out of public favor his entire life, Santa Anna was twice exiled from Mexico, but at last allowed to return in 1874.

Lost Cause: During the American Civil War, another name for the cause of the Confederate states.

Manifest Destiny: A belief among many Americans of the nineteenth century, whereby the United States was thought to possess, by the grace of God, the right to expand to fill the whole of the North American continent.

Mexican War: From 1846 to 1848, military conflict between the United States and Mexico. Growing tensions between the two nations erupted into war with the United States' decision to annex Texas in December of 1845. In the negotiated peace, the United States won some two–fifths of Mexico's territory as well as $15 million in compensation.

Military-Industrial Complex: So called by President Dwight D. Eisenhower (1890–1969), a cautionary description of the relationship between the military and the industrial forces responsible for manufacturing military equipment. Eisenhower warned that such a collaboration might one day endanger the republic.

Militia: An army of civilians with military training who can be called upon to serve in time of war or national emergency.

Naiveté: A quality of excessive trustworthiness or belief in the fundamental goodness of human nature, often limiting the ability of one to experience evil.

National American Woman's Suffrage Association: Organization of suffragettes that in 1920 became the League of Women Voters.

National Security Council Paper 68 (NSC #68): Ordered by President Harry S. Truman (1884–1972), an examination and reassessment of both the relative strengths of the Soviet Union and of the United States' strategy in containing or stopping the spread of Communism. Considered a seminal Cold War document, NSC #68 led to a massive military buildup and to increased tensions between the two global superpowers.

National Women's Party: Organization of suffragettes founded in 1916.

Nativists: Members of the American Party, known for its anti-immigration, anti-Catholic positions, and its belief that only "native born" Americans had the right to hold public office.

Nemattanew: Powhatan warrior and mystic. His murder by the English in 1622 led the Powhatan chief Opechancanough to make war against the English colonies, killing more than three hundred of the colonists.

Newburgh Conspiracy: In 1783, a plot by members of the Continental Army of the United States, stationed in Newburgh, New York, to overthrow the Congress by coup. A speech given by George Washington was instrumental in convincing the officers to set aside their plans.

Neoconservative: A political ideology in the United States that embraced the conservative policies and ideas of the Republican party, favored an active and robust military, and believed in the spread of democracy through armed intervention in undemocratic societies.

Opechancanough: Native American chief, and brother to Powhatan, Opechancanough (c. 1545–1644) was responsible for the capture of the English Captain, John Smith, and, indirectly, for Captain Smith's introduction to Opechancanough's niece, Pocahontas.

Pasha: Title used in Turkey and various Middle Eastern countries during the reign of the Ottoman Empire to denote a high-ranking official.

Patriot Missiles: A guided surface-to-air missile designed primarily to shoot down incoming missiles before they reach their targets. First widely deployed during the Gulf War in 1991, the Patriot Missile system, though at first reported to be successful, in fact shot down none of its intended targets and may have been responsible for firing on friendly Coalition aircraft.

Patriots: Before and during the Revolutionary War, the colonists who supported independence from Great Britain. Generally, anyone who proudly defends the actions or culture of his or her own country.

Policymakers: Those responsible for creating or crafting public policy, as legislators, politicians, or other elected or appointed officials.

Postwar: The period following the end of a military conflict.

Progressives: From 1900 to 1920, a political and social movement inside the United States that called for, among other things, a graduated income tax, direct election of the United States Senate, and government action to break up industrial monopolies.

Radical Republicans: Members of the Republican party during and after the American Civil War who advocated harsh Reconstruction measures as a way of punishing the former Confederate states.

Reconstruction Acts: Passed on May 31, 1870, February 28, 1870, and April 20, 1871, laws designed to curb illegal activity, such as that perpetrated by the Ku Klux Klan, in parts of the South after the end of hostilities in the Civil War. Among other things, the Reconstruction Acts levied harsh penalties against anyone who attempted to prevent recently freed slaves from voting.

Redcoats: Informal or derisive name given to British soldiers, especially those in the colonies before and during the American Revolutionary War.

Red Scare: Following the end of World War I and brought about largely by the onset of the Russian Revolution, a period of general suspicion and paranoia regarding the political beliefs of recent immigrants, a few hundred who were arrested and deported. A second scare occurred in the late 1940s as Americans began to fear that communists had infiltrated the highest levels of government and the entertainment industry.

Revolutionary War: From 1775 to 1781, the war of American independence, fought between the colonies in the New World and the forces of the British Crown.

SCUD Missiles: Short-range ballistic missiles used by the Iraqi military, especially during the Gulf War of 1991.

Senate: In the United States, the highest house of Congress.

Slaughterhouse Cases: A number of cases heard by the United States Supreme Court in 1873 involving the legality of a twenty-five year monopoly granted by the Louisiana state legislature to a single slaughterhouse operator in New Orleans for the purpose of protecting the public health. The court ruled that the state had not violated the 14th amendment, as had been charged.

Slave-Power Conspiracy: Before the American Civil War, a belief among many northerners, to some degree perpetuated by the Republican Party and abolitionist groups, that the South planned to marginalize the North by extending slavery into the western territories and Central America.

Spanish American War: In 1898, a military conflict between the United States and Spain on behalf of Cuba. Its victory increased the standing of the United States as a legitimate world power.

Sunset Laws: Laws designed with a specific date of termination.

Supreme Court: The highest federal court in the United States, composed of a chief justice and eight associate judges. The Supreme Court was established by Article 3 of the United States Constitution. Its justices are appointed by the President and serve for life.

Texas Revolution: Beginning in 1835, Texas' war of independence from Mexico. The conflict involved the famous battle at the Alamo and ended in 1836 when Samuel Houston defeated Santa Anna and forced him to recognize the independence of Texas.

Three-Fifths Compromise: An agreement reached during the Constitutional Convention of 1787. As proposed by James Madison, the Three-Fifths Compromise sought to solve the divisive issue of how to count the slaves for the purpose of establishing representation in the new Congress. Madison's compromise was that each slave would be counted as three-fifths of a free white. The 14th Amendment to the United States Constitution later repealed the Compromise.

Unionist: One who supported the Northern or Union cause during the Civil War.

Vietcong: Any supporter or member of the Communist supported armed forces of the so-called National Liberation Front, which fought to reunite South Vietnam with North Vietnam during the Vietnam War (1954–1976).

Whig Party: Political party founded in the 1830s to oppose the Democrats. Notable Whigs include Daniel Webster (1782–1852) and William Henry Harrison (1773–1841).

Women's Rights Movement: The populist activity that aimed to secure social, economic, and political equality for women.

Zacatecas: A state in north central Mexico. Also, the capital of that state.

PRIMARY SOURCE DOCUMENTS

ACTS OF CONGRESS

Congressional Act Appointing Commissioner of Indian Affairs (1832)

Commentary

By the 1820s, with the push to eliminate independent Indian tribes east of the Mississippi River, the foundations were being laid for U.S. Indian policy through the century and beyond. One of the major developments in this policy came about in a little noticed action by Secretary of War John C. Calhoun (1782–1850). Without obtaining authorization from Congress, in 1824 he established an Office of Indian Affairs. In practice, the War Department already had been handling most dealings with the Indian tribes. The army, after all, was the one branch of the government most likely to be in direct contact with them.

For eight years Congress took no action; but in 1832, when it appointed a Commissioner of Indian Affairs, it left the office within the War Department. This meant that U.S. Indian policy would henceforth speak with one voice. Beyond that, formalizing the office sent the message, whether intentionally or not, that Congress wanted dealings with the Indians to be conducted under the auspices of the department set up to deal with the nation's enemies. Although in 1849 the Bureau of Indian Affairs was moved to the Department of the Interior, the policy direction was already established.

Be it enacted by the Senate and House of Representatives of the United States of America, in Congress assembled, That the President shall appoint, by and with the advice and consent of the Senate, a commissioner of Indian affairs, who shall, under the direction of the Secretary of War, and agreeably to such regulations as the President may, from time to time, prescribe, have the direction and management of all Indian affairs, and of all matters arising out of Indian relations, and shall receive a salary of three thousand dollars per annum.

Sec. 2. And be it further enacted, That the Secretary of War shall arrange or appoint to the said office the number of clerks necessary therefor, so as not to increase the number now employed; and such sum as is necessary to pay the salary of said commissioner for the year one thousand eight hundred and thirty-two, shall be, and the same hereby is, appropriated out of any money in the treasury.

Sec. 3. And be it further enacted, That all accounts and vouchers for claims and disbursements connected with Indian affairs, shall be transmitted to the said commissioner for administrative examination, and by him passed to the proper accounting officer of the Treasury Department for settlement; and all letters and packages to and from the said commissioner, touching the business of his office, shall be free of postage.

Sec. 4. And be it further enacted, That no ardent spirits shall be hereafter introduced, under any pretence, into the Indian country.

Sec. 5. And be it further enacted, That the Secretary of War shall, under the direction of the President, cause to be discontinued the services of such agents, sub-agents, interpreters, and mechanics, as may, from time to time, become unnecessary, in consequence of the emigration of the Indians, or other causes.

Homestead Act (1862)

Commentary

The idea that the government should provide land titles directly to Western settlers dated to the early 1850s. Before that time, settlers often negotiated at a disadvantage with wealthy speculators who held title to their homesteads. In 1851, the state of Illinois and the federal government pioneered a new arrangement: the national authorities transferred thousands of acres of federal lands to the state government; in return, the state agreed to build a railroad through the grant areas, promote settlement along the line, and eventually transfer land titles directly to the emigrants as they established homesteads.

The Illinois land grant was a huge success and inspired enthusiasts of westward expansion to consider conferring federal land directly on the settlers themselves. Passage of the Kansas-Nebraska Act in 1854 with its doctrine of "popular sovereignty" gave a new incentive to Northern advocates of such a homestead law, for they saw it as a way to speed the flow of free-state emigrants to the West in order to defeat proslavery forces in territorial elections. By the 1860 presidential campaign, creation of an effective Homestead Act had become an integral part of the Republican party's program to confine slavery to the states where it already existed. Abraham Lincoln (1809–1865) and the Republicans won the election, but soon after their victory, the nation was plunged into Civil War and diverted attention from the territories. Even so, they did not forget their pledge. In May 1862, Republican leaders in Congress summoned support to pass the Homestead Act.

The law changed federal policy in two important ways. First, it curbed the activities of land speculators by limiting the acreage which an individual citizen could purchase. Second, it permitted settlers to gain title to their homesteads directly from the government for a token fee. However, the act did not apply to those who had "borne arms against the Government" or "given aid and comfort to its enemies"; in other words, slaveholding citizens of the rebellious Confederacy were forever denied the opportunity claim Western land under the terms of the law. By subsidizing Northern settlers with grants of essentially free land and barring Confederate citizens and sympathizers from benefitting by its generous terms, the Homestead Act helped accelerate the flow of free-state citizens into the West and doomed the Southern dream of an empire for slavery in the American plains.

Be it enacted by the Senate and House of Representatives of the United States of America in Congress assembled, That any person who is the head of a family, or who has arrived at the age of twenty-one years, and is a citizen of the United States, or who shall have filed his declaration of intention to become such, as required by the naturalization laws of the United States, and who has never borne arms against the United States Government or given aid and comfort to its enemies, shall, from and after the first January, eighteen hundred and sixty-three, be entitled to enter one quarter section or a less quantity of unappropriated public lands, upon which said person may have filed a preemption claim, or which may, at the time the application is made, be subject to preemption at one dollar and twenty-five cents, or less, per acre; or eighty acres or less of such unappropriated lands, at two dollars and fifty cents per acre, to be located in a body, in conformity to the legal subdivisions of the public lands, and after the same shall have been surveyed: Provided, That any person owning and residing on land may, under the provisions of this act, enter other land lying contiguous to his or her said land, which shall not, with the land so already owned and occupied, exceed in the aggregate one hundred and sixty acres.

Sec. 2. And be it further enacted, That the person applying for the benefit of this act shall, upon application to the register of the land office in which he or she is about to make such entry, make affidavit before the said register or receiver that he or she is the head of a family, or is twenty-one years or more of age, or shall have performed service in the army or navy of the United States, and that he has never borne arms against the Government of the United States or given aid and comfort to its enemies, and that such application is made for his or her exclusive use and benefit, and that said entry is made for the purpose of actual settlement and cultivation, and not either directly or indirectly for the use or benefit of any other person or persons whomsoever; and upon filing the said affidavit with the register or receiver, and on payment of ten dollars, he or she shall thereupon be permitted to enter the quantity of land specified: Provided, however, That no certificate shall be given or patent issued therefor until the expiration of five years from the date of such entry; and if, at the expiration of such time, or at any time within two years thereafter, the person making such entry; or, if he be dead, his widow; or in case of her death, his heirs or devisee; or in case of a widow making such entry, her heirs or devisee; in case of her death; shall prove by two credible witnesses that he, she, or they have resided upon or cultivated the same for the term of five years immediately succeeding, the time of filing the affidavit aforesaid, and shall make affidavit that no part of said land has been alienated, and that he has borne true allegiance to the Government of the United States; then, in such case, he, she, or they, if at that time a citizen of the United States, shall be entitled to a patent, as in other cases provided for by law: And provided, further, That in case of the death of both father and mother, leaving an infant child, or children, under twenty-one years of age, the right and fee shall enure to the benefit of said infant child or children; and the executor, administrator, or guardian may, at any time within two years after the death of the surviving parent, and in accordance with the laws of the State in which such children for the time being have their domicil, sell said land for the benefit of said infants, but for no other purpose; and the purchaser shall acquire the absolute title by the purchase, and be entitled to a patent from the United States, on payment of the office fees and sum of money herein specified.

Sec. 3. And be it further enacted, That the register of the land office shall note all such applications on the tract books and plats of his office, and keep a register of all such entries, and make return thereof to the General Land Office, together with the proof upon which they have been founded.

Sec. 4. And be it further enacted, That no lands acquired under the provisions of this act shall in any event become liable to the satisfaction of any debt or debts contracted prior to the issuing of the patent therefor.

Sec. 5. And be it further enacted, That if, at any time after the filing of the affidavit, as required in the second section of this act, and before the expiration of the five years aforesaid, it shall be proven, after due notice to the settler, to the satisfaction of the register of the land office, that the person having filed such affidavit shall have actually changed his or her residence, or abandoned the said land for more than six months at any time, then and in that event the land so entered shall revert to the government.

Sec. 6. And be it further enacted, That no individual shall be permitted to acquire title to more than one quarter section under the provisions of this act; and that the Commissioner of the General Land Office is hereby required to prepare and issue such rules and regulations, consistent with this act, as shall be necessary and proper to carry its provisions into effect; and that the registers and receivers of the several land offices shall be entitled to receive the same compensation for any lands entered under the provisions of this act that they are now entitled to receive when the same quantity of land is entered with money, one half to be paid by the person making the application at the time of so doing, and the other half on the issue of the certificate by the person to whom it may be issued; but this shall not be construed to enlarge the maximum of compensation now prescribed by law for any register or receiver: Provided, That nothing

contained in this act shall be so construed as to impair or interfere in any manner whatever with existing pre-emption rights: And provided, further, That all persons who may have filed their applications for a preemption right prior to the passage of this act, shall be entitled to all privileges of this act: Provided, further, That no person who has served, or may hereafter serve, for a period of not less than fourteen days in the army or navy of the United States, either regular or volunteer, under the laws thereof, during the existence of an actual war, domestic or foreign, shall be deprived of the benefits of this act on account of not having attained the age of twenty-one years.

Sec. 7. And be it further enacted, That the fifth section of the act entitled "An act in addition to an act more effectually to provide for the punishment of certain crimes against the United States, and for other purposes," approved the third of March, in the year eighteen hundred and fifty-seven, shall extend to all oaths, affirmations, and affidavits, required or authorized by this act.

Sec. 8. And be it further enacted, That nothing in this act shall be so construed as to prevent any person who has availed him or herself of the benefits of the first section of this act, from paying the minimum price, or the price to which the same may have graduated, for the quantity of land so entered at any time before the expiration of the five years, and obtaining a patent therefor from the government, as in other cases provided by law, on making proof of settlement and cultivation as provided by existing laws granting preemption rights.

Approved, May 20, 1862.

Thirteenth Amendment (1865)

Commentary

The Thirteenth Amendment was one of the three amendments passed in the wake of the Civil War (1861–1865) to end slavery and, it was hoped, its effects. Passed by the Senate in 1864, as the war was drawing to an end, the amendment was blocked in the House of Representatives. In 1865, however, it managed to secure enough votes to win passage in both houses of Congress. The states ratified it the same year.

Section 1 of the amendment prohibits slavery or "involuntary servitude" anywhere in the United States. The meaning of the section is mostly unambiguous: it ended the system of enslaving African Americans, especially in the South, that had been among the principal causes of the war. By also prohibiting involuntary servitude, it has been suggested, Congress sought to give itself authority for determining the nature of freedom, and what constitutes slavery beyond the most obvious forms of it.

Section 2 was almost as far-reaching as Section 1, for it says that "Congress shall have power to enforce this article by appropriate legislation." This was the first time that an amendment had specifically given the federal government authority to act against the power of the states to promote some higher good in the national interest.

For many years after it was passed, the Thirteenth Amendment was rarely cited in Supreme Court decisions. In 1883, in *United States v. Harris*, the Court ruled that it did not apply to cases of personal racial discrimination, and because the Fourteenth Amendment has since been used to argue many such cases, the Thirteenth Amendment lay more or less dormant. It had ended slavery, and that was that.

However, in 1986 the amendment reemerged in *Jones v. Alfred H. Mayer Co.*, in which the Court used it to declare unconstitutional a case of private racial discrimination in a property matter. The plaintiff, Jones, said the defendants had refused to sell him a home because he was black. In basing his case on the Thirteenth Amendment, instead of the Fourteenth, Jones and his attorneys opened up a new avenue for combating racial discrimination under the Constitution.

Section 1. Neither slavery nor involuntary servitude, except as a punishment for crime whereof the party shall have been duly convicted, shall exist within the United States, or any place subject to their jurisdiction.

Section 2. Congress shall have power to enforce this article by appropriate legislation.

Civil Rights Bill Veto (1866)

Commentary

In 1866 President Andrew Johnson (1808–1875) vetoed a civil rights bill that sought to define national citizenship, a move that would resolve a persistently ambiguous legal principle in American politics. The bill eliminated racial distinctions on citizenship confirmed by the Dred Scott decision of 1857 and established nativity (birth within the territory of the United States) as the main criteria for citizenship. Although it stopped short of giving freedmen the right to vote, it gave them the tools to make contracts and to protect themselves from extreme economic exploitation.

Johnson's veto message struck chords that were themes throughout his unsuccessful presidency. He objected to deciding such fundamental questions with inadequate input from the Southern states. He also questioned what he considered an unwarranted elevation of African-Americans from their position as defined by the Dred Scott case. To dramatize his concerns, he raised the perennial issue for opponents of racial equality—the threat of racial intermarriage—and hinted that the extension of citizenship to blacks somehow worked to the disadvantage of whites. Finally, he expressed concerns about the "centralization and concentration" of powers of the federal government. By eliminating the possibility of a middle course of compromise, Johnson gambled and lost. The Republicans' success in enacting the Civil Rights Act over his veto gave them the confidence to proceed on their own plans, without any further cooperation from the president.

By the first section of the bill all persons born in the United States and not subject to any foreign power, excluding Indians not taxed, are declared to be citizens of the United States. This provision comprehends the Chinese of the Pacific States, Indians subject to taxation, the people called gypsies, as well as the entire race designated as blacks. . . . Every individual of these races born in the United States is by the bill made a citizen. . . .

The grave question presents itself whether, when eleven of the thirty-six States are unrepresented in Congress at the present time, it is sound policy to make our entire colored population and all other excepted classes citizens of the United States. Four millions of them have just emerged from slavery into freedom. Can it be reasonably supposed that they possess the requisite qualifications to entitle them to all the privileges and immunities of citizens of the United States? Have the people of the several States expressed such a conviction? . . . The policy of the Government from its origin to the present time seems to have been that persons who are strangers to and unfamiliar with our institutions and our laws should pass through a certain probation, at the end of which, before attaining the coveted prize, they must give evidence of their fitness to receive and to exercise the rights of citizens as contemplated by the Constitution of the United States. The bill in effect proposes a discrimination against large numbers of intelligent, worthy, and patriotic foreigners, and in favor of the negro. . . .

A perfect equality of the white and colored races is attempted to be fixed by Federal law in every State of the Union over the vast field of State jurisdiction covered by these enumerated rights. In no one of these can any State ever exercise any power of discrimination between the different races. In the exercise of State policy over matters exclusively affecting the people of each State it has frequently been thought expedient to discriminate between the two races. By the statutes of some of the States, Northern as well as Southern, it is enacted, for instance, that no white person shall intermarry with a negro or mulatto. . . .

I do not say that this bill repeals State laws on the subject of marriage between the two races. . . . I cite this discrimination, however, as an instance of the State policy as to discrimination, and to inquire whether if Congress can abrogate all State laws of discrimination between the two races in the matter of real estate, of suits, and of contracts generally Congress may not also repeal the State laws as to the contract of marriage between the two races. Hitherto every subject embraced in the enumeration of rights contained in this bill has been considered as exclusively belonging to the States. They all relate to the internal police and economy of the respective States. They are matters which in each State concern the domestic condition of its people, varying in each according to its own peculiar circumstances and the safety and well-being of its own citizens. . . .

If, in any State which denies to a colored person any one of all those rights, that person should commit a crime against the laws of a State—murder, arson, rape, or any other crime—all protection and punishment through the courts of the State are taken away, and he can only be tried and punished in the Federal courts. . . . So that over this vast domain of criminal jurisprudence provided by each State for the protection of its own citizens and for the punishment of all persons who violate its criminal laws, Federal law, whenever it can be made to apply, displaces State law. . . . This section of the bill undoubtedly comprehends cases and authorizes the exercise of powers that are not, by the Constitution, within the jurisdiction of the courts of the United States. . . .

I do not propose to consider the policy of this bill. To me the details of the bill seem fraught with evil. The white race and the black race of the South have hitherto lived together under the relation of master and slave—capital owning labor. Now, suddenly, that relation is changed, and as to ownership capital and labor are divorced. They stand now each master of itself. In this new relation, one being necessary to the other, there will be a new adjustment, which both are deeply interested in making harmonious. . . .

This bill frustrates this adjustment. It intervenes between capital and labor and attempts to settle questions of political economy through the agency of numerous officials whose interest it will be to foment discord between the two races, for as the breach widens their employment will continue, and when it is closed their occupation will terminate.

In all our history, in all our experience as a people living under Federal and State law, no such system as that contemplated by the details of this bill has ever before been proposed or adopted. They establish for the security of the colored race safeguards which go infinitely beyond any that the General Government has ever provided for the white race. In fact, the distinction of race and color is by the bill made to operate in favor of the colored and against the white race. They interfere with the municipal legislation of the States, with the relations existing exclusively between a State and its citizens, or between inhabitants of the same State—an absorption and assumption of power by the General Government which, if acquiesced in, must sap and destroy our federative system of limited powers and break down the barriers which preserve the rights of the States. It is another step, or rather stride, toward centralization and the concentration of all legislative powers in the National Government. The tendency of the bill must be to resuscitate the spirit of rebellion and to arrest the progress of those influences which are more closely drawing around the States the bonds of union and peace.

Fourteenth Amendment (1868)

Commentary

The Fourteenth Amendment, proposed by Congress in 1866 and ratified by the states in 1868, was a reaction against efforts by the southern states to impose restrictions on the civil liberties of freed blacks in the aftermath of the Civil War (1861–1865). The Thirteenth Amendment had ended slavery, but in many places across the South there had been little change in the status of African Americans. In fact, a range of Black Codes had been put in place to restrict many of their civil rights—their right to vote, to own property, to testify in court, travel, speak, make contracts, and more.

Besides denying blacks their civil rights, such laws posed a political risk to Republicans in the North. Article I, Section 2, of the Constitution had counted slaves as three-fifths of a free person for purposes of representation in Congress. Suddenly, the full population of the South counted, so the number of southern congressmen was going to increase. But if blacks could not vote in the South, then whites would elect Democrats, who would outnumber the northern Republicans in Congress. For this reason as well as genuine distaste for what was happening (and, not incidentally, a desire to punish the southern former slaveowners), Congress passed the Fourteenth Amendment.

The amendment has five sections. Section 1 defines, for the first time, national citizenship: "All persons born or naturalized in the United States . . . are citizens of the United States and of the State wherein they reside." It also prohibits the states from making laws that deny U.S. citizens their lawful "privileges or immunities," deny them the "equal protection of the laws," or deprive them of "life, liberty, or property, without due process of law."

Sections 2 prescribes a punishment for states that in any way limit the right to vote of "male inhabitants . . . twenty-one years of age." Any such states would have their representation in Congress reduced.

Sections 3 and 4 deal with the status and effects of former rebels. By the terms of the amendment, no former officer of the Confederacy would be entitled to serve in the U.S. government unless Congress decides otherwise by a two-thirds vote. Nor, the amendment says, would the United States assume the public debt of the former Confederacy.

Section 5 gives Congress power to enforce the amendment by "appropriate legislation."

The amendment, and particularly the first section, had far-reaching implications for the future of constitutional interpretations. Never before had the Constitution been thrust so directly into the affairs of the states. Never before had a concept of national citizenship been expressed in the Constitution.

At first, however, the Supreme Court saw things differently. When the Court was first called upon to interpret the Fourteenth Amendment in 1873, in the *Slaughter-House Cases,* the issue in question had nothing to do with African Americans or former slaves. Instead, a group of butchers in New Orleans, Louisiana, claimed they had been unjustly deprived of their property by a law creating a monopoly in the butcher business in that city. The Court ruled against the butchers, stating that the amendment had never been intended to apply to any such situation. By a number of other decisions, notably *Bradwell v. Illinois* (1873), *Minor v. Happersett* (1875), the *Civil Rights Cases* (1883), and *Plessy v. Ferguson* (1896), the Court continued to interpret the Fourteenth Amendment narrowly, saying either that it did not apply to nonracial cases or that it did not apply to individuals but only to states. In the last of those,

Plessy, the Court even upheld a state law mandating segregation on railway cars, saying that such a law did not violate the Fourteenth Amendment's "equal-protection clause."

Gradually, however, the Court began interpreting the Fourteenth Amendment differently, so that today it is one of the cornerstones—with the Bill of Rights—guaranteeing Americans' civil liberties. In *Gitlow v. New York* (1925), the Court stated that the Fourteenth Amendment's equal protection clause prevented states from denying citizens their First Amendment freedom of speech. One by one, and at an accelerating pace, the Court applied other aspects of the Bill of Rights to the states by citing the federal government's authority to act under the Fourteenth Amendment.

Many of the major cases of the 20th century have involved "incorporating" the protections of the Constitution (and particularly the Bill of Rights) into the Fourteenth Amendment. These include *Shelley v. Kraemer* (1948), which outlawed restrictive housing covenants; *Brown v. Board of Education of Topeka, Kansas* (1954), which overturned *Plessy v. Ferguson;* and *Roe v. Wade* (1973), which made abortion legal in all the states.

Section 1. All persons born or naturalized in the United States and subject to the jurisdiction thereof, are citizens of the United States and of the State wherein they reside. No State shall make or enforce any law which shall abridge the privileges or immunities of citizens of the United States; nor shall any State deprive any person of life, liberty, or property, without due process of law; nor deny to any person within its jurisdiction the equal protection of the laws.

Section 2. Representatives shall be apportioned among the several States according to their respective numbers, counting the whole number of persons in each State, excluding Indians not taxed. But when the right to vote at any election for the choice of electors for President and Vice President of the United States, Representatives in Congress, the Executive and Judicial officers of a State, or the members of the Legislature thereof, is denied to any of the male inhabitants of such State, being twenty-one years of age, and citizens of the United States, or in any way abridged, except for participation in rebellion, or other crime, the basis of representation therein shall be reduced in the proportion which the number of such male citizens shall bear to the whole number of male citizens twenty-one years of age in such State.

Section 3. No person shall be a Senator or Representative in Congress, or elector of President and Vice President, or hold any office, civil or military, under the United States, or under any State, who, having previously taken an oath, as a member of Congress, or as an officer of the United States, or as a member of any State legislature, or as an executive or judicial officer of any State, to support the Constitution of the United States, shall have engaged in insurrection or rebellion against the same, or given aid or comfort to the enemies thereof. But Congress may by a vote of two-thirds of each House, remove such disability.

Section 4. The validity of the public debt of the United States, authorized by law, including debts incurred for payment of pensions and bounties for services in suppressing insurrection or rebellion, shall not be questioned. But neither the United States nor any State shall assume or pay any debt or obligation incurred in aid of insurrection or rebellion against the United States, or any claim for the loss or emancipation of any slave; but all such debts, obligations and claims shall be held illegal and void.

Section 5. The Congress shall have power to enforce, by appropriate legislation, the provisions of this article.

Fifteenth Amendment (1870)

Commentary

The Fifteenth Amendment was meant to guarantee the vote to African-American men, many of whom had been denied it despite the Thirteenth and Fourteenth Amendments. The later amendment, ratified in 1870, states that the right of citizens to vote could not be denied "on account of race, color, or previous condition of servitude"—including former slave status.

This was by no means an uncontroversial amendment, even in the North, where property qualifications for voters had been continued for blacks even as they had been gradually eliminated for whites over the first half of the 19th century. The immediate motivation for the amendment was that in the election of 1868, the Republican candidate, Ulysses S. Grant (1822–1885), won only about 52 percent of the vote. In fact, his margin of victory in the popular vote was decided by support from southern black voters. To ensure that those votes would not be denied to future Republican candidates, the Republican-controlled Congress proposed the Fifteenth Amendment. (The Republican party was very popular with former slaves; it was the party of Abraham Lincoln, 1809–1865, remembered as the Great Emancipator.)

The effect of the Fifteenth Amendment, however, was something less than its supporters had counted on. In a number of cases, the Supreme Court interpreted it narrowly, saying, for example, that it did not apply to poll taxes and literacy tests that were designed to keep blacks from voting. Later, when the Court became more interested in promoting civil rights, it turned to the Fourteenth Amendment with much more frequency than it did the Fifteenth.

However, almost a century after the amendment was ratified, Congress passed the Voting Rights Act of 1965 on authority granted in the Fifteenth Amendment. This legislation dramatically extended the federal authority to protect voting rights of minorities, and thus achieved the effect intended by the Fifteenth Amendment.

Section 1. The right of citizens of the United States to vote shall not be denied or abridged by the United States or by any State on account of race, color, or previous condition of servitude.

Section 2. The Congress shall have power to enforce this article by appropriate legislation.

Ku Klux Klan Act (1871)

Commentary

Despite their large majorities, Republican governments held power precariously during the early years of Southern Reconstruction. Factionalism within the party, movements to restore the voting power of former Confederates, and, most ominously, the widespread use of political violence by such groups as the Ku Klux Klan all jeopardized the stability of these biracial governments.

President Ulysses S. Grant (1822–1885) tolerated Conservative victories when a clear majority of legal voters favored the party of white supremacy. He made a strong commitment, however, to eliminating the open and organized violence that became common in the South between 1868 and 1871. The Ku Klux Klan—a vigilante group that turned to political violence after the introduction of Radical Reconstruction—typified white terrorism of the period. Claiming to represent the ghosts of dead Confederate soldiers, its members donned white robes and masks and directed their violence primarily at black voters and politicians. After barely two years of Reconstruction the Klan's effectiveness threatened to return white Southern Conservatives to power even in areas where there was a clear Republican majority.

Grant successfully lobbied Congress for a means of using federal force to combat the Klan's violent intimidation of voters. The resulting act sought to assure the provisions of the Fourteenth and Fifteenth Amendments, which guaranteed the "equal protection of the laws" and the right to vote. Under direction of U.S. Attorney General Amos Akerman, a white Republican from Alabama, the newly created Department of Justice prosecuted Klan members in several Southern states and even declared martial law in a Klan stronghold South Carolina. By 1872, the Grant administration had won its war on the Klan, which disappeared until its reappearance in the 20th century.

Republicans had difficulty continuing their program of swift, successful responses to white political violence. In 1873, the Supreme Court ruled that the federal enforcement powers extended only to violations by the states, not the misdeeds of individuals. The Court agreed with Conservatives that the punishment of individual criminals, even those who violated another's federal civil rights, should be punished by the state judicial systems. This ruling discouraged further national action to reduce white vigilantism and, as Northern opinion grew impatient with Southern issues, whites again turned to violent means in battling the fragile Reconstruction governments.

Be it enacted . . .

Sec. 2. That if two or more persons within any State or Territory of the United States . . . shall conspire together, or go in disguise upon the public highway or upon the premises of another for the purpose, either directly or indirectly, of depriving any person or any class of persons of the equal protection of the laws, or of equal privileges or immunities under the laws, or for the purpose of preventing or hindering the constituted authorities of any State from giving or securing to all persons within such State the equal protection of the laws, . . . or by force, intimidation, or threat to prevent any citizen of the United States lawfully entitled to vote from giving his support or advocacy in a lawful manner towards or in favor of the election of any lawfully qualified person as an elector of President or Vice-President of the United States, or as a member of the Congress of the United States, or to injure any such citizen in his person or property on account of such support or advocacy, each and every person so offending shall be deemed guilty of a high crime, and, upon conviction thereof in any district or supreme court of any Territory of the United States having jurisdiction of similar offenses shall be punished by a fine not less than five hundred nor more than five thousand dollars, or by imprisonment, with or without hard labor, as the court may determine, for a period of not less than six months nor more than six years, as the court may determine, or by both such fine and imprisonment as the court may determine. . . .

Sec. 3. That in all cases where insurrection, domestic violence, unlawful combinations, or conspiracies in any State shall so obstruct or hinder the execution of the laws thereof, and of the United States, as to deprive any portion or class of the people of such State of any of the rights, privileges, or immunities, or protection, named in the Constitution and secured by this act, and the constituted authorities of such State shall either be unable to protect, or shall from any cause fail in or refuse protection of the people in such rights, such facts will be deemed a denial by such State of the equal protection of the laws to which they are entitled under the Constitution of the United States; and in all such cases, . . . it shall be lawful for the President, and it shall be his duty to take such measures, by the employment of the militia or the land and naval forces of the United States, or of either, or by other means, as he may deem necessary for the suppression of such insurrection, domestic violence, or combinations. . . .

Sec. 4. That whenever in any State or part of a State the unlawful combinations named in the preceding section of this act shall be organized and armed, and so numerous and powerful as to be able, by violence, to either overthrow or set at defiance the constituted authorities of such State, and of the United States within such State, or when the constituted authorities are in complicity with, or shall connive at the unlawful purposes of, such powerful and armed combinations . . . it shall be lawful for the President of the United States, when in his judgment the public safety shall require it, to suspend the privileges of the writ of habeas corpus, to the end that such rebellion may be overthrown: Provided, . . . That the President shall first have made proclamation, as now provided by law, commanding such insurgents to disperse: And Provided also, That the provisions of this section shall not be in force after the end of the next regular session of Congress.

FIRST PERSON NARRATIVES

Excerpt from A Journey of Travels into the Arkansas Territory (1819)

Commentary

Thomas Nuttall (1786–1859), author of *A Journey of Travels Into the Arkansas Territory*, emigrated from England to Philadelphia in 1808. He took up the study of plants and went on to become one of America's foremost botanists; he also was a respected ornithologist and an early expert on paleontology. Between 1809 and 1835, he went on three major expeditions to pursue his scientific interests. On the second (1818–1820), his route took him down the Ohio and Mississippi rivers to the Arkansas River, and then up the Arkansas into Colorado. The Arkansas River region was relatively unknown at that time and much of this journal describes this particular trip. Most of his observations pertain to the region's plant and animal life, geology, and geography. In this selection, Nuttall is in the present-day state of Arkansas.

CHAPTER VIII.

Pass several inconsiderable rivulets, and obtain sight of the Tomahawk mountain and the Gascon hills—Mulberry creek—that of Vache Grasse.—Lee's creek—prairies—Sugarloaf mountain.—Arrive at the garrison of Belle Point—a change in the vegetation—The Maclura or Bow-wood—The garrison—Cedar prairie—Rare plants.

20th.] This morning I left Mr. Webber's, in a perogue with two French boatmen, in order to proceed to the garrison, about 120 miles distant by water. We proceeded nearly to Charbonniere creek, 24 miles from the place of departure. Ten miles from Webber's we passed the outlet of Piney creek, so called from the pine-hills by which it is bordered. Eight miles further we came to Rocky creek, opposite to the outlet of which, a ledge of rocks nearly traverses the Arkansa, and presents a considerable obstruction in the navigation at a low stage of water. The current even at this time broke with a considerable noise.

21st.] About six miles above Rocky creek we passed the Charbonniere, so called from the occurrence of coal in its vicinity; we also observed the outlet of Spadrie creek, on the borders of which there are considerable tracts of fertile land, well supplied with springs, and occupied by the Cherokees. The rocks which occasionally border the river, of very inconsiderable elevation, are composed of slaty sandstone, dipping about 25 degrees, sometimes towards the north-west, and at others to the south-east, or in opposite directions, and also exhibiting indications of coal. The Charbonniere rock, in particular, about 50 feet high, presents beds of a slaty sandstone, with a dip of

scarcely 20 degrees, and inclined in opposite directions so as to form a basin, in which there are indications of coal. A lofty blue ridge appears to the south, called by the French hunters the Cassetete or Tomahawk mountain, and about eight miles from hence enters the creek of the same name, beyond which we proceeded eight miles of a 12 mile bend, making a journey of about 28 miles in the course of the day, and encamped in view of another lofty ridge of mountains. We saw, as we proceeded, no less than 13 deer and a bear.

22d.] Four miles from Allmand creek the Cassetete mountain appears very distinct, and somewhat resembles the Magazine; being a long ridge abrupt at either end. Another range also was visible at a considerable distance, called the Gascon hills. We were detained awhile by a thunder-storm, but proceeded, notwithstanding, about 30 miles, and encamped on an island just below the outlet of Mulberry creek, on the banks of which, before the arrival of the Cherokees, there was a considerable settlement on a body of excellent land. It now constitutes the Cherokee line of demarkation, and they made free to occupy the deserted cabins and improvements of the whites without any compensation received either from them or the government. The bend, which we continued this morning, of 12 miles extent, is surrounded on the right hand side with an amphitheatre of lofty cliffs, 3 to 400 feet high, having a highly romantic and picturesque appearance. Nearly continuing to Mulberry creek, a fine stretch of about eight miles opens to view, affording an ample prospect of the river; its rich alluvions were now clothed in youthful verdure, and backed in the distance by bluish and empurpled hills. The beauty of the scenery was also enlivened by the melody of innumerable birds, and the gentle humming of the wild bees, feeding on the early blooming willows, which in the same manner line the picturesque banks of the Ohio. The Arkansa, in its general appearance throughout this day's voyage, bears, indeed, a considerable resemblance to that river. It is equally, diversified with islands, and obstructed in its course by gravelly rapids; two of them which we passed today, could not have a collective fall of less than 10 or 12 feet each.

The sandstone beds still present very little dip, and by contrary inclinations produce the appearance of basins or circumscribed vallies.

23d.] Two miles above Mulberry creek we passed two islands nearly opposite to each other, and a settlement of three or four families situated along the left bank of the river, on a handsome rising ground, flanked by a continued ridge of low hills. The dawn of morning was again ushered in by the songs of thousands of birds, re-echoing through the woods, and seeking shelter from the extensive plains, which every where now border the alluvion.

We proceeded about 32 miles, and experienced a scorching sun from noon till night, when at length the sky became obscured by clouds portentous of thunder. My thermometer when exposed to the sun rose to 100 degrees. Nearly opposite Vache Grasse creek we passed a rapid, over which there is scarcely more than 12 inches water, in the lowest stage. No hills now appear on either hand, and a little distance in the prairie, near Vache Grasse, stands the last habitation of the whites to be met with on the banks of the Arkansa, except those of the garrison.

Not far from Lee's creek, Perpillon of the French hunters, a low ridge again comes up to the border of the river, in which is discoverable the first calcareous rock on ascending the Arkansa. From hence also the prairies or grassy plains begin to be prevalent, and the trees to decrease in number and magnitude. Contiguous to our encampment commenced a prairie of seven miles in length, and continuing within a mile of the garrison. The river, now presenting long and romantic views, was almost exclusively bordered with groves of cotton-wood, at this season extremely beautiful, resembling so many vistas clad in the softest and most vivid verdure, and crowded with innumerable birds, but of species common to the rest of the United States.

24th.] This morning we passed the hills of Lee's creek, which for a short distance border the Arkansa; and about noon arrived at the garrison, which comes into view at the distance of about four miles, agreeably terminating a stretch of the river. Rising, as it were, out of the alluvial forest, is seen from hence, at the distance of 35 miles, a conic mountain nearly as blue as the sky, and known by the French hunters under the name of Point de Sucre, or the sugar loaf.

I met with politeness from major Bradford the commander of the garrison, but was disagreeably surprised to be given to understand, that I could not have permission to proceed any higher up the river without a special credential from the secretary of state, authorizing me to hold that intercourse with the natives, which I might deem necessary in further pursuing my journey. It appeared to me, however, sufficiently obvious, that the governor of the territory must be empowered to permit an intercourse, civil and commercial, with the Indians, and liberty to travel through their country by their concurrence. And, indeed, all difficulty was removed by a reference to the recent regulations, which empowered the commanders of the garrisons optionally to permit such intercourse; and I am happy to add, that this measure, which referred me to the hospitality of the major, was, apparently, as gratifying to him as to myself.

At the benevolent request of the commander, and agreeably to my intentions of exploring the natural history of the territory, I resolved to spend a few weeks at the garrison, and make it the depot of my collections. It is with a satisfaction, clouded by melancholy, that I now call to mind the agreeable hours I spent at this station, while accompanied by the friendly aid and kind participation of Dr. Russel, whose memory I have faintly endeavoured to commemorate in the specific name of a beautiful species of Monarda. But relentless death, whose ever-withering hand delights to pluck the fairest flowers, added, in the fleeting space of a few short days, another early trophy to his mortal garland; and Russel, the only hope of a fond and widowed mother, the last of his name and family, now sleeps obscurely in unhallowed earth! Gentle Reader, forgive this tribute of sympathy to the recollection of one, whom fully to know was surely to esteem, as a gentleman, an accomplished scholar, and a sincere admirer of the simple beauties of the field of nature.

27th.] Yesterday I took a walk of about five miles up the banks of the Pottoe, and found my labour well repayed by the discovery of several new or undescribed plants. In this direction the surface of the ground is gently broken or undulated, and thinly scattered with trees, resembling almost in this respect a cultivated park. The whole expanse of forest, hill, and dale, was now richly enamelled with a profusion of beautiful and curious flowers; among the most conspicuous was the charming Daisy of America, of a delicate lilac colour, and altogether corresponding in general aspect with the European species; intermingled, appears a new species of Collinsia, a large-flowered Tradescantia, various species of Phlox, the Verbena aubletia, and the esculent Scilla. From a low hill, the neighbouring prairie appeared circumscribed by forests, but the mountains of the Pottoe were not visible. The soil, even throughout the uplands, appeared nearly as fertile as the alluvions, and affords a most productive pasture to the cattle.

On the 28th, a slow rise in the river was perceptible, produced by the Canadian, or similar branches, and communicating a chocolate-red colour to the stream.

In the course of the day, I walked over the hills bordering the Pottoe, about six miles, in order to see some trees of the yellow-wood (Maclura), but they were scarcely yet in leaf, and showed no indications of producing bloom. Some of them were as much as 12 inches in diameter, with a crooked and spreading trunk, 50 or 60 feet high. Its wood dies yellow, and scarcely differs from the Fustick of the West Indies. From appearances, those few insulated trees of the Pottoe, are on the utmost limit of their northern range, and, though old and decayed, do not appear to be succeeded by others, or to produce any perfect fruit. The day was so warm, that at 9 o'clock in the evening, the thermometer still stood at 75 degrees.

The soil, wherever there is the slightest depression, is of a superior quality, and thickly covered with vegetable earth. The trees appear scattered as if planted by art, affording an unobstructed range for the hunter, equal to that of a planted park.

On the 29th, I took an agreeable walk into the adjoining prairie, which is about two miles wide and seven long. I found it equally undulated with the surrounding woodland, and could perceive no reason for the absence of trees, except the annual conflagration. A ridge of considerable elevation divides it about the centre, from whence the hills of the Pottoe, the Cavaniol, and the Sugar-loaf, at the distance of about 30 miles, appear partly enveloped in the mists of the horizon. Like an immense meadow, the expanse was now covered with a luxuriant herbage, and beautifully decorated with flowers, amongst which I was pleased to see the Painted Cup of the eastern states, accompanied by occasional clusters of a white flowered Dodecatheon or American primrose. The numerous rounded elevations which chequer this verdant plain, are so many partial attempts at shrubby and arborescent vegetation, which nature has repeatedly made, and which have only been subdued by the reiterated operation of annual burning, employed by the natives, for the purpose of hunting with more facility, and of affording a tender pasturage for the game.

May 1st.] The river still continued rising, and also red and turbid from an admixture of the clay of the salt formation.

The garrison, consisting of two block-houses, and lines of cabins or barracks for the accommodation of 70 men whom it contains, is agreeably situated at the junction of the Pottoe, on a rising ground of about 50 feet elevation, and surrounded by alluvial and up-lands of unusual fertility. The view is more commanding and picturesque, than any other spot of equal elevation on the banks of the Arkansa. The meanders of the river to the eastward, backed by the hills of Lee's creek, are visible for more than six miles. The basis of the fort is a dark-coloured slaty micaceous sandstone, the lamina of which, nearly horizontal, and occasionally traversed by calcareous illinitions, are about four to six inches in thickness, and denudated for some hundreds of yards by the washing of the current, which, in an elevated stage, roars and foams with great velocity. About three or four miles up the Pottoe, this rock is underlayed by a bituminous state-clay, indicative of coal, beneath which, no doubt, would be found calcareous rock; neither this nor the sandstone, however, present any organic remains.

3d.] To-day, accompanied by Doctor Russel, and another gentleman of the fort, I rode to Cedar prairie, lying about 10 miles south-east of the garrison, and presenting an irregular or undulating surface. I here found a second species of that interesting plant, which my venerable friend, William Bartram, called Ixia caelestina, the flowers of this species are also of a beautiful blue, and white at the base. The whole plain was, in places, enlivened with the Syshtuchium anceps, producing flowers of an uncommon magnitude; amidst this assemblage it was not easy to lose sight of the azure larkspur, whose flowers are of the brightest ultramarine; in the depressions also grew the ochroleucous Baptisia loaded with papilionaceous flowers, nearly as large as those of the garden pea.

From this prairie, and more particularly from a hill which partly traverses it, the mountains of the Pottoe appeared quite distinct, the Sugar-loaf on the east, and the Cavaniol, about three miles apart, on the west side of the river; the latter is to all appearance much the highest, and presents a tabular summit. The extensive and verdant meadow, in every direction appeared picturesquely bounded by woody hills of different degrees of elevation and distance, and lacked nothing but human occupation to reclaim it from barren solitude, and cast over it the air of rural cheerfulness and abundance.

7th.] The Pottoe and the Arkansa were now at their utmost elevation, and their waters of a pale or milky colour, in consequence of being swelled by the northern streams. The sand-bars and beaches were entirely submerged, and the river still also continued augmenting on the 8th.

On the 9th, I again rode out to Cedar prairie, accompanied by the Doctor, and one of the soldiers, whose intention was to hunt. Several deer were discovered, but all too shy to be approached. We spent the night about the centre of the first portion of the prairie, which is divided into two parts by the intersection of a small wooded rivulet; and though the evening was mild and delightfully tranquil, the swarms of musquetoes, augmented since the recent freshet, would not permit us to sleep.

It is truly remarkable how greatly the sound of objects, becomes absorbed in these extensive woodless plains. No echo answers the voice, and its tones die away in boundless and enfeebled undulations. Even game will sometimes remain undispersed at the report of the gun. Encamping near a small brook, we were favoured by the usual music of frogs, and among them heard a species which almost exactly imitated the lowing of a calf. Just as night commenced, the cheerless howling of a distant wolf accosted our ears amidst the tranquil solitude, and the whole night we were serenaded with the vociferations of the two species of whip-poor-will.

The dawn of a cloudy day, after to us a wakeful night, was ushered in by the melodious chorus of many thousands of birds, agreeably dispersing the solemnity of the ambiguous twilight.

Amongst other objects of nature, my attention was momentarily arrested by the curious appearance of certain conic hillocks, about three feet high, generally situated in denudated places, and covered over with minute pebbles; these on closer examination proved to be the habitations of swarms of large red ants, who entered and came out by one or two common apertures.

On the wooded margin of the prairie, the doctor and myself were gratified by the discovery of a very elegant plant, which constitutes a new genus allied reciprocally to Phacelia and Hydrophyllum.

Excerpt of Narrative of the Life of Frederick Douglass: An American Slave (1845)

Source: Douglass, Frederick. *Narrative of the Life of Frederick Douglass: An American Slave* (1845). Belmont, CA: Wadsworth, 2004.

Commentary

Frederick Douglass's *Narrative* is perhaps the most famous slave narrative in American history. Born on a Maryland plantation, Douglass (c. 1817–1895) escaped from slavery in 1838. He moved first to Boston and eventually settled in Rochester, New York. He was one of many former slaves who toured the North before the Civil War telling personal stories about the harsh injustices of slavery and sought to educate white audiences about the realities of the institution. Douglass published his narrative in 1845, the same year that he began a speaking tour in Britain. He returned to the United States in 1847, settled in Rochester, and established a newspaper called *The North Star*. Throughout his life, Douglass worked tirelessly for the political rights of blacks. In 1889 he was appointed United States Minister to Haiti.

Douglass's personal story graphically relates the violence and cruelty of slavery on southern plantations. In this excerpt, he describes how overseers and masters viciously whipped slaves for the most minor of infractions. Douglass also portrays the physical privations that slaves suffered, including lack of food, clothing, and sleep that were the norm on many plantations. Equally important, he documents slavery's psychological violence, showing how bondage obliterated the slave's identity as a human being. Douglass, who knew neither his birth date nor his father's identity and was separated from his mother, was therefore deprived of normal familial bonds. His master viewed his slaves as nothing more than property.

At the end of this excerpt, Douglass counters these examples of inhumanity with the image of slaves singing. He observes that the slaves were human beings with complex emotions, despite the conditions under which they lived. Douglass tells the story as he does and includes certain details in order to convince his audience that slavery is an immoral institution.

CHAPTER I.

I was born in Tuckahoe, near Hillsborough, and about twelve miles from Easton, in Talbot county, Maryland. I have no accurate knowledge of my age, never having seen any authentic record containing it. By far the larger part of the slaves know as little of their ages as horses know of theirs, and it is the wish of most masters within my knowledge to keep their slaves thus ignorant. I do not remember to have ever met a slave who could tell of his birthday. They seldom come nearer to it than planting-time, harvest-time, cherry-time, spring-time, or fall-time. A want of information concerning my own was a source of unhappiness to me even during childhood. The white children could tell their ages. I could not tell why I ought to be deprived of the same privilege. I was not allowed to make any inquiries of my master concerning it. He deemed all such inquiries on the part of a slave improper and impertinent, and evidence of a restless spirit. The nearest estimate I can give makes me now between twenty-seven and twenty-eight years of age. I come to this, from hearing my master say, some time during 1835, I was about seventeen years old.

My mother was named Harriet Bailey. She was the daughter of Isaac and Betsey Bailey, both colored, and quite dark. My mother was of a darker complexion than either my grandmother or grandfather.

My father was a white man. He was admitted to be such by all I ever heard speak of my parentage. The opinion was also whispered that my master was my father; but of the correctness of this opinion, I know nothing; the means of knowing was withheld from me. My mother and I were separated when I was but an infant—before I knew her as my mother. It is a common custom, in the part of Maryland from which I ran away, to part children from their mothers at a very early age. Frequently, before the child has reached its twelfth month, its mother is taken from it, and hired out on some farm a considerable distance off, and the child is placed under the care of an old woman, too old for field labor. For what this separation is done, I do not know, unless it be to hinder the development of the child's affection toward its mother, and to blunt and destroy the natural affection of the mother for the child. This is the inevitable result.

I never saw my mother, to know her as such, more than four or five times in my life; and each of those times was very short in duration, and at night. She was hired by a Mr. Stewart, who lived about twelve miles from my home. She made her journeys to see me in the night, travelling the whole distance on foot, after the performance of her day's work. She was a field hand, and a whipping is the penalty of not being in the field at sunrise, unless a slave has special permission from his or her master to the contrary—a permission which they seldom get, and one that gives to him that gives it the proud name of being a kind master. I do not recollect of ever seeing my mother by the light of day. She was with me in the night. She would lie down with me, and get me to sleep, but long before I waked she was gone. Very little communication ever took place between us. Death soon ended what little we could have while she lived, and with it her hardships and suffering. She died when I was about seven years old, on one of my master's farms, near Lee's Mill. I was not allowed to be present during her illness, at her death, or burial. She was gone long before I knew any thing about it. Never having enjoyed, to any considerable extent, her soothing presence, her tender and watchful care, I received the tidings of her death with much the same emotions I should have probably felt at the death of a stranger.

Called thus suddenly away, she left me without the slightest intimation of who my father was. The whisper that my master was my father, may or may not be true; and, true or false, it is of but little consequence to my purpose whilst the fact remains, in all its glaring odiousness, that slaveholders have ordained, and by law established, that the children of slave women shall in all cases follow the condition of their mothers; and this is done too obviously to administer to their own lusts, and make a gratification of their wicked desires profitable as well as pleasurable; for by this cunning arrangement, the slaveholder, in cases not a few, sustains to his slaves the double relation of master and father.

I know of such cases; and it is worthy of remark that such slaves invariably suffer greater hardships, and have more to contend with, than others. They are, in the first place, a constant offence to their mistress. She is ever disposed to find fault with them; they can seldom do any thing to please her; she is never better pleased than when she sees them under the lash, especially when she suspects her husband of showing to his mulatto children favors which he witholds from his black slaves. The master is frequently compelled to sell this class of his slaves, out of deference to the feelings of his white wife; and, cruel as the deed may strike any one to be, for a man to sell his own children to human flesh-mongers, it is often the dictate of humanity for him to do so; for, unless he does this, he must not only whip them himself, but must stand by and see one white son tie up his brother, of but few shades darker complexion than himself, and ply the gory lash to his naked back; and if he lisp one word of disapproval, it is set down to his parental partiality, and only makes a bad matter worse, both for himself and the slave whom he would protect and defend.

Every year brings with it multitudes of this class of slaves. It was doubtless in consequence of a knowledge of this fact, that one great statesman of the south predicted the downfall of slavery by the inevitable laws of population. Whether this prophecy is ever fulfilled or not, it is nevertheless plain that a very different-looking class of people are springing up at the south, and are now held

in slavery, from those originally brought to this country from Africa; and if their increase will do no other good, it will do away the force of the argument, that God cursed Ham, and therefore American slavery is right. If the lineal descendants of Ham are alone to be scripturally enslaved, it is certain that slavery at the south must soon become unscriptural; for thousands are ushered into the world, annually, who, like myself, owe their existence to white fathers, and those fathers most frequently their own masters.

I have had two masters. My first master's name was Anthony. I do not remember his first name. He was generally called Captain Anthony—a title which, I presume, he acquired by sailing a craft on the Chesapeake Bay. He was not considered a rich slaveholder. He owned two or three farms, and about thirty slaves. His farms and slaves were under the care of an overseer. The overseer's name was Plummer. Mr. Plummer was a miserable drunkard, a profane swearer, and a savage monster. He always went armed with a cowskin and a heavy cudgel. I have known him to cut and slash the women's heads so horribly, that even master would be enraged at his cruelty, and would threaten to whip him if he did not mind himself. Master, however, was not a humane slaveholder. It required extraordinary barbarity on the part of an overseer to affect him. He was a cruel man, hardened by a long life of slaveholding. He would at times seem to take great pleasure in whipping a slave. I have often been awakened at the dawn of day by the most heart-rending shrieks of an own aunt of mine, whom he used to tie up to a joist, and whip upon her naked back till she was literally covered with blood. No words, no tears, no prayers, from his gory victim, seemed to move his iron heart from its bloody purpose. The louder she screamed, the harder he whipped; and where the blood ran fastest, there he whipped longest. He would whip her to make her scream, and whip her to make her hush; and not until overcome by fatigue, would he cease to swing the blood-clotted cowskin. I remember the first time I ever witnessed this horrible exhibition. I was quite a child, but I well remember it. I never shall forget it whilst I remember any thing. It was the first of a long series of such outrages, of which I was doomed to be a witness and a participant. It struck me with awful force. It was the blood-stained gate, the entrance to the hell of slavery, through which I was about to pass. It was a most terrible spectacle. I wish I could commit to paper the feelings with which I beheld it.

This occurrence took place very soon after I went to live with my old master, and under the following circumstances. Aunt Hester went out one night, —where or for what I do not know, —and happened to be absent when my master desired her presence.

He had ordered her not to go out evenings, and warned her that she must never let him catch her in company with a young man, who was paying attention to her belonging to Colonel Lloyd. The young man's name was Ned Roberts, generally called Lloyd's Ned. Why master was so careful of her, may be safely left to conjecture. She was a woman of noble form, and of graceful proportions, having very few equals, and fewer superiors, in personal appearance, among the colored or white women of our neighborhood.

Aunt Hester had not only disobeyed his orders in going out, but had been found in company with Lloyd's Ned; which circumstance, I found, From what he said while whipping her, was the chief offence. Had he been a man of pure morals himself, he might have been thought interested in protecting the innocence of my aunt; but those who knew him will not suspect him of any such virtue. Before he commenced whipping Aunt Hester, he took her into the kitchen, and stripped her from neck to waist, leaving her neck, shoulders, and back, entirely naked. He then told her to cross her hands, calling her at the same time a d - - b - - h. After crossing her hands, he tied them with a strong rope, and led her to a stool under a large hook in the joist, put in for the purpose. He made her get upon the stool, and tied her hands to the hook. She now stood fair for his infernal purpose. Her arms were stretched up at their full length, so that she stood upon the ends of her toes. He then said to her, "Now, you d - - d b - - h, I'll learn you how to disobey my orders!" and after rolling up his sleeves, he commenced to lay on the heavy cowskin, and soon the warm, red blood (amid heartrending shrieks from her, and horrid oaths from him) came dripping to the floor. I was so terrified and horror-stricken at the sight, that I hid myself in a closet, and dared not venture out till long after the bloody transaction was over. I expected it would be my turn next. It was all new to me. I had never seen any thing like it before. I had always lived with my grandmother on the outskirts of the plantation, where she was put to raise the children of the younger women. I had therefore been, until now, out of the way of the bloody scenes that often occurred on the plantation.

CHAPTER II

My master's family consisted of two sons, Andrew and Richard; one daughter, Lucretia, and her husband, Captain Thomas Auld. They lived in one house, upon the home plantation of Colonel Edward Lloyd. My master was Colonel Lloyd's clerk and superintendent. He was what might be called the overseer of the overseers. I spent two years of childhood on this plantation in my old master's family. It was here that I witnessed the bloody transaction recorded in the first chapter; and as I received my first impressions of slavery on this plantation, I will give some description of it, and of slavery as it there existed. The plantation is about twelve miles north of Easton, in Talbot county, and is situated on the border of Miles River. The principal products raised upon it were tobacco, corn, and wheat. These were raised in great abundance; so that, with the products of this and the other farms belonging to him, he was able to keep in almost constant employment a large sloop, in carrying them to market at Baltimore. This sloop was named Sally Lloyd, in honor of one of the colonel's daughters. My master's son-in-law, Captain Auld, was master of the vessel; she was otherwise manned by the colonel's own slaves. Their names were Peter, Isaac, Rich, and Jake. These were esteemed very highly by the other slaves, and looked upon as the privileged ones of the plantation; for it was no small affair, in the eyes of the slaves, to be allowed to see Baltimore.

Colonel Lloyd kept from three to four hundred slaves on his home plantation, and owned a large number more on the neighboring farms belonging to him. The names of the farms nearest to the home plantation were Wye Town and New Design. "Wye Town" was under the overseership of a man named Noah Willis. New Design was under the overseership of a Mr. Townsend. The overseers of these, and all the rest of the farms, numbering over twenty, received advice and direction from the managers of the home plantation. This was the great business place. It was the seat of government for the whole twenty farms. All disputes among the overseers were settled here. If a slave was convicted of any high misdemeanor, became unmanageable, or evinced a determination to run away, he was brought immediately here, severely whipped, put on board the sloop, carried to Baltimore, and sold to Austin Woolfolk, or some other slave-trader, as a warning to the slaves remaining.

Here, too, the slaves of all the other farms received their monthly allowance of food, and their yearly clothing. The men and women slaves received, as their monthly allowance of food, eight pounds of pork, or its equivalent in fish, and one bushel of corn meal. Their yearly clothing consisted of two coarse linen shirts, one pair of linen trousers, like the shirts, one jacket, one pair of trousers for winter, made of coarse negro cloth, one pair of stockings, and one pair of shoes; the whole of which could not have cost more than seven dollars. The allowance of the slave children was given to their mothers, or the old women having the care of them. The children unable to work in the field had neither shoes, stockings, jackets, nor trousers, given to them; their clothing consisted of two coarse linen shirts per year. When these failed them, they went naked until the next allowance-day. Children from seven to ten years old, of both sexes, almost naked, might be seen at all seasons of the year.

There were no beds given the slaves, unless one coarse blanket be considered such, and none but the men and women had these. This, however, is not considered a very great privation. They find less difficulty from the want of beds, than from the want of time to sleep; for when their day's work in the field is done, the most of them having their washing, mending, and cooking to do, and having few or none of the ordinary facilities for doing either of these, very many of their sleeping hours are consumed in preparing for the field the coming day; and when this is done, old and young, male and female, married and single, drop down side by side, on one common bed,—the cold, damp floor,—each covering himself or herself with their miserable blankets; and here they sleep till they are summoned to the field by the driver's horn. At the sound of this, all must rise, and be off to the field. There must be no halting; every one must be at his or her post; and woe betides them who hear not this morning summons to the field; for if they are not awakened by the sense of hearing, they are by the sense of feeling: no age nor sex finds any favor. Mr. Severe, the overseer, used to stand by the door of the quarter, armed with a large hickory stick and heavy cowskin, ready to whip any one who was so unfortunate as not to hear, or, from any other cause, was prevented from being ready to start for the field at the sound of the horn.

Mr. Severe was rightly named: he was a cruel man. I have seen him whip a woman, causing the blood to run half an hour at the time; and this, too, in the midst of her crying children, pleading for their mother's release. He seemed to take pleasure in manifesting his fiendish barbarity. Added to his cruelty, he was a profane swearer. It was enough to chill the blood and stiffen the hair of an ordinary man to hear him talk. Scarce a sentence escaped him but that was commenced or concluded by some horrid oath. The field was the place to witness his cruelty and profanity. His presence made it both the field of blood and of blasphemy. From the rising till the going down of the sun, he was cursing, raving, cutting, and slashing among the slaves of the field, in the most frightful manner. His career was short. He died very soon after I went to Colonel Lloyd's; and he died as he lived, uttering, with his dying groans, bitter curses and horrid oaths. His death was regarded by the slaves as the result of a merciful providence.

Mr. Severe's place was filled by a Mr. Hopkins. He was a very different man. He was less cruel, less profane, and made less noise, than Mr. Severe. His course was characterized by no extraordinary demonstrations of cruelty. He whipped, but seemed to take no pleasure in it. He was called by the slaves a good overseer.

The home plantation of Colonel Lloyd wore the appearance of a country village. All the mechanical operations for all the farms were performed here. The shoe-making and mending, the blacksmithing, cartwrighting, coopering, weaving, and grain-grinding, were all performed by the slaves on the home plantation. The whole place wore a business-like aspect very unlike the neighboring farms. The number of houses, too, conspired to give it advantage over the neighboring farms. It was called by the slaves the Great House Farm. Few privileges were esteemed higher, by the slaves of the out-farms, than that of being selected to do errands at the Great House Farm. It was associated in their minds with greatness. A representative could not be prouder of his election to a seat in the American Congress, than a slave on one of the out-farms would be of his election to do errands at the Great House Farm. They regarded it as evidence of great confidence reposed in them by their overseers; and it was on this account, as well as a constant desire to be out of the field from under the driver's lash, that they esteemed it a high privilege, one worth careful living for. He was called the smartest and most trusty fellow, who had this honor conferred upon him the most frequently. The competitors for this office sought as diligently to please their overseers, as the office-seekers in the political parties seek to please and deceive the people. The same traits of character might be seen in Colonel Lloyd's slaves, as are seen in the slaves of the political parties.

The slaves selected to go to the Great House Farm, for the monthly allowance for themselves and their fellow-slaves, were peculiarly enthusiastic. While on their way, they would make the dense old woods, for miles around, reverberate with their wild songs, revealing at once the highest joy and the deepest sadness. They would compose and sing as they went along, consulting neither time nor tune. The thought that came up, came out—if not in the word, in the sound;—and as frequently in the one as in the other. They would sometimes sing the most pathetic sentiment in the most rapturous tone, and the most rapturous sentiment in the most pathetic tone. Into all of their songs they would manage to weave something of the Great House Farm. Especially would they do this, when leaving home. They would then sing most exultingly the following words:—

"I am going away to the Great House Farm! O, yea! O, yea! O!"

This they would sing, as a chorus, to words which to many would seem unmeaning jargon, but which, nevertheless, were full of meaning to themselves. I have sometimes thought that the mere hearing of those songs would do more to impress some minds with the horrible character of slavery, than the reading of whole volumes of philosophy on the subject could do.

I did not, when a slave, understand the deep meaning of those rude and apparently incoherent songs. I was myself within the circle; so that I neither saw nor heard as those without might see and hear. They told a tale of woe which was then altogether beyond my feeble comprehension; they were tones loud, long, and deep; they breathed the prayer and complaint of souls boiling over with the bitterest anguish. Every tone was a testimony against slavery, and a prayer to God for deliverance from chains. The hearing of those wild notes always depressed my spirit, and filled me with ineffable sadness. I have frequently found myself in tears while hearing them. The mere recurrence to those songs, even now, afflicts me; and while I am writing these lines, an expression of feeling has already found its way down my cheek. To those songs I trace my first glimmering conception of the dehumanizing character of slavery. I can never get rid of that conception. Those songs still follow me, to deepen my hatred of slavery, and quicken my sympathies for my brethren in bonds. If any one wishes to be impressed with the soul-killing effects of slavery, let him go to Colonel Lloyd's plantation, and, on allowance-day, place himself in the deep pine woods, and there let him, in silence, analyze the sounds that shall pass through the chambers of his soul,—and if he is not thus impressed, it will only be because "there is no flesh in his obdurate heart."

I have often been utterly astonished, since I came to the north, to find persons who could speak of the singing, among slaves, as evidence of their contentment and happiness. It is impossible to conceive of a greater mistake. Slaves sing most when they are most unhappy. The songs of the slave represent the sorrows of his heart; and he is relieved by them, only as an aching heart is relieved by its tears. At least, such is my experience. I have often sung to drown my sorrow, but seldom to express my happiness. Crying for joy, and singing for joy, were alike uncommon to me while in the jaws of slavery. The singing of a man cast away upon a desolate island might be as appropriately considered as evidence of contentment and happiness, as the singing of a slave; the songs of the one and of the other are prompted by the same emotion.

Excerpt of Incidents in the Life of a Slave-Girl (1861)

Source: Jacobs, Harriet A. *Incidents in the Life of A Slave-Girl* (1861). West Berlin, NJ: Townsend Press, 2004.

Commentary

Harriet Jacobs (1813–1897) was born in Edenton, North Carolina. Her *Incidents in the Life of a Slave Girl*, which recounts her experiences as a slave in the South and as a fugitive slave in the North,

is the most comprehensive female slave narrative. Jacobs wrote the autobiography anonymously and, in the book, her narrator calls herself Linda Brent. Jacobs first ran away in 1835 and hid for seven years in a crawl space in her grandmother's home in Edonton, North Carolina. In 1842, she escaped to New York, where she eventually joined Frederick Douglass's circle and helped fugitive and freed slaves. After the Civil War, she established a school for freed blacks in Alexandria, Virginia. Despite the social mores of her time, in her book Jacobs described her master's sexual abuse of her and the relationship she had with a white man on a neighboring plantation. The relationship with the white neighbor produced two children, whom she joined in New York at the time of her escape.

In the first chapter, Jacobs' narrator describes the reaction of local plantation owners and overseers to the 1831 Nat Turner rebellion, when Turner led sixty fellow slaves in a uprising in which fifty five whites were killed. In retaliation, whites searched the slaves' homes, destroying property and stealing whatever they wanted. The chapter also reveals the stratification of Southern white society. The landless whites are illiterate and oppressed; in contrast, Brent, a slave, can read and receives some protection from a white slaveholder. The second chapter recounts the racial prejudice Brent experienced in the North as a domestic servant for a white family. In her book, Jacobs shows the ways her life in the North differs from and yet is similar to her life in the South.

XII.
Fear of Insurrection.

Not far from this time Nat Turner's insurrection broke out; and the news threw our town into great commotion. Strange that they should be alarmed, when their slaves were so "contented and happy"! But so it was.

It was always the custom to have a muster every year. On that occasion every white man shouldered his musket. The citizens and the so-called country gentlemen wore military uniforms. The poor whites took their places in the ranks in every-day dress, some without shoes, some without hats. This grand occasion had already passed; and when the slaves were told there was to be another muster, they were surprised and rejoiced. Poor creatures! They thought it was going to be a holiday. I was informed of the true state of affairs, and imparted it to the few I could trust. Most gladly would I have proclaimed it to every slave; but I dared not. All could not be relied on. Mighty is the power of the torturing lash.

By sunrise, people were pouring in from every quarter within twenty miles of the town. I knew the houses were to be searched; and I expected it would be done by country bullies and the poor whites. I knew nothing annoyed them so much as to see colored people living in comfort and respectability; so I made arrangements for them with especial care. I arranged every thing in my grandmother's house as neatly as possible. I put white quilts on the beds, and decorated some of the rooms with flowers. When all was arranged, I sat down at the window to watch. Far as my eye could reach, it rested on a motley crowd of soldiers. Drums and fifes were discoursing martial music. The men were divided into companies of sixteen, each headed by a captain. Orders were given, and the wild scouts rushed in every direction, wherever a colored face was to be found.

It was a grand opportunity for the low whites, who had no negroes of their own to scourge. They exulted in such a chance to exercise a little brief authority, and show their subserviency to the slaveholders; not reflecting that the power which trampled on the colored people also kept themselves in poverty, ignorance, and moral degradation. Those who never witnessed such scenes can hardly believe what I know was inflicted at this time on innocent men, women, and children, against whom there was not the slightest ground for suspicion. Colored people and slaves who lived in remote parts of the town suffered in an especial manner. In some cases the searchers scattered powder and shot among their clothes, and then sent other parties to find them, and bring them forward as proof that they were plotting insurrection. Every where men, women, and children were whipped till the blood stood in puddles at their feet. Some received five hundred lashes; others were tied hands and feet, and tortured with a bucking paddle, which blisters the skin terribly. The dwellings of the colored people, unless they happened to be protected by some influential white person, who was nigh at hand, were robbed of clothing and every thing else the marauders thought worth carrying away. All day long these unfeeling wretches went round, like a troop of demons, terrifying and tormenting the helpless. At night, they formed themselves into patrol bands, and went wherever they chose among the colored people, acting out their brutal will. Many women hid themselves in woods and swamps, to keep out of their way. If any of the husbands or fathers told of these outrages, they were tied up to the public whipping post, and cruelly scourged for telling lies about white men. The consternation was universal. No two people that had the slightest tinge of color in their faces dared to be seen talking together.

I entertained no positive fears about our household, because we were in the midst of white families who would protect us. We were ready to receive the soldiers whenever they came. It was not long before we heard the tramp of feet and the sound of voices. The door was rudely pushed open; and in they tumbled, like a pack of hungry wolves. They snatched at every thing within their reach. Every box, trunk, closet, and corner underwent a thorough examination. A box in one of the drawers containing some silver change was eagerly pounced upon. When I stepped forward to take it from them, one of the soldiers turned and said angrily, "What d'ye foller us fur? D'ye s'pose white folks is come to steal?"

I replied, "You have come to search; but you have searched that box, and I will take it, if you please."

At that moment I saw a white gentleman who was friendly to us; and I called to him, and asked him to have the goodness to come in and stay till the search was over. He readily complied. His entrance into the house brought in the captain of the company, whose business it was to guard the outside of the house, and see that none of the inmates left it. This officer was Mr. Litch, the wealthy slaveholder whom I mentioned, in the account of neighboring planters, as being notorious for his cruelty. He felt above soiling his hands with the search. He merely gave orders; and, if a bit of writing was discovered, it was carried to him by his ignorant followers, who were unable to read.

My grandmother had a large trunk of bedding and table cloths. When that was opened, there was a great shout of surprise; and one exclaimed, "Where'd the damned niggers git all dis sheet an' table clarf?"

My grandmother, emboldened by the presence of our white protector, said, "You may be sure we didn't pilfer 'em from your houses."

"Look here, mammy," said a grim-looking fellow without any coat, "you seem to feel mighty gran' 'cause you got all them 'ere fixens. White folks oughter have 'em all."

His remarks were interrupted by a chorus of voices shouting, "We's got 'em! We's got 'em! Dis 'ere yaller gal's got letters!"

There was a general rush for the supposed letter, which, upon examination, proved to be some verses written to me by a friend. In packing away my things, I had overlooked them. When their captain informed them of their contents, they seemed much disappointed. He inquired of me who wrote them.

I told him it was one of my friends. "Can you read them?" he asked. When I told him I could, he swore, and raved, and tore the paper into bits. "Bring me all your letters!" said he, in a commanding tone. I told him I had none. "Don't be afraid," he continued, in an insinuating way. "Bring them all to me. Nobody shall do you any harm." Seeing I did not move to obey him, his pleasant tone changed to oaths and threats. "Who writes to you? half free niggers?" inquired he. I replied, "O, no; most of my letters are from white people. Some request me to burn them after they are read, and some I destroy without reading."

An exclamation of surprise from some of the company put a stop to our conversation. Some silver spoons which ornamented an old-fashioned buffet had just been discovered. My grandmother was in the habit of preserving fruit for many ladies in the town, and of preparing suppers for parties; consequently she had many jars of preserves. The closet that contained these was next invaded, and the contents tasted. One of them, who was helping himself freely, tapped his neighbor on the shoulder, and said, "Wal done! Don't wonder de niggers want to kill all de white folks, when dey live on 'sarves" [meaning preserves]. I stretched out my hand to take the jar, saying, "You were not sent here to search for sweetmeats."

"And what were we sent for?" said the captain, bristling up to me. I evaded the question.

The search of the house was completed, and nothing found to condemn us. They next proceeded to the garden, and knocked about every bush and vine, with no better success. The captain called his men together, and, after a short consultation, the order to march was given. As they passed out of the gate, the captain turned back, and pronounced a malediction on the house. He said it ought to be burned to the ground, and each of its inmates receive thirty-nine lashes. We came out of this affair very fortunately; not losing any thing except some wearing apparel.

Towards evening the turbulence increased. The soldiers, stimulated by drink, committed still greater cruelties. Shrieks and shouts continually rent the air. Not daring to go to the door, I peeped under the window curtain. I saw a mob dragging along a number of colored people, each white man, with his musket upraised, threatening instant death if they did not stop their shrieks. Among the prisoners was a respectable old colored minister. They had found a few parcels of shot in his house, which his wife had for years used to balance her scales. For this they were going to shoot him on Court House Green. What a spectacle was that for a civilized country! A rabble, staggering under intoxication, assuming to be the administrators of justice!

The better class of the community exerted their influence to save the innocent, persecuted people; and in several instances they succeeded, by keeping them shut up in jail till the excitement abated. At last the white citizens found that their own property was not safe from the lawless rabble they had summoned to protect them. They rallied the drunken swarm, drove them back into the country, and set a guard over the town.

The next day, the town patrols were commissioned to search colored people that lived out of the city; and the most shocking outrages were committed with perfect impunity. Every day for a fortnight, if I looked out, I saw horsemen with some poor panting negro tied to their saddles, and compelled by the lash to keep up with their speed, till they arrived at the jail yard. Those who had been whipped too unmercifully to walk were washed with brine, tossed into a cart, and carried to jail. One black man, who had not fortitude to endure scourging, promised to give information about the conspiracy. But it turned out that he knew nothing at all. He had not

even heard the name of Nat Turner. The poor fellow had, however, made up a story, which augmented his own sufferings and those of the colored people.

The day patrol continued for some weeks, and at sundown a night guard was substituted. Nothing at all was proved against the colored people, bond or free. The wrath of the slaveholders was somewhat appeased by the capture of Nat Turner. The imprisoned were released. The slaves were sent to their masters, and the free were permitted to return to their ravaged homes. Visiting was strictly forbidden on the plantations. The slaves begged the privilege of again meeting at their little church in the woods, with their burying ground around it. It was built by the colored people, and they had no higher happiness than to meet there and sing hymns together, and pour out their hearts in spontaneous prayer. Their request was denied, and the church was demolished. They were permitted to attend the white churches, a certain portion of the galleries being appropriated to their use. There, when every body else had partaken of the communion, and the benediction had been pronounced, the minister said, "Come down, now, my colored friends." They obeyed the summons, and partook of the bread and wine, in commemoration of the meek and lowly Jesus, who said, "God is your Father, and all ye are brethren."

XXXV.
Prejudice Against Color.

It was a relief to my mind to see preparations for leaving the city. We went to Albany in the steamboat *Knickerbocker*. When the gong sounded for tea, Mrs. Bruce said, "Linda, it is late, and you and baby had better come to the table with me." I replied, "I know it is time baby had her supper, but I had rather not go with you, if you please. I am afraid of being insulted." "O no, not if you are with me," she said. I saw several white nurses go with their ladies, and I ventured to do the same. We were at the extreme end of the table. I was no sooner seated, than a gruff voice said, "Get up! You know you are not allowed to sit here." I looked up, and, to my astonishment and indignation, saw that the speaker was a colored man. If his office required him to enforce the by-laws of the boat, he might, at least, have done it politely. I replied, "I shall not get up, unless the captain comes and takes me up." No cup of tea was offered me, but Mrs. Bruce handed me hers and called for another. I looked to see whether the other nurses were treated in a similar manner. They were all properly waited on.

Next morning, when we stopped at Troy for breakfast, every body was making a rush for the table. Mrs. Bruce said, "Take my arm, Linda, and we'll go in together." The landlord heard her, and said, "Madam, will you allow your nurse and baby to take breakfast with my family?" I knew this was to be attributed to my complexion; but he spoke courteously, and therefore I did not mind it.

At Saratoga we found the United States Hotel crowded, and Mr. Bruce took one of the cottages belonging to the hotel. I had thought, with gladness, of going to the quiet of the country, where I should meet few people, but here I found myself in the midst of a swarm of Southerners. I looked round me with fear and trembling, dreading to see some one who would recognize me. I was rejoiced to find that we were to stay but a short time.

We soon returned to New York, to make arrangements for spending the remainder of the summer at Rockaway. While the laundress was putting the clothes in order, I took an opportunity to go over to Brooklyn to see Ellen. I met her going to a grocery store, and the first words she said, were, "O, mother, don't go to Mrs. Hobbs's. Her brother, Mr. Thorne, has come from the south, and may be he'll tell where you are." I accepted the warning. I told her I was going away with Mrs. Bruce the next day, and would try to see her when I came back.

Being in servitude to the Anglo-Saxon race, I was not put into a "Jim Crow car," on our way to Rockaway, neither was I invited to ride through the streets on the top of trunks in a truck; but every where I found the same manifestations of that cruel prejudice, which so discourages the feelings, and represses the energies of the colored people. We reached Rockaway before dark, and put up at the Pavilion—a large hotel, beautifully situated by the sea-side—a great resort of the fashionable world. Thirty or forty nurses were there, of a great variety of nations. Some of the ladies had colored waiting-maids and coachmen, but I was the only nurse tinged with the blood of Africa. When the tea bell rang, I took little Mary and followed the other nurses. Supper was served in a long hall. A young man, who had the ordering of things, took the circuit of the table two or three times, and finally pointed me to a seat at the lower end of it. As there was but one chair, I sat down and took the child in my lap. Whereupon the young man came to me and said, in the blandest manner possible, "Will you please to seat the little girl in the chair, and stand behind it and feed her? After they have done, you will be shown to the kitchen, where you will have a good supper."

This was the climax! I found it hard to preserve my self-control, when I looked round, and saw women who were nurses, as I was, and only one shade lighter in complexion, eyeing me with a defiant look, as if my presence were a contamination. However, I said nothing. I quietly took the child in my arms, went to our room, and refused to go to the table again. Mr. Bruce ordered meals to be sent to the room for little Mary and I. This answered for a few days; but the waiters of the establishment were white, and they soon began to complain, saying they were not hired to wait on negroes. The landlord requested Mr. Bruce to send me down to my meals, because his servants rebelled against bringing them up, and the colored servants of other boarders were dissatisfied because all were not treated alike.

My answer was that the colored servants ought to be dissatisfied with themselves, for not having too much self-respect to submit to such treatment; that there was no difference in the price of board for colored and white servants, and there was no justification for difference of treatment. I staid a month after this, and finding I was resolved to stand up for my rights, they concluded to treat me well. Let every colored man and woman do this, and eventually we shall cease to be trampled under foot by our oppressors.

A Slave's Letter to His Former Master (1865)

Commentary

The antagonistic antebellum relationships between masters and slaves did not disappear with emancipation. Though whites could no longer claim blacks as "property," many landowners hoped that the freedpeople would continue to work for them as wage-earning employees. Working out the exact nature of the new relationships prompted tensions on both sides, as new expectations and old demands repeatedly clashed.

This letter from Jourdon Anderson to his former master in Tennessee dramatically conveyed the new framework of free labor negotiations. Anderson, who apparently had fled to Nashville and then to Ohio during the war, responded to Colonel P.H. Anderson's offer of employment on his farm. The letter documents serious hostilities between the two men, which had culminated with the colonel's shooting at his slave. Nevertheless, the former master's pressing need for farm workers forced him to offer a pledge of fair treatment if his former slave would return.

Jourdon Anderson clearly enjoyed relating his new good fortune to the man who had earlier threatened his life. He gladly detailed his high wages, the educational opportunities available to his children, and the respect displayed towards he and his wife, who others now addressed as "Mrs. Anderson." He expected to be assured of at least these conditions before he would return to Tennessee. Most boldly, he also argued that in order to "have faith in your promises in the future," the colonel would have to pay him back wages for his thirty-two years of slavery, a sum totalling several thousand dollars. These conditions made any agreement between the two unlikely, a result probably intended by the former slave, who relished his life outside the South.

For most, however, there were limits to the bargaining power that Jourdon Anderson had so shrewdly displayed in his letter. While he and his family enjoyed bright prospects in Ohio, most remaining in the South had to accept a far less satisfying situation in order to support themselves. Still, the passing of slavery gave freedpeople the basic right to select the employer offering the best terms.

Dayton, Ohio, August 7, 1865
To My Old Master, Colonel P. H. Anderson, Big Spring, Tennessee

Sir: I got your letter and was glad to find you had not forgotten Jourdon, and that you wanted me to come back and live with you again, promising to do better for me than anybody else can. I have often felt uneasy about you. I thought the Yankees would have hung you long before this for harboring Rebs they found at your house. I suppose they never heard about your going to Col. Martin's to kill the Union soldier that was left by his company in their stable. Although you shot at me twice before I left you, I did not want to hear of your being hurt, and am glad you are still living. It would do me good to go back to the dear old home again and see Miss Mary and Miss Martha and Allen, Esther, Green, and Lee. Give my love to them all, and tell them I hope we will meet in the better world, if not in this. I would have gone back to see you all when I was working in the Nashville hospital, but one of the neighbors told me Henry intended to shoot me if he ever got a chance.

I want to know particularly what the good chance is you propose to give me. I am doing tolerably well here; I get $25 a month, with victuals and clothing; have a comfortable home for Mandy (the folks here call her Mrs. Anderson), and the children, Milly, Jane and Grundy, go to school and are learning well; the teacher says Grundy has a head for a preacher. They go to Sunday-School, and Mandy and me attend church regularly. We are kindly treated; sometimes we overhear others saying, "Them colored people were slaves" down in Tennessee. The children feel hurt when they hear such remarks, but I tell them it was no disgrace in Tennessee to belong to Col. Anderson. Many darkies would have been proud, as I used to was, to call you master. Now, if you will write and say what wages you will give me, I will be better able to decide whether it would be to my advantage to move back again.

As to my freedom, which you say I can have, there is nothing to be gained on that score, as I got my free-papers in 1864 from the Provost-Marshall-General of the Department at Nashville. Mandy says she would be afraid to go back without some proof that you are sincerely disposed to treat us justly and kindly—and we have concluded to test your sincerity by asking you to send us our wages for the time we served you. This will make us forget and forgive old scores, and rely on your justice and friendship in the future. I served you faithfully for thirty-two years and Mandy twenty years. At $25 a month for me, and $2 a week for Mandy, our earnings would amount to $11,680. Add to this the interest for the time our wages has been kept back and deduct what you paid for our clothing and three doctor's visits to me, and

pulling a tooth for Mandy, and the balance will show what we are in justice entitled to. Please send the money by Adams Express, in care of V. Winters, esq, Dayton, Ohio. If you fail to pay us for faithful labors in the past we can have little faith in your promises in the future. We trust the good Maker has opened your eyes to the wrongs which you and your fathers have done to me and my fathers, in making us toil for you for generations with out recompense. Here I draw my wages every Saturday night, but in Tennessee there was never any pay day for the negroes any more than for the horses and cows. Surely there will be a day of reckoning for those who defraud the laborer of his hire.

In answering this letter please state if there would be any safety for my Milly and Jane, who are now grown up and both good-looking girls. You know how it was with poor Matilda and Catherine. I would rather stay here and starve and die if it comes to that than have my girls brought to shame by the violence and wickedness of their young masters. You will also please state if there has been any schools opened for the colored children in your neighborhood, the great desire of my life now is to give my children an education, and have them form virtuous habits.

P.S.—Say howdy to George Carter, and thank him for taking the pistol from you when you were shooting at me.

From your old servant,
Jourdon Anderson

Southern Women Make Do During the Blockade (1888)

Source: Hague, Parthenia A. *A Blockaded Family: Life in Southern Alabama During the Civil War.* Bedford, MA: Applewood Press, 1995.

Commentary
The Union blockade of Southern ports caused shortages of vital household goods. In these excerpts from her 1888 book *A Blockaded Family*, Parthenia Hague describes how families in the Confederacy dealt with some of them. Hague lived on a plantation in Alabama during the Civil War.

The obtaining of salt became extremely difficult when the war had cut off our supply. This was true especially in regions remote from the sea-coast and border States, such as the interior of Alabama and Georgia. Here again we were obliged to have recourse to whatever expedient ingenuity suggested. All the brine left in troughs and barrels, where pork had been salted down, was carefully dipped up, boiled down, and converted into salt again. In some cases the salty soil under old smoke-houses was dug up and placed in hoppers, which resembled backwoods ash-hoppers, make for leaching ashes in the process of soap-manufacture. Water was then poured upon the soil, the brine which percolated through the hopper was boiled down to the proper point, poured into vessels, and set in the sun, which by evaporation completed the rude process. Though never of immaculate whiteness, the salt which resulted from these methods served well enough for all our purposes and we accepted it without complaining.

Before the war there were in the South but few cotton mills. These were kept running night and day, as soon as the Confederate army was organized, and we were ourselves prevented by the blockade from purchasing clothing from the factories at the North, or clothing from France or England. The cotton which grew in the immediate vicinity of the mills kept them well supplied with raw material. Yet notwithstanding the great push of the cotton mills, they proved totally inadequate, after the war began, to our vast need for clothing of every kind. Every household now became a miniature factory in itself, with its cotton, cards, spinning-wheels, warping frames, looms, and so on. Wherever one went, the hum of the spinning wheel and the clang of the batten of the loom was borne on the ear.

Great trouble was experienced, in the beginning to find dyes with which to color our stuffs; but in the course of time, both at the old mills and at smaller experimental factories, which were run entirely by hand, barks, leaves, roots, and berries were found containing coloring properties. I was well acquainted with a gentleman in southwestern Georgia who owned a small cotton mill, and who, when he wanted coloring substances, used to send his wagons to the woods and freight them with a shrub known as myrtle, that grew teeming in low moist places near his mill. This myrtle yielded a nice gray for woolen goods.

That the slaves might be well clad, the owners kept, according to the number of slaves owned, a number of Negro women carding and spinning, and had looms running all the time. Now and then a planter would be so fortunate as to secure a bale or more of white sheeting and osnaburgs from the cotton mills, in exchange for farm products, which would be quite a lift, and give a little breathing-spell from the almost incessant whirr, hum, and clang of the spinning wheel and loom. . . .

One of our most difficult tasks was to find a good substitute for coffee. This palatable drink, if not a real necessary of life, is almost indespensable to the enjoyment of a good meal, and some Southerners took it three times a day. Coffee soon rose to thirty dollars per pound; from that it went to sixty and seventy dollars per pound. Good workmen received thirty dollars per day; so it took two days' hard labor to buy one pound of coffee, and scarcely any could be had even at that fabulous price.

Some imagined themselves much better in health for the absence of coffee, and wondered why they had ever used it at all, and declared it good for nothing any way; but "Sour grapes" would be the reply for such as they. Others saved a few handfuls of coffee, and used it on very important occasions, and then only as an extract, so to speak, for flavoring substitutes for coffee.

There were those who planted long rows of the okra plant on the borders of their cotton or corn fields, and cultivated this with the corn and cotton. The seeds of this, when mature and nicely browned, came nearer in flavor to the real coffee than any other substitute I now remember. Yam potatoes used to be peeled, sliced thin, cut into small squares, dried and then parched brown; they were thought to be next best to okra for coffee. Browned wheat, meal, and burnt corn made passable beverages; even meal-bran was browned and used for coffee if other substitutes were not obtainable.

We had several substitutes for tea which were equally as palatable, and, I fancy, more wholesome, than much that it snow sold for tea. Prominent among these substitutes were raspberry leaves. Many during the blockade planted and cultivated the raspberry-vine all around their garden palings, as much for tea as the berries for jam or pies; these leaves were considered the best substitute for tea. The leaves of the blackberry bush, huckleberry leaves, and the leaves of the holly-tree when dried in the shade, also made a palatable tea. . . .

In place of kerosene for lights, the oil of cotton seed and ground peas, together with the oil of compressed lard, was used, and served well the need of the times. For lights we had also to fall back on moulding candles, which had long years lain obsolete. When beeswax was plentiful it was mixed with tallow for moulding candles. Long rows of candles so moulded would be hung on the lower limbs of widespreading oaks, where, sheltered by the dense foliage from the direct rays of the sun, they would remain suspended day and night until they were bleached as white as the sperm candles we had been wont to buy, and almost as transparent as wax candles.

A Female Nurse at the Frontlines (1889)

Source: Livermore, Mary Ashton Rice. *My Story of the War* (1889). New York: Arno Press, 1972.

Commentary

The author of this account, Mary A. Livermore (1820–1905), spent most of her adult life in Chicago, where she worked with her husband, a Universalist clergyman, on the magazine *The New Covenant*. She was a Chicago-area founder of the United States Sanitary Commission (USSC) and served as a national director of that organization. After the war, she put her energies into the women's suffrage movement.

In this excerpt of Livermore's Civil War memoir, she describes another formidable woman: Mary Ann Ball Bickerdyke (1817–1901), a woman formally trained as a nurse, who was known affectionately as Mother Bickerdyke. She served with the USSC in nineteen battles in the war's western theater. Her contributions were so valuable that General William Tecumseh Sherman specifically requested her for his corps. At the war's end, she rode at the head of her corps in the Grand Review in Washington. After the war, she worked to secure pensions for wounded soldiers. In 1886, she was awarded her own pension.

Among the hundreds of women who devoted a part or the whole of the years of the war to the care of the sick and wounded of the army, "Mother Bickerdyke" stands pre-eminent. Others were as heroic and consecrated as she, as unwearied in labors, and as unselfish and self-sacrificing. But she was unique in method, extraordinary in executive ability, enthusiastic in devotion, and indomitable in will. After her plans were formed, and her purposes matured, she carried them through triumphantly, in the teeth of the most formidable opposition. She gave herself to the rank and file of the army,—the private soldiers,—for whom she had unbounded tenderness, and developed almost limitless resources of help and comfort.

To them she was strength and sweetness; and for them she exercised sound, practical sense, a ready wit, and a rare intelligence, that made her a power in the hospital, or on the field. There was no peril she would not dare for a sick and wounded man, no official red tape of formality for which she cared more than for a common tow string, if it interfered with her in her work of relief. To their honor be it said, the "boys" reciprocated her affection most heartily. "That homely figure, clad in calico, wrapped in a shawl, and surmounted with a 'Shaker' bonnet, is more to this army than the Madonna to a Catholic!" said an officer, pointing to Mother Bickerdyke, as she emerged from the Sanitary Commission head-quarters, in Memphis, laden with an assortment of supplies. Every soldier saluted her as she passed; and those who were at leisure relieved her of her burden, and bore it to its destination. To the entire army of the West she was emphatically "Mother Bickerdyke." Nor have the soldiers forgotten her in her poverty and old age. They remember her to-day in many a tender letter, and send her many a small donation to eke out her scanty and irregular income. . . .

[Bickerdyke] was living in Galesburg, Ill., and was a member of Rev. Dr. Edward Beecher's church when the war of the rebellion broke out. Hardly had the troops reached Cairo, when, from the sudden change in their habits, their own imprudence, and the ignorance of their commanders on all sanitary points, sickness broke out among them. At the suggestion of the ladies of Galesburg, who had organized to do something for the country—they hardly knew what at that time—Mrs. Bickerdyke went down among them. Her well-known skill as a nurse, the fertility of her resources, her burning patriotism, and her possession of that rare combination of qualities which we call "common sense," had always enabled her to face any emergency.

There was at that time little order, system, or discipline anywhere. In company with Mary Safford, then living in Cairo, she commenced an immediate systematic work in the camp and regimental hospitals at Cairo and Bird's Point. In the face of obstacles of every kind, she succeeded in working a great change for the better in the condition of the sick. The influence of her energetic, resolute, and systematic spirit was felt everywhere; and the loyal people of Cairo gladly aided her in her voluntary and unpaid labors. A room was hired for her, and a cooking-stove set up for her especial use. She improvised a sick-diet kitchen, and carried thence to the sick in the hospitals the food she had prepared for them. The first assortment of delicacies for the sick sent to Cairo by the Chicago Sanitary Commission, were given to her for distribution. Almost all the hospital supplies sent from the local societies of Chicago or Illinois, were, for a time, given to her trustworthy care.

After the battle of Belmont she was appointed matron of the large post hospital at Cairo, which was filled with the wounded. She found time, however, to work for, and to visit daily, every other hospital in the town. The surgeon who appointed her was skillful and competent, but given to drunkenness; and he had little sympathy with his patients. He had filled all the positions in the hospitals with surgeons and officers of his sort, and bacchanalian carousals in the "doctor's room" were of frequent occurrence. In twenty-four hours Mother Bickerdyke and he were at swords' points. She denounced him to his face; and, when the garments and delicacies sent her for the use of the sick and wounded disappeared mysteriously, she charged their theft upon him and his subordinates.

He ordered her out of his hospital, and threatened to put her out if she did not hasten her departure. She replied that "she should stay as long as the men needed her—that if he put her out of one door she should come in at another; and if he barred all the doors against her, she should come in at the windows, and that the patients would help her in. When anybody left it would be he, and not she," she assured him, "as she had already lodged complaints against him at headquarters." "Conscience makes cowards of us all"; and he did not proceed to expel her, as he might have done, and probably would, if his cause had been just.

But though she was let alone, this was not the case with her supplies for the sick and wounded—they were stolen continually. She caught a ward-master dressed in the shirt, slippers, and socks that had been sent her, and, seizing him by the collar, in his own ward, she disrobed him sans ceremony before the patients. Leaving him nude save his pantaloons, she uttered this parting injunction: "Now, you rascal, let's see what you'll steal next!" To ascertain who were the thieves of the food she prepared, she resorted to a somewhat dangerous ruse. Purchasing a quantity of tartar emetic at a drug store, she mixed it with some stewed peaches that she had openly cooked in the kitchen, telling Tom, the cook, that "she wanted to leave them on the kitchen table over night to cool." Then she went to her own room to await results.

She did not wait long. Soon the sounds of suffering from the terribly sick thieves reached her ears, when, like a Nemesis, she stalked in among them. There they were, cooks, table-waiters, stewards, ward-masters,—all save some of the surgeons—suffering terribly from the emetic, but more from the apprehension that they were poisoned. "Peaches don't seem to agree with you, eh?" she said, looking on the pale, retching, groaning fellows with a sardonic smile. "Well, let me tell you that you will have a worse time than this if you keep on stealing! You may eat something seasoned with ratsbane one of these nights." . . .

After the battle of Donelson, Mother Bickerdyke went from Cairo in the first hospital boat, and assisted in the removal of the wounded to Cairo, St. Louis, and Louisville, and in nursing those too badly wounded to be moved. The Sanitary Commission had established a depot of stores at Cairo, and on these she was allowed to make drafts ad libitum: for she was as famous for her economical use of sanitary stores as she had been before the war for her notable housewifery. The hospital boats at that time were poorly equipped for the sad work of transporting the wounded. But this thoughtful woman, who made five of the terrible trips from the battle-field of Donelson to the hospital, put on board the boat with which she was connected, before it started from Cairo, an abundance of necessaries. There was hardly a want expressed for which she could not furnish some sort of relief.

On the way to the battle-field, she systematized matters perfectly. The beds were ready for the occupants, tea, coffee, soup and gruel, milk punch and ice water were prepared in large quantities, under her supervision, and sometimes by her own hand. When the wounded were brought on board,—mangled almost out of human shape; the frozen ground from which they had been cut adhering to them; chilled with the intense cold in which some had lain for twenty-four hours; faint with loss of blood, physical agony, and lack of nourishment; racked with a terrible five-mile ride over frozen roads, in ambulances, or common Tennessee farm wagons, without springs; burning with fever; raving in delirium, or in the faintness

of death,—Mother Bickerdyke's boat was in readiness for them.

"I never saw anybody like her," said a volunteer surgeon who came on the boat with her. "There was really nothing for us surgeons to do but dress wounds and administer medicines. She drew out clean shirts or drawers from some corner, whenever they were needed. Nourishment was ready for every man as soon as he was brought on board. Every one was sponged from blood and the frozen mire of the battle-field, as far as his condition allowed. His blood-stiffened, and sometimes horribly filthy uniform, was exchanged for soft and clean hospital garments. Incessant cries of 'Mother! Mother! Mother!' rang through the boat, in every note of beseeching and anguish. And to every man she turned with a heavenly tenderness, as if he were indeed her son. She moved about with a decisive air, and gave directions in such decided, clarion tones as to ensure prompt obedience. We all had an impression that she held a commission from the Secretary of War, or at least from the Governor of Illinois. To every surgeon who was superior, she held herself subordinate, and was as good at obeying as at commanding." And yet, at that time, she held no position whatever, and was receiving no compensation for her services; not even the beggarly pittance of thirteen dollars per month allowed by government to army nurses.

At last it was believed that all the wounded had been removed from the field, and the relief parties discontinued their work. Looking from his tent at midnight, an officer observed a faint light flitting hither and thither on the abandoned battle-field, and, after puzzling over it for some time, sent his servant to ascertain the cause. It was Mother Bickerdyke, with a lantern, still groping among the dead. Stooping down, and turning their cold faces towards her, she scrutinized them searchingly, uneasy lest some might be left to die uncared for. She could not rest while she thought any were overlooked who were yet living. . . .

After the wounded of Donelson were cared for, Mrs. Bickerdyke left the hospitals, and went back into the army. There was great sickness among our troops at Savannah, Tenn. She had already achieved such a reputation for devotion to the men, for executive ability, and versatility of talent, that the spirits of the sick and wounded revived at the very sound of her voice, and at the sight of her motherly face. While busy here, the battle of Shiloh occurred, nine miles distant by the river, but only six in a direct line. There had been little provision made for the terrible needs of the battle-field in advance of the conflict. The battle occurred unexpectedly, and was a surprise to our men,—who nearly suffered defeat,—and again there was utter destitution and incredible suffering.

Three days after the battle, the boats of the Sanitary Commission arrived at the Landing, laden with every species of relief,—condensed food, stimulants, clothing, bedding, medicines, chloroform, surgical instruments, and carefully selected volunteer nurses and surgeons. They were on the ground some days in advance of the government boats.

Here Mother Bickerdyke was found, carrying system, order, and relief wherever she went. One of the surgeons went to the rear with a wounded man, and found her wrapped in the gray overcoat of a rebel officer, for she had disposed of her blanket shawl to some poor fellow who needed it. She was wearing a soft slouch hat, having lost her inevitable Shaker bonnet. Her kettles had been set up, the fire kindled underneath, and she was dispensing hot soup, tea, crackers, panado, whiskey and water, and other refreshments, to the shivering, fainting, wounded men.

"Where did you get these articles?" he inquired; "and under whose authority are you at work?"

She paid no heed to his interrogatories, and, indeed, did not hear them, so completely absorbed was she in her work of compassion. Watching her with admiration for her skill, administrative ability, and intelligence,—for she not only fed the wounded men, but temporarily dressed their wounds in some cases,—he approached her again.

"Madam, you seem to combine in yourself a sick-diet kitchen and a medical staff. May I inquire under whose authority you are working?"

Without pausing in her work, she answered him, "I have received my authority from the Lord God Almighty; have you anything that ranks higher than that?" The truth was, she held no position whatever at that time. She was only a "volunteer nurse," having received no appointment, and being attached to no corps of relief.

The Chicago boat took down over one hundred boxes of sanitary stores, on which she was allowed to draw. But they were only as a drop in the bucket among the twelve thousand wounded, lying in extemporized hospitals in and around Savannah. Other consignments of sanitary goods were made to her from Chicago and Springfield, Ill. The agents of the St. Louis and Cincinnati Commissions gave to her freely, when she made requisition on them. When every other resource failed, Mother Bickerdyke would take an ambulance, and one of her detailed soldiers as driver, and go out foraging. Never returned she empty-handed. The contrabands were her friends and allies; and she always came back with eggs, milk, butter, and fowls, which were the main objects of her quest. These foraging expeditions sometimes placed her in great peril; but she scorned any thought of danger where the welfare of the boys was concerned.

Excerpt from My Life by Geronimo (1906)

Source: Geronimo and Barret, S. M. *Geronimo: His Own Story* (1906). New York: E. P. Dutton, 1970.

Commentary

Geronimo (1829–1909) was a chief, later war chief, of the Chiricahua Apaches of southern Arizona. After evading the Mexican Army and 5,000 U.S. soldiers for 18 months as one of the last holdouts for Indian independence, he surrendered his band of 144, including 101 women and children in 1886. Most subsequently died in Florida, where they were imprisoned at Fort Marion. The children were forcibly removed to the Indian School at Carlisle, Pennsylvania. Geronimo was later brought to Fort Sill, Oklahoma, effectively a prisoner of war until his death in 1909.

In 1906, with permission from President Theodore Roosevelt, he dictated his autobiography to S. M. Barret, an educator who lived near Fort Sill. In the portions reproduced here, Geronimo speaks of the massacre of "Kaskiyeh," in 1858, in which his mother, wife, and children were killed by Mexicans. He also describes his first contacts with the United States and his efforts to keep his people alive and his tribe intact.

About the time of the massacre of "Kaskiyeh" (1858) we heard that some white men were measuring land to the south of us. In company with a number of other warriors, I went to visit them. We could not understand them very well, for we had no interpreter, but we made a treaty with them by shaking hands and promising to be brothers. Then we made our camp near their camp, and they came to trade with us. We gave them buckskin, blankets, and ponies in exchange for shirts and provisions. We also brought them game, for which they gave us some money. We did not know the value of this money, but we kept it and later learned from the Navajo Indians that it was very valuable.

Every day they measured land with curious instruments and put down marks which we could not understand. They were good men, and we were sorry when they had gone on into the west. They were not soldiers. These were the first white men I ever saw.

About ten years later some more white men came. These were all warriors. They made their camp on the Gila River south of Hot Springs. At first they were friendly and we did not dislike them, but they were not as good as those who came first.

After about a year some trouble arose between them and the Indians, and I took the warpath as a warrior, not as a chief. I had not been wronged, but some of my people had been, and I fought with my tribe; for the soldiers and not the Indians were at fault.

Not long after this some of the officers of the United States troops invited our leaders to hold a conference at Apache Pass (Fort Bowie). Just before noon the Indians were shown into a tent and told that they would be given something to eat. When in the tent they were attacked by soldiers. Our chief, Mangus-Colorado, and several other warriors, by cutting through the tent, escaped; but most of the warriors were killed or captured. Among the Bedonkohe Apaches killed at this time were Sanza, Kladetahe, Niyokahe, and Gopi. After this treachery the Indians went back to the mountains and left the fort entirely alone. I do not think that the agent had anything to do with planning this, for he had always treated us well. I believe it was entirely planned by the soldiers.

From the very first the soldiers sent out to our western country, and the officers in charge of them, did not hesitate to wrong the Indians. They never explained to the Government when an Indian was wronged, but always reported the misdeeds of the Indians. Much that was done by mean white men was reported at Washington as the deeds of my people.

The Indians always tried to live peaceably with the white soldiers and settlers. One day during the time that the soldiers were stationed at Apache Pass I made a treaty with the post. This was done by shaking hands and promising to be brothers. Cochise and Mangus-Colorado did likewise. I do not know the name of the officer in command, but this was the first regiment that ever came to Apache Pass. This treaty was made about a year before we were attacked in a tent, as above related. In a few days after the attack at Apache Pass we organized in the mountains and returned to fight the soldiers. There were two tribes—the Bedonkohe and the Chokonen Apaches, both commanded by Cochise. After a few days' skirmishing we attacked a freight train that was coming in with supplies for the Fort. We killed some of the men and captured the others. These prisoners our chief offered to trade for the Indians whom the soldiers had captured at the massacre in the tent. This the officers refused, so we killed our prisoners, disbanded, and went into hiding in the mountains. Of those who took part in this affair I am the only one now living.

In a few days troops were sent out to search for us, but as we were disbanded, it was, of course, impossible for them to locate any hostile camp. During the time they were searching for us many of our warriors (who were thought by the soldiers to be peaceable Indians) talked to the officers and men, advising them where they might find the camp they sought, and while they searched we watched them from our hiding places and laughed at their failures.

After this trouble all of the Indians agreed not to be friendly with the white men any more. There was no general engagement, but a long struggle followed. Sometimes we attacked the white men—sometimes they attacked us. First a few Indians would be killed and then a few soldiers. I think the killing was about equal on each side. The number killed in these troubles did not amount to

much, but this treachery on the part of the soldiers had angered the Indians and revived memories of other wrongs, so that we never again trusted the United States troops.

Perhaps the greatest wrong ever done to the Indians was the treatment received by our tribe from the United States troops about 1863. The chief of our tribe, Mangus-Colorado, went to make a treaty of peace for our people with the white settlement at Apache Tejo, New Mexico. It had been reported to us that the white men in this settlement were more friendly and more reliable than those in Arizona, that they would live up to their treaties and would not wrong the Indians.

Mangus-Colorado, with three other warriors, went to Apache Tejo and held a council with these citizens and soldiers. They told him that if he would come with his tribe and live near them, they would issue to him, from the Government, blankets, flour, provisions, beef, and all manner of supplies. Our chief promised to return to Apache Tejo within two weeks. When he came back to our settlement he assembled the whole tribe in council. I did not believe that the people at Apache Tejo would do as they said and therefore I opposed the plan, but it was decided that with part of the tribe Mangus-Colorado should return to Apache Tejo and receive an issue of rations and supplies. If they were as represented, and if these white men would keep the treaty faithfully, the remainder of the tribe would join him and we would make our permanent home at Apache Tejo. I was to remain in charge of that portion of the tribe which stayed in Arizona. We gave almost all of our arms and ammunition to the party going to Apache Tejo, so that in case there should be treachery they would be prepared for any surprise. Mangus-Colorado and about half of our people went to New Mexico, happy that now they had found white men who would be kind to them, and with whom they could live in peace and plenty.

No word ever came to us from them. From other sources, however, we heard that they had been treacherously captured and slain. In this dilemma we did not know just exactly what to do, but fearing that the troops who had captured them would attack us, we retreated into the mountains near Apache Pass.

During the weeks that followed the departure of our people we had been in suspense, and failing to provide more supplies, had exhausted all of our store of provisions. This was another reason for moving camp. On this retreat, while passing through the mountains, we discovered four men with a herd of cattle. Two of the men were in front in a buggy and two were behind on horse-back. We killed all four, but did not scalp them; they were not warriors. We drove the cattle back into the mountains, made a camp, and began to kill the cattle and pack the meat.

Before we had finished this work we were surprised and attacked by United States troops, who killed in all seven Indians—one warrior, three women, and three children. The Government troops were mounted and so were we, but we were poorly armed, having given most of our weapons to the division of our tribe that had gone to Apache Tejo, so we fought mainly with spears, bows, and arrows. At first I had a spear, a bow, and a few arrows; but in a short time my spear and all my arrows were gone. Once I was surrounded, but by dodging from side to side of my horse as he ran I escaped. It was necessary during this fight for many of the warriors to leave their horses and escape on foot. But my horse was trained to come at call, and as soon as I reached a safe place, if not too closely pursued, I would call him to me. During this fight we scattered in all directions and two days later reassembled at our appointed place of rendezvous, about fifty miles from the scene of this battle.

About ten days later the same United States troops attacked our new camp at sunrise. The fight lasted all day, but our arrows and spears were all gone before ten o'clock, and for the remainder of the day we had only rocks and clubs with which to fight. We could do little damage with these weapons, and at night we moved our camp about four miles back into the mountains where it would be hard for the cavalry to follow us. The next day our scouts, who had been left behind to observe the movements of the soldiers, returned, saying that the troops had gone back toward San Carlos Reservation.

A few days after this we were again attacked by another company of United States troops. Just before this fight we had been joined by a band of Chokonen Indians under Cochise, who took command of both divisions. We were repulsed, and decided to disband.

After we had disbanded our tribe the Bedonkohe Apaches reassembled near their old camp vainly waiting for the return of Mangus-Colorado and our kinsmen. No tidings came save that they had all been treacherously slain. Then a council was held, and as it was believed that Mangus-Colorado was dead, I was elected Tribal Chief.

For a long time we had no trouble with anyone. It was more than a year after I had been made Tribal Chief that United States troops surprised and attacked our camp. They killed seven children, five women, and four warriors, captured all our supplies, blankets, horses, and clothing, and destroyed our tepees. We had nothing left; winter was beginning, and it was the coldest winter I ever knew. After the soldiers withdrew I took three warriors and trailed them. Their trail led back toward San Carlos.

While returning from trailing the Government troops we saw two men, a Mexican and a white man, and shot them off their horses. With these two horses we returned and moved our camp. My people were suffering much and it was deemed advisable to go where we could get more provisions. Game was scarce in our range then, and since I had been Tribal Chief I had not asked for rations from the Government, nor did I care to do so, but we did not wish to starve.

We had heard that Chief Victoria of the Chihenne (Oje Caliente) Apaches was holding a council with the white men near Hot Springs in New Mexico, and that he had plenty of provisions. We had always been on friendly terms with this tribe, and Victoria was especially kind to my people. With the help of the two horses we had captured, to carry our sick with us, we went to Hot Springs. We easily found Victoria and his band, and they gave us supplies for the winter. We stayed with them for about a year, and during this stay we had perfect peace. We had not the least trouble with Mexicans, white men, or Indians. When we had stayed as long as we should, and had again accumulated some supplies, we decided to leave Victoria's band. When I told him that we were going to leave he said that we should have a feast and dance before we separated.

The festivities were held about two miles above Hot Springs, and lasted for four days. There were about four hundred Indians at this celebration. I do not think we ever spent a more pleasant time than upon this occasion. No one ever treated our tribe more kindly than Victoria and his band. We are still proud to say that he and his people were our friends.

When I went to Apache Pass (Fort Bowie) I found General Howard in command, and made a treaty with him. This treaty lasted until long after General Howard had left our country. He always kept his word with us and treated us as brothers. We never had so good a friend among the United States officers as General Howard. We could have lived forever at peace with him. If there is any pure, honest white man in the United States army, that man is General Howard. All the Indians respect him, and even to this day frequently talk of the happy times when General Howard was in command of our Post. After he went away he placed an agent at Apache Pass who issued to us from the Government clothing, rations, and supplies, as General Howard directed. When beef was issued to the Indians I got twelve steers for my tribe, and Cochise got twelve steers for his tribe. Rations were issued about once a month, but if we ran out we only had to ask and we were supplied. Now, as prisoners of war in this Reservation, we do not get such good rations.

Excerpt from My Army Life (1910)

Source: Carrington, Frances C. *My Army Life and the Fort Phil Kearney Massacre, with an Account of the Celebration of "Wyoming Opened."* Freeport, NY: Books for Libraries Press, 1971.

Commentary

Fort Phil Kearny was built near present-day Story, Wyoming in 1866 to protect travelers on the Bozeman Trail from attacks by the Sioux. In the first six months of its existence, it was attacked repeatedly by the Sioux, who surrounded the compound with the so-called "Circle of Death." After more than 150 soldiers were killed, the fort was abandoned under the terms of the 1868 Treaty of Fort Laramie.

Frances Carrington was the second wife of Colonel Henry B. Carrington, who oversaw the construction of Fort Phil Kearny. Her memoir, published about forty years after the fort was abandoned, gives a revealing account of the privations and dangers of life in the northern Wyoming encampment. Though under constant attack from both the elements and the Sioux, Mrs. Carrington makes it clear she worked hard to achieve and maintain basic standards of housekeeping and domestic order.

CHAPTER XIII.

Domesticities and New Friendships.

The residents of Fort Phil. Kearney were not troubled with ennui. While the men were busy in their departments of labor, the ladies were no less occupied in their accustomed activities. "Baking, brewing, stewing, and sewing" was the alliterative expression of the daily routine. With little fresh meat other than juiceless wild game, buffalo, elk, deer, or mountain sheep, and no vegetables, canned stuffs were in immediate and constant requisition. Once, indeed, Mr. Bozeman sent a few sacks of potatoes from his ranch in Montana to headquarters, as precious as grain in the sacks of Israels sons in Egypt; but these were doled out in small quantities to officers families, while the remainder, the major part, was sent to the hospital for men afflicted or threatened with scurvy.

The preparation of edible from canned fruits, meats, and vegetables taxed all ingenuity to evolve some product, independent of mere stewing, for successful results. Calico, flannel, and linsey woolsey, procured from the sutlers store, with gray army blankets as material for little boys overcoats, composed the staple goods required, and ladies garments, evolved after the "hit or miss" style, came in due time without the aid of sewing machines, of which none were at the post. Our buffalo boots were of a pattern emanating from or necessitated by our frontier locality, a counterpart of the leggings worn by the men, except that theirs did not have the shoe attachment. They were made by the company shoemakers of harness leather, to which was attached buffalo skin, with the hair inside, reaching almost to the knee and fastened on the outside with leather straps and brass buttons. The brass buttons were not for ornament, but a necessity in lieu of any other available kind. Nothing could exceed them in comfort, as a means adapted to an end.

There were hours when one could sit down composedly for a bit of sewing in a comfortable chair, with additional pleasure in the possession of a table sufficiently large for the double duty of dining and work table. With the few books I had carried with me for companionship distributed about, there was just a bit of homelikeness in tent life. My cooking experiments were never a great success, especially in the attempt at making pies, though I tried to emulate the ladies of larger experience in the effort. The cook-stove rested upon boards somewhat inclined, which was fatal to pie-making, which I did attempt a few times from canned fruit only to find in due time well developed crusts minus the fruit, which had oozed out gradually during the process, still in evidence of my good intentions, and to be eaten with as much philosophy as one could command with a straight face, disguising laughter, or tears.

Through the kind consideration of Mrs. Carrington, a large double bedstead was made by the carpenters, a luxury indeed, with mattress stuffed with dried grass, army blankets, and a large gay-colored shawl for counterpane, and surely no four-poster of mahogany, with valences of richest texture and downy pillows, and, for that matter, no Chippendale table, with these furniture accessories, could have been more prized during my life at the fort, as a demonstration of the simple life theory in every detail, whether enforced or otherwise.

Often, while reading or sewing quietly by myself, I would be startled by a rustling at my tent door, but fears were soon allayed when I discovered the beautiful head of Mrs. Hortons pet antelope protruding within. Its large, melting eyes would look at me appealingly, and, with sufficient encouragement, it would approach for the accustomed caress and favorite bite to eat.

Of the little children at the fort there were four boys, and many pleasant hours were spent in my tent with Jimmy Carrington, my little favorite, whose loving disposition made him a welcome guest. No picknickers of the pine woods ever enjoyed a repast so much as we did, after our simple preparations, involving a trip to the sutlers store, where cans of sugar were obtained, each with a mysterious-looking little bottle of lemon essence deposited therein, from which we produced lemonade, and this, together with ginger-snaps and nuts, made a "dainty dish fit for a King," never mind about the birds. After the repast was the song. He possessed a remarkably sweet voice, and together we sang familiar Sunday School hymns his mother had taught him, one of which I especially recall, "There is a light in the window for me," and his sweet childish tones sang the words deeply into my heart.

Sunday evening singing at headquarters was a feature of the day. Neither was Sunday morning service neglected, for, though no chapel had as yet been erected, each new building in turn was utilized for the service. With a fine string band to accompany the voices, and sometimes additional instruments, the presence of God was felt and recognized in this impromptu worship. Several of the band were German Catholics and good singers. On one occasion especial pains had been taken by the Colonel to make the music an attractive specialty to interest the men. The chaplain, Rev. David White, was a devout Methodist, of good heart and excellent in teaching the soldiers children at the fort, for there were several, but very unsophisticated in general society matters. On one occasion, when great care had secured the rendition of "Te Deum Laudamus," in which the band took part, he very solemnly asked the Colonel, "Isnt that a Catholic tune?" and upon answer by the Colonel, "Why, that is one of the oldest and most glorious hymns of the Church all over Christendon," he expressed surprise, but thought himself that "it seemed to be quite religious, but it was new to him."

With a coterie of five ladies at the post, each had four places to visit, and the most was made of it in comparing notes upon the important matters of cooking, sewing, and our various steps of advancement in the different arts, quite independently of prevailing fashions of dress in the States, and yet this did not signify entire emancipation, for the problem was still a little perplexing in the evolution of new ideas, while mutual helpfulness simplified all our efforts. There was often an all-round social dance, games of cards, the "authors game," and other contrivances for recreation and amusement, in addition to the receptions at headquarters, which were spirited and congenial, and, with a band having the deserved reputation of being the finest in the army, their choice music was no small feature in the cheer on the frontier.

LITERATURE AND SONGS

"Battle Hymn of the Republic" (1861)

Commentary

"The Battle Hymn of the Republic" was a popular marching song among Union troops during the Civil War. Julia Ward Howe (1801–1876) wrote the rousing lyrics in November 1861. She set the words to the tune of a hymn composed by William Steffe around 1856. The tune was already an infantry favorite because of its snappy cadence and soldiers often created their own verses to match its tempo. Howe reportedly heard an obscene version of the song while visiting a Union army encampment and decided to write words more fitting the tune's origin as a hymn. Her "Battle Hymn" was included in Union Army hymnbooks carried by many soldiers. Its religious motif is interlaced with military themes, epitomized in the famous line "As [Christ] died to make men holy, / Let us die to make men free." The song represents the soldiers' adoption of the shift in federal war aims from preserving the Union to ending slavery.

Mine eyes have seen the glory of the coming of the
    Lord;
He is trampling out the vintage where the grapes of
    wrath are stored;
He hath loos'd the fateful lightning of His terrible
    swift sword,
His truth is marching on.

Chorus:
Glory, glory Hallelujah! Glory, glory Hallelujah! Glory,
    glory Hallelujah! His truth is marching on.

I have seen Him in the watch fires of a hundred
    circling camps;
They have builded Him an altar in the ev'ning
    dews and damps;
I can read His righteous sentence by the dim and
    flaring lamps,
His day is marching on.

Chorus

I have read a fiery gospel writ in burnish'd rows of
    steel:
"As ye deal with My contemners, so with you My
    grace shall deal";
Let the Hero born of woman crush the serpent
    with His heel,
Since God is marching on.

Chorus

He has sounded forth the trumpet that shall never
    call retreat;
He is sifting out the hearts of men before His
    judgment seat,
Oh, be swift, my soul, to answer Him! Be jubilant
    my feet!
Our God is marching on.

Chorus

In the beauty of the lilies Christ was born across
    the sea,
With a glory in His bosom that transfigures you
    and me;
As He died to make men holy let us die to make
    men free,
While God is marching on.

Chorus

"Vacant Chair" (1861)

Commentary

George F. Root (1820–1895) wrote the words and music to many of the tunes most popular with Union soldiers and others in the North during the Civil War. Soldiers still sang his "Tramp, Tramp, Tramp" nearly a century later. While this song made a less enduring impression, it appealed to both Union and Confederate families. It is representative of the sentimental style of its day, as well as of the very real suffering of so many families who lost men to the battlefield.

We shall meet but we shall miss him,
There will be one vacant chair;
░░░░░░░░░░░░░░░░░░░░░░
While we breathe our evening prayer.
When a year ago we gathered,
Joy was in his mild blue eye;
But a golden cord is severed,
And our hopes in ruins lie.

Chorus:
We shall meet but we shall miss him,
There will be one vacant chair;
We shall linger to caress him
While we breathe our evening prayer.

At our fireside sad and lonely,
Often will the bosom swell
At remembrance of the story
How our noble soldier fell;
How he strove to bear our banner
Through the thickest of the fight
And uphold our country's honor
In the strength of manhood's might.

Chorus

"New Colossus" (1883)

Source: Lazarus, Emma. *The Poems of Emma Lazarus*. Boston and New York: Houghton, Mifflin, 1889.

Commentary

Her first book, published when she was not yet eighteen years old, earned Emma Lazarus (1849–1887) the attention of Ralph Waldo Emerson and other eminent writers. In addition to her writings, she became active on behalf of Russian Jews in 1882, supporting the Zionist cause as well as working with immigrants in New York City. Her devotion to refugees fueled this, her most famous poem. It was auctioned along with contributions from Longfellow, Whitman, and Twain in an 1883 effort to raise funds for the pedestal of the Statue of Liberty. Years after Lazarus's death at age thirty-eight, a campaign by one of her friends resulted in a bronze plaque inscribed with its text being mounted on the statue's base in 1903. Over the years it has been set to music and memorized by generations of school children.

Not like the brazen giant of Greek fame,
With conquering limbs astride from land to land;
Here at our sea-washed, sunset gates shall stand
A mighty woman with a torch, whose flame
Is the imprisoned lightning, and her name
Mother of Exiles. From her beacon-hand
Glows world-wide welcome; her mild eyes command
The air-bridged harbor that twin cities frame.
"Keep, ancient lands, your storied pomp!" cries she

With silent lips. "Give me your tired, your poor,
Your huddled masses yearning to breathe free,
The wretched refuse of your teeming shore.
Send these, the homeless, tempest-tost tome,
I lift my lamp beside the golden door!"

REPORTS, SPEECHES, AND DECLARATIONS

Unanimous Declaration of Independence by Texans (1836)

Commentary

In 1820 Moses Austin, acting as a private U.S. citizen, negotiated an agreement with Spain that granted him a large tract of land in northern Mexico where he was to settle three hundred families. The families were to practice the Catholic religion and in time become properly Mexicanized. The settlers, born and raised in the United States, resented the restrictions imposed by a "foreign" government as well as the presence of Mexican soldiers. Furthermore, free from Spain by 1830, Mexico abolished slavery and prohibited the importation of slaves, but the majority of Texans hailed from southern states and continued the practice.

With roughly 30,000 Texas-Americans inhabiting the region , relations between Texas and Mexico deteriorated. When Stephen Austin, Moses's son, attempted to negotiate their differences, the Mexican leader Antonio Lopez de Santa Anna imprisoned him for eight months. In 1835, Santa Anna eliminated all local rights and began to organize a military reprisal. Later that year, Texans issued a preliminary declaration of independence. In March of 1836, a Mexican army under Santa Anna crossed the border and wiped out a band of Texans at the Alamo in San Antonio. That same month a Texas convention wrote a formal declaration of independence and also a constitution modeled closely on that of the United States. The following month, Santa Anna was defeated at San Jacinto. Texas gained its independence, and remained an independent republic until joining the United States in 1845.

When a government has ceased to protect the lives liberty and property of its people, from whom its legitimate powers are derived, and for the advancement of whose happiness it was instituted, and so far from being a guarantee for the enjoyment of those inestimable and inalienable rights, becomes an instrument in the hands of evil rulers for their oppression: When the Federal Republican Constitution of their country, which they have sworn to support, no longer has a substantial existence, and the whole nature of their government has been forcibly changed without their consent, from a restricted federative republic, composed of sovereign states to a consolidated central military despotism in which every interest is disregarded but that of the army and the priesthood—both the eternal enemies of civil liberty, the ever-ready minions of power, and the usual instruments of tyrants:

When, long after the spirit of the constitution has departed, moderation is at length so far lost by those in power that even the semblance of freedom is removed, and the forms, themselves, of the constitution discontinued; and so far from their petitions and remonstrances being regarded, the agents who bear them are thrown into dungeons; and mercenary armies sent forth to force a new government upon them at the point of the bayonet: When, in consequence of such acts of malfeasance and abdication, on the part of the government, anarchy prevails, and Civil Society is dissolved into its original elements. In such a crisis, the first law of nature, the right of self-preservation—the inherent and unalienable right of the people to appeal to first principles and take their political affairs into their own hands in extreme cases enjoins it as a right towards themselves and a sacred obligation to their posterity to abolish such government and create another in its stead, calculated to rescue them from impending dangers, and to secure their future welfare and happiness.

Nations, as well as individuals, are amenable for their acts to the public opinion of mankind. Statement of a part of our grievance is, therefore, submitted to an impartial world, in justification of the hazardous but unavoidable step now taken of severing our political connection with the Mexican people, and assuming an independent attitude among the nations of the earth.

The Mexican government, by its colonization laws, invited and induced the Anglo-American population of Texas to colonize its wilderness under the pledged faith of a written constitution that they should continue to enjoy that constitutional liberty and republican government to which they had been habituated in the land of their birth, the United States of America. In this expectation they have been cruelly disappointed, in as much as the Mexican nation has acquiesced in the late changes made in the government by General Antonio Lopez de Santa Anna, who, having overturned the constitution of his country, now offers as the cruel alternative either to abandon our homes, acquired by so many privations, or submit to the most intolerable of all tyranny, the combined despotism of the sword and the priesthood.

It has sacrificed our welfare to the State of Coahuila, by which our interests have been continually depressed through a jealous and partial course of legislation carried on at a far distant seat of government by a hostile majority, in an unknown tongue; and this too, notwithstanding we have petitioned in the humblest terms, for the establishment of a separate state government, and have, in accordance with the provisions of the national constitution presented to the General Congress a republican constitution which was, without just cause, contemptuously rejected.

It incarcerated in a dungeon, for a long time, one of our citizens, for no other cause but a zealous endeavor to procure the acceptance of our constitution and the establishment of a state government.

It has failed and refused to secure on a firm basis, the right of trial by jury, that palladium of civil liberty, and only safe guarantee for the life, liberty and property of the citizen.

It has failed to establish any public system of education, although possessed of almost boundless resources (the public domain) and although it is an axiom in political science, that unless a people are educated and enlightened it is idle to expect the continuance of civil liberty, or the capacity for self-government.

It has suffered the military commandants stationed among us to exercise arbitrary acts of oppression and tyranny; thus trampling upon the most sacred rights of the citizen and rendering the military superior to the civil power.

It has dissolved by force of arms, the State Congress of Cohuila and Texas, and obliged our representatives to fly for their lives from the seat of government; thus depriving us of the fundamental political right of representation.

It has demanded the surrender of a number of our citizens and ordered military detachments to seize and carry them into the Interior for trial; in contempt of the civil authorities, and in defiance of the laws and the constitution.

It has made piratical attacks upon our commerce, by commissioning foreign desperadoes, and authorizing them to seize our vessels, and convey the property of our citizens to far distant ports for confiscation.

It denies us the right of worshipping the Almighty according to the dictates of our own conscience, by the support of a national religion calculated to promote the temporal interest of its human functionaries rather than the glory of the true and living God.

It has demanded us to deliver up our arms, which are essential to our defence, the rightful property of freemen, and formidable only to tyranical governments.

It has invaded our country by sea and by land, with intent to lay waste our territory and drive us from our homes, and has now a large mercenary army advancing to carry on against us a war of extermination.

It has, through its emisaries, incited the merciless savage, with the tomahawk and scalping knife, to massacre the inhabitants of our defenceless frontiers.

It hath been, during the whole time of our connection with it, the contemptible sport and victim of successive military revolutions, and hath continually exhibited every characteristic of a weak, corrupt, and tyrannical government.

These, and other grievances, were patiently borne by the people of Texas untill they reached that point at which forbearance ceases to be a virtue. We then took up arms in defence of the national constitution. We appealed to our Mexican brethren for assistance. Our appeal has been made in vain. Though months have elapsed, no sympathetic response has yet been heard from the Interior. We are, therefore, forced to the melancholy conclusion that the Mexican people have acquiesced in the destruction of their liberty and the substitution therefore of a Military Government—that they are unfit to be free and incapable of self-government.

The necessity of self-preservation, therefore, now decrees our eternal political separation.

We therefore, the delegates with plenary powers, of the people of Texas, in solemn convention assembled, appealing to a candid world for the necessities of our condition, do hereby resolve and declare that our political connection with the Mexican Nation has forever ended; and that the people of Texas do now constitute a free sovereign and independent republic, and are fully invested with all the rights and attributes which properly belong to independent nations; and conscious of the rectitude of our intentions, we fearlessly and confidently commit the issue to the decision of the Supreme Arbiter of the destinies of Nations.

Richard Ellis, President.
Test:
H. S. Kimble, Secretary.

Seneca Falls Declaration of Rights and Sentiments (1848)

Source: Anthony, Susan B.; Stanton, Elizabeth Cady; and Gage, Matilda Joslyn, eds. *The History of Woman Suffrage.* Rochester, NY: S. Anthony, 1889.

Commentary

In drafting *The Declaration of Rights and Sentiments* the day before the first women's rights convention at Seneca Falls, New York (July 19 and 20, 1848) Elizabeth Cady Stanton, Mary Ann McClintock, Martha Wright, Lucretia Mott, and Jane Hunt read aloud the Declaration of Independence. Instantly they decided to pattern their *Declaration of Rights and Sentiments* on the historic document of 1776. First, they changed the dictatorial "King George" to "all men." Then, seeing that the Declaration listed 18 grievances, they also listed 18 injuries felt by women. Demanding that the rights in the Declaration of Independence apply to women as well as men, they reworded this document to include women: "We hold these truths to be self-evident: that all men are created equal . . . " became "We hold these truths to be self-evident: that all men and women are created equal . . . " The *Declaration of Sentiments* was followed by a list of resolutions demanding that women be allowed to speak in public, be accorded equal treatment under the law, receive equal education, equal access to trades and professions, equality in marriage, the right to sue and be sued, to testify in court, to have guardianship over children and, at the insistence of Elizabeth Cady Stanton, be granted the vote. Stanton's husband, Henry, was so upset over the demand for the vote that he left town the day of the convention.

On July 19, "crowds in carriages and on foot, wended their way to the Wesleyan church." Elizabeth Cady Stanton, terrified, gave her first speech. And quite a speech it was, holding the attention of everyone in the chapel. Then followed the resolutions and discussions. All resolutions passed unanimously except resolution nine, calling for the vote. This one squeaked by, with Cady Stanton and famed African-American speaker and editor Frederick Douglass persisting until it was approved.

When, in the course of human events, it becomes necessary for one portion of the family of man to assume among the people of the earth a position different from that which they have hitherto occupied, but one to which the laws of nature and of nature's God entitle them, a decent respect to the opinions of mankind requires that they should declare the causes that impel them to such a course.

We hold these truths to be self-evident: that all men and women are created equal; that they are endowed by their Creator with certain inalienable rights; that among these are life, liberty, and the pursuit of happiness; that to secure these rights governments are instituted, deriving their just powers from the consent of the governed. Whenever any form of government becomes destructive of these ends, it is the right of those who suffer from it to refuse allegiance to it, and to insist upon the institution of a new government, laying its foundation on such principles, and organizing its powers in such form, as to them shall seem most likely to effect their safety and happiness. Prudence indeed, will dictate that governments long established should not be changed for light and transient causes; and accordingly all experience hath shown that mankind are more disposed to suffer, while evils are sufferable, than to right themselves by abolishing the forms to which they were accustomed. But when a long train of abuses and usurpations, pursuing invariably the same object evinces a design to reduce them under absolute despotism, it is their duty to throw off such government, and to provide new guards for their future security. Such has been the patient sufferance of the women under this government, and such is now the necessity which constrains them to demand the equal station to which they are entitled.

The history of mankind is a history of repeated injuries and usurpations on the part of man toward woman, having in direct object the establishment of an absolute tyranny over her. To prove this, let facts be submitted to a candid world.

He has never permitted her to exercise her inalienable right to the elective franchise.

He has compelled her to submit to laws, in the formation of which she had no voice.

He has withheld from her rights which are given to the most ignorant and degraded men—both natives and foreigners.

Having deprived her of this first right of a citizen, the elective franchise, thereby leaving her without representation in the halls of legislation, he has oppressed her on all sides.

He has made her, if married, in the eye of the law, civilly dead.

He has taken from her all right in property, even to the wages she earns.

He has made her, morally, an irresponsible being, as she can commit many crimes with impunity, provided they be done in the presence of her husband. In the covenant of marriage, she is compelled to promise obedience to her husband, he becoming, to all intents and purposes, her master—the law giving him power to deprive her of her liberty, and to administer chastisement.

He has so framed the laws of divorce, as to what shall be the proper causes, and in the case of separation, to whom the guardianship of the children shall be given, as to be wholly regardless of the happiness of women—the law, in all cases, going upon a false supposition of the supremacy of man, and giving all power into his hands.

After depriving her of all rights as a married woman, if single, and the owner of property, he has taxed her to support a government which recognizes her only when her property can be made profitable to it.

He has monopolized nearly all the profitable employments, and from those she is permitted to follow, she receives but a scanty remuneration. He closes against her all the avenues to wealth and distinction which he considers most honorable to himself. As a teacher of theology, medicine, or law, she is not known.

He has denied her the facilities for obtaining a thorough education, all colleges being closed against her.

He allows her in Church, as well as State, but a subordinate position, claiming Apostolic authority for her exclusion from the ministry, and, with some exceptions, from any public participation in the affairs of the Church.

He has created a false public sentiment by giving to the world a different code of morals for men and women, by which moral delinquencies which exclude women from society, are not only tolerated, but deemed of little account in man.

He has usurped the prerogative of Jehovah himself, claiming it as his right to assign for her a sphere of action, when that belongs to her conscience and to her God.

He has endeavored, in every way that he could, to destroy her confidence in her own powers, to lessen her self-respect, and to make her willing to lead a dependent and abject life.

Now, in view of this entire disfranchisement of one-half the people of this country, their social and religious degradation—in view of the unjust laws above mentioned, and because women do feel themselves aggrieved, oppressed, and fraudulently deprived of their most sacred rights, we insist that they have immediate admission to all the rights and privileges which belong to them as citizens of the United States.

In entering upon the great work before us, we anticipate no small amount of misconception, misrepresentation, and ridicule; but we shall use every instrumentality within our power to effect our object. We shall employ agents, circulate tracts, petition the State and National legislatures, and endeavor to enlist the pulpit and the press in our behalf. We hope this Convention will be followed by a series of Conventions embracing every part of the country.

[RESOLUTIONS]

Whereas, The great precept of nature is conceded to be, that "man shall pursue his own true and substantial happiness." Blackstone in his Commentaries remarks, that this law of Nature being coeval with mankind, and dictated by God himself, is of course superior in obligation to any other. It is binding over all the globe, in all countries and at all times; no human laws are of any validity if contrary to this, and such of them as are valid, derive all their force, and all their validity, and all their authority, mediately and immediately, from this original; therefore,

Resolved, That such laws as conflict, in any way, with the true and substantial happiness of woman, are contrary to the great precept of nature and of no validity, for this is "superior in obligation to any other."

Resolved, That all laws which prevent woman from occupying such a station in society as her conscience shall dictate, or which place her in a position inferior to that of man, are contrary to the great precept of nature, and therefore of no force or authority.

Resolved, That woman is man's equal—was intended to be so by the Creator, and the highest good of the race demands that she should be recognized as such.

Resolved, That the women of this country ought to be enlightened in regard to the laws under which they live, that they may no longer publish their degradation by declaring themselves satisfied with their present position, nor their ignorance, by asserting that they have all the rights they want.

Resolved, That inasmuch as man, while claiming for himself intellectual superiority, does accord to woman moral superiority, it is pre-eminently his duty to encourage her to speak and teach, as she has an opportunity, in all religious assemblies.

Resolved, That the same amount of virtue, delicacy, and refinement of behavior that is required of woman in the social state, should also be required of man, and the same transgressions should be visited with equal severity on both man and woman.

Resolved, That the objection of indelicacy and impropriety, which is so often brought against woman when she addresses a public audience, comes with a very ill-grace from those who encourage, by their attendance, her appearance on the state, in the concert, or in feats of the circus.

Resolved, That woman has too long rested satisfied in the circumscribed limits which corrupt customs and a perverted application of the Scriptures have marked out for her, and that it is time she should move in the enlarged sphere which her great Creator has assigned her.

Resolved, That it is the duty of the women of this country to secure to themselves their sacred right to the elective franchise.

Resolved, That the equality of human rights results necessarily from the fact of the identity of the race in capabilities and responsibilities.

Resolved, therefore, That, being invested by the Creator with the same capabilities, and the same consciousness of responsibility for their exercise, it is demonstrably the right and duty of woman, equally with man, to promote every righteous cause by every righteous means; and especially in regard to the great subjects of morals and religion, it is self-evidently her right to participate with her brother in teaching them, both in private and in public, by writing and by speaking, by any instrumentalities proper to be used, and in any assemblies proper to be held; and this being a self-evident truth growing out of the divinely implanted principles of human nature, any custom or authority adverse to it, whether modern or wearing the hoary sanction of antiquity, is to be regarded as a self-evident falsehood, and at war with mankind.

At the last session Lucretia Mott offered and spoke to the following resolution:

Resolved, That the speedy success of our cause depends upon the zealous and untiring efforts of both men and women, for the overthrow of the monopoly of the pulpit, and for the securing to woman an equal participation with men in the various trades, professions, and commerce.

Excerpt of Report of the New York City Draft Riots (1863)

Commentary

In the summer of 1863 there was ample reason for tension in New York City. Having failed to meet their federally prescribed enlistment quotas, most city wards faced forced conscription. Meanwhile, the issuance of President Abraham Lincoln's Emancipation Proclamation back in January—and the subsequent decision to arm black troops—had introduced a new element into the conflict. Now the war was about slavery as well as about the Union. New York had a powerful Democratic party as well as a sizable population of working-class immigrants who objected to conscription, disliked emancipation, and worried about their own economic futures if they were going to have to compete with black laborers.

The draft typically occurred over the course of several days, with names announced at public drawings. Those who were selected were to come forward and either furnish a substitute, claim an exemption, or prepare for service. Following a calm first day, New York City erupted in three days of rioting after a mob attacked one of the draft offices. More than a hundred people, mostly rioters, died in the draft riot. One of the most tragic—and revealing—aspects of the riot was the vicious treatment of African-Americans. This probably reflected both hostility to federal policies and long-standing racial tensions in the city.

This newspaper story provides an assortment of information to help explain what happened and how it was interpreted by local citizens. The author blames "a few wire-pullers" for the actions of the mob, implying that the rioters were (figuratively) controlled by unseen elite puppeteers. And although he attributes the violence to men, he notes that they were urged on by crowds of women and children. Other accounts found women among the rioters; they made up nearly ten percent of those arrested.

Order was finally restored in New York when Union troops arrived, fresh from the Battle of Gettysburg, Pennsylvania. Other towns and cities watched the violence in horror and were spurred on to more rigorous recruiting so that they would be spared a potentially disastrous draft day.

The initiation of the draft on Saturday in the Ninth Congressional District was characterized by so much order and good feeling as to well nigh dispel the foreboding of tumult and violence which many entertained in connection with the enforcement of the conscription in this City. Very few, then, were prepared for the riotous demonstrations which yesterday, from 10 in the morning until late at night, prevailed almost unchecked in our streets. The authorities had counted upon more or less resistance to this measure of the Government after the draft was completed and the conscripts were required to take their place in the ranks, and at that time they would have been fully prepared to meet it; but no one anticipated resistance at so early a stage in the execution of the law, and consequently, both the City and National authorities were totally unprepared to meet it. The abettors of the riot knew this, and in it they saw their opportunity. We say abettors of the riot, for it is abundantly manifest that the whole affair was concocted on Sunday last by a few wire-pullers, who, after they saw the ball fairly in motion yesterday morning prudently kept in the background. Proof of this is found in the fact that as early as 9 o'clock, some laborers employed by two or three railroad companies, and in the iron foundries on the eastern side of the City, formed in procession in the Twenty-second Ward, and visited the different workshops in the upper wards, where large numbers were employed, and compelled them, by threats in some instances, to cease their work. As the crowd augmented, their shouts and disorderly demonstrations became more formidable. The number of men who thus started out in their career of violence and blood, did not probably at first exceed three-score. Scarcely had two dozen names been called, when a crowd, numbering perhaps 500, suddenly made an irruption in front of the building (corner of Third Avenue and Forty-sixth street,) attacking it with clubs, stones, brickbats and other missiles. . . . Following these missiles, the mob rushed furiously into the office on the first floor, where the draft was going on, seizing the books, papers, records, lists, &c., all of which they destroyed, except those contained in a large iron safe. The drafting officers were set upon with stones and clubs, and, with the reporters for the Press and others, had to make a hasty exit through the rear.

At 11 a.m. word reached the Park Barracks of the disturbance, and Lieut. Ried and a detachment of the Invalid corps immediately repaired to the scene of the riot. They went by the Third avenue route, the party occupying one car. On the way up, crowds of men, women and children gathered at the street corners, hissed and jeered them, and some even went so far as to pick up stones, which they defiantly threatened to throw at the car. When near the scene of the disturbance, Lieut. Ried and command alighted, and formed in company line, in which order they marched up to the mob. Facing the rioters the men were ordered to fire, which many of them did, the shots being blank cartridges, but the smoke had scarce cleared away when the company (which did not number more than fifty men, if as many) were attacked and completely demoralized by the mob, who were armed with clubs, sticks, swords and other implements. The soldiers had their bayonets taken away, and they themselves were compelled [to] seek refuge in the side streets, but in attempting to flee thither, several, it is said, were killed, while those that escaped, did so only to be hunted like dogs, but in a more inhuman and brutal manner. They were chased by the mob, who divided themselves into squads, and frequently a single soldier would be caught in a side street, with each end blocked up by the rioters. The houses and stores were all closed (excepting a few liquor shops, which had their shutters up, but kept the back door open,) no retreat was, therefore, open for him, and the poor fellow would be beaten almost to death. . . .

Elated with success, the mob, which by this time had been largely reinforced, next formed themselves into marauding parties, and paraded through the neighboring streets, looking more like so many infuriated demons, the men being more or less intoxicated, dirty and half clothed. . . . The streets were thronged with women and children, many of whom instigated the men to further work of blood.

As soon as the Provost-Marshal's office has been gutted of its contents, and the adjoining building—a wheelwright's shop, in which there was much combustible material—had been fired, the telegraph wires were cut. Parties and bands of men and boys then visited the various workshops in the vicinity, and compelled the men to leave their work and join. . . .

By this time the Fire Department of the District arrived on the ground, and were preparing to work on the fire; but were prevented from doing so by the mob, who threatened them with instant death if their orders were disobeyed. The cars were stopped from running either way; the horses in several instances were killed, and the cars broken to pieces. . . .

The fire, which had now consumed the wheelwright's shop, had extended to the Provost-Marshal's office, which was soon enveloped in flames, from which issued a large and dark volume of smoke.

The rioters meantime danced with fiendish delight before the burning building, . . . sent showers of stones against the office, smashing in the doors and windows. . . . The murky atmosphere and the heavy black clouds which lined the horizon, formed a strange, weird spectacle, which was made the more complete by the demoniac yells of the mobs.

The Orphan Asylum for Colored Children was visited by the mob about 4 o'clock. This Institution is situated on Fifth-avenue, and the building, with the grounds and gardens adjoining, extended from Forty-third to Forty-fourth street. Hundreds, and perhaps thousands of the rioters, the majority of whom were women and children, entered the premises, and in the most excited and violent manner they ransacked and plundered the building from cellar to garret. The building was located in the most pleasant and healthy portion of the City. It was purely a charitable institution. In it there are on an average 600 or 800 homeless colored orphans. The building was a large four-story one, with two wings of three stories each.

After the entire building had been ransacked, and every article deemed worth carrying away had been taken—and this included even the little garments for the orphans, which were contributed by the benevolent ladies of this City—the premises were fired on the first floor. . . .

. . . The institution was destined to be burned, and after an hour and a half of labor on the part of the mob, it was in flames in all parts. . . . There is now scarcely one brick left upon another of the Orphan Asylum.

Among the most cowardly features of the riot, and one which indicated its political animus . . . was the causeless and inhuman treatment of the negroes of the City. It seemed to be an understood thing throughout the City that the negroes should be attacked wherever found, whether then [sic] offered any provocation or not. As son as one of these unfortunate people was spied, whether on a cart, a railroad car, or in the street, he was immediately set upon by a crowd of men and boys, and unless some man of pluck came to his rescue, or he was fortunate enough to escape into a building, he was inhumanly beaten and perhaps killed. There were probably not less than a dozen negroes beaten to death in different parts of the City during the day. Among the most diabolical of these outrages . . . is that of a negro cartman living in Carmine street. About 8 o'clock in the evening as he was coming out of the stable, after having put up his horses, he was attacked by a crowd of about 400 men and boys, who beat him with clubs and paving-stones till he was lifeless, and then hung him to a tree opposite the burying-ground. Not being yet satisfied with their devilish work, they set fire to his clothes and danced and yelled and swore their horrid oaths around his burning corpse. The charred body of the poor victim was still hanging upon the tree at a late hour last evening.

Early in the afternoon the proprietors of such saloons and other places of business as had negroes in their employ, were obliged to close up for fear that the rioters would destroy their premises. In most of them the negroes were compelled to remain over night, not daring to go home lest they be mobbed on the way. . . .

Gettysburg Address (1865)

Commentary

President Abraham Lincoln (1809–1865) attended the dedication of the military cemetery at the Gettysburg battlefield on November 19, 1863. Following an oration of several hours by former Secretary of State Edward Everett, Lincoln rose and delivered a speech of less than 300 words. This brief statement, because of its exceptional eloquence, became one of Lincoln's most famous speeches.

Lincoln stressed the same themes that he had made in numerous other speeches about the war—namely, that the nation was historically a single entity and it would remain a single nation for the future. Echoing his 1860 speeches in New York and New Haven, he reminded his listeners that eighty-seven years earlier, the nation's founders had established one nation, dedicated to the idea that all men were created equal.

Standing on the field where thousands of men had lost their lives just a few months earlier, Lincoln urged the nation to rededicate itself to the Union cause. Speaking nearly a year after the Emancipation Proclamation went into effect, Lincoln called for "a new birth of freedom" throughout the country. In a now famous statement, Lincoln closed his speech with a reaffirmation of his commitment to a government of, by, and for the people.

Fourscore and seven years ago our fathers brought forth on this continent a new nation, conceived in liberty, and dedicated to the proposition that all men are created equal. Now we are engaged in a great civil war, testing whether that nation, or any nation so conceived and so dedicated, can long endure. We are met on a great battlefield of that war. We have come to dedicate a portion of that field as a final resting-place for those who here gave their lives that the nation might live. It is altogether fitting and proper that we should do this. But, in a larger sense, we cannot dedicate—we cannot consecrate—we cannot hallow—this ground. The brave men, living and dead, who struggled here have consecrated it, far above our poor power to add or detract. The world will little note, nor long remember, what we say here, but it can never forget what they did here. It is for us the living, rather, to be dedicated here to the unfinished work which they who fought here have thus far so nobly advanced. It is rather for us to be here dedicated to the great task remaining before us—that from these honored dead we take increased devotion to that cause for which they gave the last full measure of devotion—that we here highly resolve that these dead shall not have died in vain—that this nation, under God, shall have a new birth of freedom and that government of the people, by the people, for the people, shall not perish from the earth.

Second Inaugural Address, by Abraham Lincoln (1865)

Commentary

On March 4, 1865, only a few weeks before Confederate General Robert E. Lee (1807–1870) surrendered at Appomattox Courthouse, Virginia, President Abraham Lincoln (1809–1865) delivered his second inaugural address. As in the election of 1860, the votes of Northerners alone had elected Lincoln to the highest office in the land. Nevertheless, Lincoln directed his remarks to the nation as a whole, as he had four years earlier in his first inaugural address. In the address, notable for its brevity, Lincoln reflected on the war and its origins. He identified slavery as a cause of the armed conflict and reminded his audience that his initial policy had been to restrict the growth of slavery, not to abolish it entirely. The speech is also notable in that Lincoln expressed no enmity toward the South, but rather set a tone of reconciliation and peace.

Historians have long debated the impact of religion of Lincoln's ideas, and one of the most striking aspects of this address is Lincoln's use of theological concepts and biblical paraphrases.

Although Lincoln was not a member of any church, in this speech, Lincoln used religious language to stress the nation's common bonds. He observed that both North and South read from the same Bible and turned to the same God for help.

The address's last paragraph is perhaps one of the most famous statements by any American president. After four years of bloody war, Lincoln asked the country to move on, with "malice toward none" and "charity for all." Lincoln was killed just over a month later and so did not live to see the process of Reconstruction—and era during which the country would often recall the president's plea.

Fellow-Countrymen:

At this second appearing to take the oath of the Presidential office there is less occasion for an extended address than there was at the first. Then a statement somewhat in detail of a course to be pursued seemed fitting and proper. Now, at the expiration of four years, during which public declarations have been constantly called forth on every point and phase of the great contest which still absorbs the attention and engrosses the energies of the nation, little that is new could be presented. The progress of our arms, upon which all else chiefly depends, is as well known to the public as to myself, and it is, I trust, reasonably satisfactory and encouraging to all. With high hope for the future, no prediction in regard to it is ventured.

On the occasion corresponding to this four years ago all thoughts were anxiously directed to an impending civil war. All dreaded it, all sought to avert it. While the inaugural address was being delivered from this place, devoted altogether to saving the Union without war, urgent agents were in the city seeking to destroy it without war—seeking to dissolve the Union and divide effects by negotiation. Both parties deprecated war, but one of them would make war rather than let the nation survive, and the other would accept war rather than let it perish, and the war came.

One-eighth of the whole population were colored slaves, not distributed generally over the Union, but localized in the southern part of it. These slaves constituted a peculiar and powerful interest. All knew that this interest was somehow the cause of the war. To strengthen, perpetuate, and extend this interest was the object for which the insurgents would rend the Union even by war, while the Government claimed no right to do more than to restrict the territorial enlargement of it. Neither party expected for the war the magnitude or the duration which it has already attained. Neither anticipated that the cause of the conflict might cease with or even before the conflict itself should cease. Each looked for an easier triumph, and a result less fundamental and astounding. Both read the same Bible and pray to the same God, and each invokes His aid against the other. It may seem strange that any men should dare to ask a just God's assistance in wringing their bread from the sweat of other men's faces, but let us judge not, that we be not judged. The prayers of both could not be answered. That of neither has been answered fully. The Almighty has His own purposes. "Woe unto the world because of offenses; for it must needs be that offenses come, but woe to that man by whom the offense cometh." If we shall suppose that American slavery is one of those offenses which, in the providence of God, must needs come, but which, having continued through His appointed time, He now wills to remove, and that He gives to both North and South this terrible war as the woe due to those by whom the offense came, shall we discern therein any departure from those divine attributes which the believers in a living God always ascribe to Him? Fondly do we hope, fervently do we pray, that this mighty scourge of war may speedily pass away. Yet, if God wills that it continue until all the wealth piled by the bondsman's two hundred and fifty years of unrequited toil shall be sunk, and until every drop of blood drawn with the lash shall be paid by another drawn with the sword, as was said three thousand years ago, so still it must be said "the judgments of the Lord are true and righteous altogether."

With malice toward none, with charity for all, with firmness in the right as God gives us to see the right, let us strive on to finish the work we are in, to bind up the nation's wounds, to care for him who shall have borne the battle and for his widow and his orphan, to do all which may achieve and cherish a just and lasting peace among ourselves and with all nations.

Address from the Committee on Education (1866)

Commentary

Reconstruction raised hopes and expectations for Northern blacks as well former slaves in the South. In this excerpt, from the Committee on Education address at the Illinois State Convention of Colored Men condemns their state's exclusion of blacks from the public schools. In extending educational privileges to "a persecuted race," it concludes, the state would uphold the loftiest of American ideals.

While in some areas blacks accepted segregated schooling, many insisted on going to school with whites. Everywhere African Americans placed great hope in the ability of public education to bring them into the mainstream of American life, as this address demonstrates. In 1870, a new Illinois constitution replaced the earlier stipulations that public education be limited to whites with a new commitment to the education of "all children." After several local communities failed to open their schools to black residents or attempted to construct separate facilities, the state legislature took stronger action. In 1874, it passed a law that barred racial discrimination in schools and fined school officials who attempted to intimidate black children.

Fellow Citizens of the State of Illinois,—Among the great questions which claim our special consideration, is that of education. The past and present history of our native country, as well as of all other countries which have attained to any degree of greatness, has proven that, without education, they are lost to virtue, intelligence, and to that usefulness which have made a people great, good, happy, and contented.

If a nation, republican in form, loses her virtue, she can no longer claim prestige with her sister republics. The same is with communities and individuals.

What is it that makes a nation, a people, a community, or even an individual, great, good, and happy? It is a pure, unsullied love of virtue! And how shall this virtue be obtained, so as to become beneficial to all, irrespective of color or condition?

Judging from the past and looking at the present, we can see, through the dim vista, the future of a race of people, who are giants in intellect, whose energies have been crushed by the power of might—a people claiming the admiration of men and angels, still entreating you, by all that is patriotic in government and sacred in religion, to be the witness of what they will do to establish their claim to be recognized as men worthy of a chance in this your noble State, to earn their bread, to educate themselves and their children—a people full of love and humanity, ever ready to yield to those christian impulses and feelings which characterize those whom God has chosen for his elect from all eternity. Such characteristics must eventually have their reward; such virtues must ever live. And, as a part of that race, living in your midst, tilling your soil, loading your ships, and by our labor enriching you—willing to forget that you have oppressed, trampled us under foot, shot us down like dogs, treated us as beasts of burden, having watered the soil of our fair country with the blood of our fathers, mothers, brothers and sisters—still, we feel it to be our duty to show, not only to the people of the State of Illinois, but to the nation, that we are men and American citizens; that we desire to acquire all your virtues, shunning every evil calculated to retard our moral, physical, and social condition. To do this, we ask you, in the name of twenty-two thousand colored citizens of the State, to open wide your doors, and admit our children into your public schools and colleges. We appeal to you, in behalf of eight thousand colored boys and girls, with expansive minds, ready and willing to drink from the fountain of literature and learning.

Slaves, many of us have been; but if you give us those advantages which the Constitution guarantees to all citizens, we shall soon rise in the scale of being so high that it will blush the cheek of many who have spent their golden moments at the shrine of vice and infamy.

Looking at the educational statistics of our State, we find less than one hundred of our colored children in public schools, or less than one in every eighty. How long shall such a state of things exist; how long will you encourage pauperism, and charge us with having minds not susceptible of culture. Your legislature, less than two years ago, wiped from the escutcheon of our great and noble State, a part of her black code.

Three years ago, you took from your midst twenty-five hundred true and loyal blacks, to help fill up your quota, and your generals led them to a scene of carnage and death. As men and soldiers of Illinois they fought; as American citizens they died, defending the honor of the State and the government. Believing that the State, the government, and the entire people, irrespective of all political differences, would honor their memory by doing justice in the education of their children, the protection of their widows and orphans, and proving to the world that the genius of the American people is liberty unproscribed to all. How can you hope for success in the establishment of the government on the eternal foundation on which your fathers built, if you persist in denying an education to a persecuted race. This is a world of compensations, and he who would himself be great through the means of education, must not enslave the mind of his fellow-being. Then, fellow citizens, accept the aphorism, and enlarge upon it: say that, as the colored man is now free, he may live a better patriot, a better man and a better christian.

Joseph Stanley, Chairman of Com. on Education. Geo. T. Fountain, Adams Co. Walter Coleman, Will C. S. Jacobs, Mercer H. Hicklin, Sangamon

Page numbers in **bold** indicate the main article on a subject. Page numbers in *italics* indicate illustrations. Page numbers followed by *t* indicate tables. The number preceding the colon indicates the volume number, and the number after the colon indicates the page number. This index is sorted word by word.

Shays's Rebellion, **1**:165–166
  significance, **1**:157
  slavery, **1**:40, 168, 169–171, **2**:162
  states' rights, **2**:153, 164
  Supreme Court, **1**:42
  three-fifths clause, **1**:40, 45, 168, 170–171, **2**:162
  Thirteenth Amendment, **2**:203
  treaties, **1**:184
  war, **1**:88
  War Powers Resolution (1973), **4**:206
  Washington, George, **1**:40, 42
  See also Articles of Confederation; Bill of Rights; Federalist Papers
Constitution, U.S.S., **1**:140, 141, *141*
Constitutional Convention, **1**:13, 75, 165–166, 168, 198
Constitutional Union Party, **2**:57, 133
Constitutions, state, **1**:37, 156–157, 178
Consummation (Cole), **1**:138
Containment and détente, **4**:45–47
  arms control debate, **4**:9
  Kennan, George F., **4**:46, 147–148
  Kissinger, Henry, **4**:46, 103, 143
  Korean War, **4**:46, 105
  labor, 1946-present, **4**:108
  McCarthyism, **4**:119
  National Security Memorandum No. 68, **4**:46, 147–148
  Nixon, Richard M., **4**:46, 143, 144
  See also Arms control debate; Communism and anticommunism
Continental Association, **1**:15, 175
  See also Association test
Continental Congresses, **1**:42–45
  American Revolution, **1**:44
  Articles of Confederation, **1**:12, 44
  Constitution, **1**:40–41
  Continental Army, **1**:120, 121
  Continental Association, **1**:14–15
  Declaration of Independence, **1**:44, 47, 49
  First Continental Congress, **1**:12, *13*, 14–15, 42–43
  George III (king of England), **1**:43–44
  Indian removal and response, **2**:85
  Loyalists, **1**:111
  Madison, James, **1**:115
  Northwest Ordinance, **1**:44, **2**:85
  and Parliament, **1**:42, 44
  purpose, **1**:12
  Second, **1**:12, 43–44, 47, 49, 120, 121, 198, **2**:85
  veterans' benefits, **1**:189–190
  Washington, George, **1**:198
"Contraband," former slaves as, **2**:106, 147, 162, 189
Convention Against Torture and Other Cruel, Inhuman, or Degrading Treatment or Punishment, **4**:85

Convention of 1800, **1**:146
Convention on Genocide, **4**:85
Convention on the Elimination of All Forms of Racial Discrimination, **4**:85
Convention on the Rights of the Child, **4**:85
Cooke, Jay, **2**:18, 67–68
Coolidge, Calvin, **3**:67, 161, **4**:45
Cooper, James Fenimore, **1**:45, **70–71**, 132, 175–176
Copey, John Singleton, *1:3*
Copland, Aaron, **3**:127
Copley, John Singleton, **1**:137
Copperheads. *See* Peace Democrats
Coppola, Francis Ford, **4**:62
Corbin, Margaret, **1**:31
CORE. *See* Congress of Racial Equality (CORE)
Cosmatos, George P., **4**:42
Cotton
  Civil War, **2**:64, 65–66
  exports, **2**:68
  as industry, **2**:52, 53
  labor and labor movements, **2**:99, 100
  sharecropping and tenant farming, **2**:157
  slavery, **1**:171, **2**:52, 160, *161*
Cotton gin, **1**:170, 171, *2:27*, 27–28, 160
Council of National Defense, **3**:20, 48
Country Joe and the Fish, **4**:130
Country music, **4**:127, 128
"The Country of Pointed Firs" (Jewett), **2**:108
The Course of the Empire (Cole), **1**:138
"Courtesy of the Red, White, and Blue (The Angry American)" (Keith), **4**:127
Cousens, Charles, **3**:183
Cowboys in art, **2**:183
CPD (Committee on the Present Danger), **4**:101, 142
Crane, Stephen, **2**:108, 146, **3**:86
Craven, John J., *2:113*
Crazy Horse, **2**:88
Creedence Clearwater Revival, **4**:130
Creek Indians, **1**:91, **2**:86
Creek-Cherokee war, **1**:57
Creel, George, **3**:124, 150, 151, 161
Cret, Paul, **3**:116
Criner, Greg, *4:17*
Crisis, **3**:45

The Crisis (Paine), **1**:135
Crittenden, John J., **2**:129
Crockett, David, **2**:9–10
Croix de Guerre, **3**:3, *4*, 95, 180
Cromwell, Oliver, **1**:182, 198
Cronkite, Walter, **4**:187, 190–191
Crosby, Stills, and Nash, **4**:130
The Crucible (Miller), **4**:163
Crusade in Europe (Eisenhower), **3**:99
The Crusaders (Heym), **3**:98
Cuba
  American Red Cross, **3**:159
  Communism and anticommunism, **4**:44
  Eisenhower, Dwight D., **4**:56
  imperialism, **3**:78–79
  journalism, Spanish-American War, **3**:83–86, *85*
  McKinley, William, **3**:104
  quarantine, **4**:48, 98
Cuba: The Missile Crisis, **4**:188
Cuban Americans, **4**:126
Cuban Missile Crisis, **4**:9, *47–49*, *48*, 98
  See also Kennedy, John Fitzgerald
Cuffee, Paul, **1**:167, 171
Cultural exchange programs, **4**:10
Cummings, E. E., **3**:97
Curfew, for Japanese Americans, **3**:22
Currier and Ives, **2**:81
Curtis, Charles, *3:40*
Custer, George A., **2**:88

D

Dances with Wolves, **1**:161
Dangling Man (Bellow), **3**:98
Dark Star, **4**:62
Dartmouth College v. Woodward (1819), **1**:182–183
Dartmouth (ship), **1**:23–24
Davis, Angela, **4**:51–52, *52*
Davis, Benjamin O., Jr., **4**:172
Davis, Elmer, **3**:87, 151, 156
Davis, Jefferson, **2**:43–44, *44*
  and Chesnut, Mary Boykin, **2**:23
  civil liberties, Civil War, **2**:26
  Civil War, **2**:44, 133–134
  Confederate States of America, **2**:36, 38, 44
  and Davis, Varina Howell, **2**:45
  Emancipation Proclamation, **2**:59
  and Lee, Robert E., **2**:102

Shepard, William, 1:165

Sherman, Roger, 1:40, 49

Sherman, William T., 2:15, 123, 125–126, 140

Sherman Antitrust Act (1890), 2:20

Sherman's march to the sea, 2:24, 58, 157–159, *158*

Short, Walter C., 3:139, 140

A Short Narrative of the Horrid Massacre, 1:22

Shute, Nevil, 4:40

Sierra Leone, 1:111, 170, 171

Simcoe, John, 1:29–30

Simmons, William Joseph, 2:97

Sioux Indians, 2:86–88

Sisson, Jack, 1:168

Sit-in movement, 4:34, 146

Sitting Bull, 2:8, 86, 88

Six Days of the Condor (Grady), 4:41

Six Nations, 1:57–58, 59, 200

Six-Day War, 4:79, 90, 168

Sixteenth Amendment, 3:57

Sixth Amendment, 1:38
   See also Bill of Rights

Slaughterhouse Cases (1873), 2:40, 165–166

Slaughterhouse-Five (Vonnegut), 3:98, 111, 4:215

Slave music, 2:118–119

Slave narratives, 2:48–49

Slave rebellions, 1:8, 9, 172
   See also Stono Rebellion

Slave trade, 1:169–170, 2:159, 160

Slavery, 2:159–162, *161*
   in America, 1:167, **169–174,** *173*
   American Revolution, 1:172–173, 2:155
   Chesnut, Mary Boykin, 2:23–24
   Christianity, 2:173, 174
   Compromise of 1850, 2:13
   Constitution, 1:40, 168, 169–171, 2:162
   cotton production, 1:171, 2:52, 160, *161*
   and Declaration of Independence, 1:49–50
   economic aspects, 2:52, 53, 160
   farming, 2:66, 67
   Fourth of July, 1:73
   Greeley, Horace, 2:76
   Hartford Convention, 1:87, 88
   and the homefront, 1775-1783, **1:167–169**
   Impact of American Revolution on, 1:62, 157–158

and Jefferson, Thomas, 1:94–95
journalism, 2:123
justification of, 2:159–160
laws, 2:160 161
Lincoln, Abraham, 2:39, 103, 104
in literature, 2:106–107
Manifest Destiny, 2:111–112
Monroe, James, 1:123
religion, 2:150, 159, 161–162
and secession, 2:153–154
Supreme Court, 1815-1900, 2:165–166
and violence, 2:179–180
Virginia, 1:168, 171, 172, 2:159
westward expansion, 2:8, 77–78
women, 2:190
See also Abolitionists; Compromise of 1850; Emancipation Proclamation; Kansas-Nebraska Act (1854); Thirteenth Amendment

Slaves
   American Revolution mobilization, 1:121–122
   family life, 2:64, 162
   food shortages during Civil War, 2:69
   labor and labor movements, 2:99
   as Loyalists, 1:109, 111
   recreation and social life, 2:144–145
   War of 1812, 1:196

Slaves in Algiers (Rowson), 1:151

Slave's Letter to His Former Master (Anderson), 2:218

Smith, Al, 2:98

Smith, Charles Henry, 2:82

Smith, Kate, 3:127

Smith, Oliver P., *4:114*

Smith, William Gardner, 3:98

Smith Act (1940), 4:119–120

Smith-Connally Act, 3:93

Smithson, James, 2:28

Smithsonian Institution, 2:28

SNCC. *See* Student Nonviolent Coordinating Committee (SNCC)

Social life and recreation, 2:144–146, *145,* 3:165

Socialist Party of America, 3:31, 39, 41, 79, 138

Society of Cincinnati, 1:159

Society of Friends. *See* Quakers

Soft money, 2:18

Soldiers' Adjusted Compensation Act, 3:192

Soldiers' Bonus, 3:192

Soldier's Pay (Faulkner), 3:97

"Soledad Brothers," 4:52, *53*

Somalia, 4:36–37, 172

Son of Star Wars, 4:184, 192

Sons of Liberty, *1:174,* 174–175
   Boston Massacre, 1:20, 21, 22
   Boston Tea Party, 1:22–24, *23*
   decline of, 1:175
   peace movements, 2:130
   protesting the Stamp Act, 1:174–175
   See also Boston Massacre; Boston Tea Party

Soto, Hernando de, 1:56

The Souls of Black Folk (Du Bois), 3:45, 78

"The Sources of Soviet Conduct" (Kennan), 4:46, 147–148

South
   economy, 2:52–53
   farming, 2:65–66
   food shortages, 2:69–70
   occupation of, 2:125–127, *126*
   political humor, 2:82
   Reconstruction, 2:143

South Carolina
   Davis, Jefferson, 2:38
   nullification controversy, 2:21–22, 164
   secession, 2:154
   slavery, 1:170, 171, 172
   Stono Rebellion, 1:8, 179–181
   warfare between Native Americans and Europeans, 1:107

South Vietnam bombing, *4:2*

Southern Baptist Convention, 4:23

Southern Christian Leadership Conference (SCLC)
   antiwar movement, 4:7
   Civil Rights movement, 4:34, 35
   Jackson, Jesse Louis, 4:91
   King, Martin Luther, Jr., 4:99
   nonviolence, 3:44, 4:146, 147
   Operation Breadbasket, 4:91

Southern Historical Society, 2:109

Southern Punch, 2:81, 82

Southern Women Make Do During the Blockade, *2:219*

The Sovereignty and Goodness of God (Rowlandson), 1:100, 132, 159–161

Soviet Union
   and aerospace industry, 4:1
   arms control debate, 4:9
   Berlin as symbol, 4:15–16
   Bush, George H. W., 4:18
   churches, Evangelical, 4:24
   CIA and espionage, 4:27, 28
   Communism and anticommunism, 4:43–45
   containment and détente, 4:45–47
   Eisenhower, Dwight D., 4:56–57
   as "evil empire," 4:162, 173, 187
   foreign aid, 1946-present, 4:65
   H-bomb, decision to build, 4:75–76
   image among World War II Allies, 3:8–9

Strategic Offensive Reductions Treaty (2002), **4:**9

Stride toward Freedom (King), **4:**99

Strikes, labor, **2:**100, **3:**93, 94, 161
See also Labor and labor movements

Strong, Caleb, **1:**87

Struble, Arthur, *4:114*

Stuart, Gilbert, **1:**114, 137

Student Nonviolent Coordinating Committee (SNCC), **4:**16, 34, 35, 100, 146

Students for a Democratic Society (SDS), **4:**6–7, 16, 128, 189

Sugar Act (1764) (Britain), **1:**139, 177

Sukarno, **4:**145

Sullivan, John, **1:**29

Sullivan, New York Times v. (1964), **4:**32

Sully, T., Jr., *2:135*

Sumner, Charles, **2:**179–180

The Sun Also Rises (Hemingway), **3:**70

Surgery, **2:**113, *113*, **3:**108

The Surrender of Burgoyne (Trumbull), **1:**137

The Surrender of Cornwallis (Trumbull), **1:**137

Surveillance, **4:**32, 59–60

Susan B. Anthony Amendment, **3:**208
See also Nineteenth Amendment; Women's suffrage movement

Susquehanna Company, **1:**200

Susquehannock Indians, **1:**17, 18

Sutter, John, **2:**7

Suu, Vu, *4:191*

Swaine, Charles, *3:40*

Sweet Act (1921), **3:**192

T

Taft, Howard H., **3:**92

Taft, William Howard, **3:**48

Taft-Hartley Act (1947), **3:**94, **4:**107

Taiwan, **4:**55

Taliban. See Al-Qaida and Taliban

Tammany Society, **1:**142

Taney, Roger B., **2:**25, 39, 104, 165

Taylor, Maxwell D., **4:**123

Tea Act (1773) (Britain), **1:**23, 175

Teachers, **2:**189–190, **3:**43

Tear gas, **4:**209

Tecumseh, **1:**10, 107, 194, **2:**86

Teenagers, 1946-present, **4:**185–187

Tehran Conference (1943), **3:**187

Tejanos, **2:**10–11, 168

Telegraph, **2:**123, 124

Television, 1946-present, **4:**157, 162–163, **187–189**
See also Photojournalism; Popular culture and Cold War

Teller, Edward, **3:**101, **4:**75, 76, 183

Ten Percent Plan, **2:**141

Tenant farming. See Sharecropping and tenant farming

Tenement buildings, *2:176*, 177

Tennessee Valley Authority, **3:**132

Tenth Amendment, **1:**5–6, 33, 38, 95, **2:**136
See also Bill of Rights

Tenure of Office Act, **2:**93

Terrorism, **4:**19–20, 37, **189–190**
See also Al-Qaida and Taliban; Homeland security; 9-11; War on terrorism

Testimony of Paul Robeson Before the House Committee on Un-American Activities, **4:**

Testimony of Walter E. Disney Before the House Committee on Un-American Activities, **4:**

Tet Offensive, **4:**7, 95, 140, **190–192**, *191*
See also Johnson, Lyndon Baines; Vietnam War

Texas, Republic of, **2:**10–11, **167–169**, *168*

Texas annexation, **2:**135, 168–169

Textile industry, **2:**51, 99

Thailand, **4:**202, 203

Thames, Battle of the, **1:**10, 194, **2:**86

Them!, **4:**40

Thermonuclear devices. See H-bombs

"They Are There!" (Ives), **3:**126

They Were Expendable, **3:**123, 197

The Thin Red Line (Jones), **3:**98

Think tanks, **4:**192

Third Amendment, **1:**38, 155
See also Bill of Rights

"Third World neutralism," **4:**44, 145

Thirteenth Amendment
abolitionists, **2:**2
content, **2:**38, 39
excerpt, **2:**142, 203
Ku Klux Klan, **2:**96
Reconstruction, **2:**142
Supreme Court, **2:**166
See also Abolitionists

This Is Nazi Brutality (Shahn), **3:**195–196

This Is the Army (Berlin), **3:**127

"This Is War" (Duncan), **4:**157

Thomason, John, **3:**97

Thompson, Hugh, **4:**132

Thoreau, Henry David, **2:**107

Thoughts on Government (Adams), **1:**3

Thoughts upon Female Education (Rush), **1:**151

Three Days of the Condor, **4:**41

Three Mile Island nuclear accident, **4:**12

The Three Servicemen (Hart), **4:**200, 201

Three Soldiers (Dos Passos), **3:**96

Three-fifths clause
Constitution, **1:**40, 45, 168, 170–171, **2:**162

Three-Power Treaty (1930), *3:40*

Through the Wheat (Boyd), **3:**96–97

Tilden, Samuel J., **2:**5, 58

Tillman, Ben "Pitchfork," **3:**137

Time, **3:**87, 196, **4:**157–158

Time lines
armed conflicts in America, 1587-1815, **1:**7
Indian wars, 1607-1826, **1:**106
slavery in America, **1:**170

Time standardization, **2:**139

Timucua Indians, **1:**55, 56

Tin Pan Alley, **3:**124

Tires, rationing of, **3:**157

To Hell and Back (Murphy), **3:**111

Tobias, Charlie, **3:**127

Tocqueville, Alexis de, **1:**149

Tojo, Hideki, *3:51*

Tokyo Rose, **3:183–185**, *184*
See also Japanese Americans, World War II

Tokyo subway station chemical attack, **4:**207, *208*, 209

Tolan Committee, **3:**163

Tomb of the Unknowns, **2:**31, **3:**11, 14, 115, *117*

Tommy (Who), **4:**186

Tonkin Gulf episode, **4:**94

Tora! Tora! Tora!, **4:**216

Tories, American. See Loyalists

"Tories," as term, **1:**109, 111

Torture, **3:**78, **4:**85, 164

Total war, **2:**70, **3:**157, 203

Tourneur, Jacques, **4:**40

Town, Laura, **2:**55–56